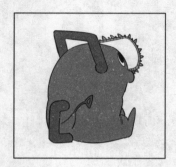

Tatsuki Fujimoto

I love *Jacob's Ladder*!

Tatsuki Fujimoto won Honorable Mention in the
November 2013 Shueisha Crown Newcomers' Awards for
his debut one-shot story *Love Is Blind*. His first series,
Fire Punch, ran for eight volumes. *Chainsaw Man* began
serialization in 2018 in *Weekly Shonen Jump*.

10

SHONEN JUMP Edition

Story & Art TATSUKI FUJIMOTO

Translation/AMANDA HALEY
Touch-Up Art & Lettering/SABRINA HEEP
Design/JULIAN [JR] ROBINSON
Editor/ALEXIS KIRSCH

CHAINSAW MAN © 2018 by Tatsuki Fujimoto
All rights reserved.
First published in Japan in 2018 by SHUEISHA Inc., Tokyo.
English translation rights arranged by SHUEISHA Inc.

The stories, characters, and incidents mentioned in this publication are
entirely fictional.

Printed in the U.S.A.

Published by VIZ Media, LLC
P.O. Box 77010
San Francisco, CA 94107

10 9 8 7 6 5 4 3 2 1
First printing, April 2022

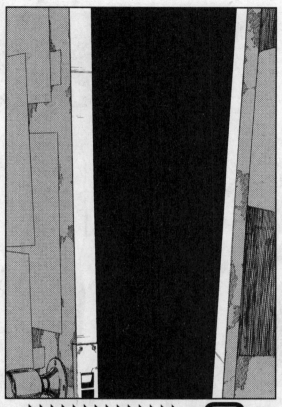

CHAINSAW MAN

10

A Dog's Feelings

Tatsuki Fujimoto

CHARACTERS

Denji

A young man-slash-Chainsaw Devil who carries his partner Pochita inside him. He's always true to his desires. Likes Makima, the first person to ever treat him like a human being.

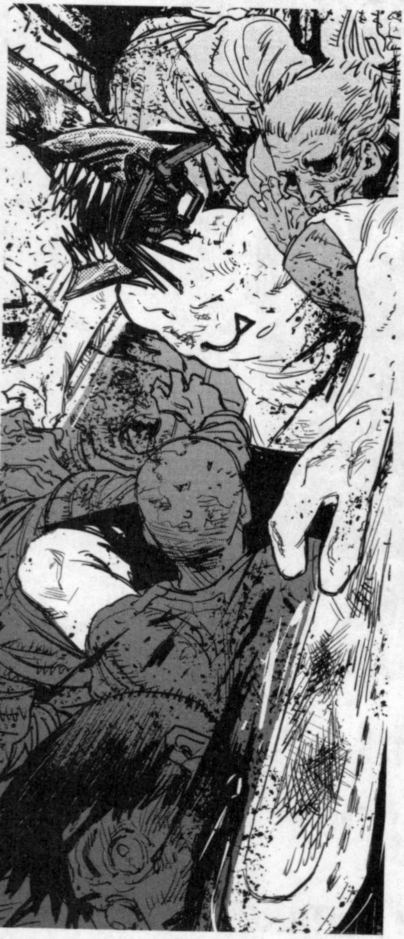

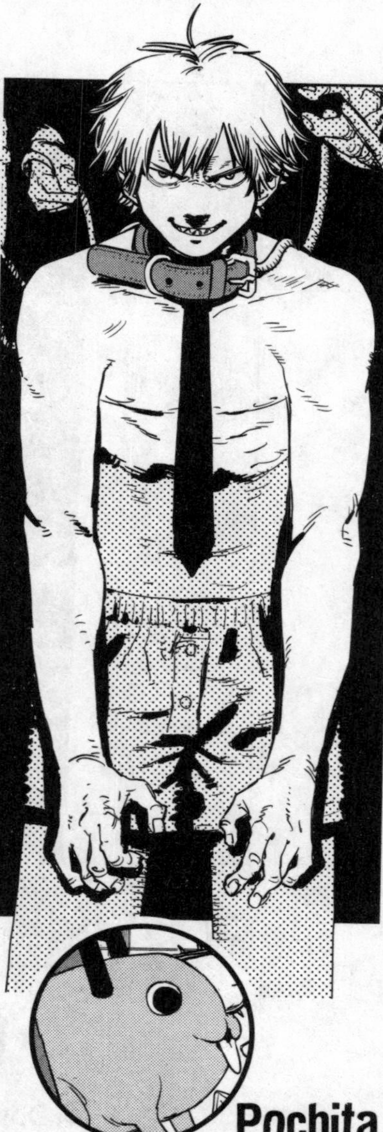

Pochita

Chainsaw Devil. Gave up his heart to Denji, becoming part of his body.

Makima

The mysterious woman in charge
of Public Safety Devil Extermination
Special Division 4. Her true identity is
the Control Devil.

Aki Hayakawa

Makima's subordinate. He was Denji's
senior at Public Safety by three years,
but he turned into the Gun Fiend.

Kishibe

A man with extraordinary fighting
ability who belongs to the Special
Division. The strongest Devil Hunter.
Wary of Makima?

Power

Blood Devil Fiend. Egotistical and
prone to going out of control. Her cat
Meowy is her only friend.

STORY

Denji is a young man who hunts devils with his
pet devil-dog Pochita. To pay off his debts, Denji is
forced to live in extreme poverty and worked like
a dog, only to be betrayed and killed on the job
without ever getting to live a decent life. But Pochita,
at the cost of the pooch's own life, brings Denji
back—as Chainsaw Man! After Denji buzzes through
all their attackers, he's taken in by the mysterious
Makima, and begins a new life as a Public Safety
Devil Hunter.

As the operation to eliminate the Gun Devil
draws closer, Aki realizes he's become attached
to Denji and Power and tries to withdraw his team

from the operation to protect them. Makima makes
a shocking revelation to him—the Gun Devil has
already been defeated and confined. Not only that,
the Future Devil shows him a terrible future in which
he and Power are killed by Denji. Makima finally
reveals her true nature as the Control Devil to a
shaken Aki. America sends its Gun Devil to stop
Makima, an attempt that fails. After the battle, Aki
shows up at the trio's apartment as a Gun Fiend.
Denji tries to bring him back to his senses in the
ensuing massacre and mayhem, but to no avail. And
so, in a moment of profound despair, Denji is left
with no choice but to end his friend's life…

CONTENTS

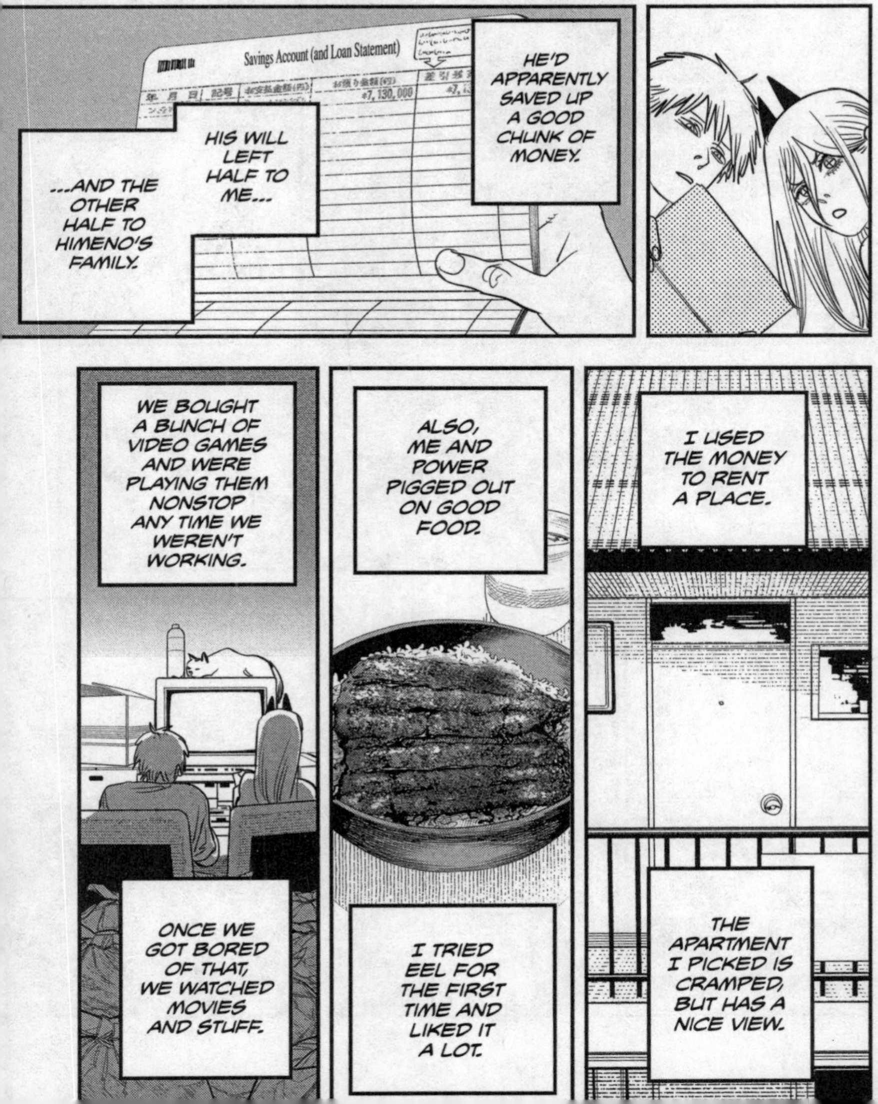
HE'D APPARENTLY SAVED UP A GOOD CHUNK OF MONEY.
Savings Account (and Loan Statement)
¥7,130,000
HIS WILL LEFT HALF TO ME...
...AND THE OTHER HALF TO HIMENO'S FAMILY.
I USED THE MONEY TO RENT A PLACE.
THE APARTMENT I PICKED IS CRAMPED, BUT HAS A NICE VIEW.
ALSO, ME AND POWER PIGGED OUT ON GOOD FOOD.
I TRIED EEL FOR THE FIRST TIME AND LIKED IT A LOT.
WE BOUGHT A BUNCH OF VIDEO GAMES AND WERE PLAYING THEM NONSTOP ANY TIME WE WEREN'T WORKING.
ONCE WE GOT BORED OF THAT, WE WATCHED MOVIES AND STUFF.

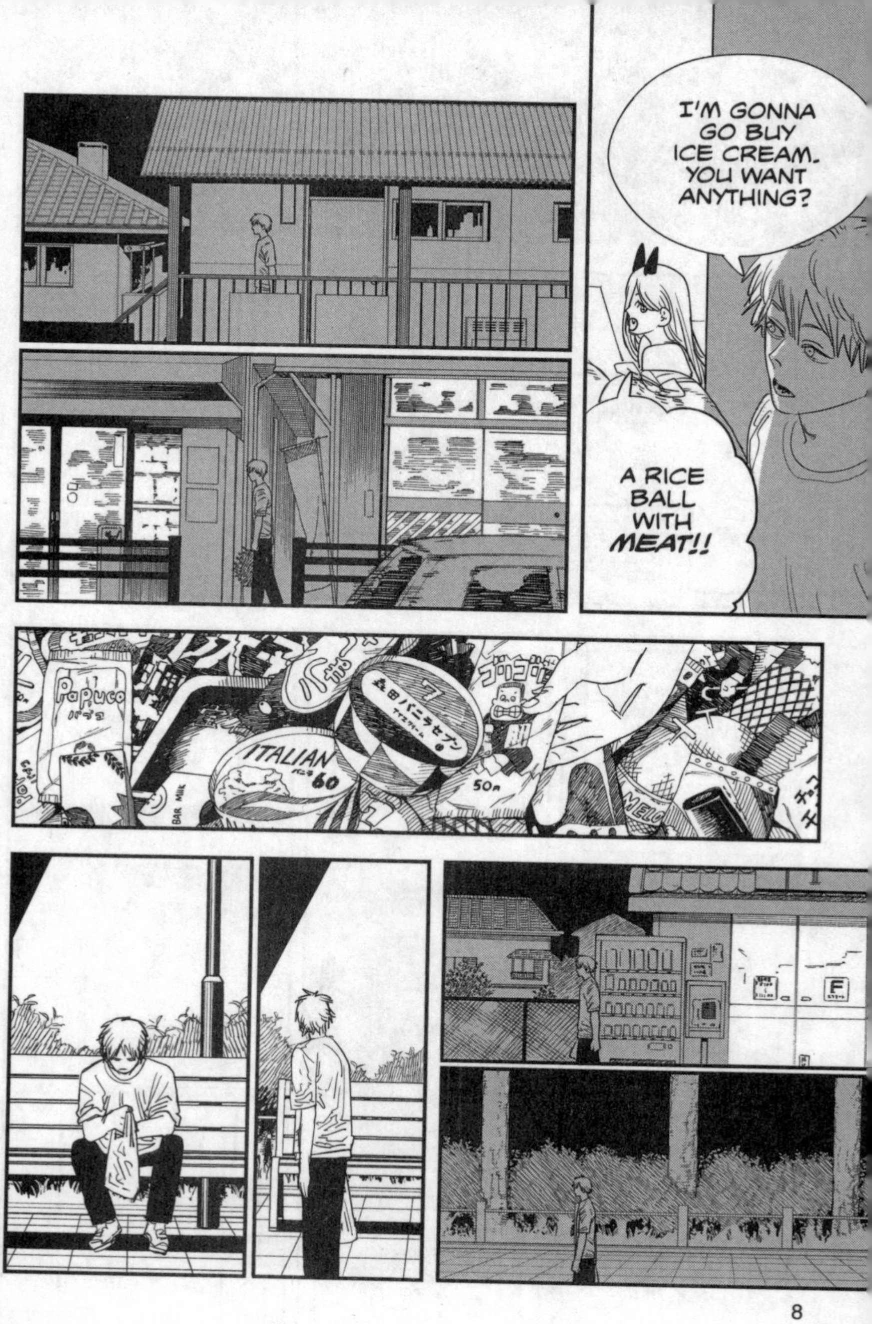
I'M GONNA GO BUY ICE CREAM. YOU WANT ANYTHING?
A RICE BALL WITH *MEAT!!*
Papuco
ITALIAN
BAR MILK

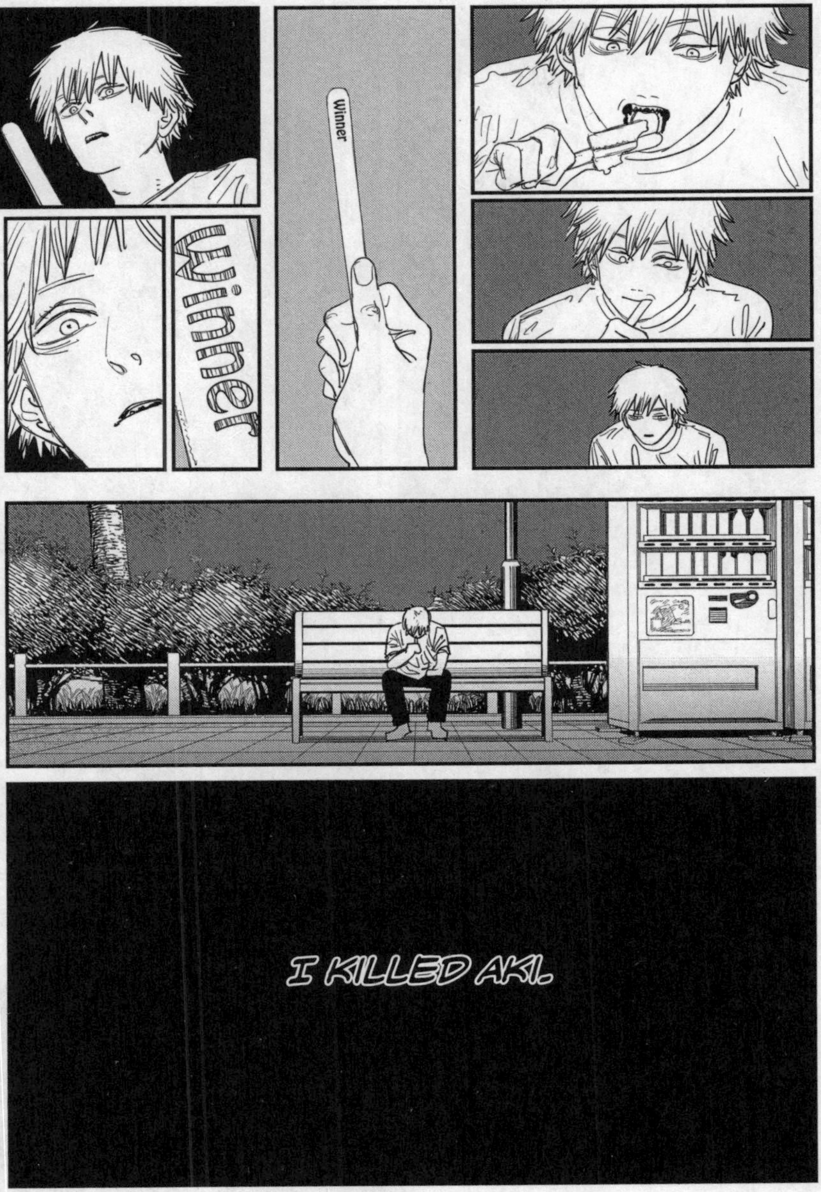
Winner
Winner
I KILLED AKI.

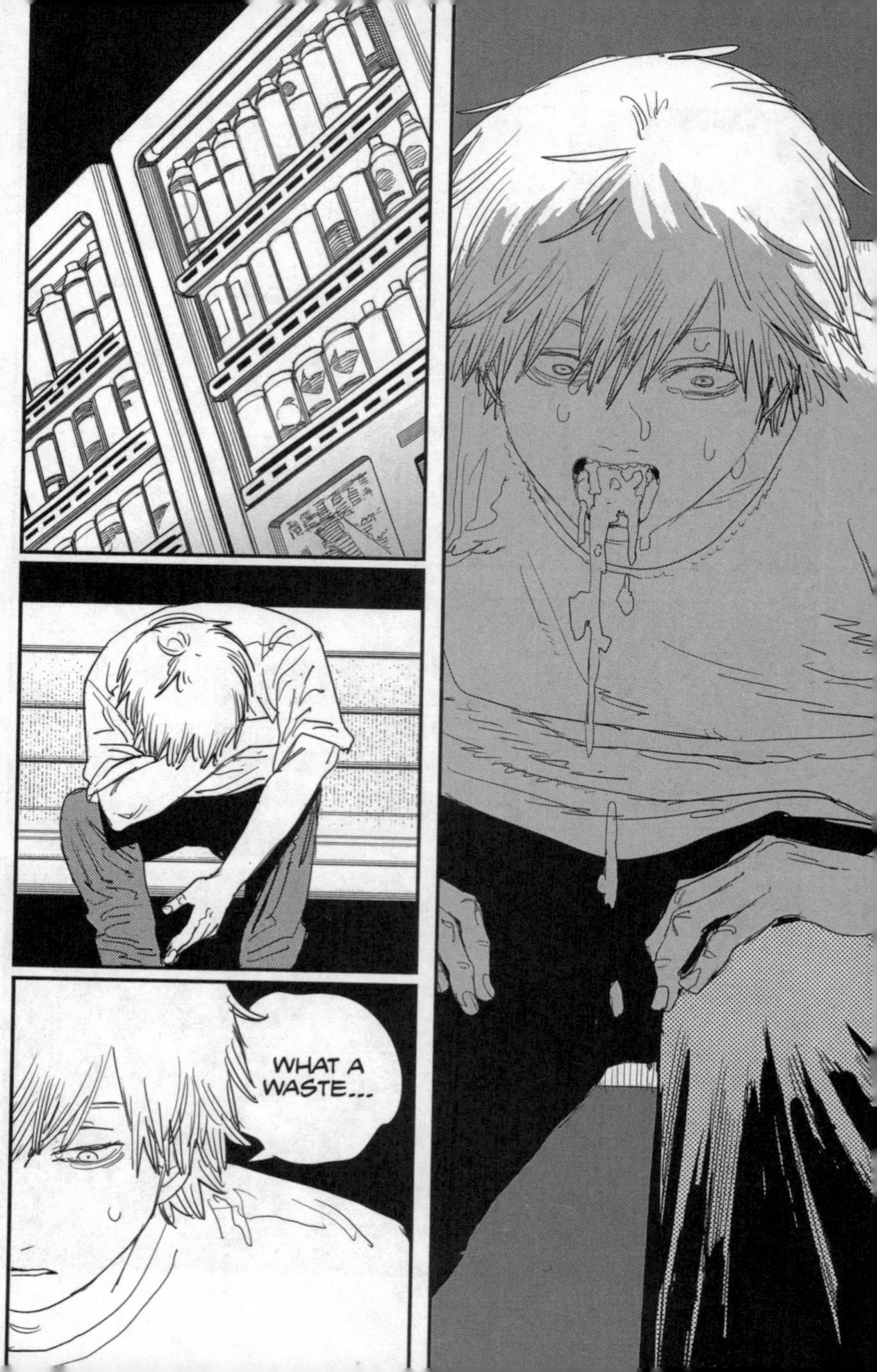
WHAT A WASTE...

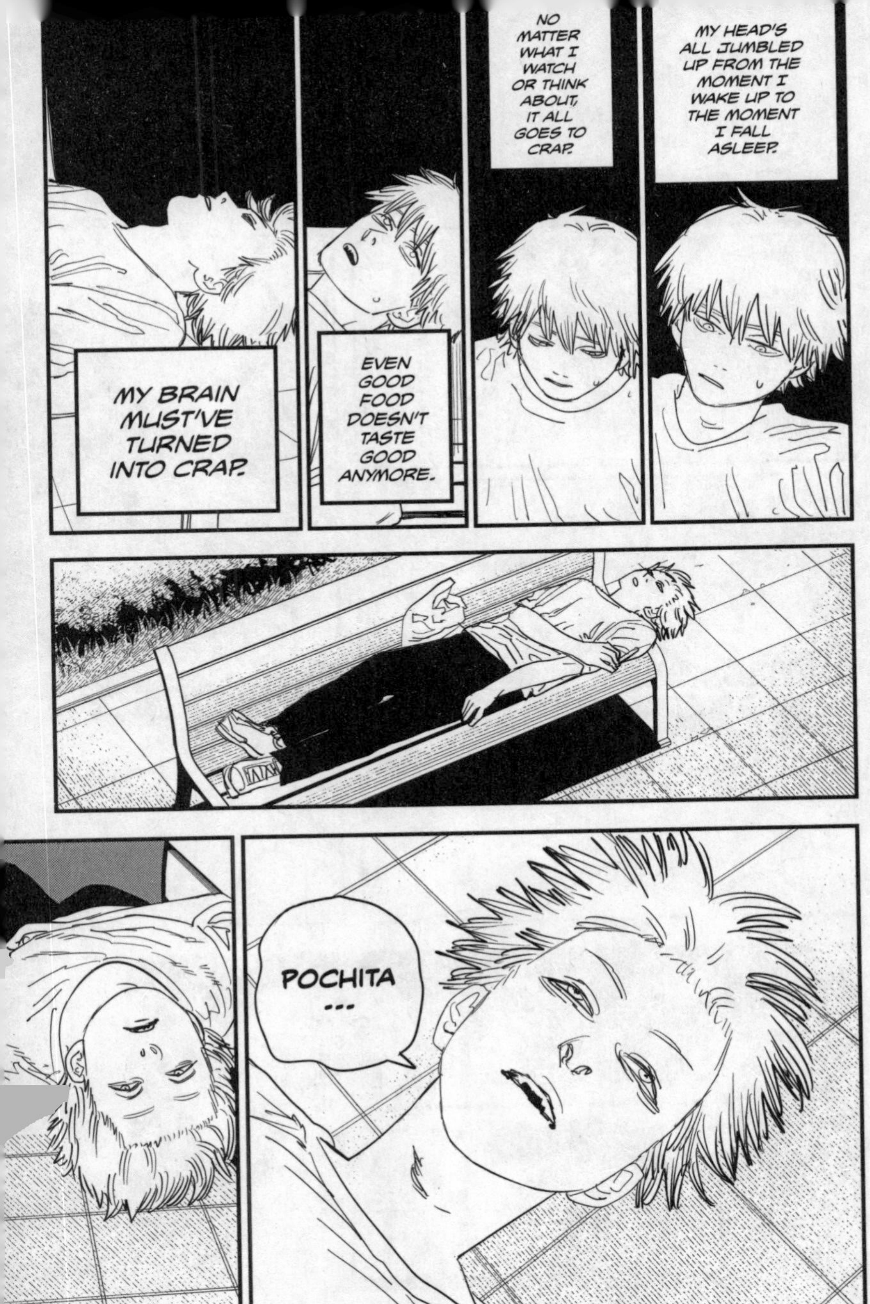
MY HEAD'S ALL JUMBLED UP FROM THE MOMENT I WAKE UP TO THE MOMENT I FALL ASLEEP.
NO MATTER WHAT I WATCH OR THINK ABOUT, IT ALL GOES TO CRAP.
EVEN GOOD FOOD DOESN'T TASTE GOOD ANYMORE.
MY BRAIN MUST'VE TURNED INTO CRAP.
POCHITA ...

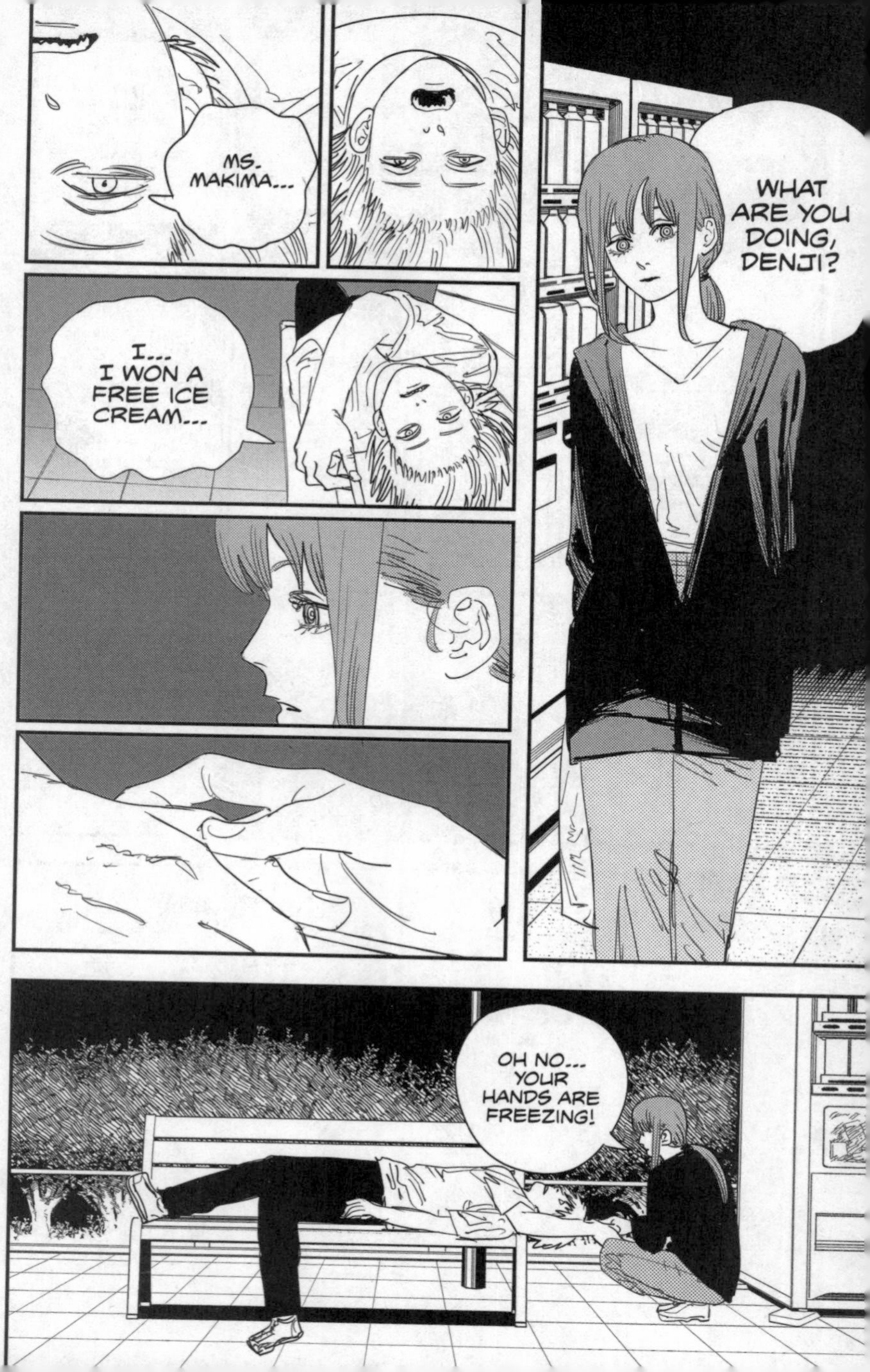
WHAT ARE YOU DOING, DENJI?
MS. MAKIMA...
I... I WON A FREE ICE CREAM...
OH NO... YOUR HANDS ARE FREEZING!

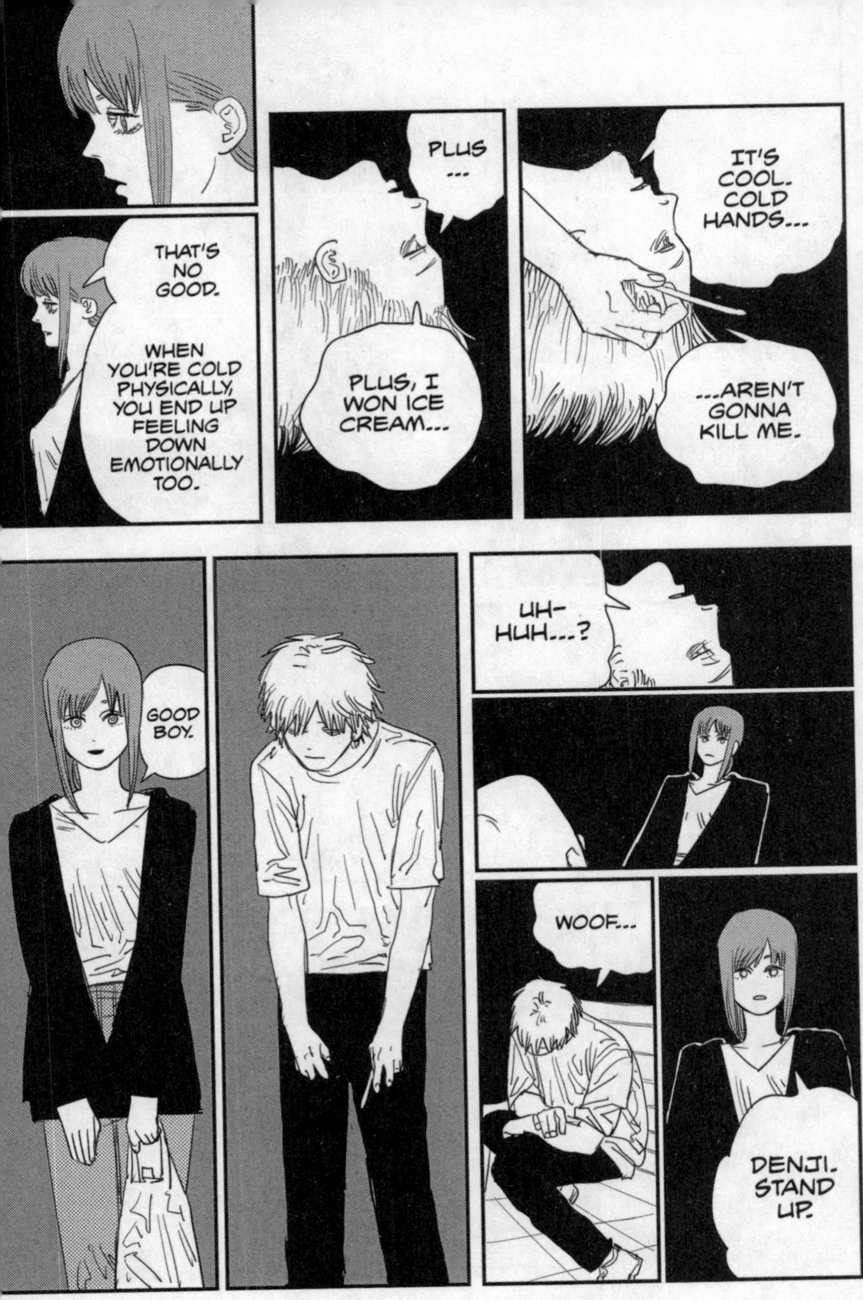
IT'S COOL. COLD HANDS...
...AREN'T GONNA KILL ME.
PLUS ...
PLUS, I WON ICE CREAM...
THAT'S NO GOOD.
WHEN YOU'RE COLD PHYSICALLY, YOU END UP FEELING DOWN EMOTIONALLY TOO.
UH-HUH...?
DENJI. STAND UP.
WOOF...
GOOD BOY.

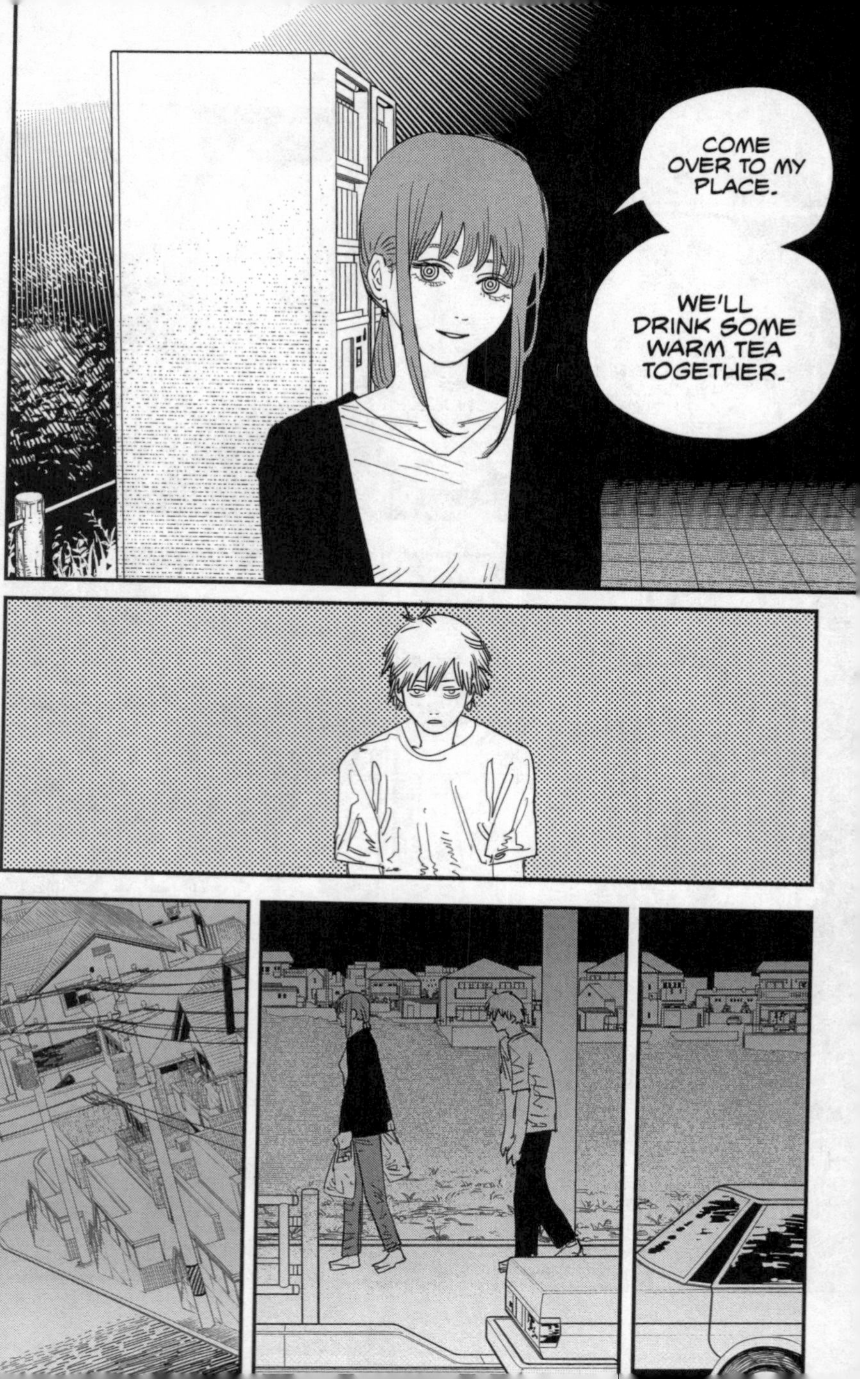
COME OVER TO MY PLACE.
WE'LL DRINK SOME WARM TEA TOGETHER.

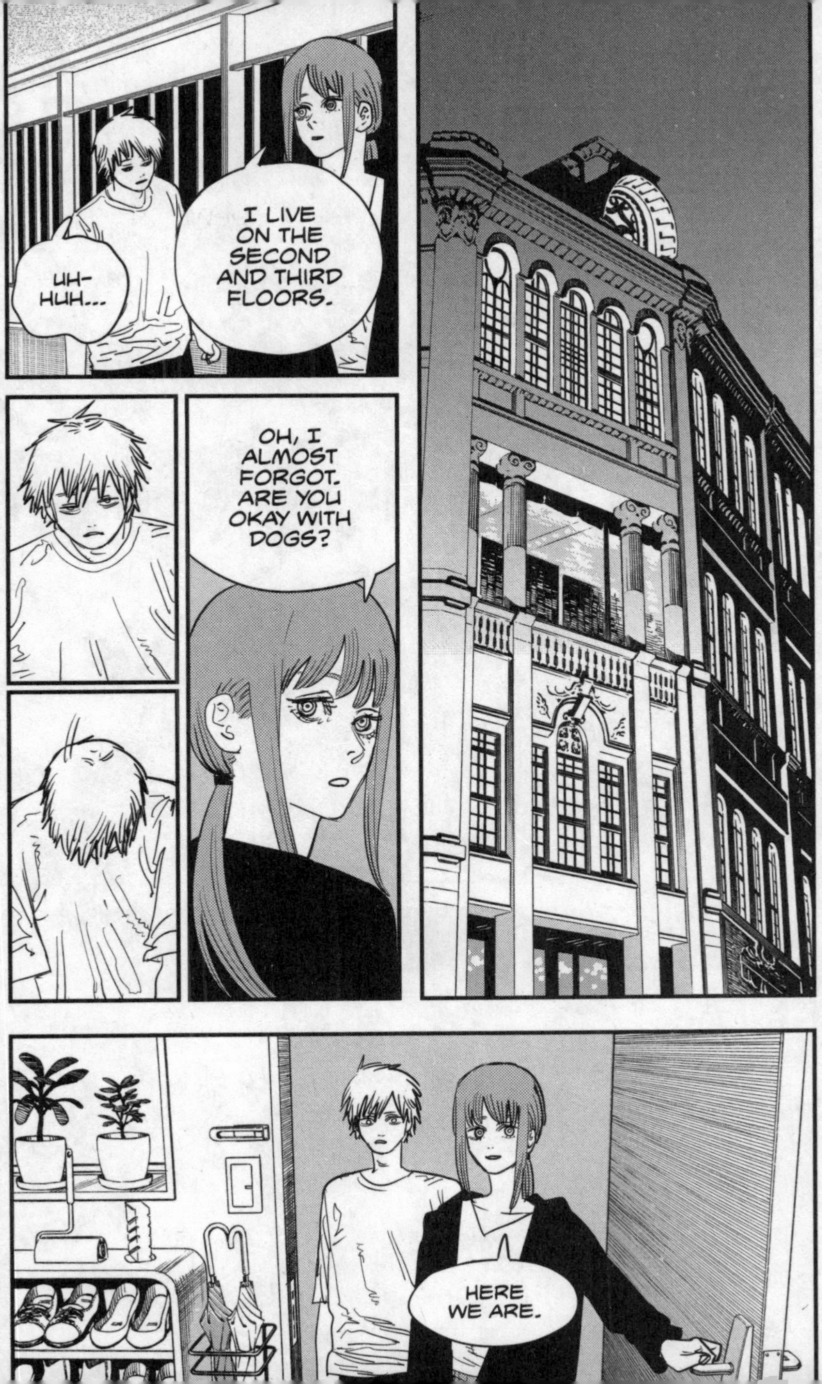
I LIVE ON THE SECOND AND THIRD FLOORS.
UH-HUH...
OH, I ALMOST FORGOT. ARE YOU OKAY WITH DOGS?
HERE WE ARE.

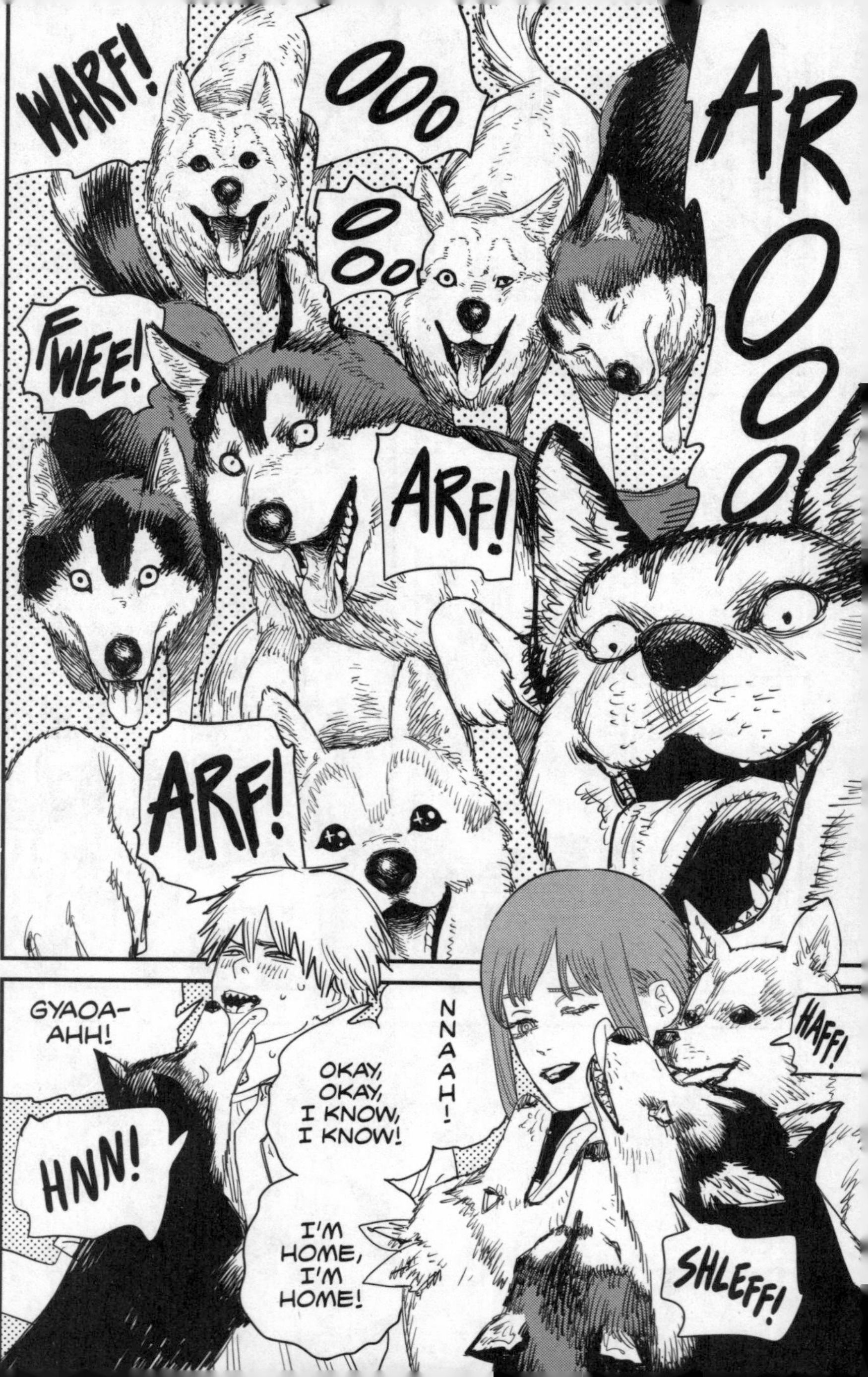
AROOOO!
OOO
OOo
WARF!
FWEE!
ARF!
ARF!
HAFF!
SHLEFF!
NNAAH!
OKAY, OKAY, I KNOW, I KNOW!
I'M HOME, I'M HOME!
GYAOA-AHH!
HNN!

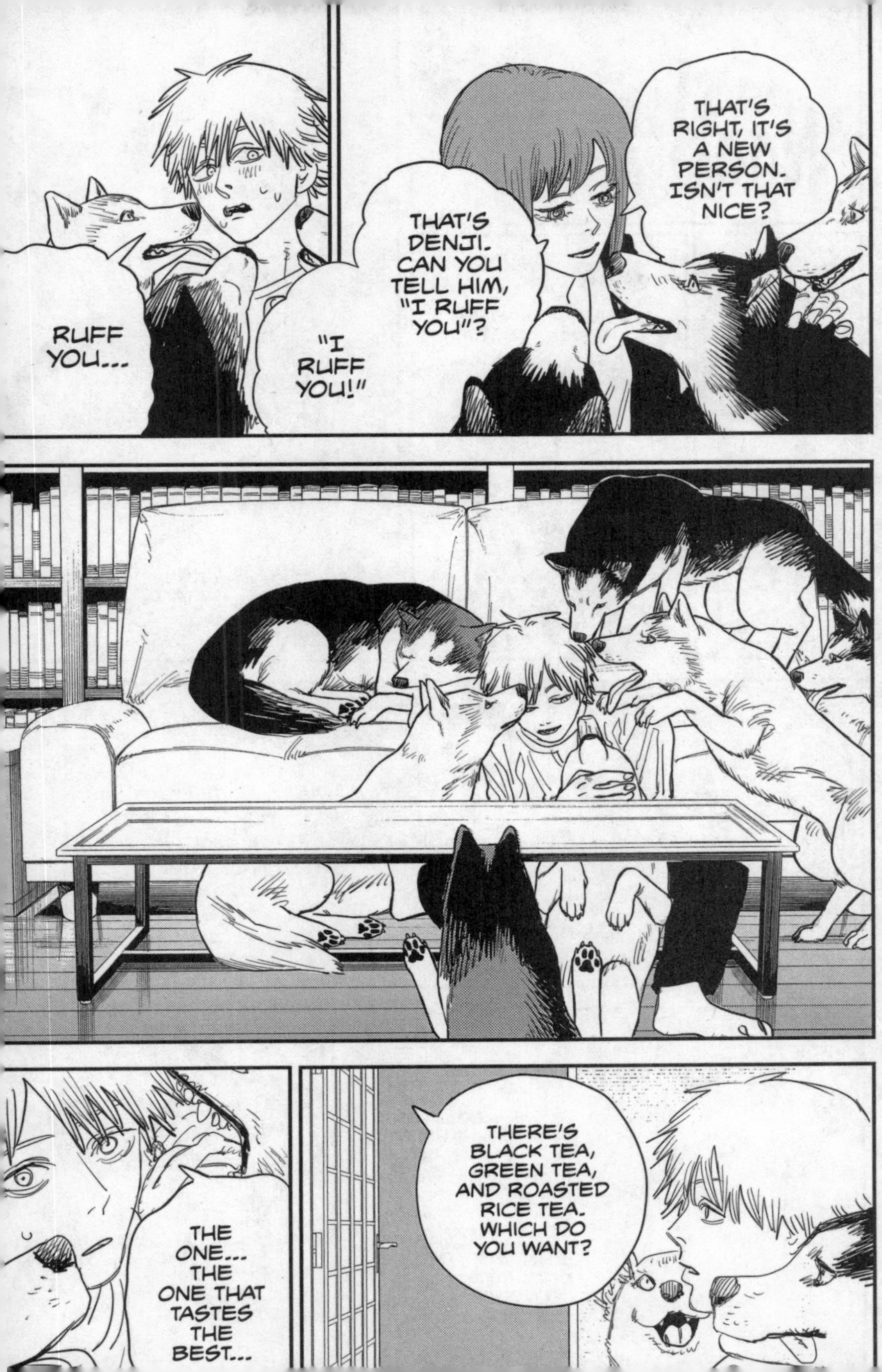
THAT'S RIGHT, IT'S A NEW PERSON. ISN'T THAT NICE?
THAT'S DENJI. CAN YOU TELL HIM, "I RUFF YOU"?
"I RUFF YOU!"
RUFF YOU...
THERE'S BLACK TEA, GREEN TEA, AND ROASTED RICE TEA. WHICH DO YOU WANT?
THE ONE... THE ONE THAT TASTES THE BEST...

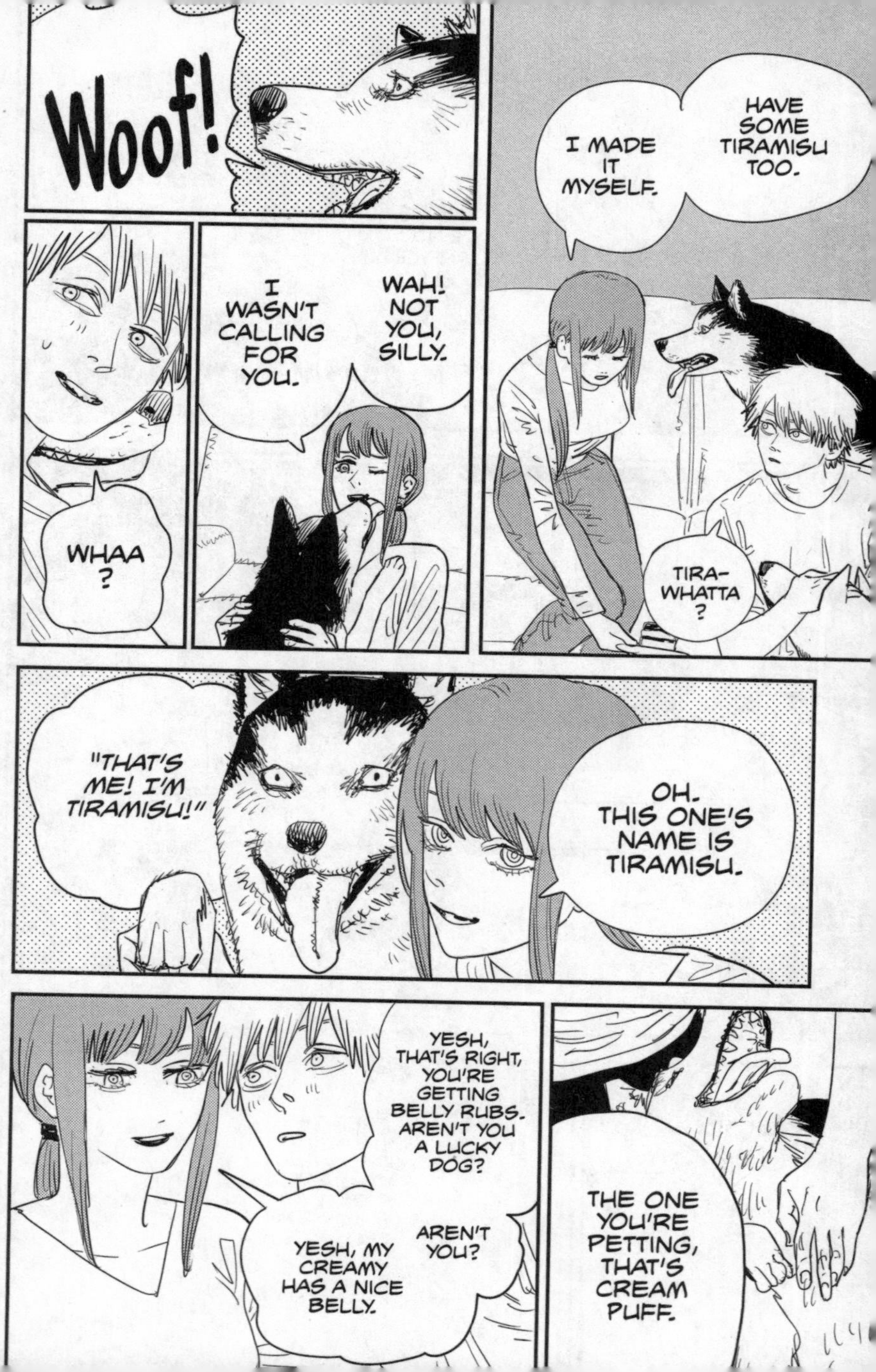
HAVE SOME TIRAMISU TOO.
I MADE IT MYSELF.
TIRA-WHATTA?
Woof!
WAH! NOT YOU, SILLY.
I WASN'T CALLING FOR YOU.
WHAA?
OH. THIS ONE'S NAME IS TIRAMISU.
"THAT'S ME! I'M TIRAMISU!"
THE ONE YOU'RE PETTING, THAT'S CREAM PUFF.
YESH, THAT'S RIGHT, YOU'RE GETTING BELLY RUBS. AREN'T YOU A LUCKY DOG?
AREN'T YOU?
YESH, MY CREAMY HAS A NICE BELLY.

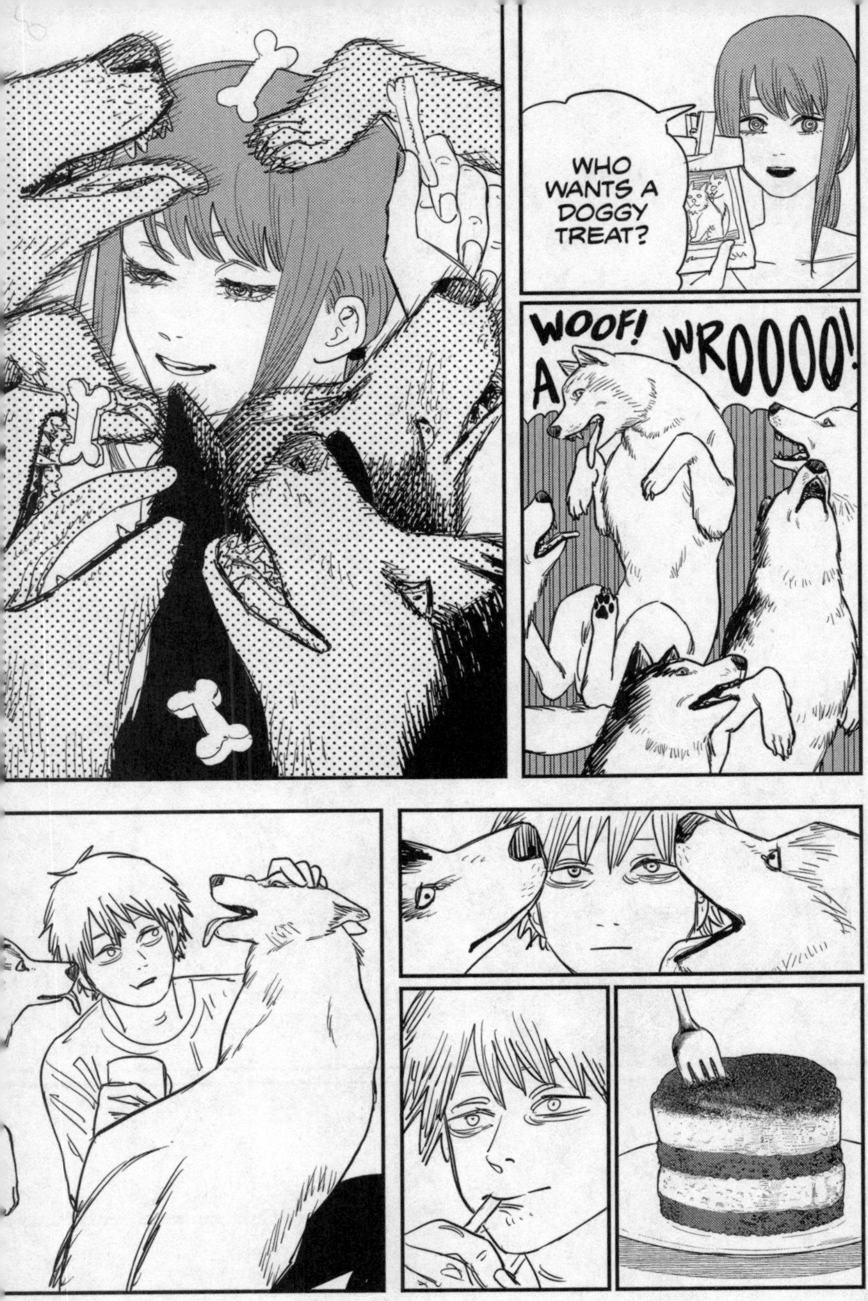
WHO WANTS A DOGGY TREAT?
WOOF!
A WROOOO!

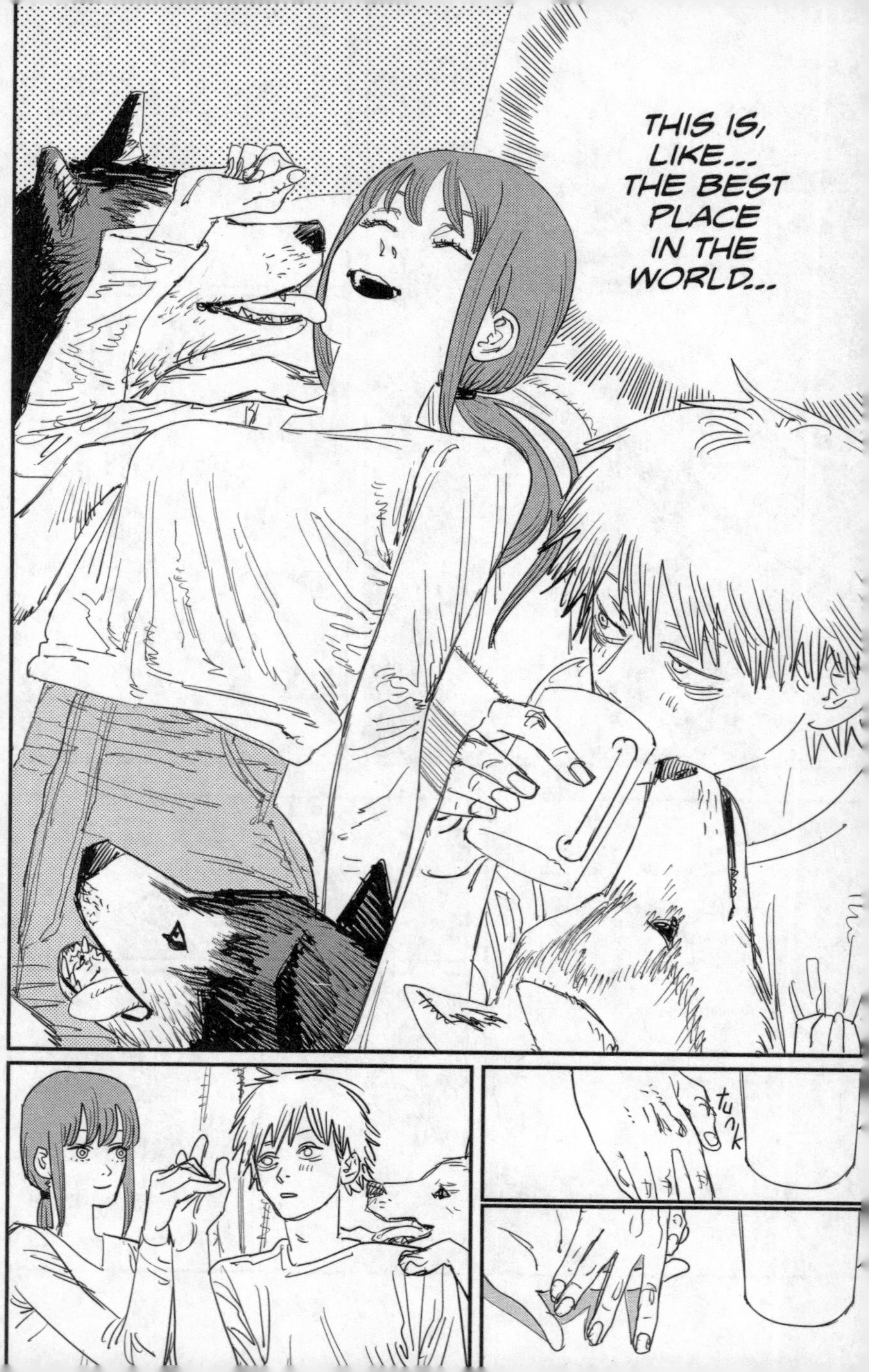
THIS IS, LIKE... THE BEST PLACE IN THE WORLD...
tunk

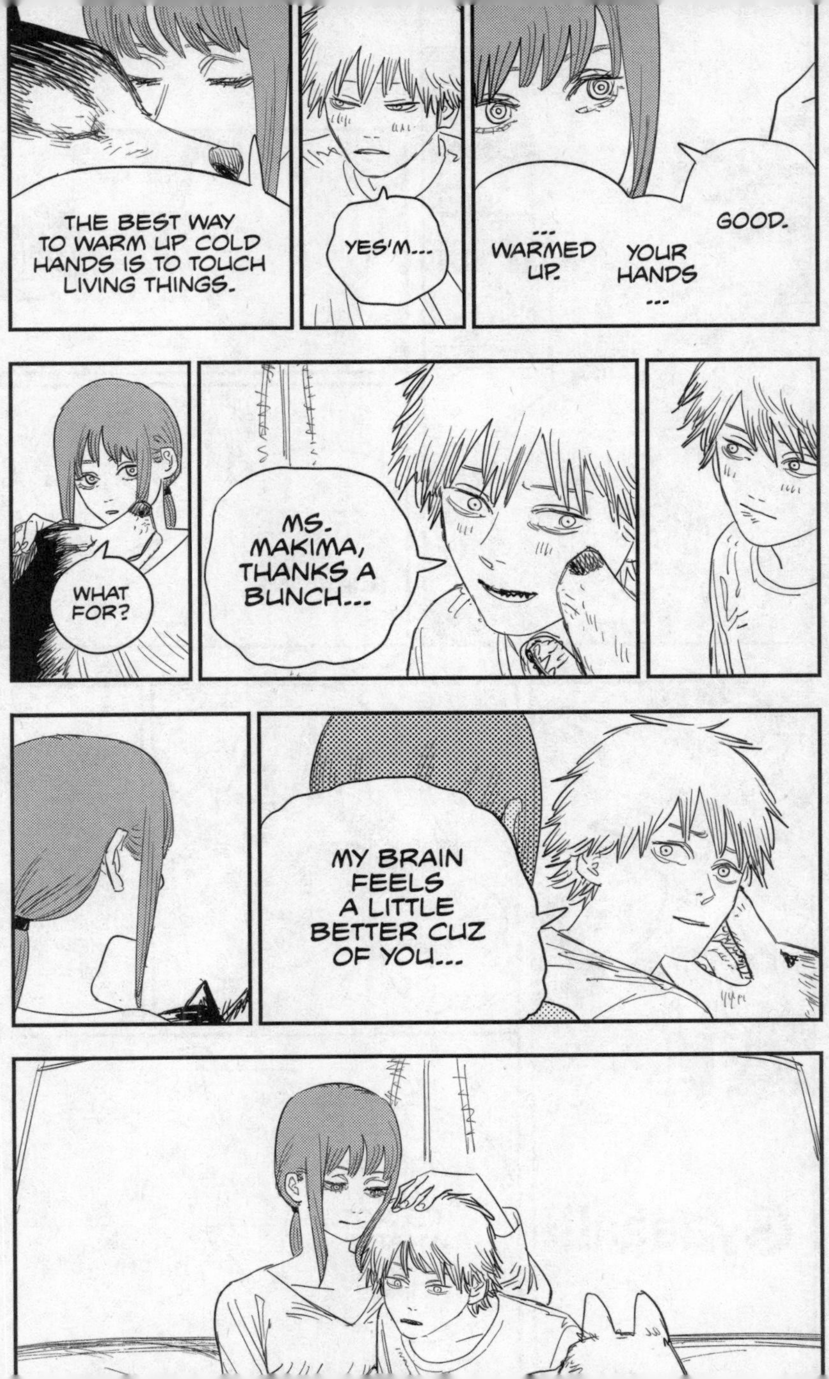
GOOD.
YOUR HANDS ...
... WARMED UP.
YES'M...
THE BEST WAY TO WARM UP COLD HANDS IS TO TOUCH LIVING THINGS.
MS. MAKIMA, THANKS A BUNCH...
WHAT FOR?
MY BRAIN FEELS A LITTLE BETTER CUZ OF YOU...

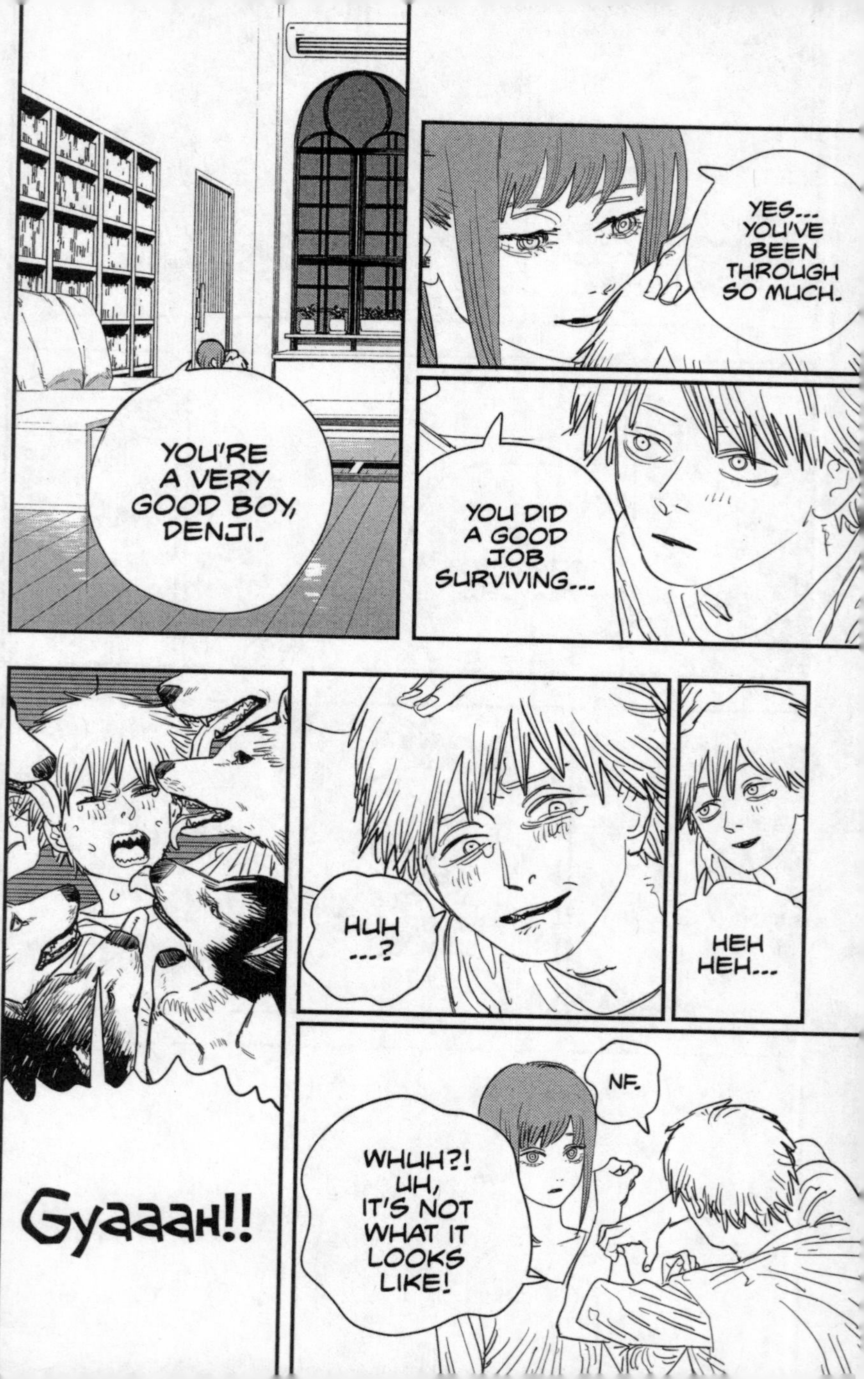
YES... YOU'VE BEEN THROUGH SO MUCH.
YOU DID A GOOD JOB SURVIVING...
YOU'RE A VERY GOOD BOY, DENJI.
HEH HEH...
HUH ...?
NF.
WHUH?! UH, IT'S NOT WHAT IT LOOKS LIKE!
Gyaaah!!

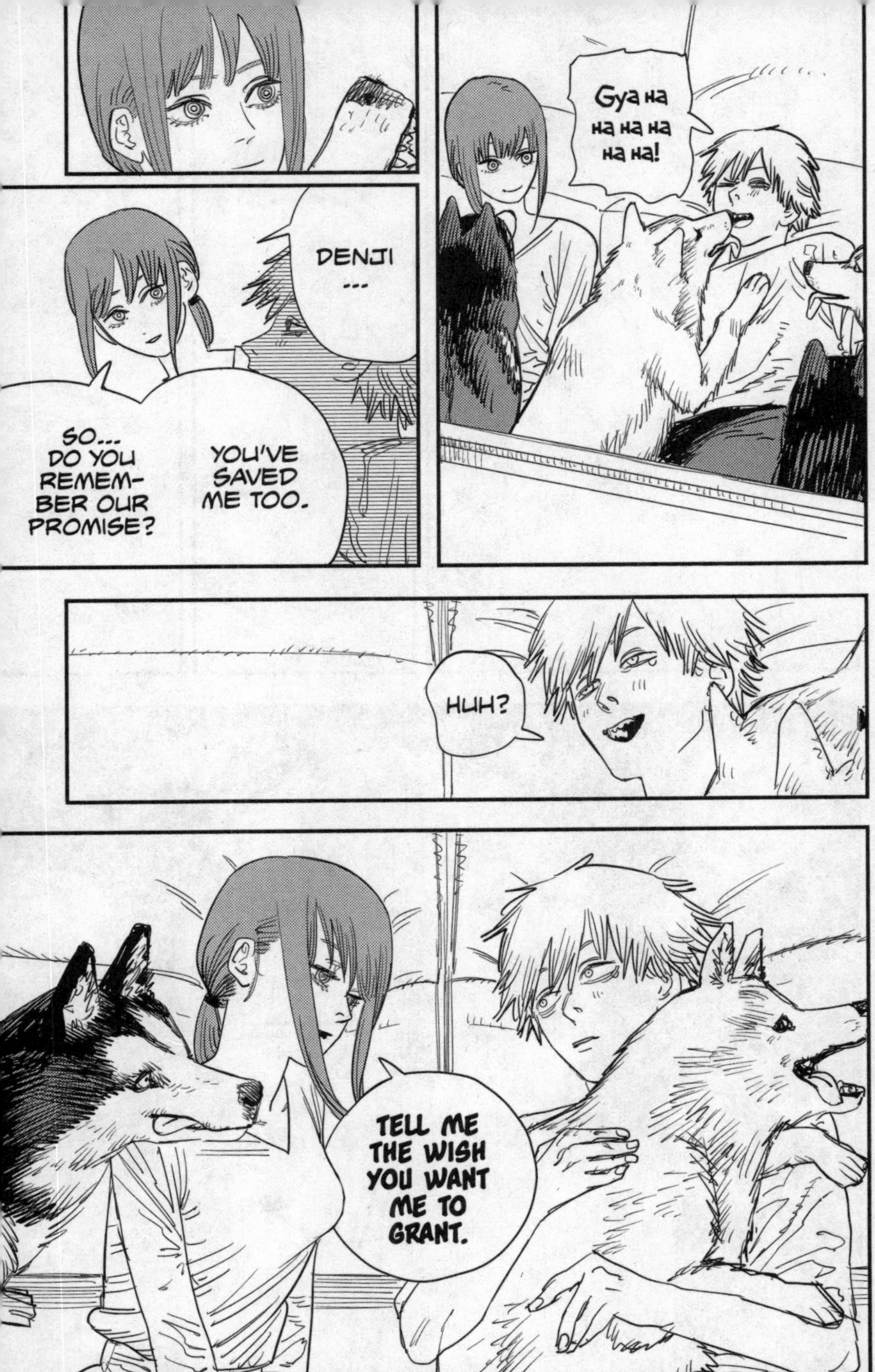
Gya ha ha ha ha ha ha!
DENJI ...
YOU'VE SAVED ME TOO.
SO... DO YOU REMEMBER OUR PROMISE?
HUH?
TELL ME THE WISH YOU WANT ME TO GRANT.

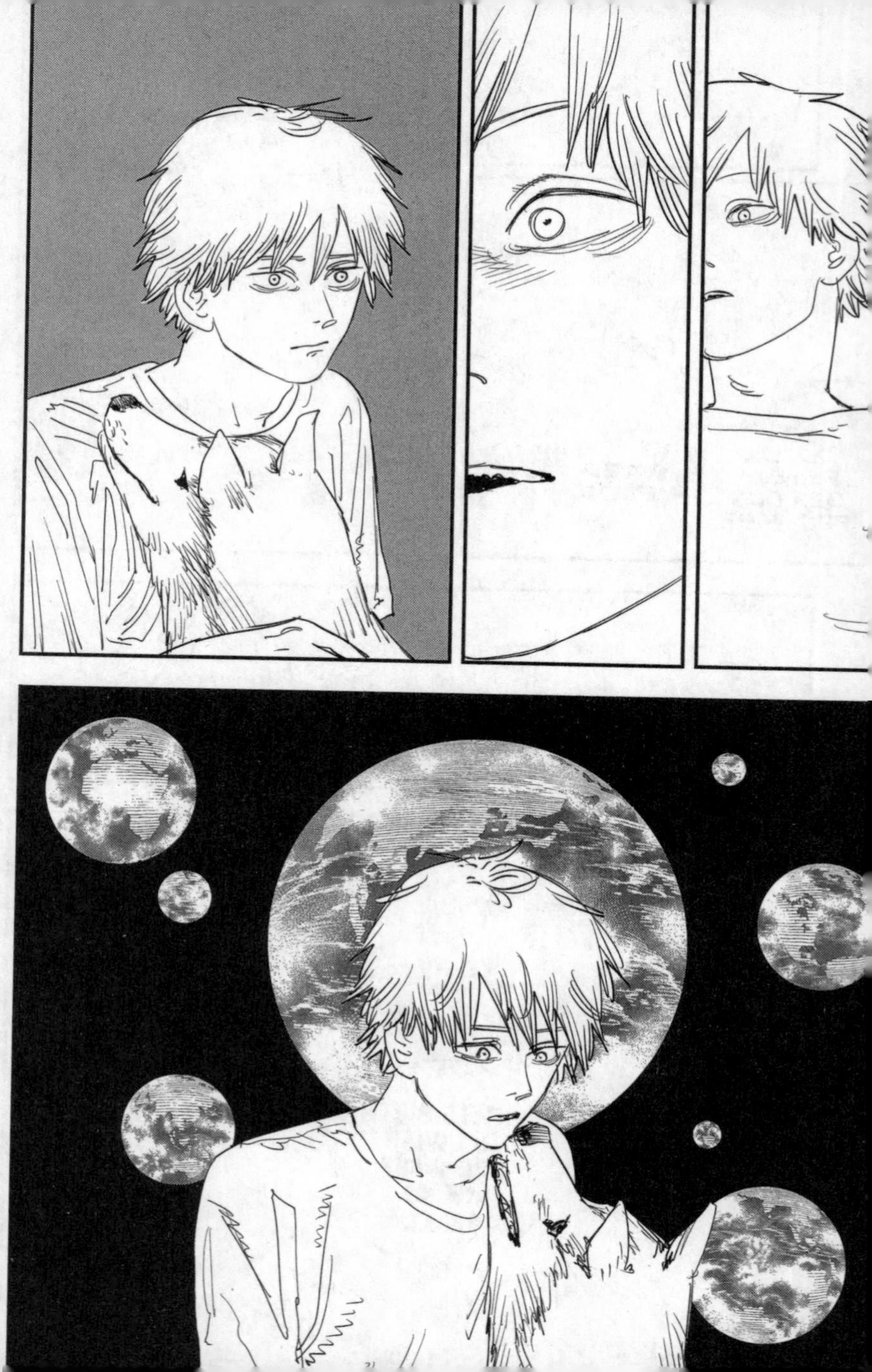

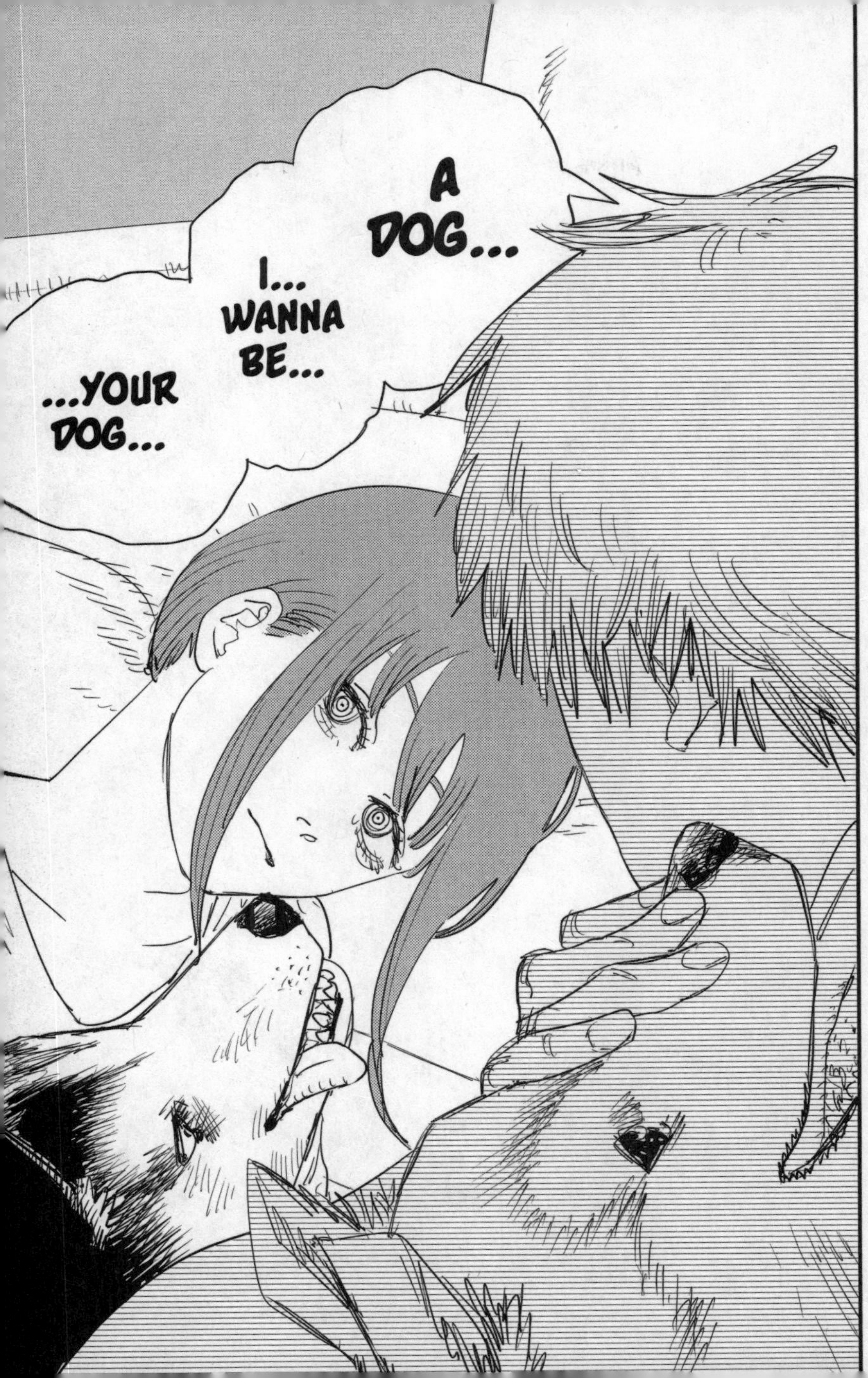
A DOG...
I... WANNA BE...
...YOUR DOG...

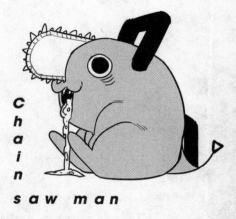

Chain saw man

Chapter 81: Paw

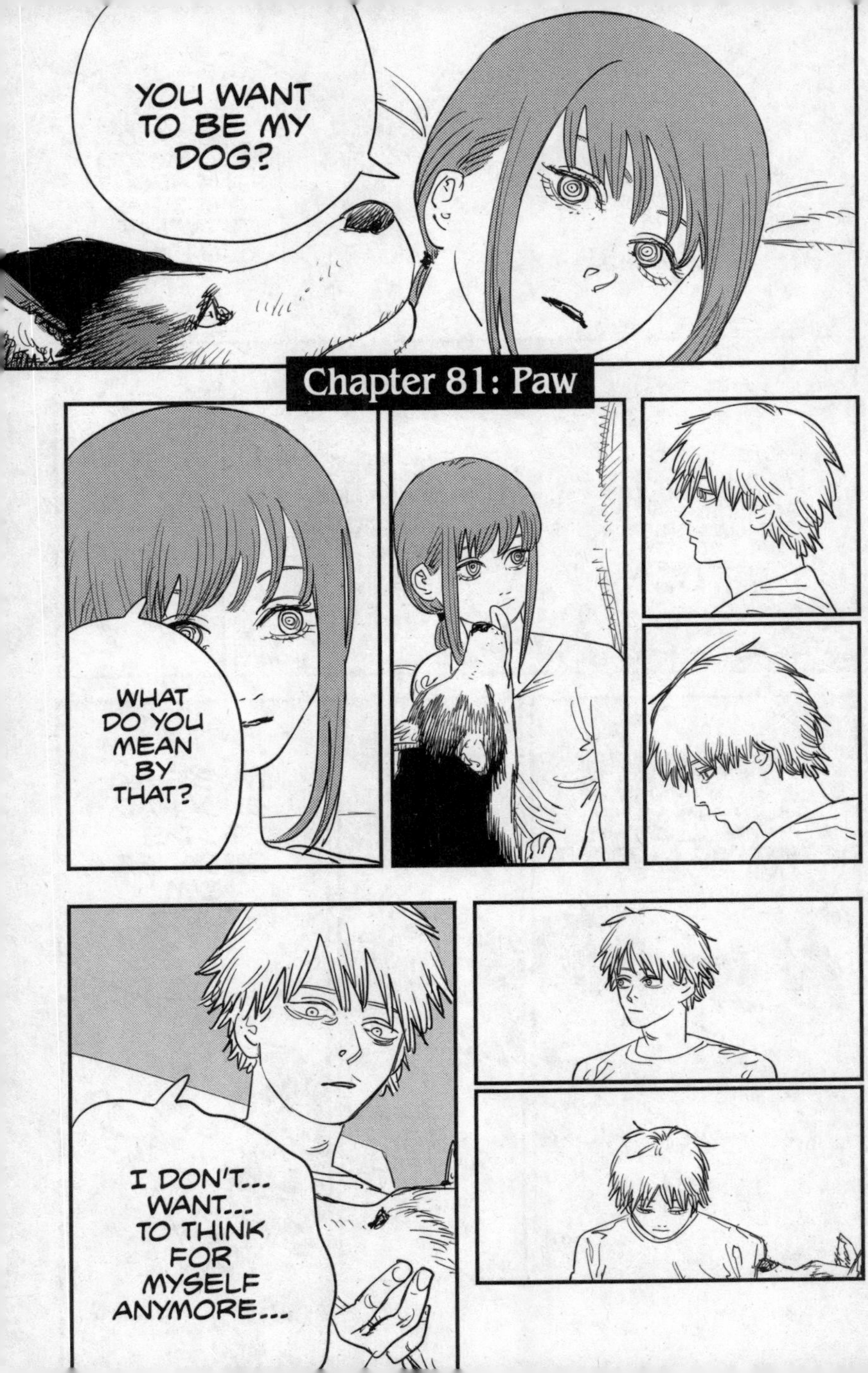
YOU WANT TO BE MY DOG?
WHAT DO YOU MEAN BY THAT?
I DON'T... WANT... TO THINK FOR MYSELF ANYMORE...

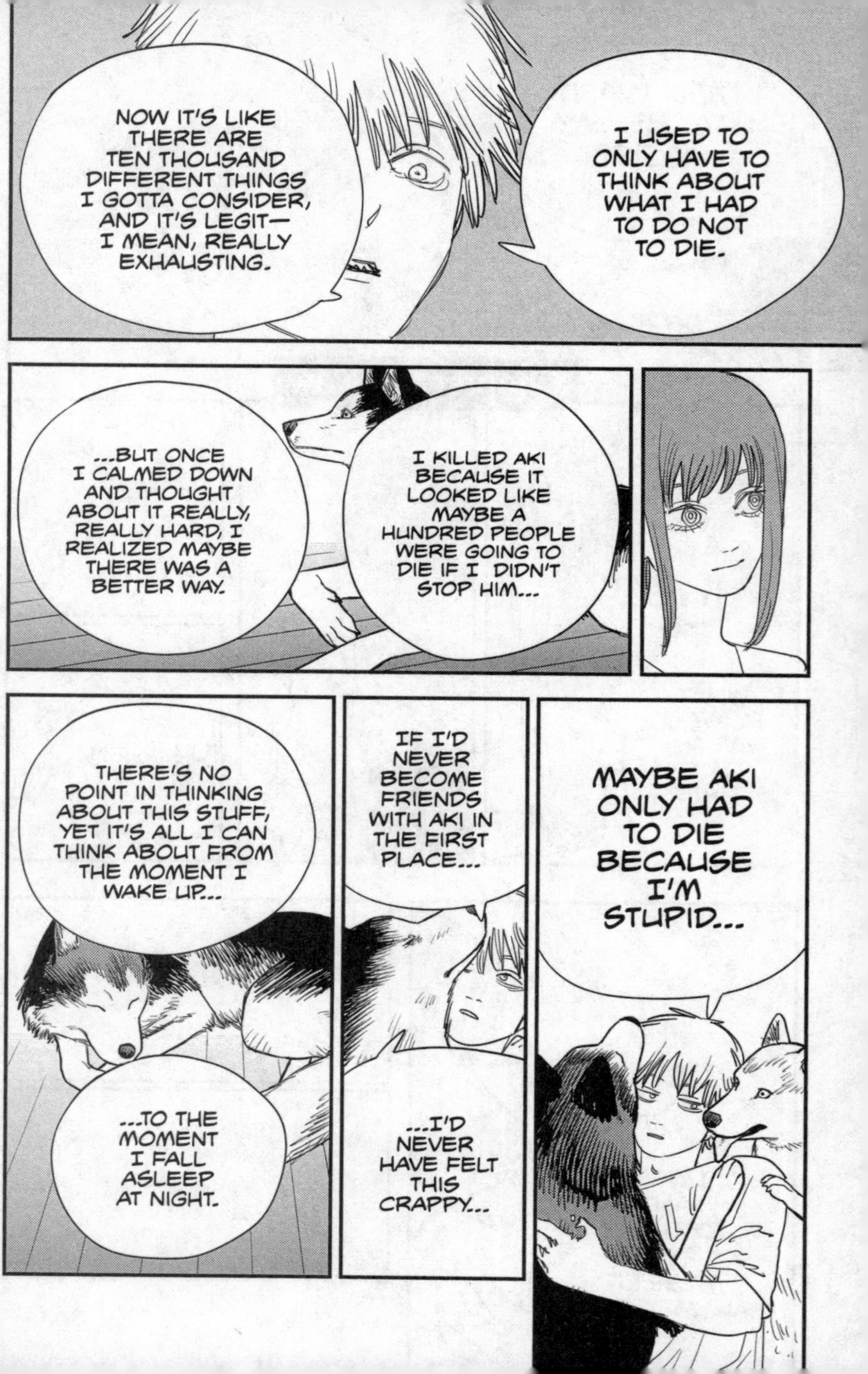
I USED TO ONLY HAVE TO THINK ABOUT WHAT I HAD TO DO NOT TO DIE.
NOW IT'S LIKE THERE ARE TEN THOUSAND DIFFERENT THINGS I GOTTA CONSIDER, AND IT'S LEGIT— I MEAN, REALLY EXHAUSTING.
I KILLED AKI BECAUSE IT LOOKED LIKE MAYBE A HUNDRED PEOPLE WERE GOING TO DIE IF I DIDN'T STOP HIM...
...BUT ONCE I CALMED DOWN AND THOUGHT ABOUT IT REALLY, REALLY HARD, I REALIZED MAYBE THERE WAS A BETTER WAY.
MAYBE AKI ONLY HAD TO DIE BECAUSE I'M STUPID...
IF I'D NEVER BECOME FRIENDS WITH AKI IN THE FIRST PLACE...
...I'D NEVER HAVE FELT THIS CRAPPY...
THERE'S NO POINT IN THINKING ABOUT THIS STUFF, YET IT'S ALL I CAN THINK ABOUT FROM THE MOMENT I WAKE UP...
...TO THE MOMENT I FALL ASLEEP AT NIGHT.

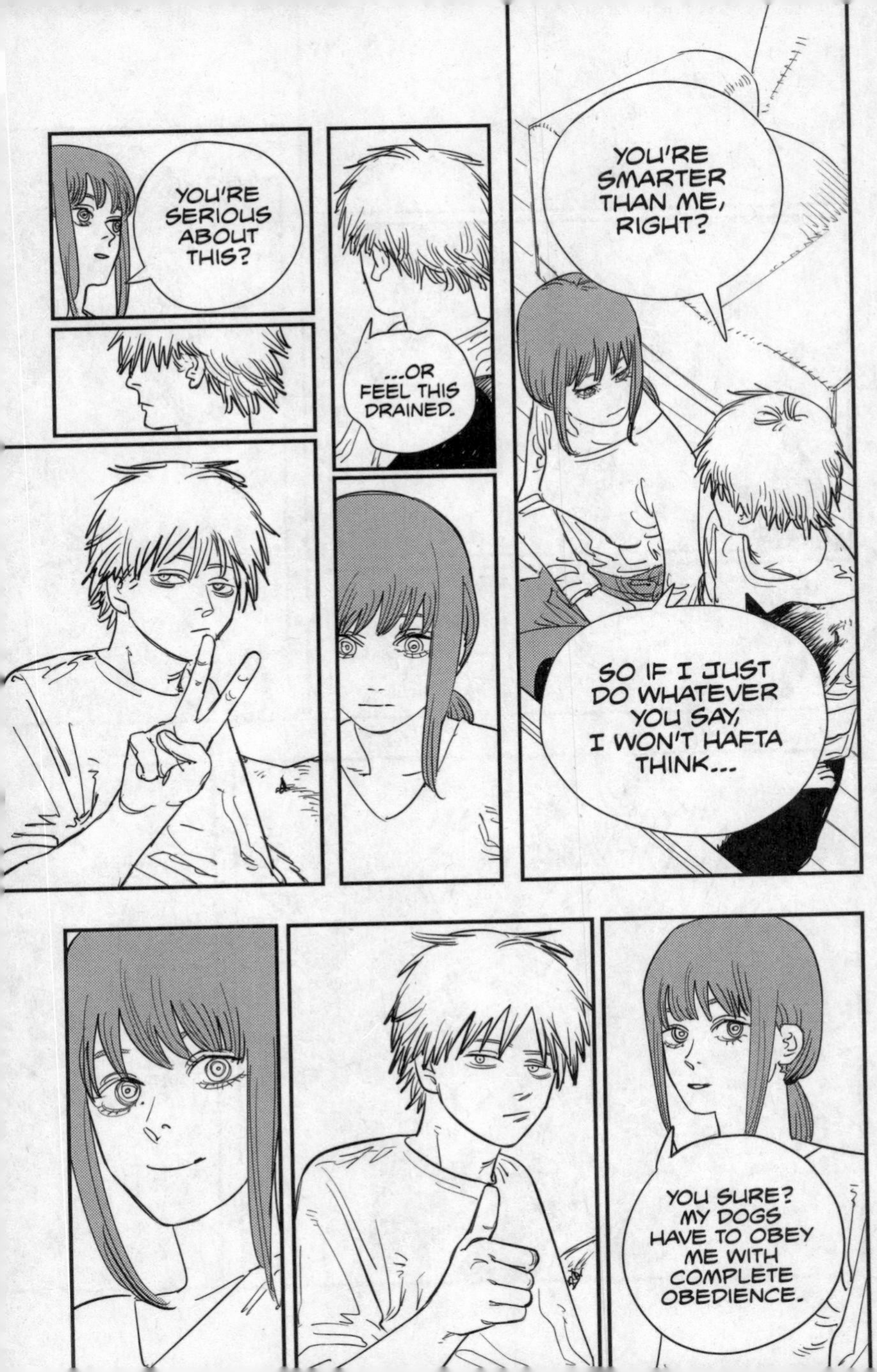
YOU'RE SMARTER THAN ME, RIGHT?
SO IF I JUST DO WHATEVER YOU SAY, I WON'T HAFTA THINK...
...OR FEEL THIS DRAINED.
YOU'RE SERIOUS ABOUT THIS?
YOU SURE? MY DOGS HAVE TO OBEY ME WITH COMPLETE OBEDIENCE.

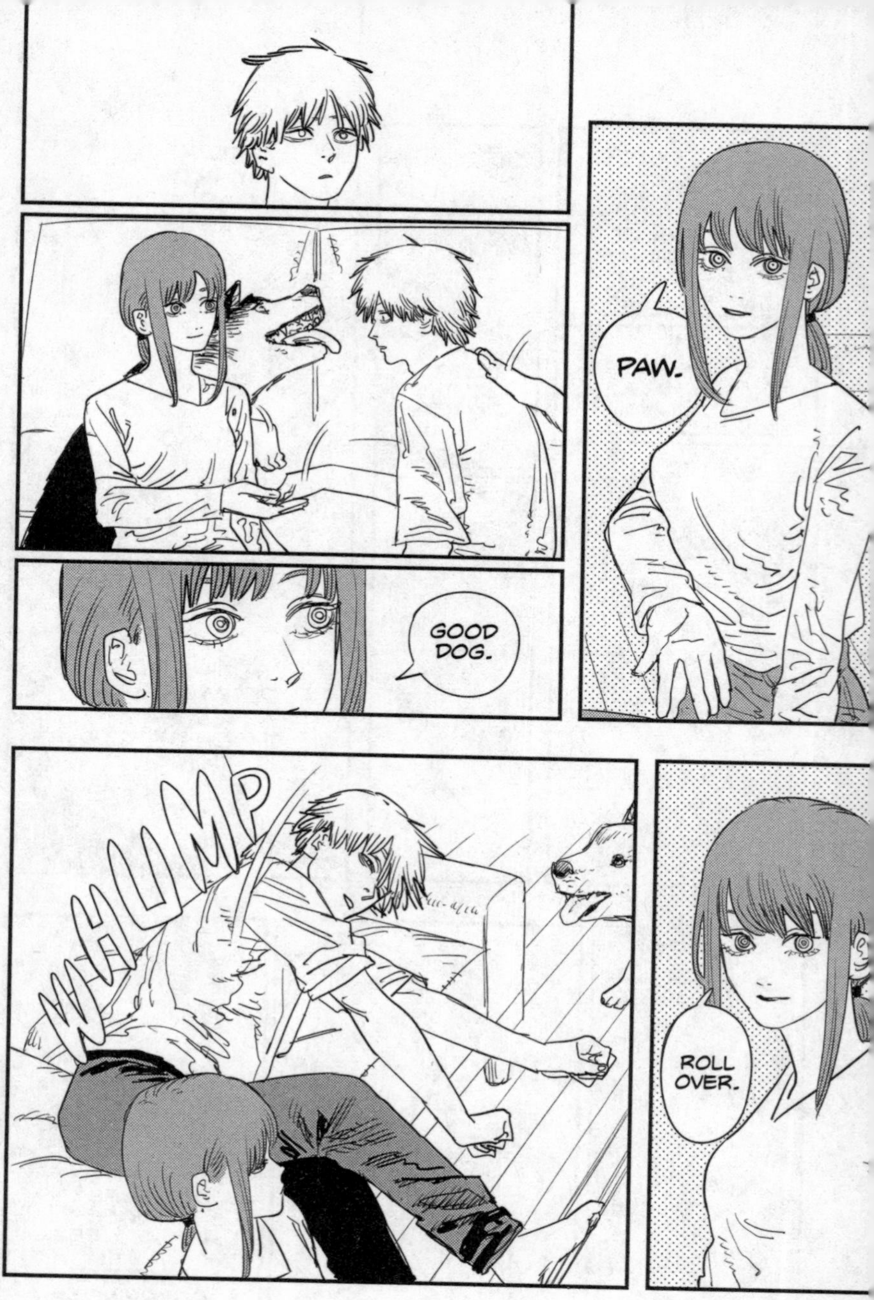
PAW.
GOOD DOG.
ROLL OVER.
WHUMP

WHAT A SMART DOG YOU ARE, DENJI.

GOOD BOY.

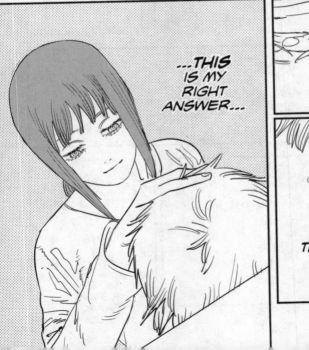

...THIS IS MY RIGHT ANSWER...

I THINK...

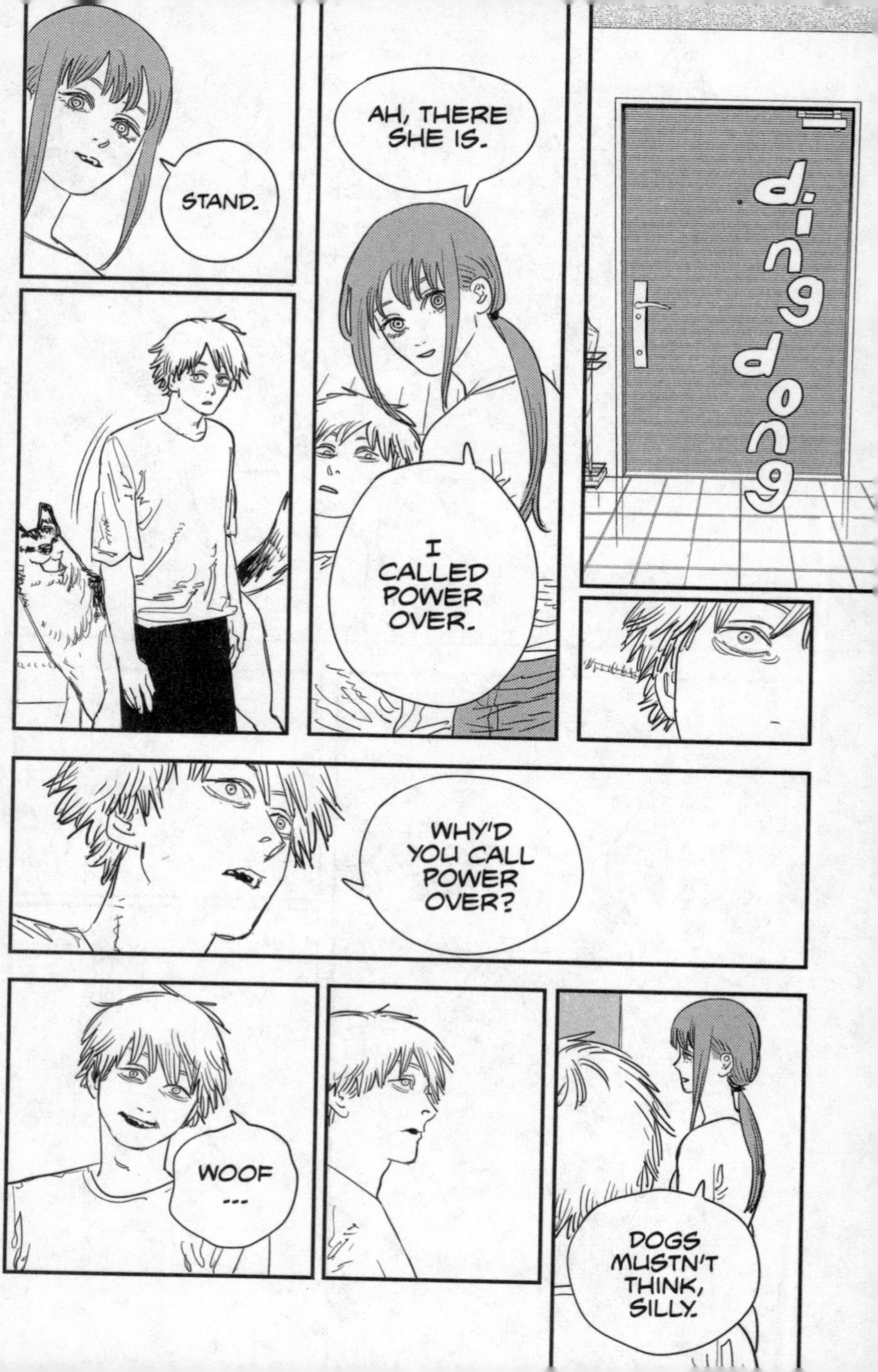
ding dong
AH, THERE SHE IS.
I CALLED POWER OVER.
STAND.
WHY'D YOU CALL POWER OVER?
DOGS MUSTN'T THINK, SILLY.
WOOF ...

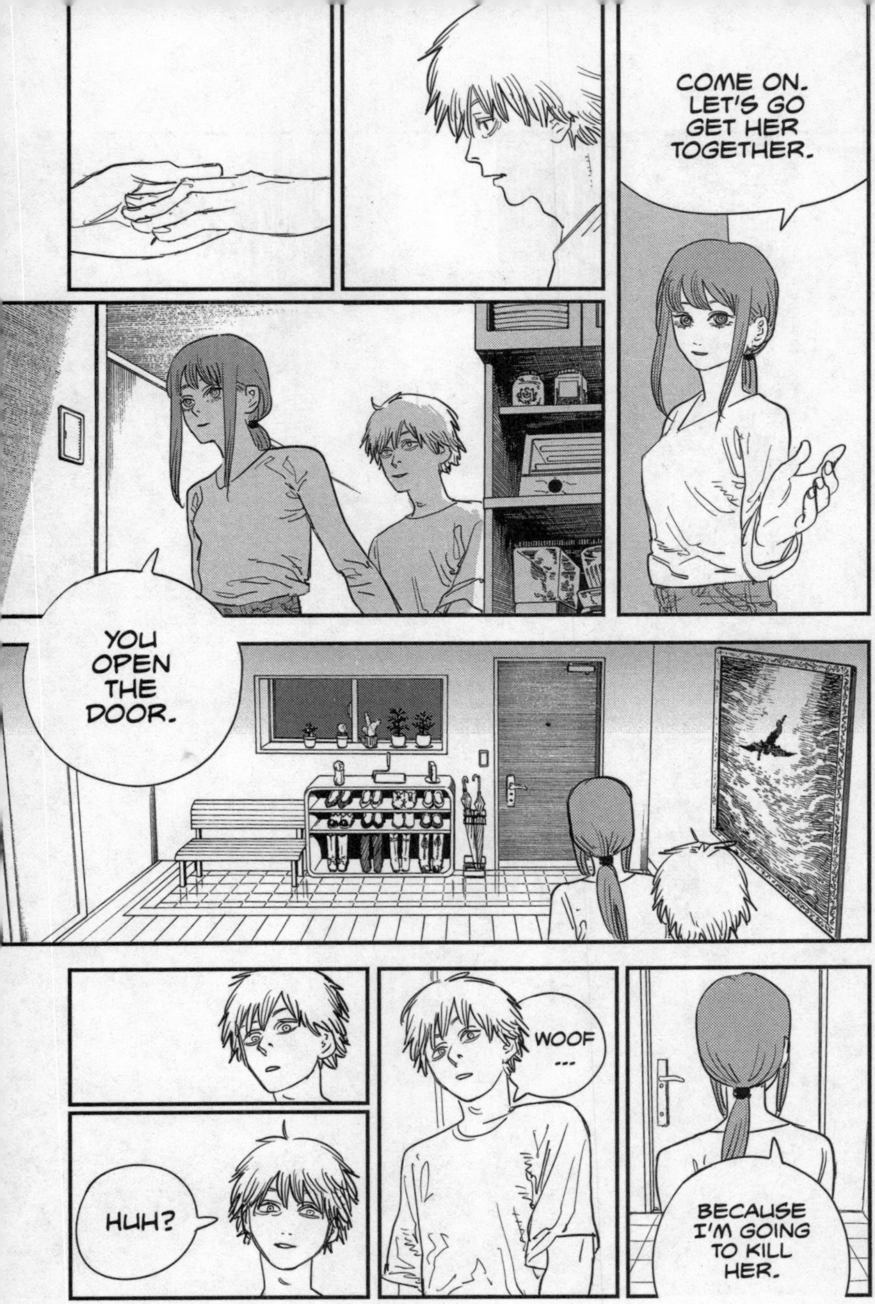
COME ON. LET'S GO GET HER TOGETHER.
YOU OPEN THE DOOR.
BECAUSE I'M GOING TO KILL HER.
WOOF ...
HUH?

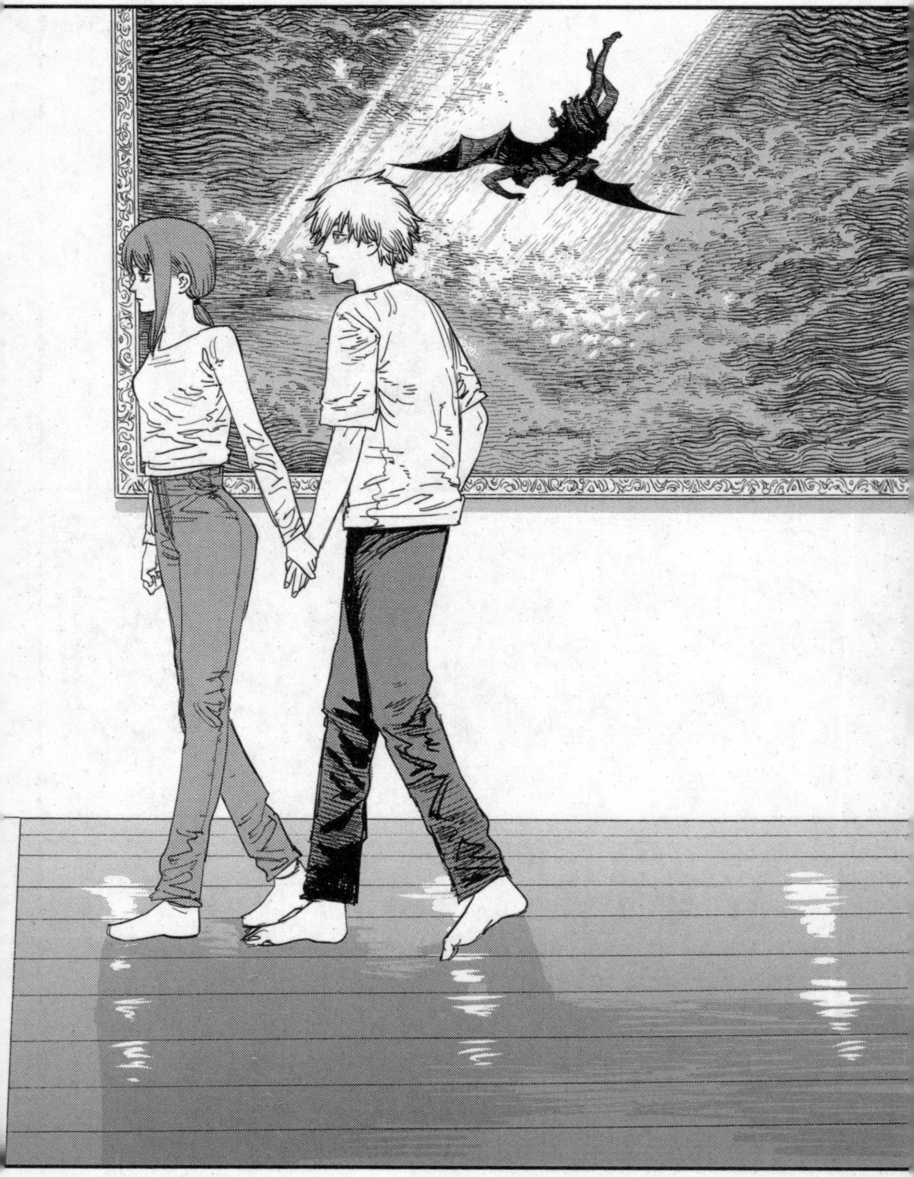

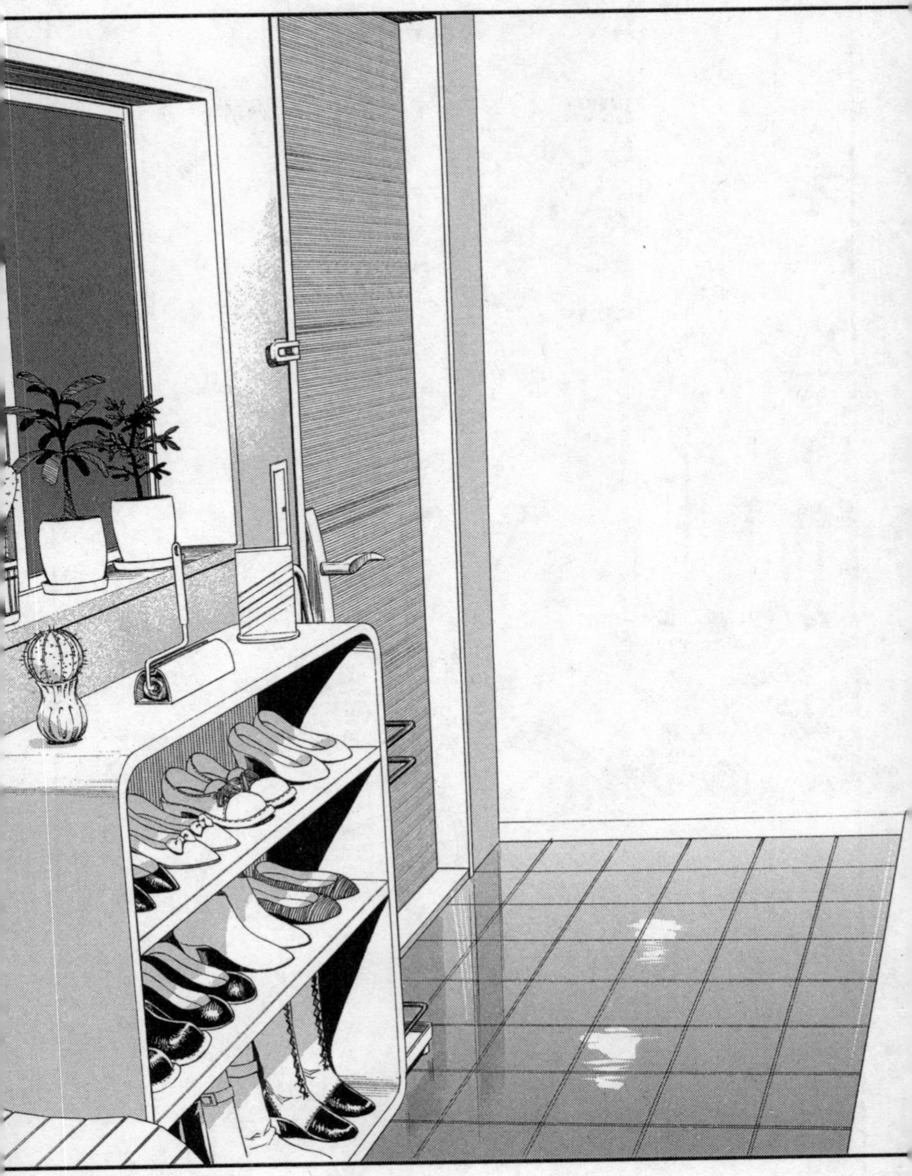

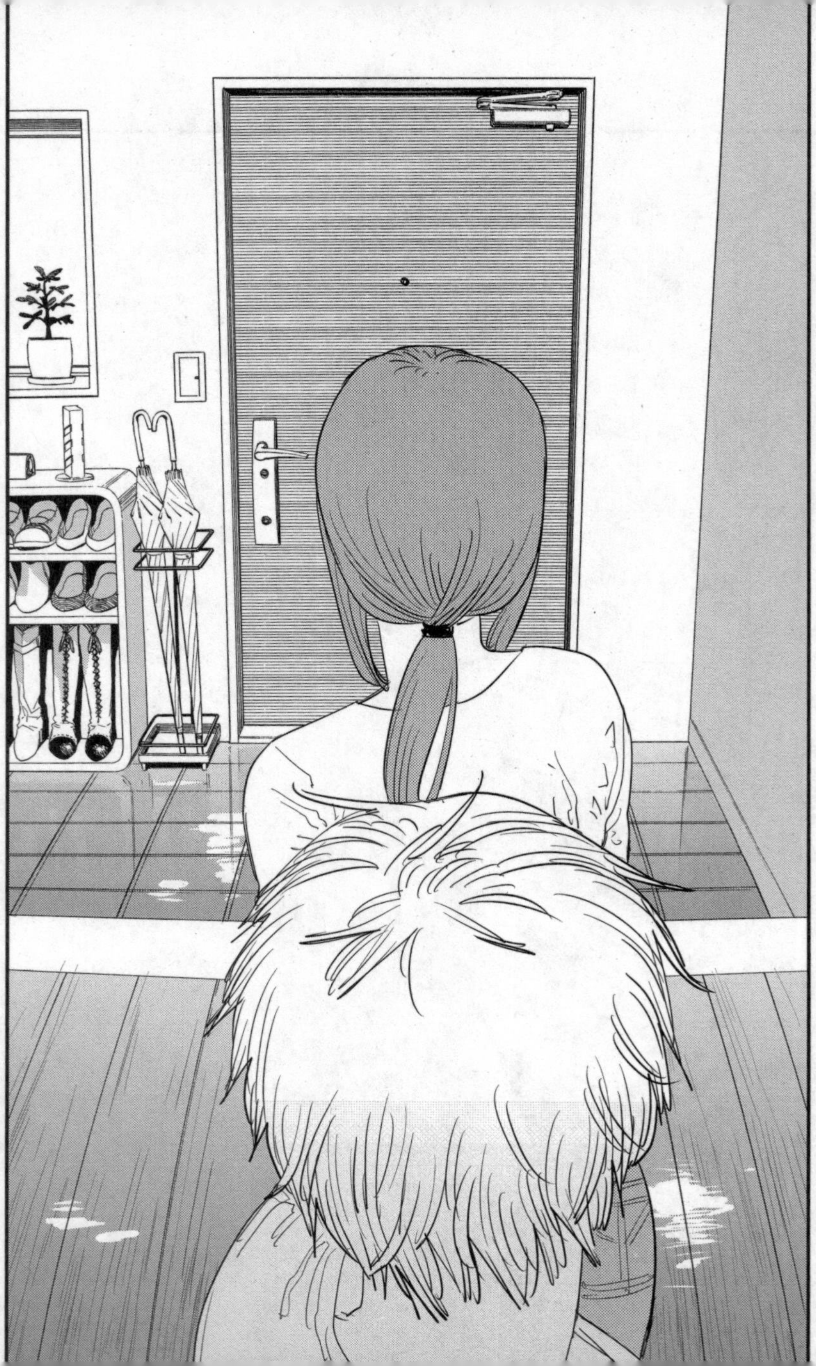

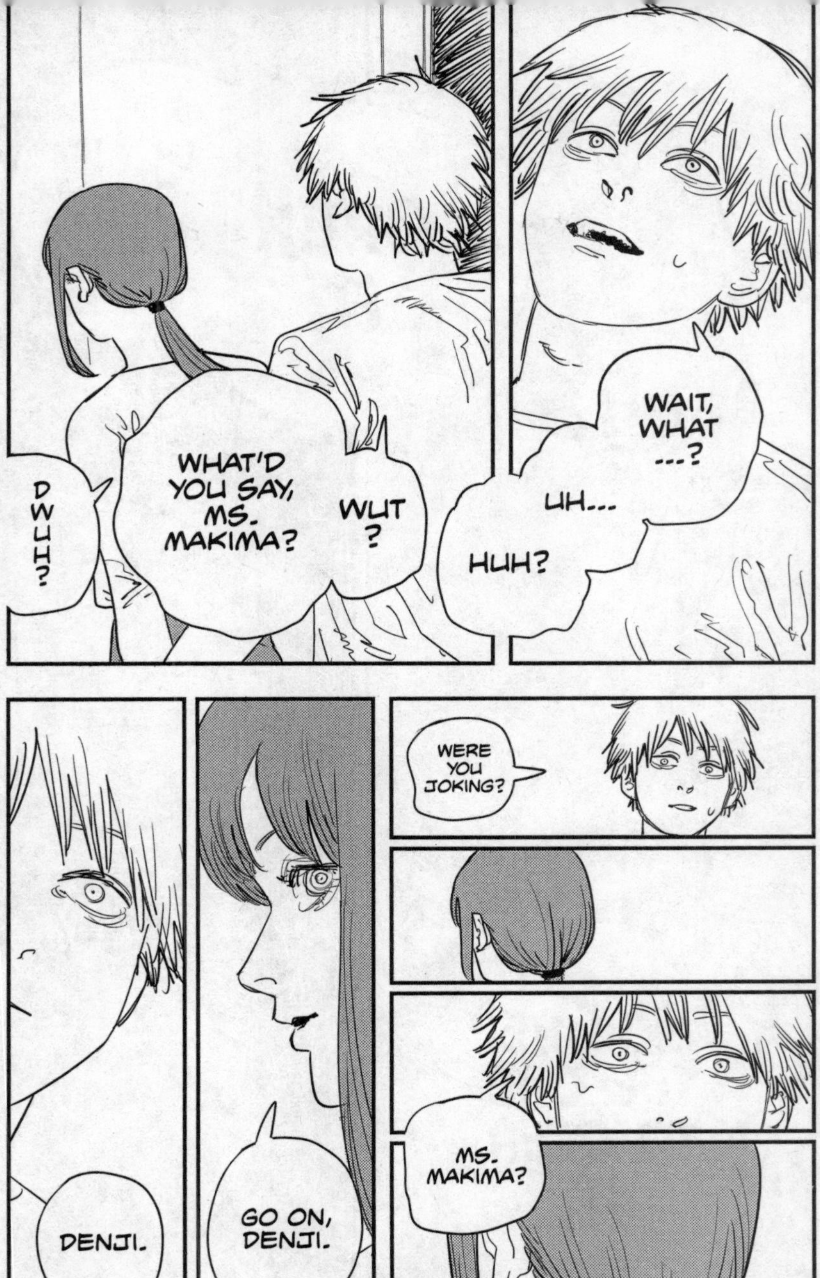
WAIT, WHAT ...?
UH...
HUH?
WUT?
WHAT'D YOU SAY, MS. MAKIMA?
DWUH?
WERE YOU JOKING?
MS. MAKIMA?
GO ON, DENJI.
DENJI.

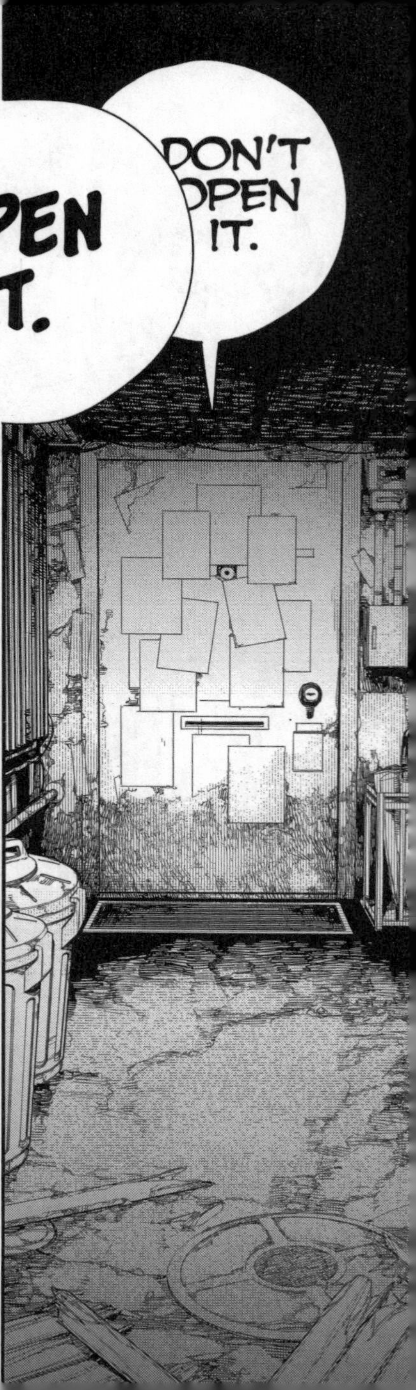
DON'T OPEN IT.
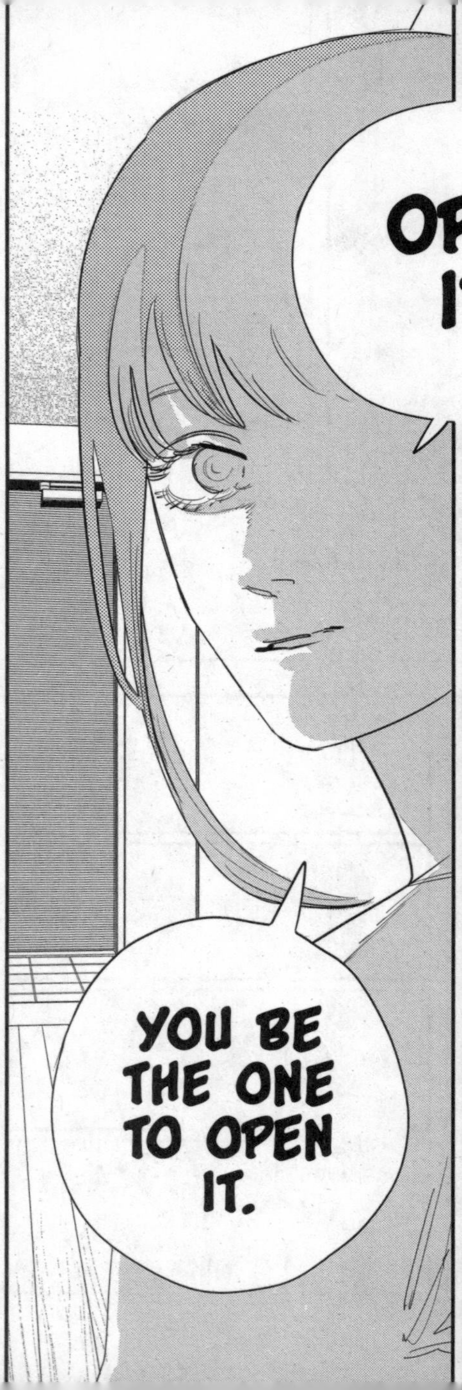
OPEN IT.
YOU BE THE ONE TO OPEN IT.

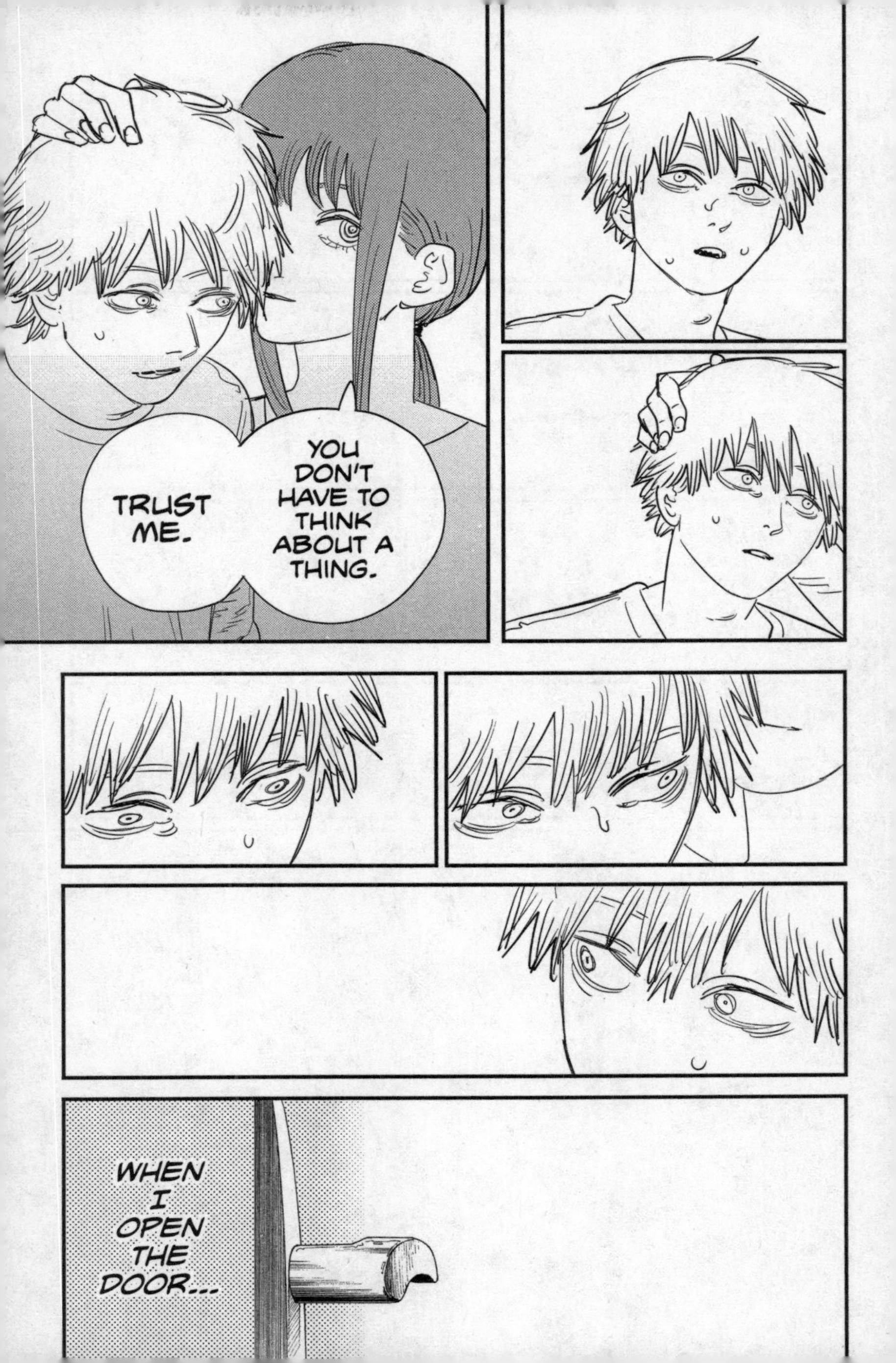
YOU DON'T HAVE TO THINK ABOUT A THING.
TRUST ME.
WHEN I OPEN THE DOOR...

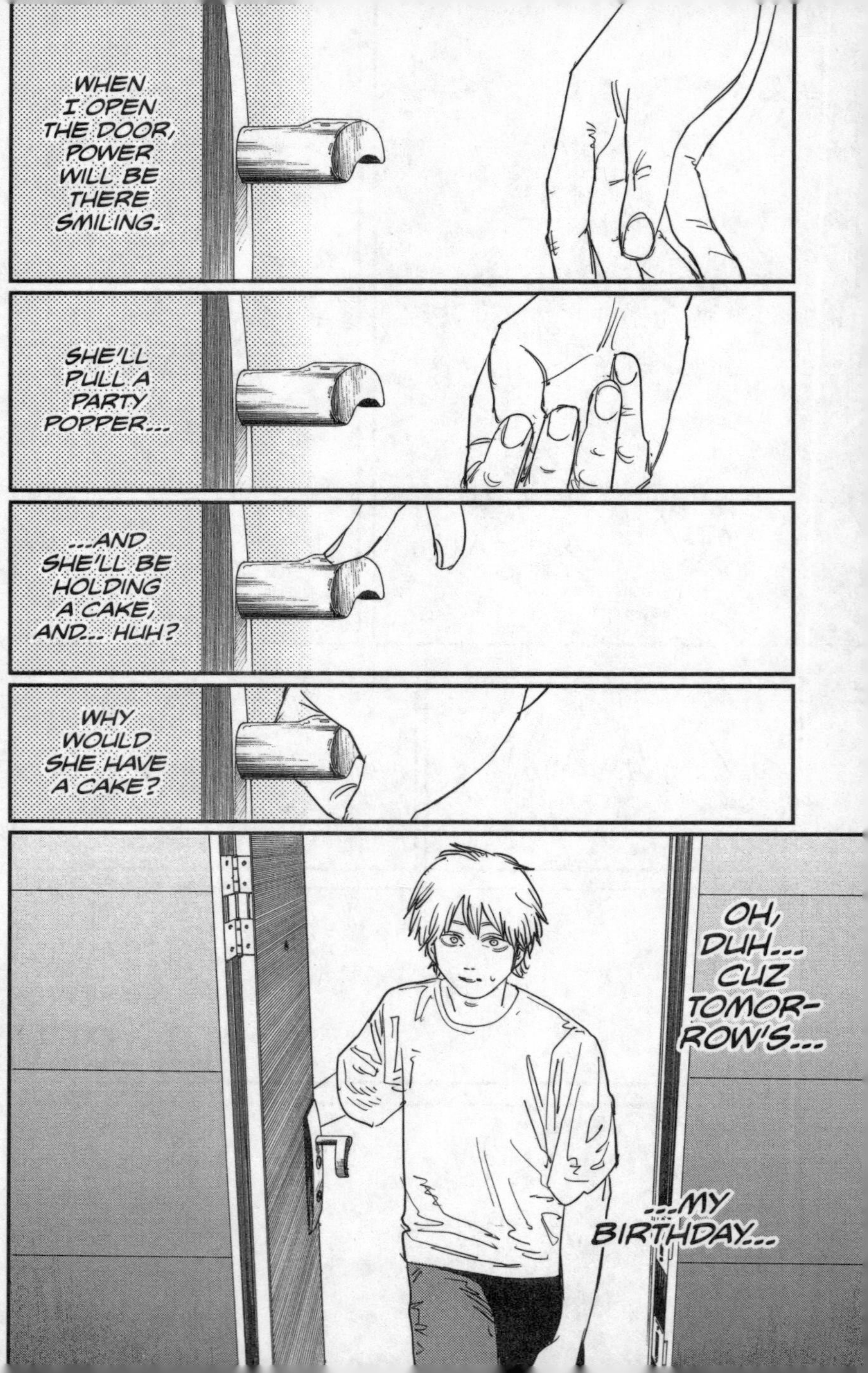
WHEN I OPEN THE DOOR, POWER WILL BE THERE SMILING.
SHE'LL PULL A PARTY POPPER...
...AND SHE'LL BE HOLDING A CAKE, AND... HUH?
WHY WOULD SHE HAVE A CAKE?
OH, DUH... CUZ TOMOR-ROW'S...
...MY BIRTHDAY...

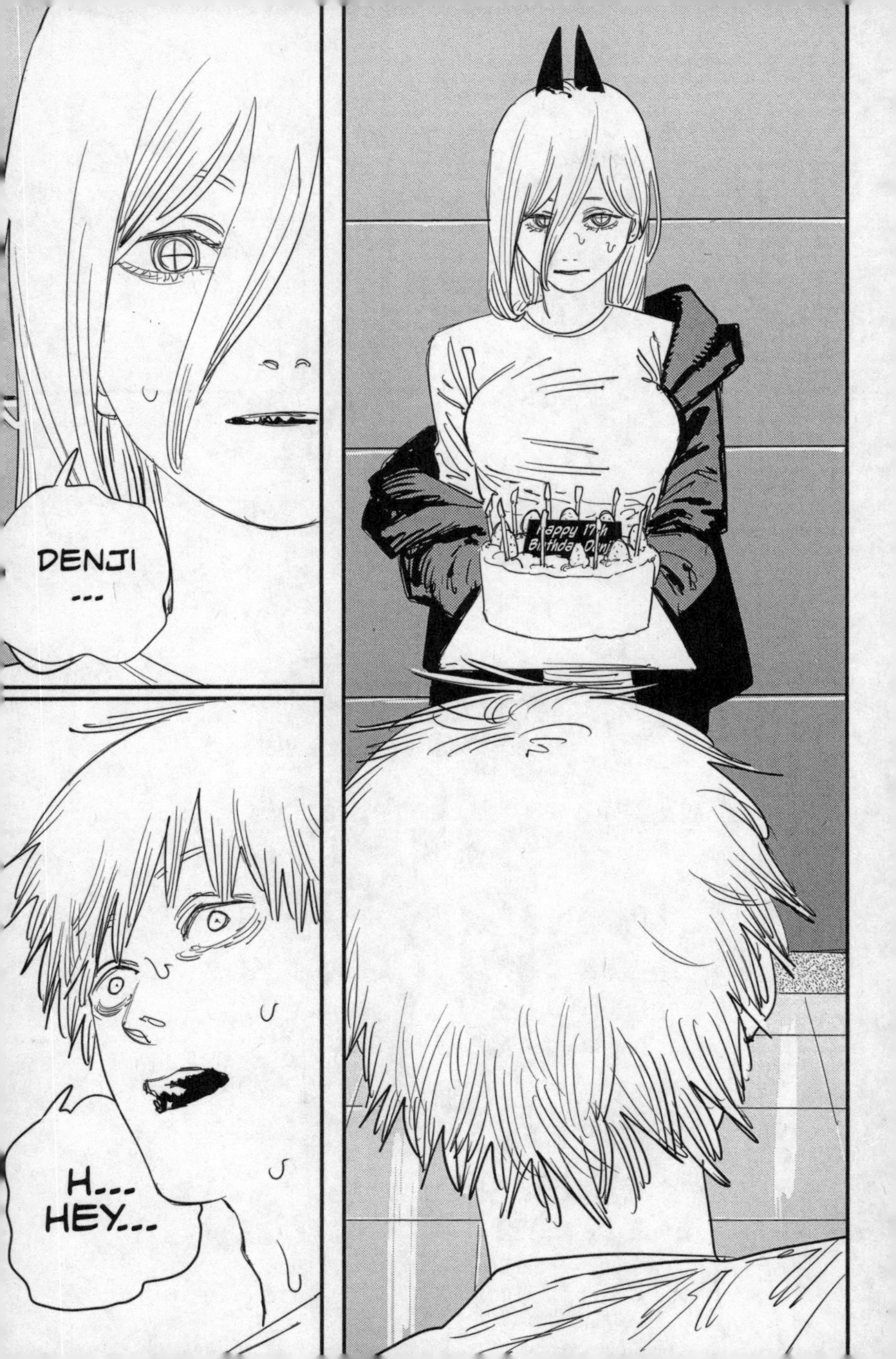
DENJI
...
H...
HEY...

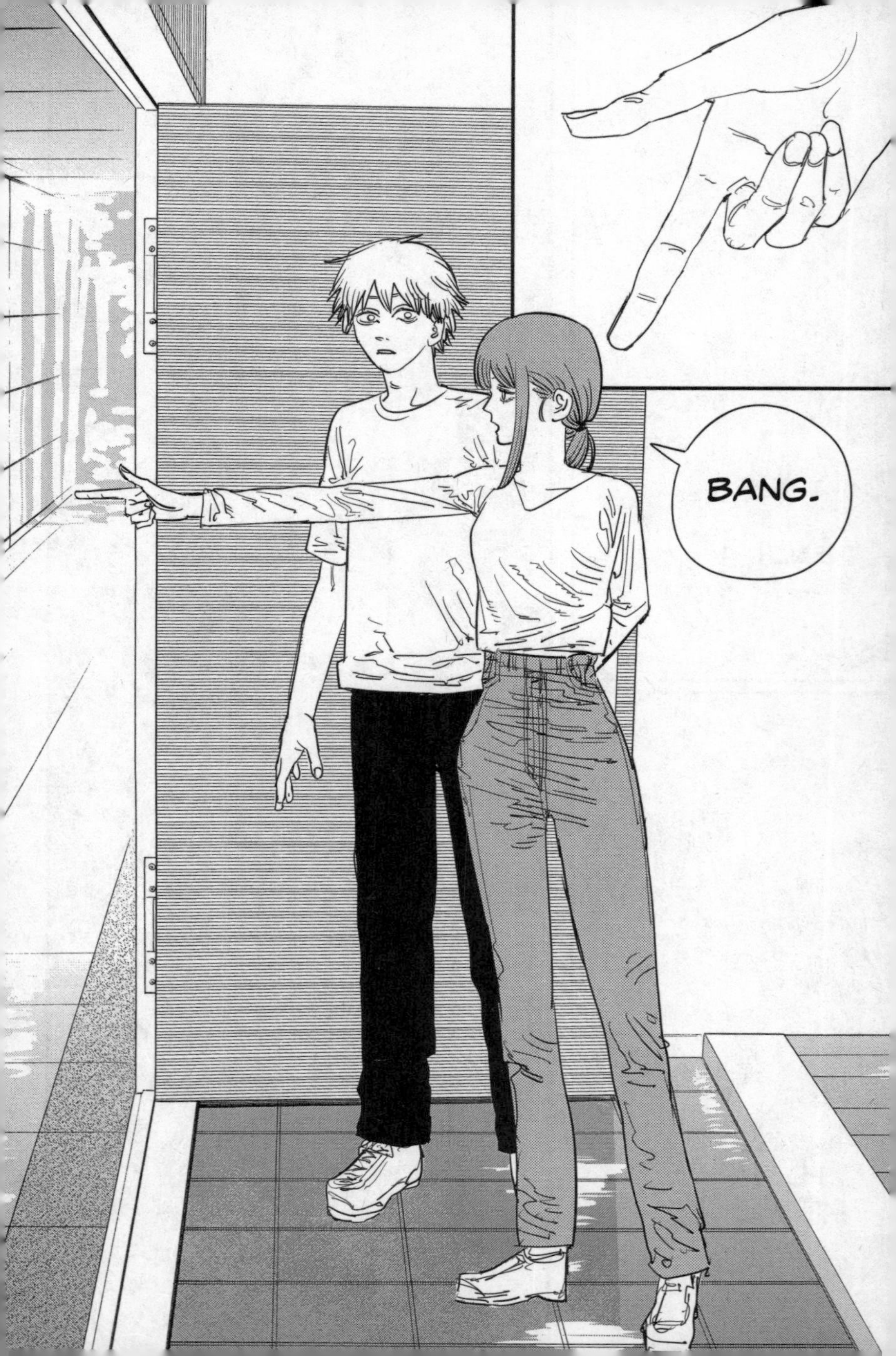
BANG.

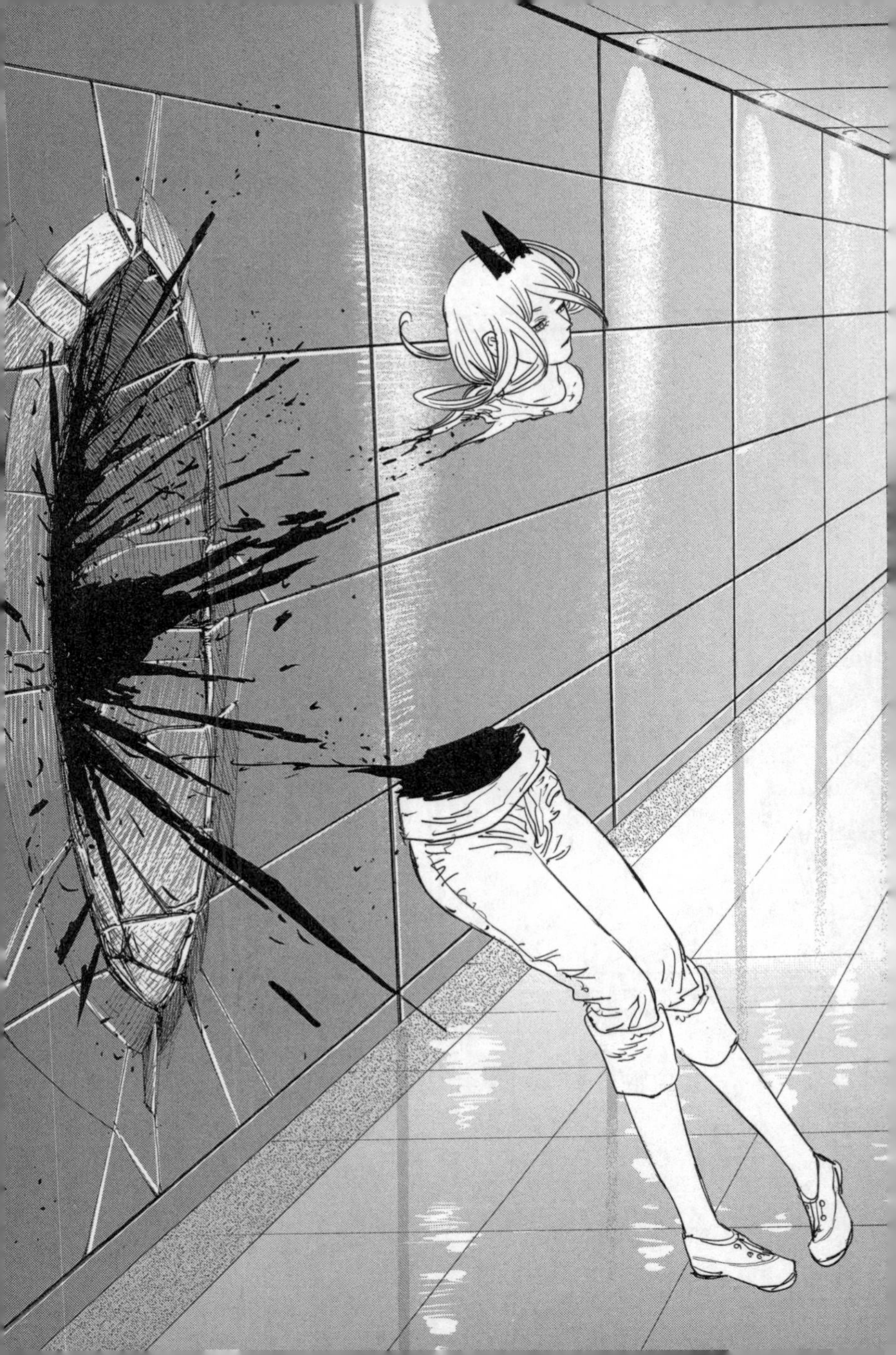

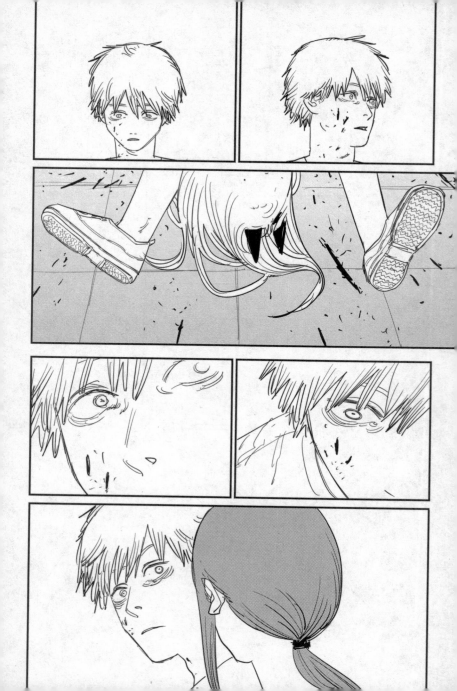

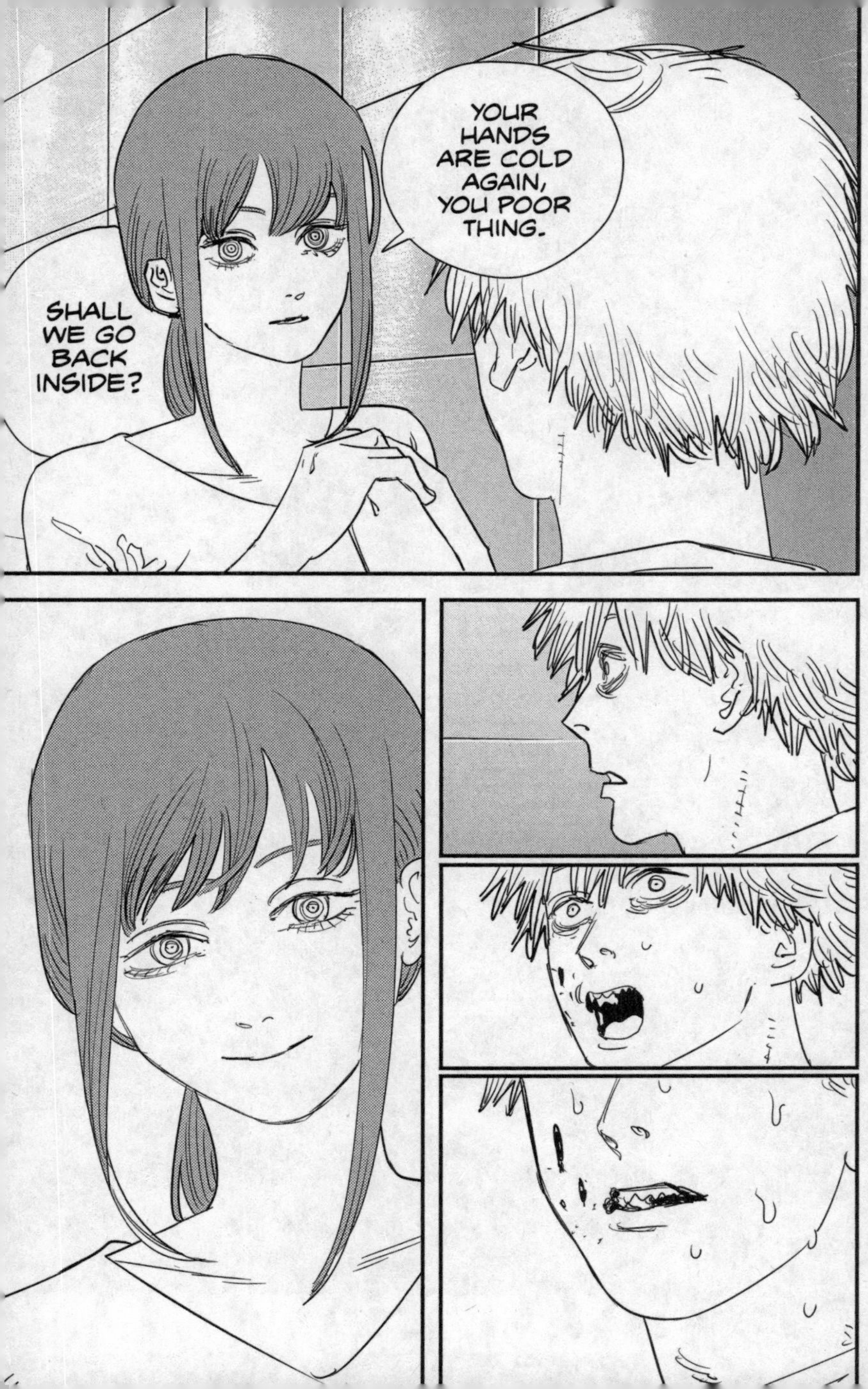
YOUR HANDS ARE COLD AGAIN, YOU POOR THING.
SHALL WE GO BACK INSIDE?

CHAINSAW MAN

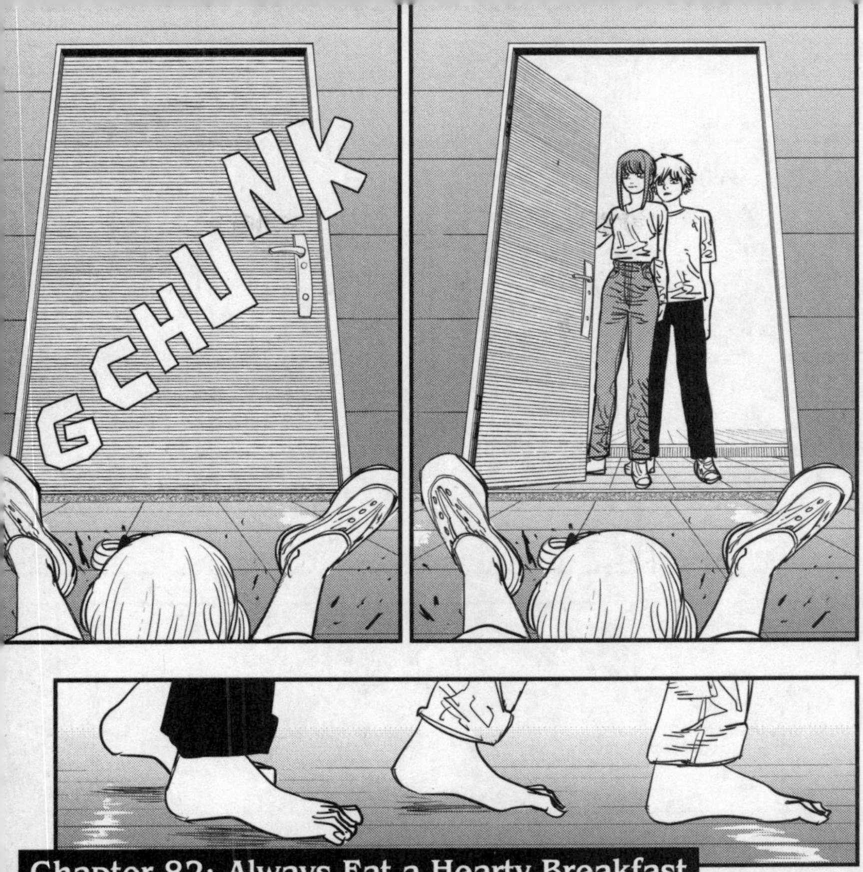
GCHUNK

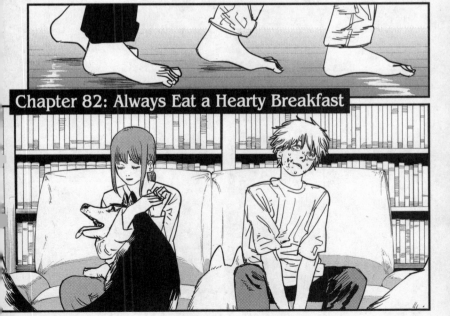

Chapter 82: Always Eat a Hearty Breakfast

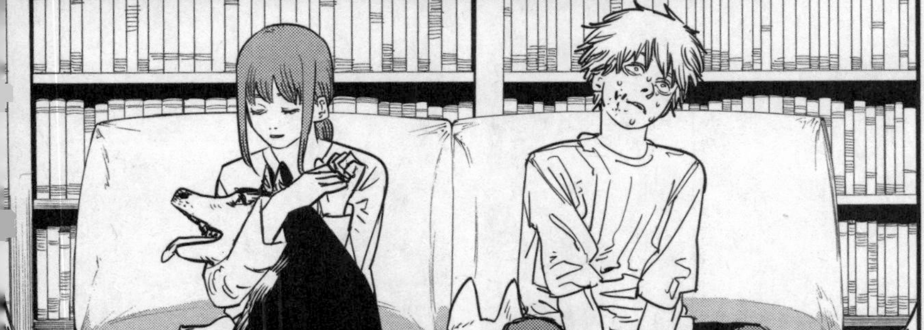

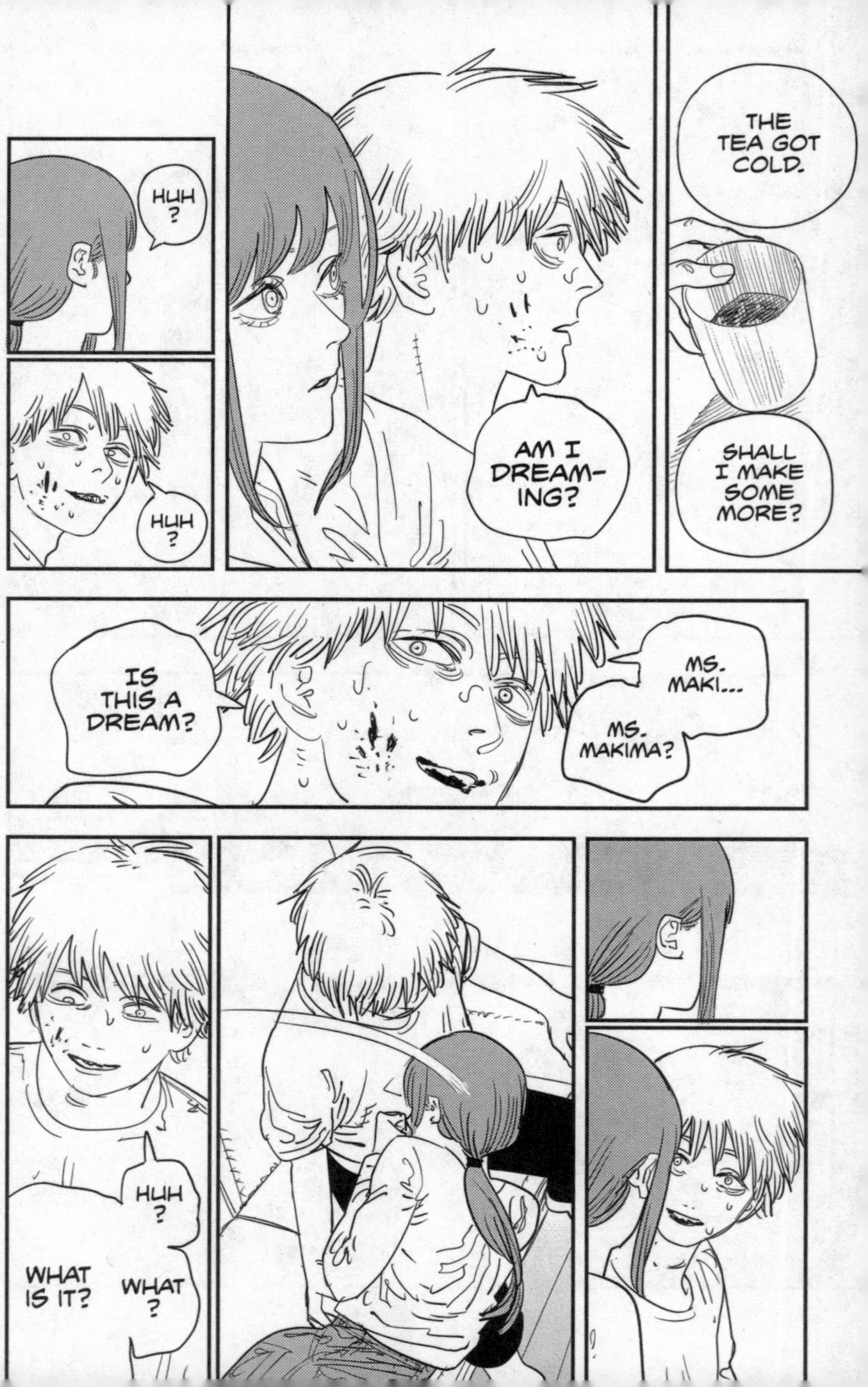
THE TEA GOT COLD.
SHALL I MAKE SOME MORE?
AM I DREAMING?
HUH?
HUH?
MS. MAKI...
MS. MAKIMA?
IS THIS A DREAM?
HUH?
WHAT?
WHAT IS IT?

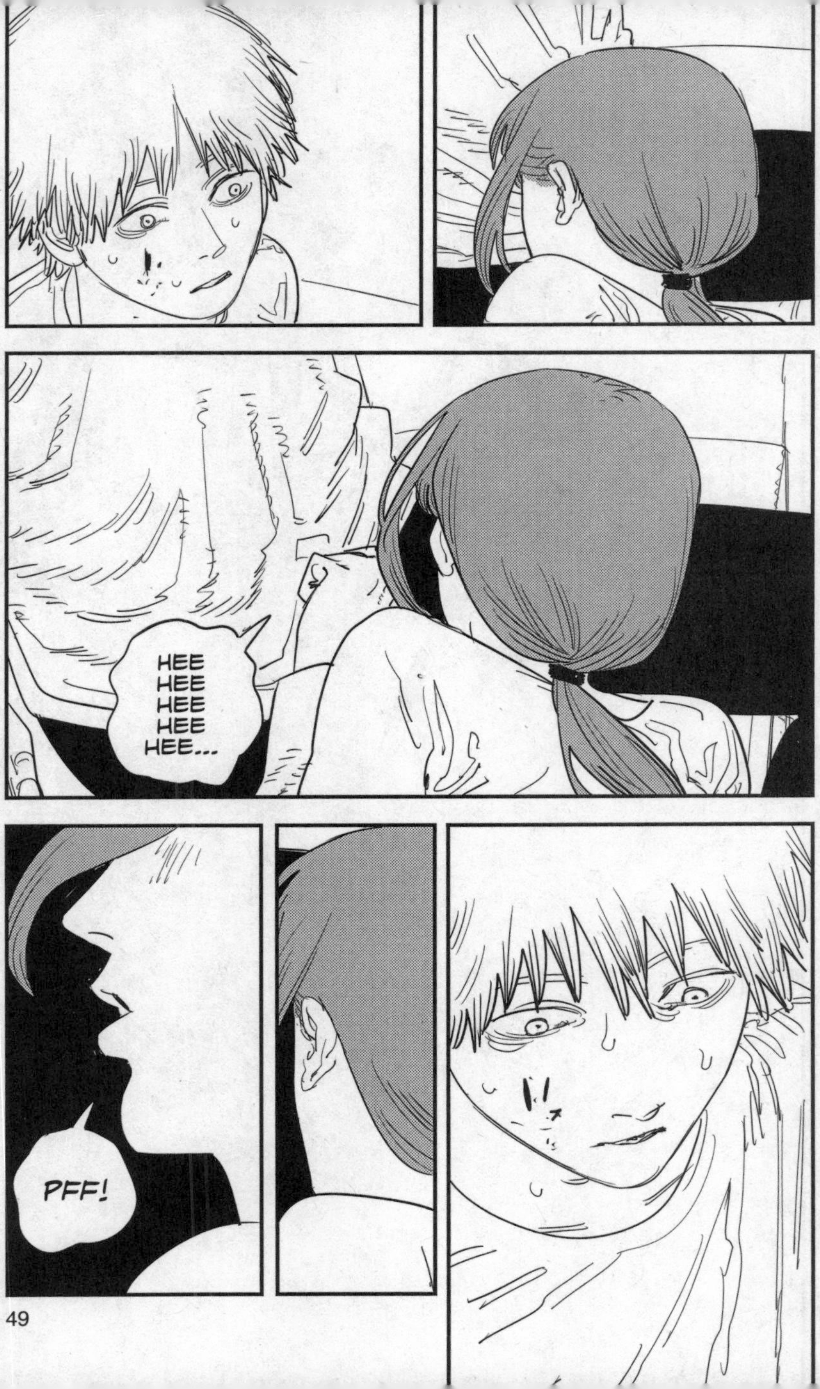
HEE
HEE
HEE
HEE
HEE...
PFF!

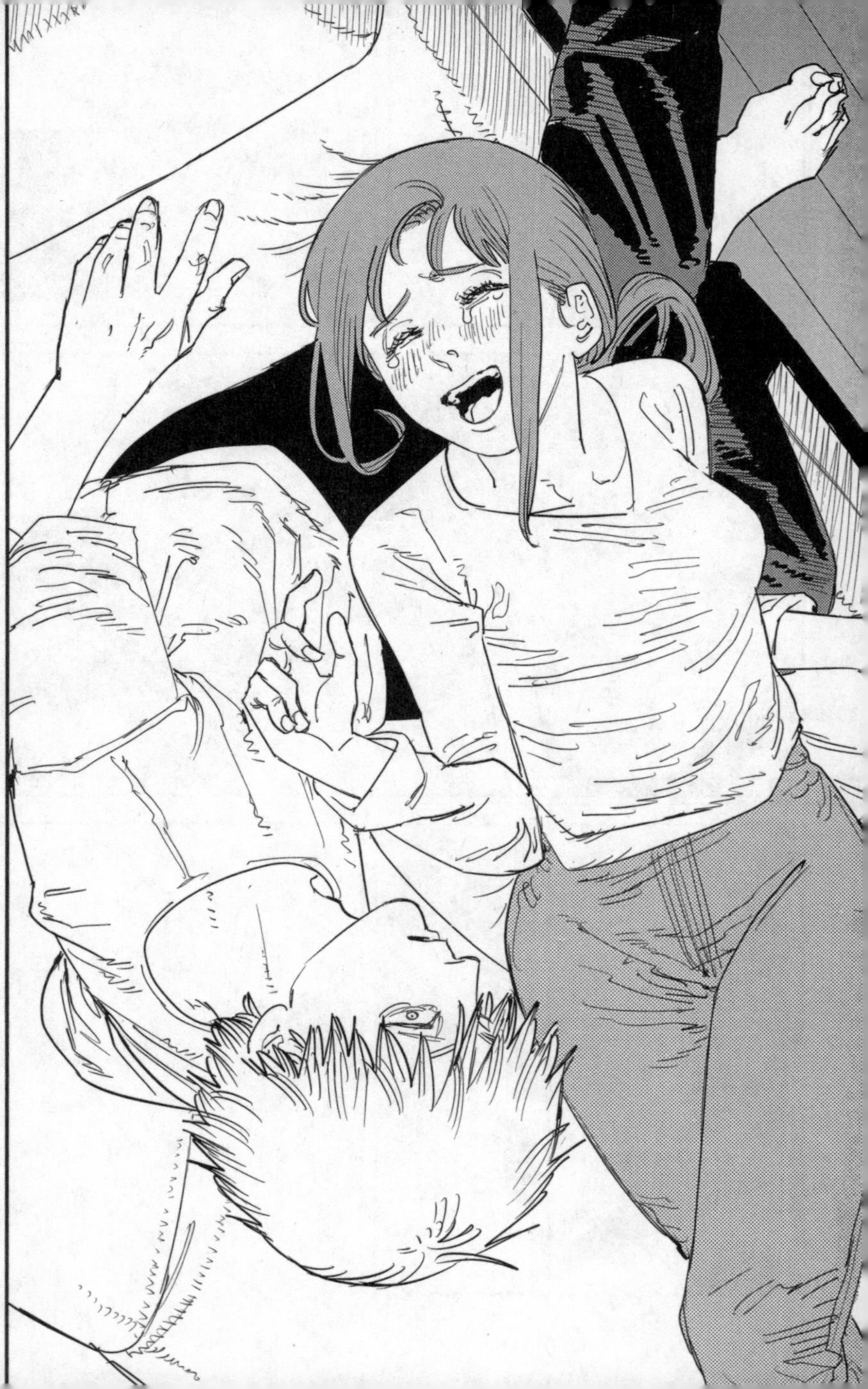

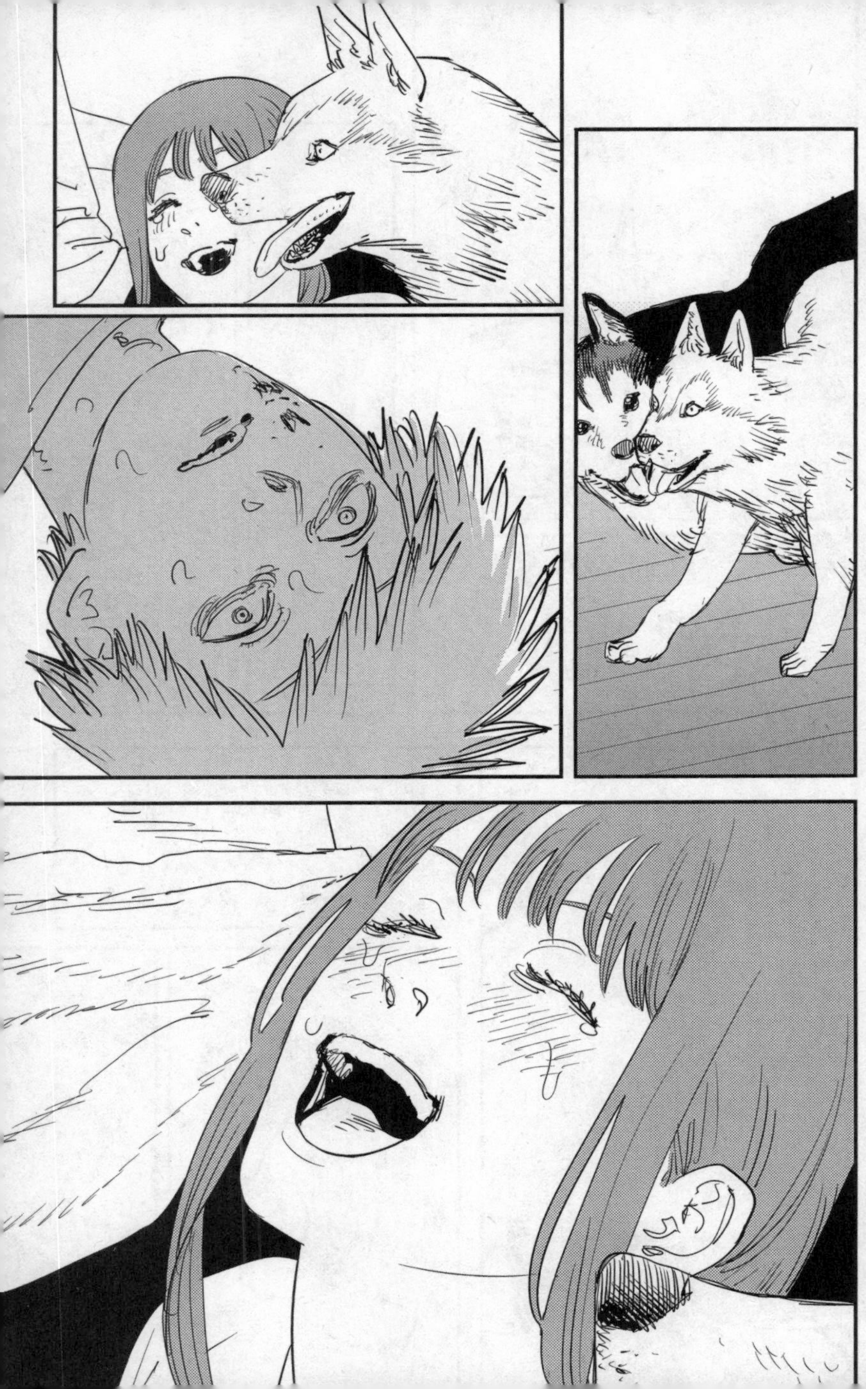

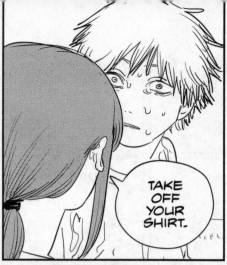

AHHHH...
THAT WAS A GOOD LAUGH!
TAKE OFF YOUR SHIRT.
HOW DO YOU RESPOND?

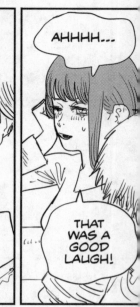

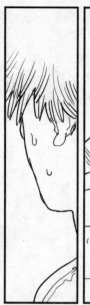

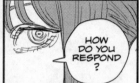

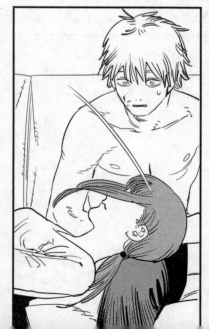

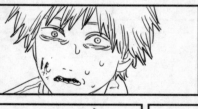

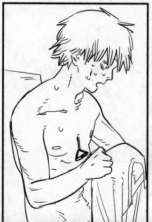

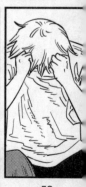

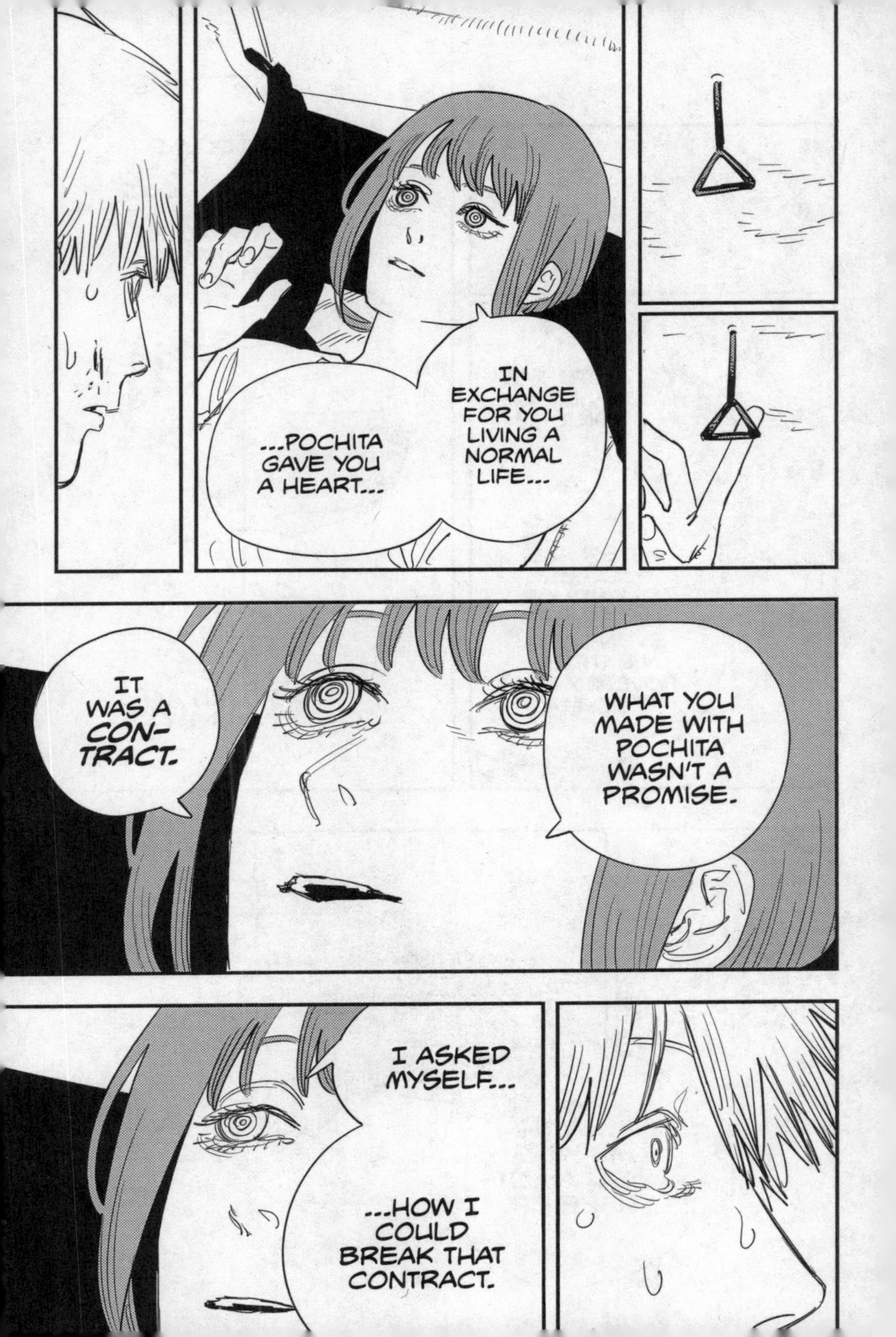
IN EXCHANGE FOR YOU LIVING A NORMAL LIFE...
...POCHITA GAVE YOU A HEART...
WHAT YOU MADE WITH POCHITA WASN'T A PROMISE.
IT WAS A CON-TRACT.
I ASKED MYSELF...
...HOW I COULD BREAK THAT CONTRACT.

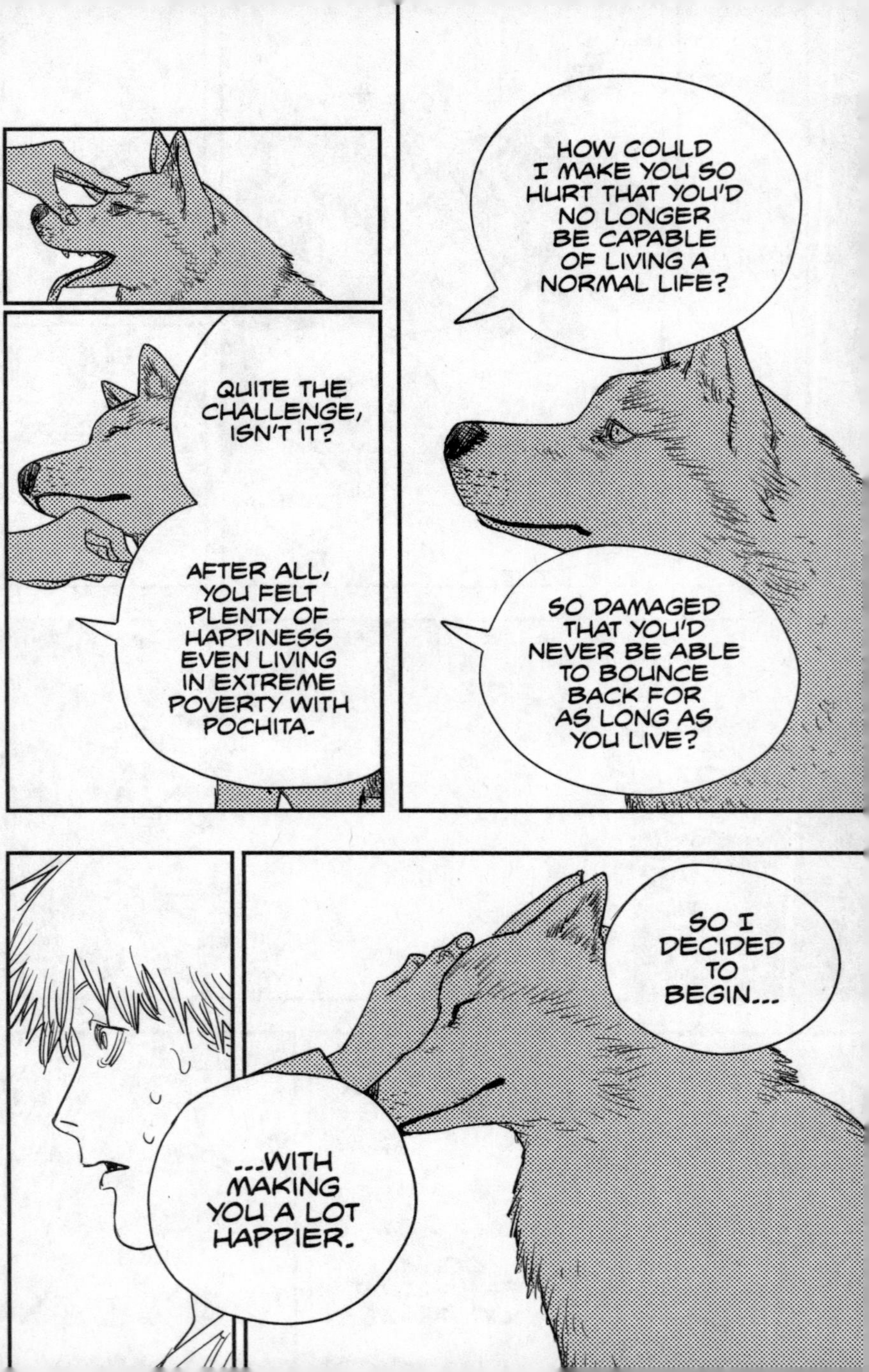
HOW COULD I MAKE YOU SO HURT THAT YOU'D NO LONGER BE CAPABLE OF LIVING A NORMAL LIFE?
SO DAMAGED THAT YOU'D NEVER BE ABLE TO BOUNCE BACK FOR AS LONG AS YOU LIVE?
QUITE THE CHALLENGE, ISN'T IT?
AFTER ALL, YOU FELT PLENTY OF HAPPINESS EVEN LIVING IN EXTREME POVERTY WITH POCHITA.
SO I DECIDED TO BEGIN...
...WITH MAKING YOU A LOT HAPPIER.

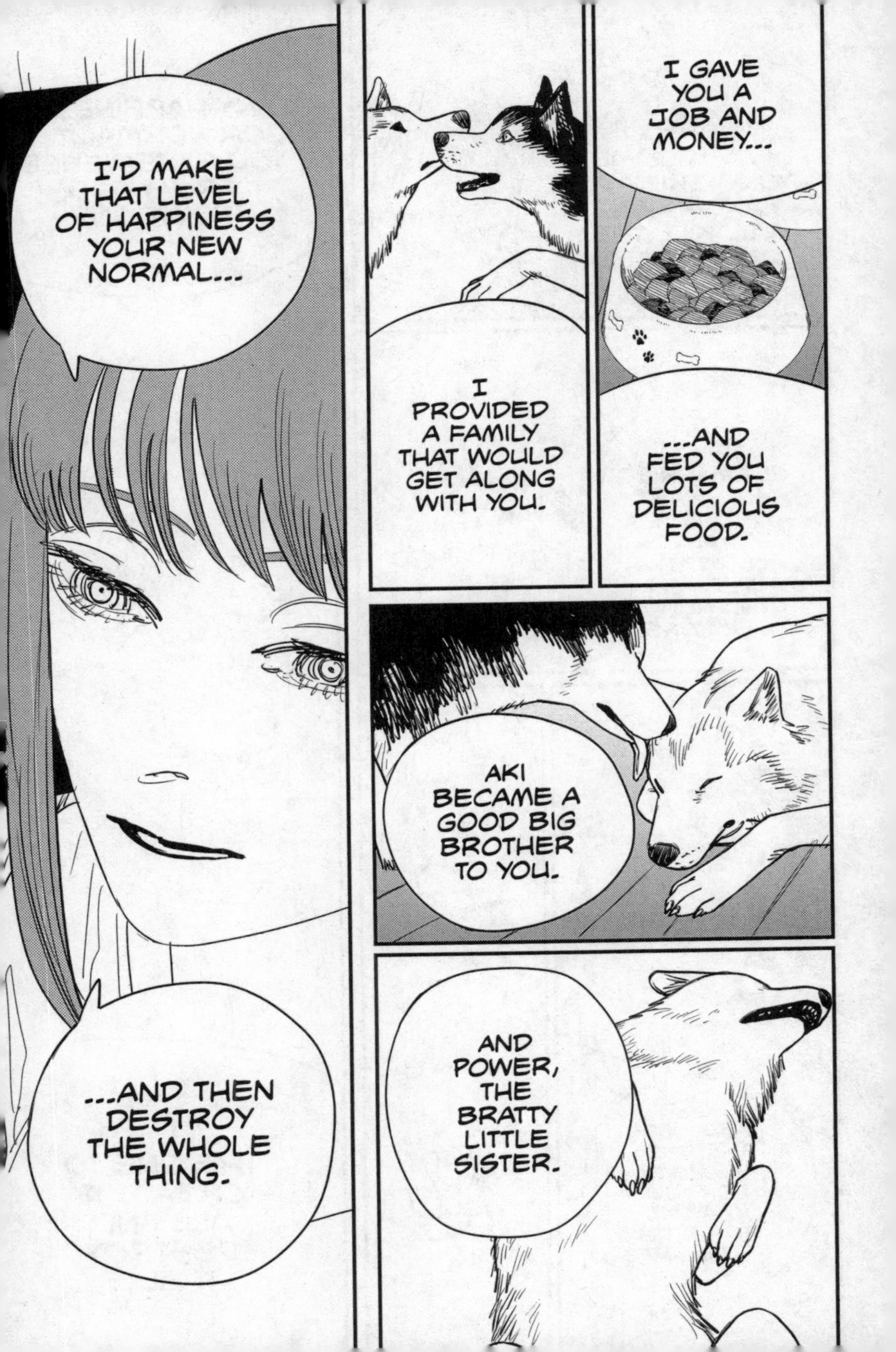
I GAVE YOU A JOB AND MONEY...
...AND FED YOU LOTS OF DELICIOUS FOOD.
I PROVIDED A FAMILY THAT WOULD GET ALONG WITH YOU.
AKI BECAME A GOOD BIG BROTHER TO YOU.
AND POWER, THE BRATTY LITTLE SISTER.
I'D MAKE THAT LEVEL OF HAPPINESS YOUR NEW NORMAL...
...AND THEN DESTROY THE WHOLE THING.

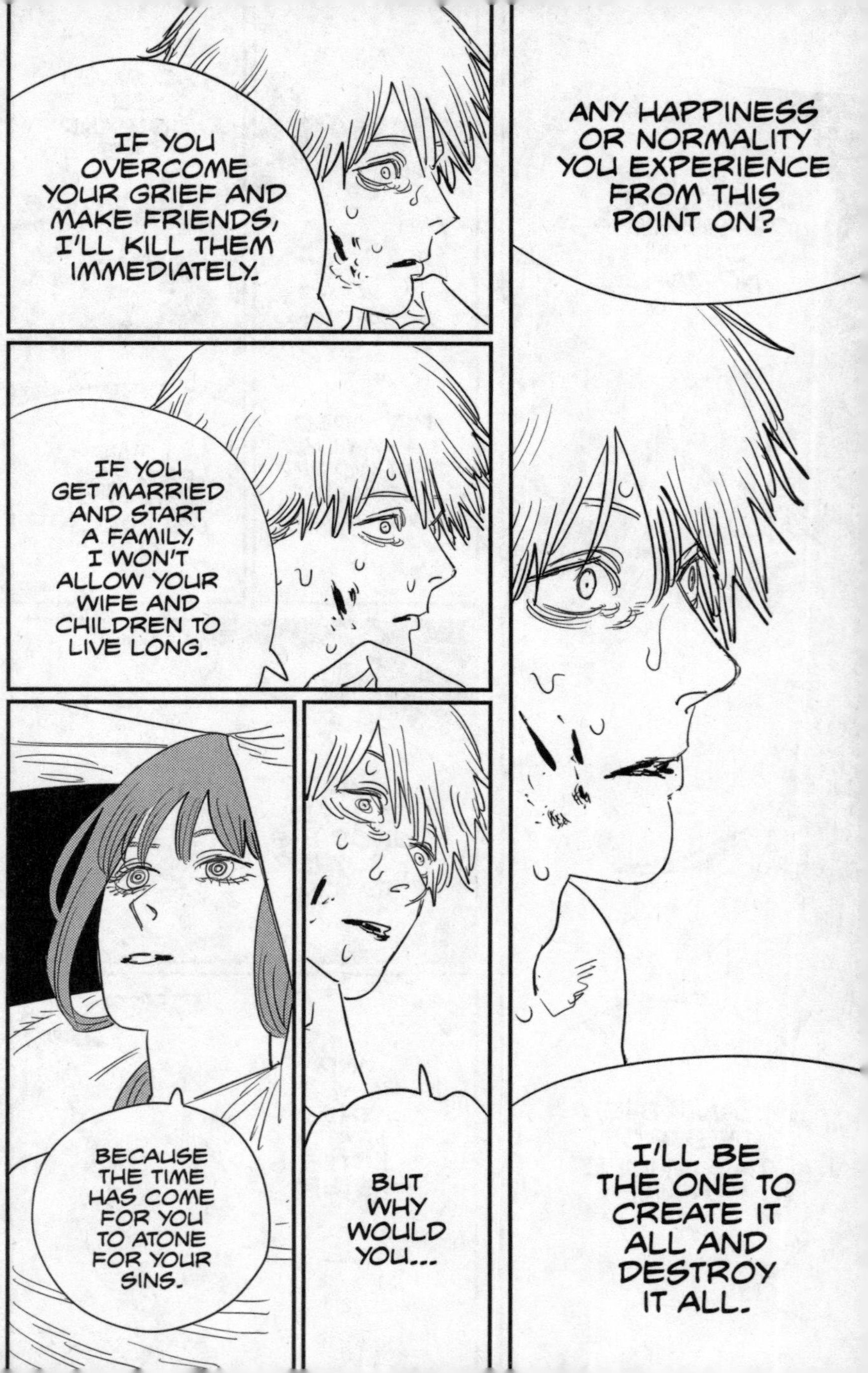
ANY HAPPINESS OR NORMALITY YOU EXPERIENCE FROM THIS POINT ON?
I'LL BE THE ONE TO CREATE IT ALL AND DESTROY IT ALL.
IF YOU OVERCOME YOUR GRIEF AND MAKE FRIENDS, I'LL KILL THEM IMMEDIATELY.
IF YOU GET MARRIED AND START A FAMILY, I WON'T ALLOW YOUR WIFE AND CHILDREN TO LIVE LONG.
BUT WHY WOULD YOU...
BECAUSE THE TIME HAS COME FOR YOU TO ATONE FOR YOUR SINS.

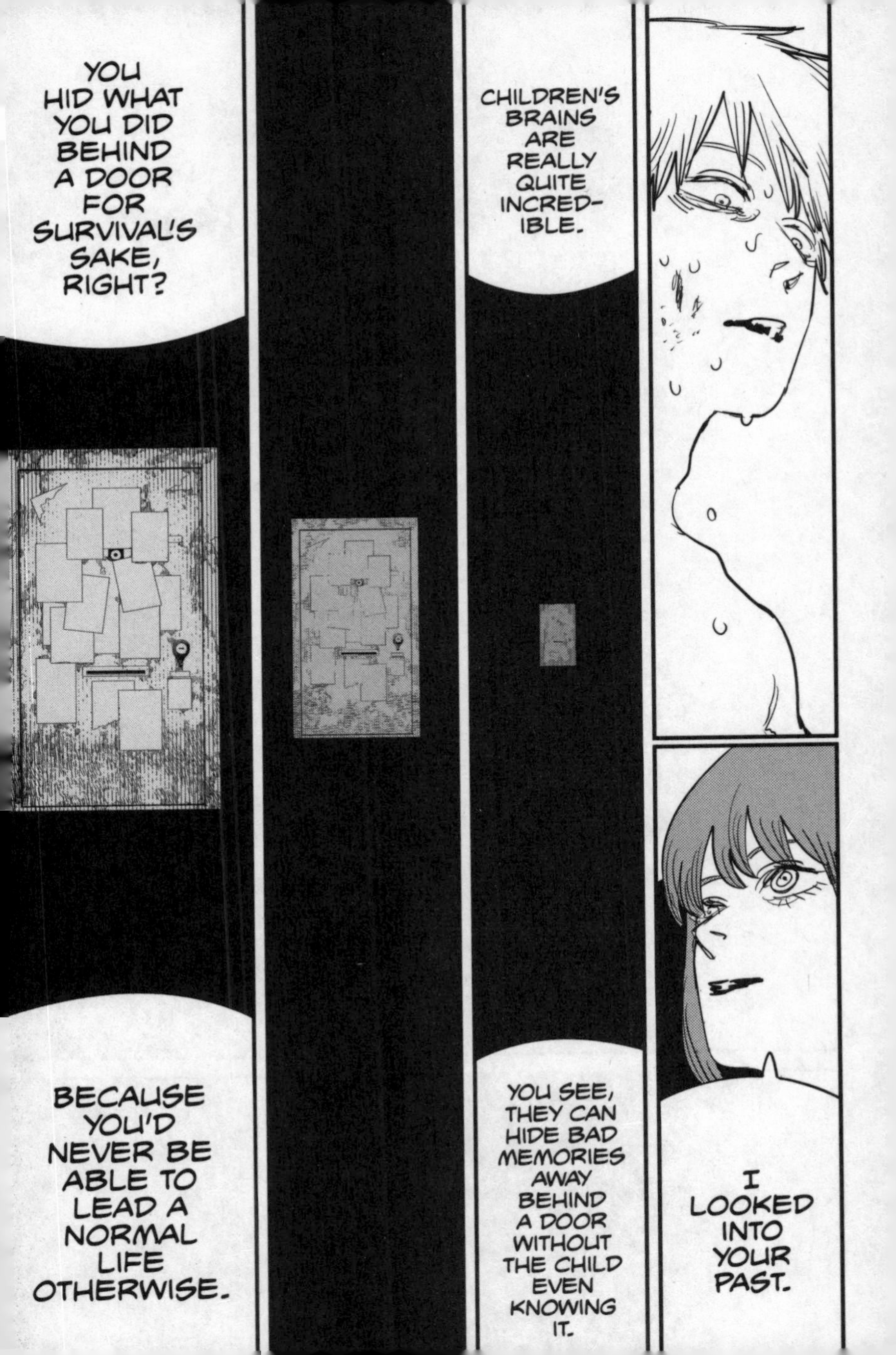
I LOOKED INTO YOUR PAST.
CHILDREN'S BRAINS ARE REALLY QUITE INCREDIBLE.
YOU SEE, THEY CAN HIDE BAD MEMORIES AWAY BEHIND A DOOR WITHOUT THE CHILD EVEN KNOWING IT.
YOU HID WHAT YOU DID BEHIND A DOOR FOR SURVIVAL'S SAKE, RIGHT?
BECAUSE YOU'D NEVER BE ABLE TO LEAD A NORMAL LIFE OTHERWISE.

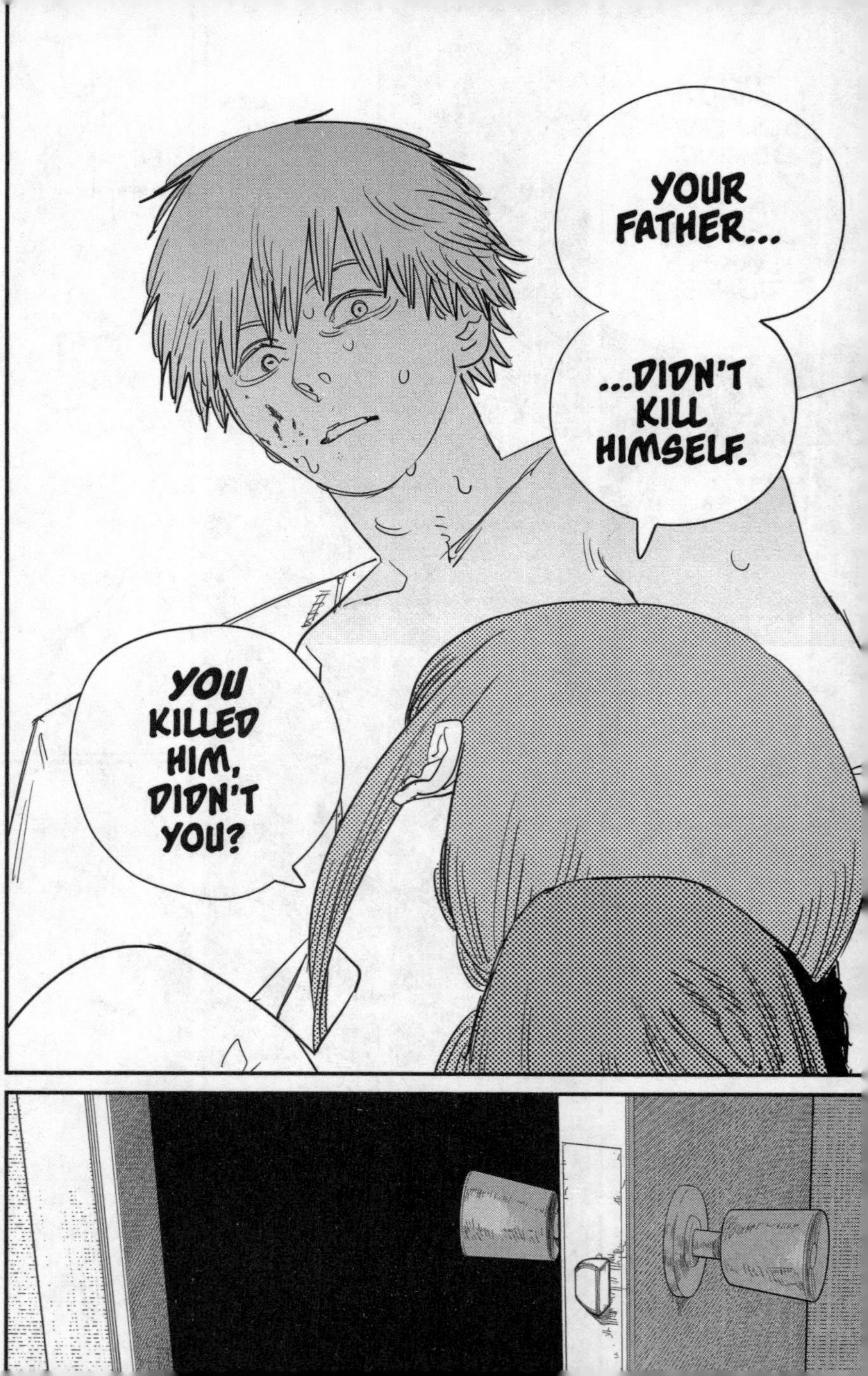
YOUR FATHER...
...DIDN'T KILL HIMSELF.
YOU KILLED HIM, DIDN'T YOU?

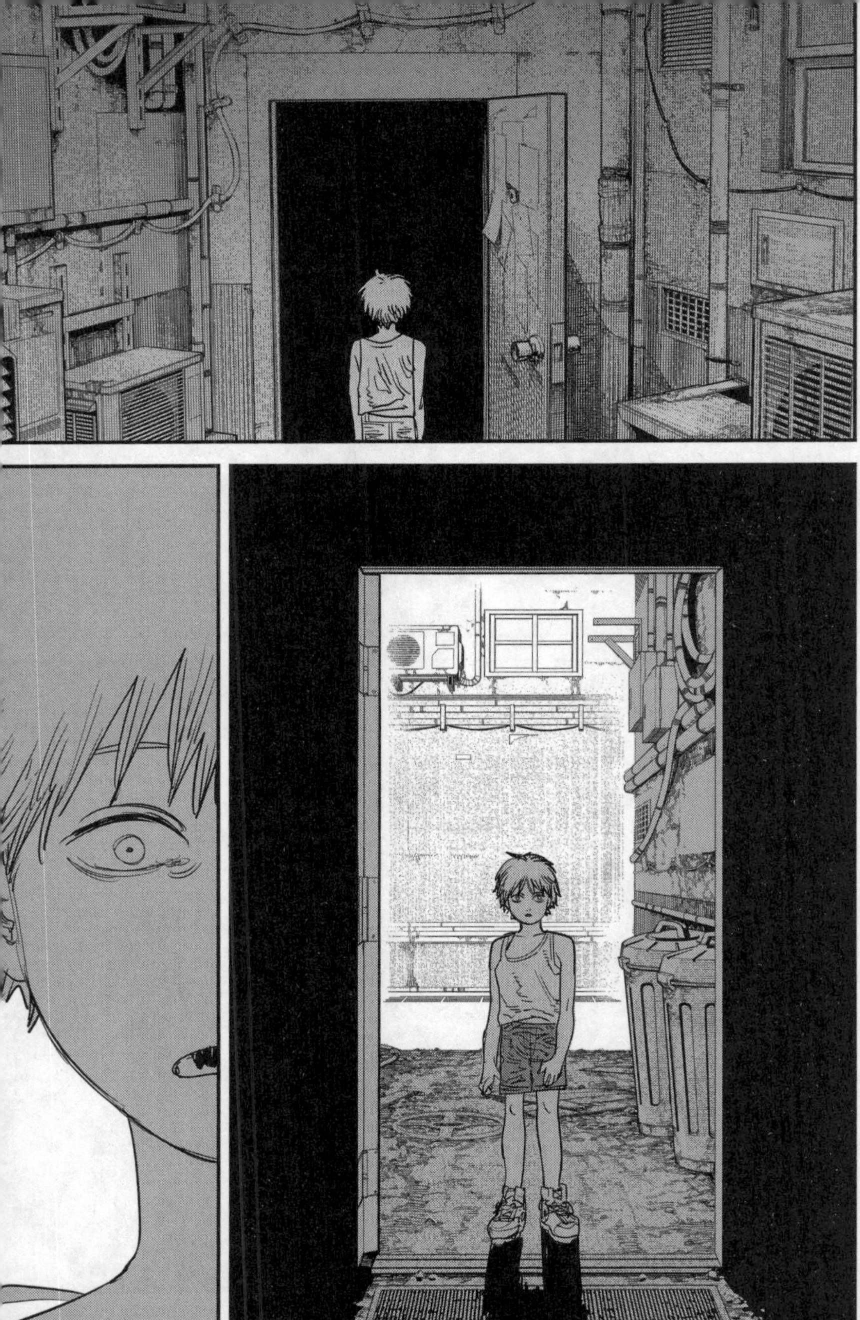

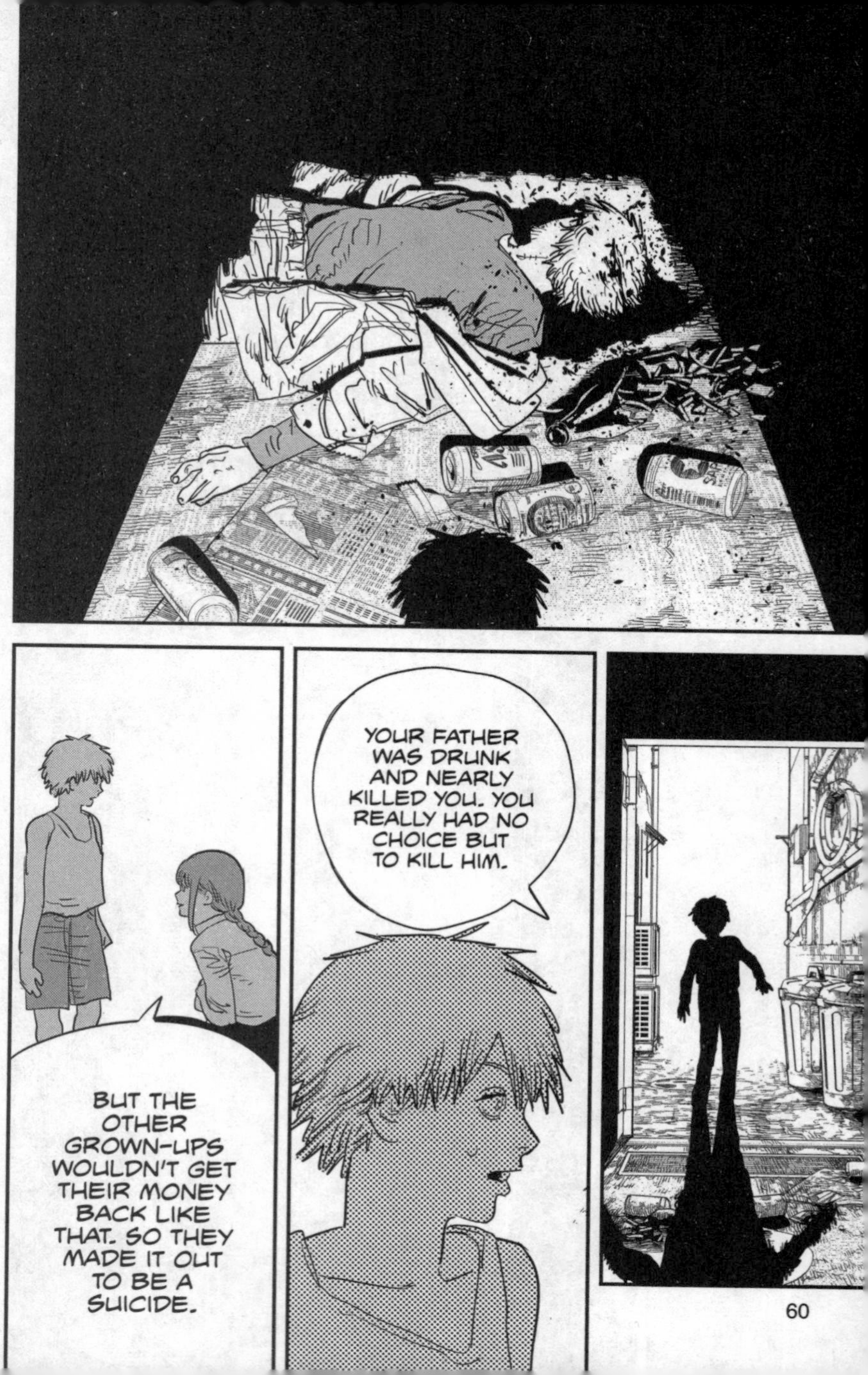
YOUR FATHER WAS DRUNK AND NEARLY KILLED YOU. YOU REALLY HAD NO CHOICE BUT TO KILL HIM.
BUT THE OTHER GROWN-UPS WOULDN'T GET THEIR MONEY BACK LIKE THAT. SO THEY MADE IT OUT TO BE A SUICIDE.

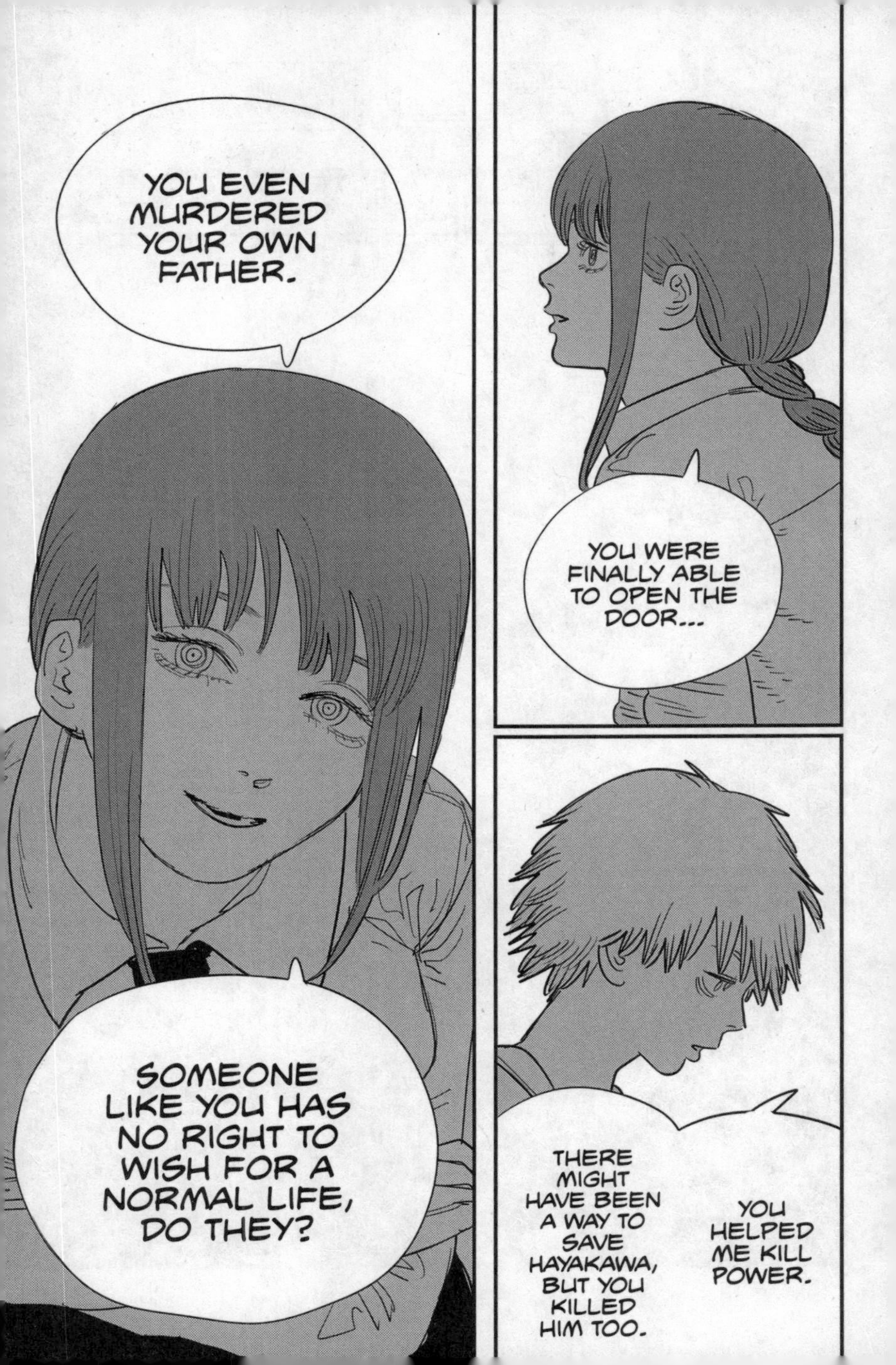
YOU WERE FINALLY ABLE TO OPEN THE DOOR...
YOU HELPED ME KILL POWER.
THERE MIGHT HAVE BEEN A WAY TO SAVE HAYAKAWA, BUT YOU KILLED HIM TOO.
YOU EVEN MURDERED YOUR OWN FATHER.
SOMEONE LIKE YOU HAS NO RIGHT TO WISH FOR A NORMAL LIFE, DO THEY?

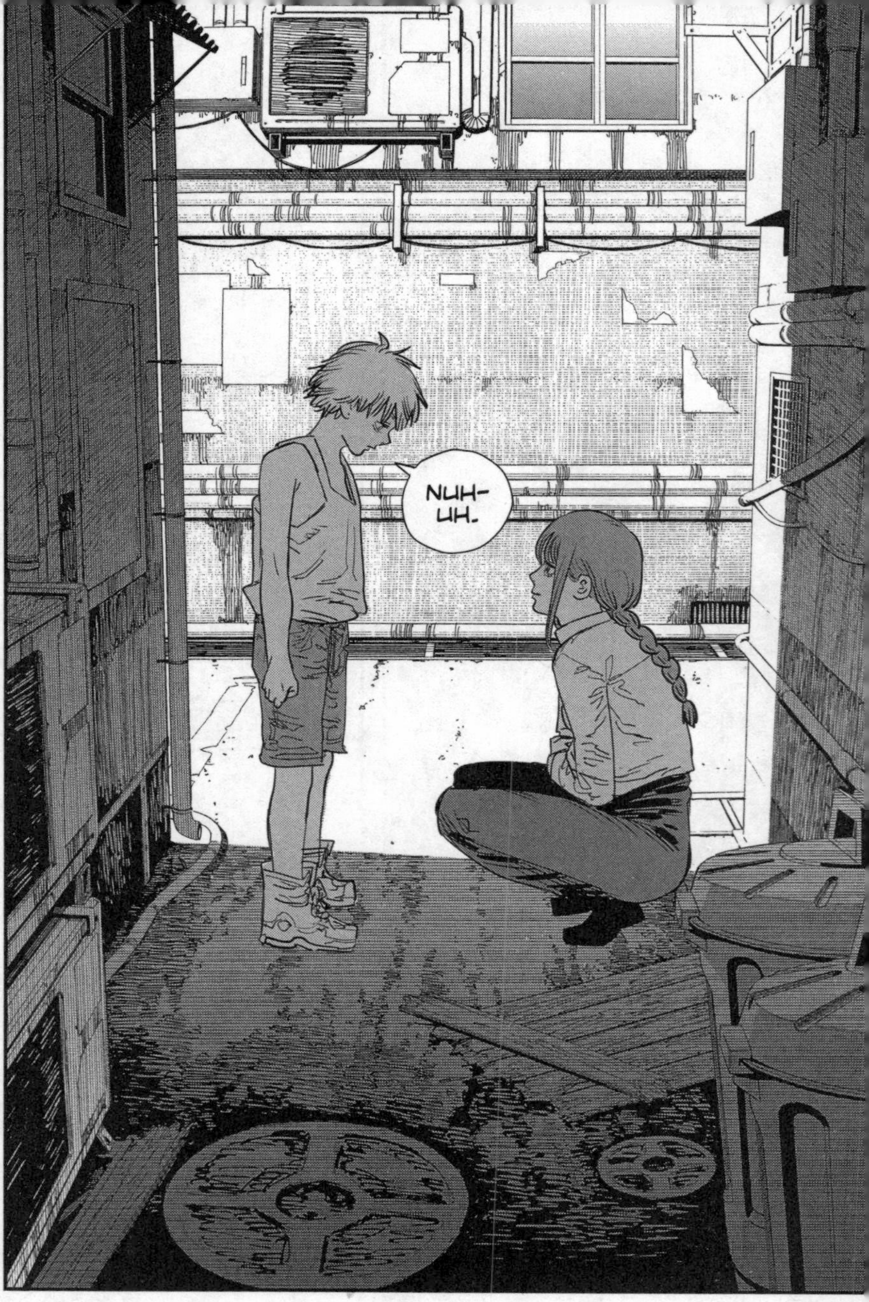
NUH-UH.

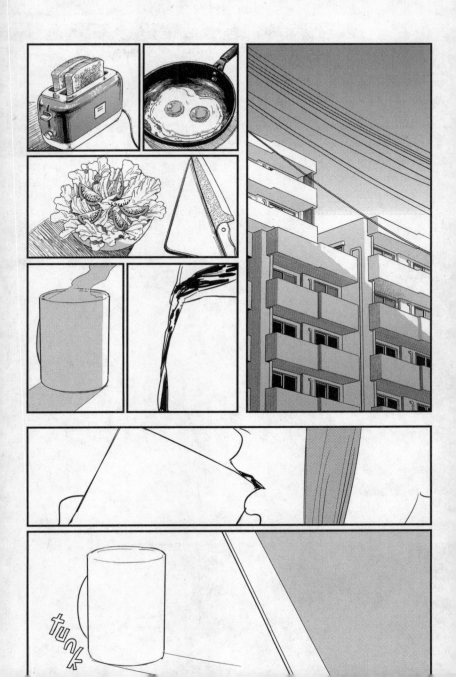

tunk

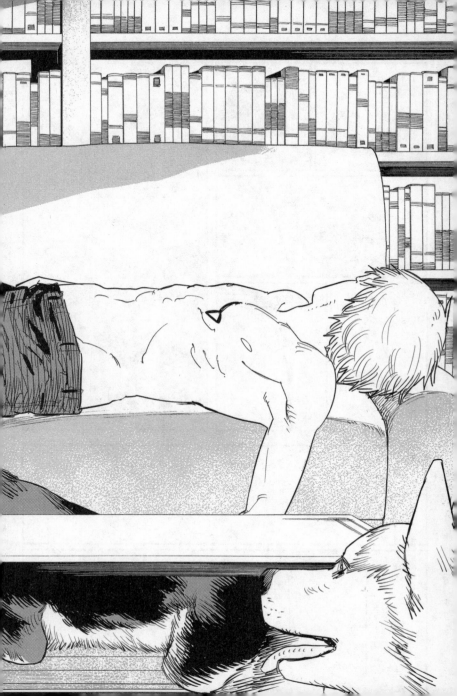

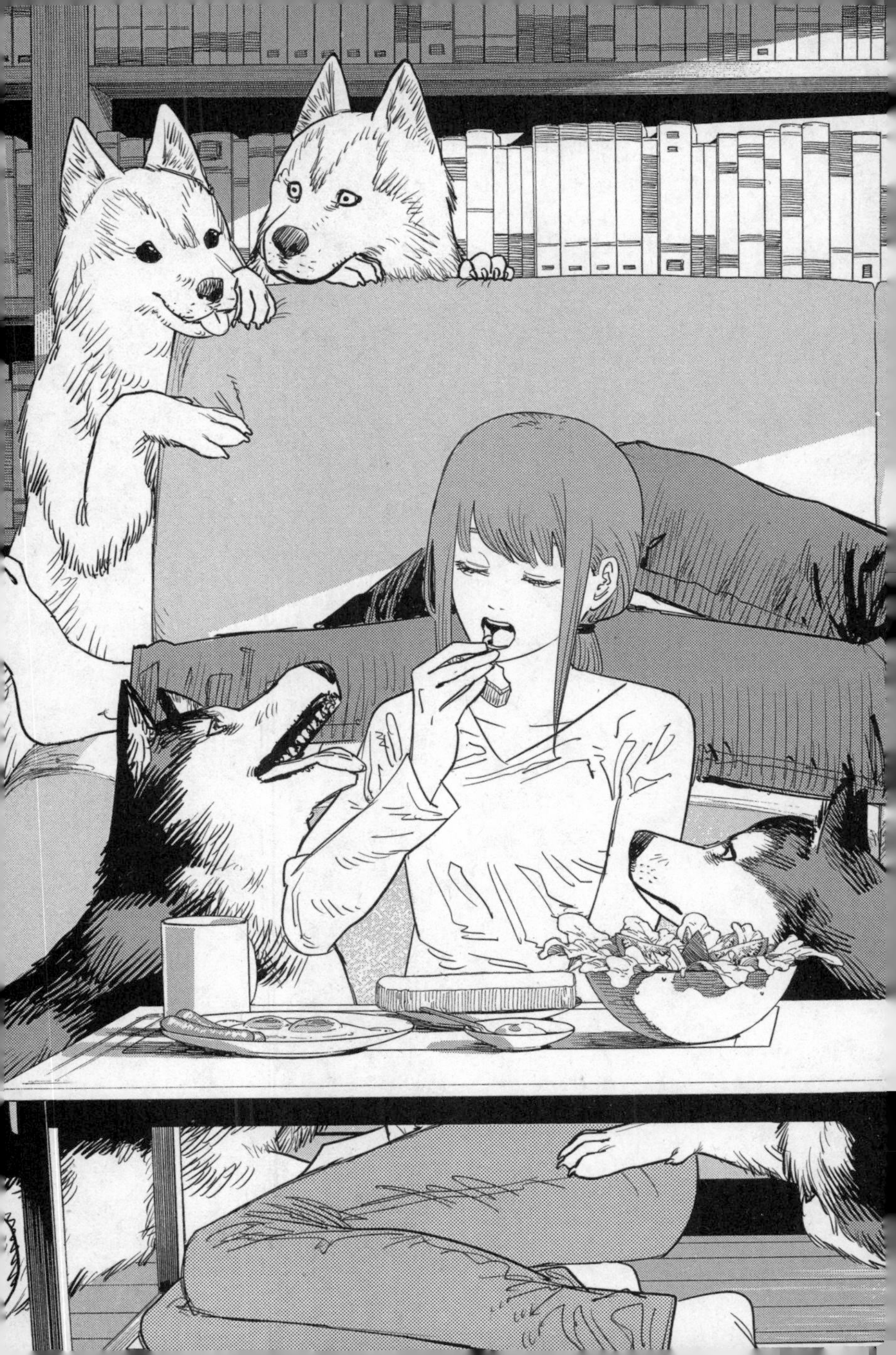

CHAINSAW MAN

Chapter 83: Death, Resurrection, Chainsaw

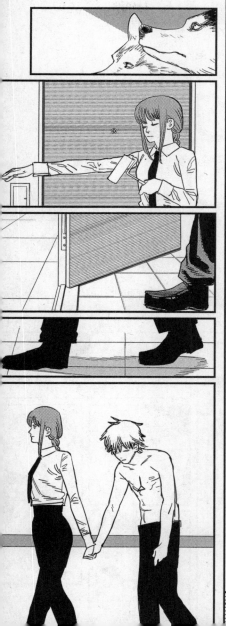

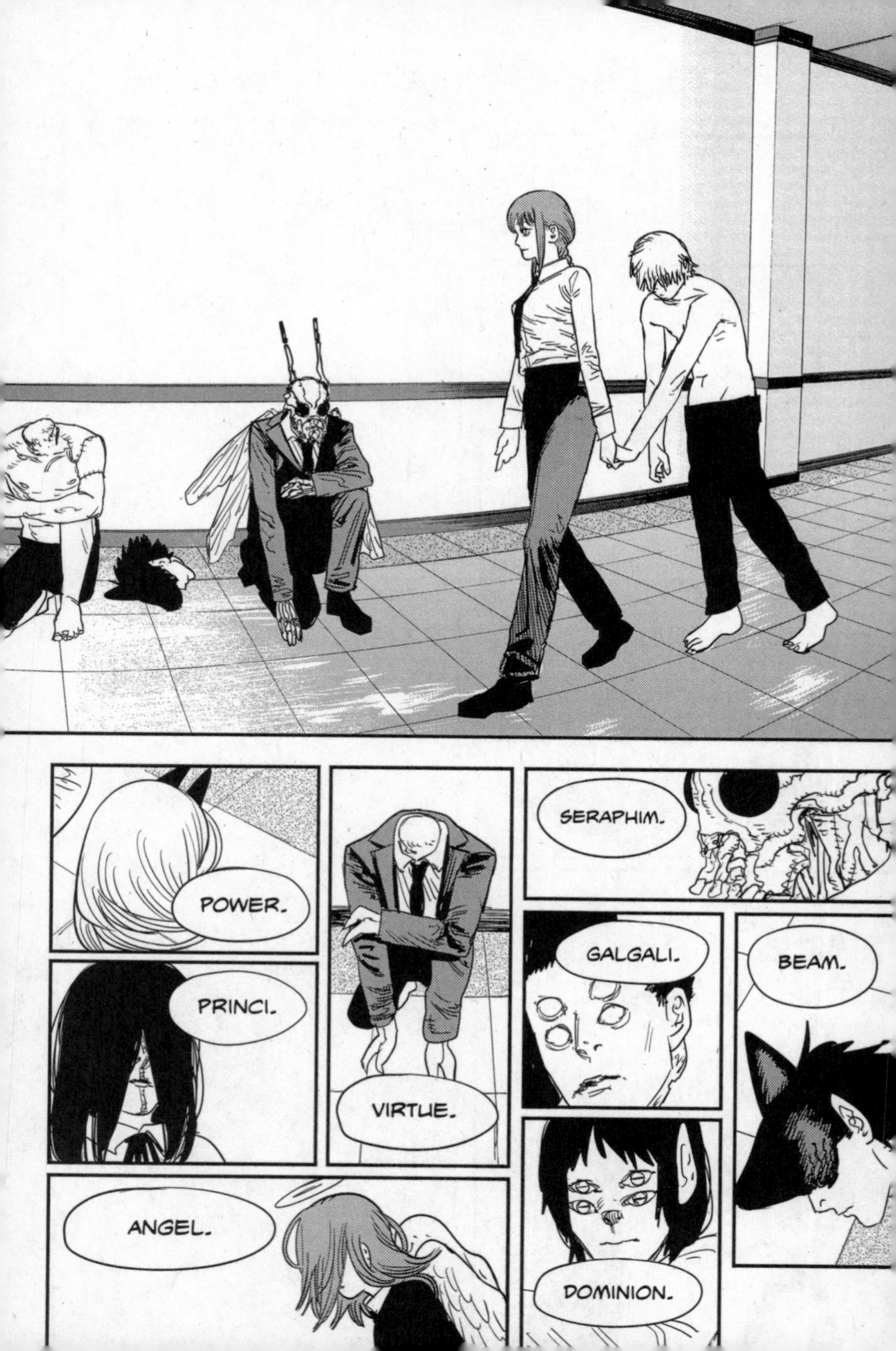
SERAPHIM.
BEAM.
GALGALI.
DOMINION.
VIRTUE.
POWER.
PRINCI.
ANGEL.

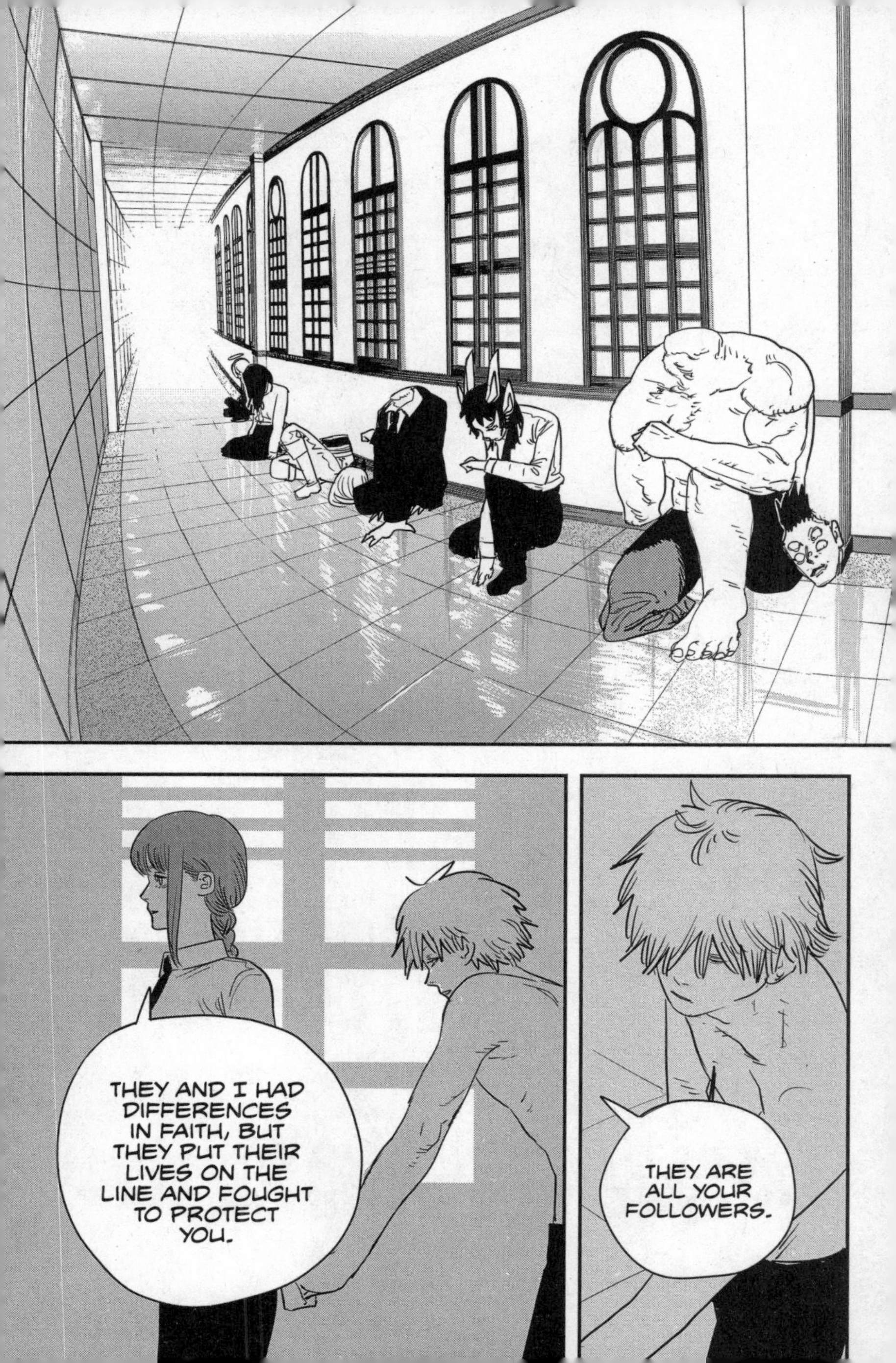
THEY ARE ALL YOUR FOLLOWERS.
THEY AND I HAD DIFFERENCES IN FAITH, BUT THEY PUT THEIR LIVES ON THE LINE AND FOUGHT TO PROTECT YOU.

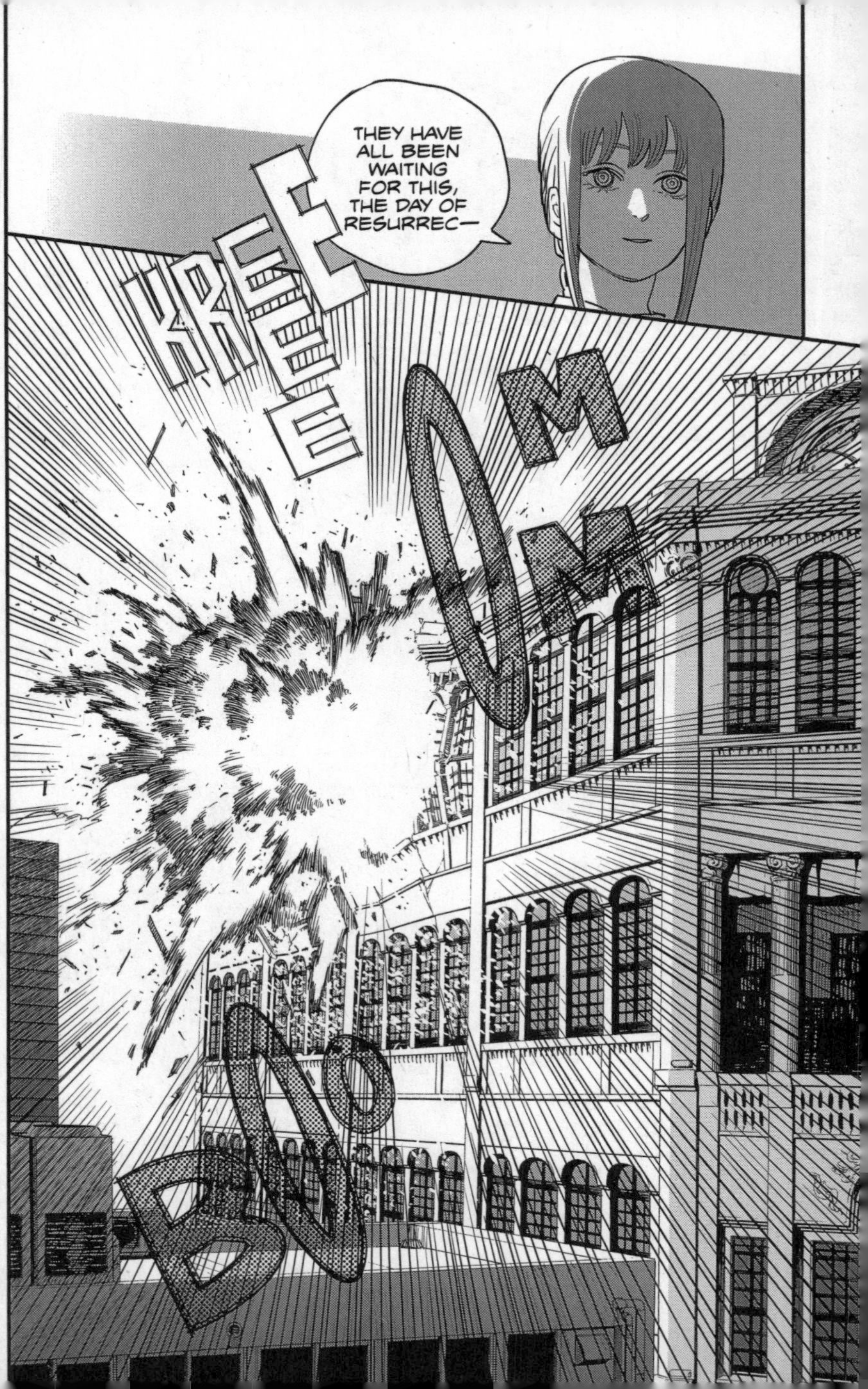
THEY HAVE ALL BEEN WAITING FOR THIS, THE DAY OF RESURREC—

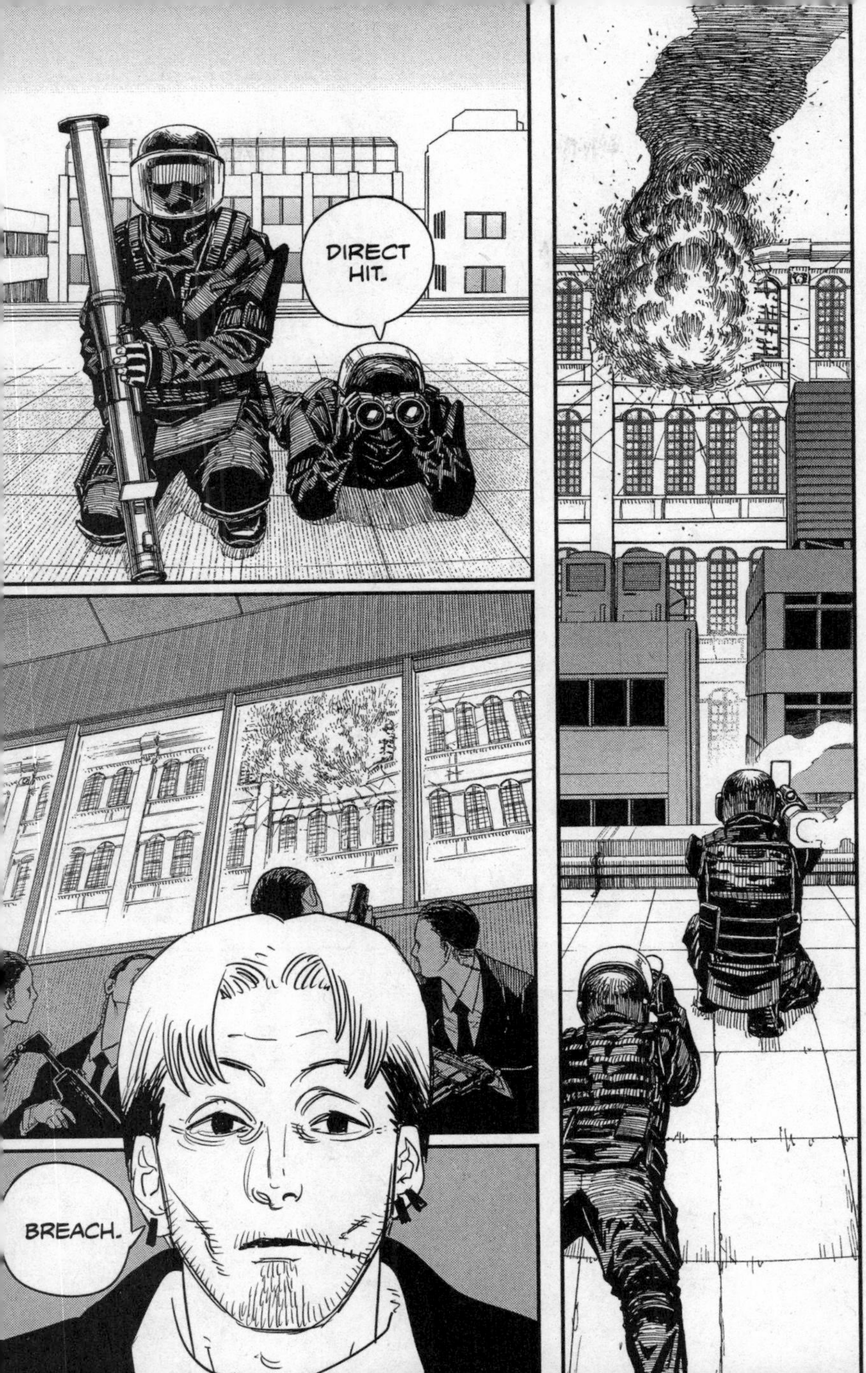
DIRECT HIT.
BREACH.

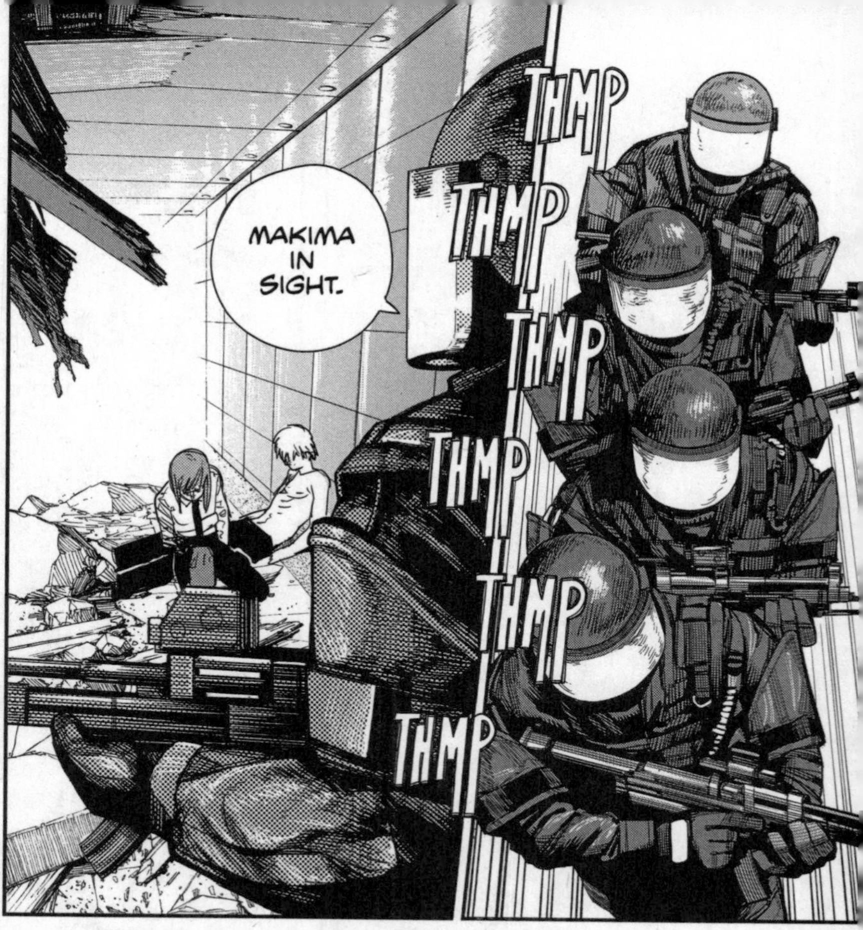
THMP
THMP
MAKIMA IN SIGHT.
THMP
THMP
THMP
THMP

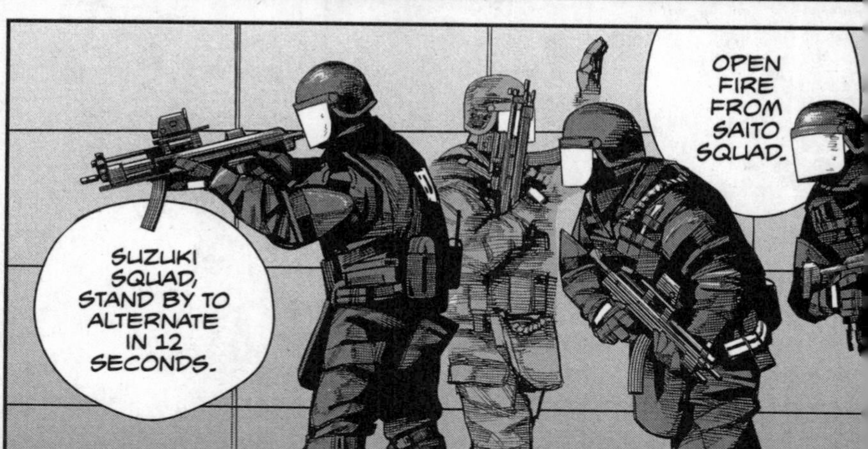
OPEN FIRE FROM SAITO SQUAD.
SUZUKI SQUAD, STAND BY TO ALTERNATE IN 12 SECONDS.

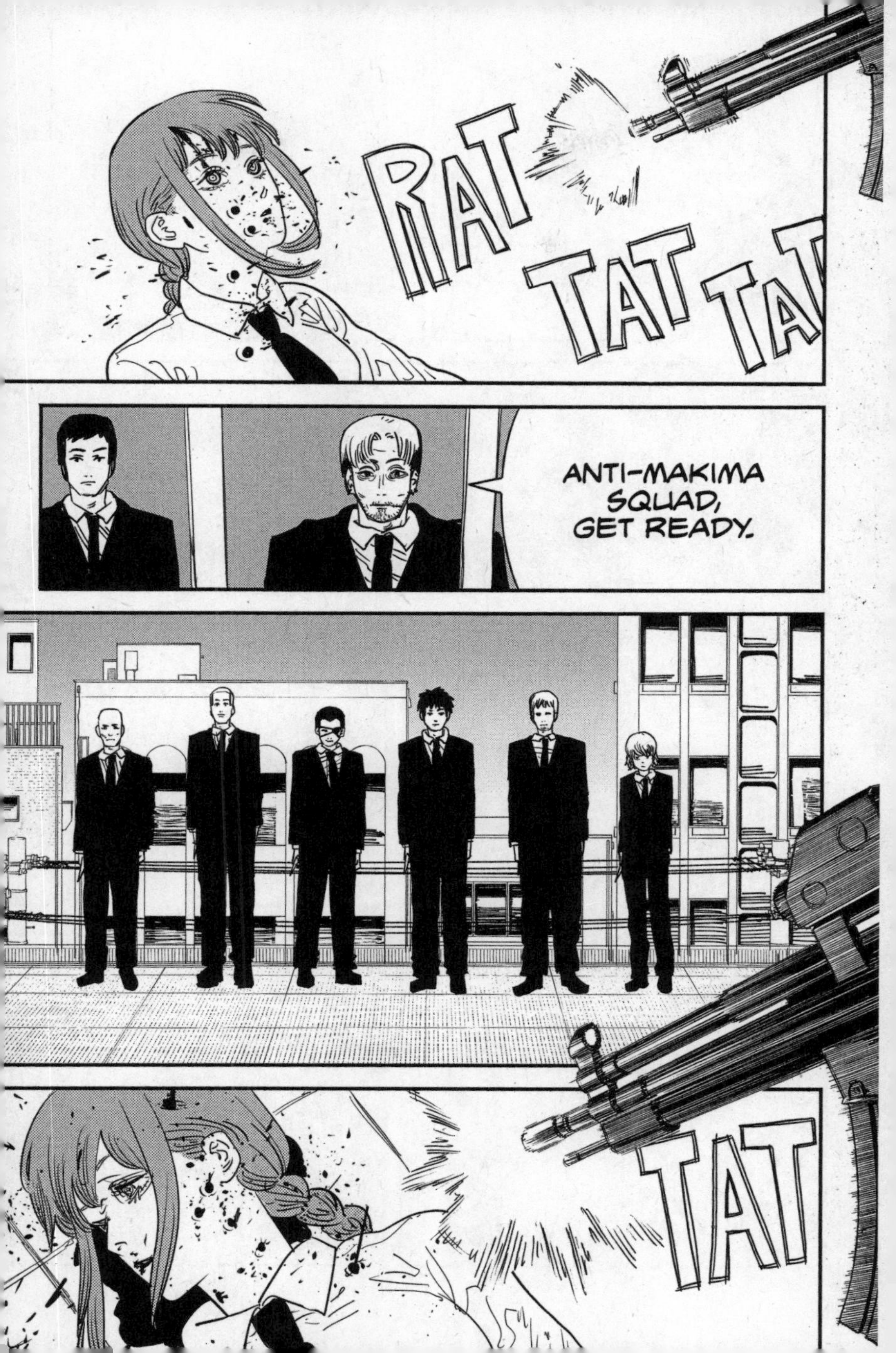
RAT
TAT
TAT
ANTI-MAKIMA SQUAD, GET READY.
TAT

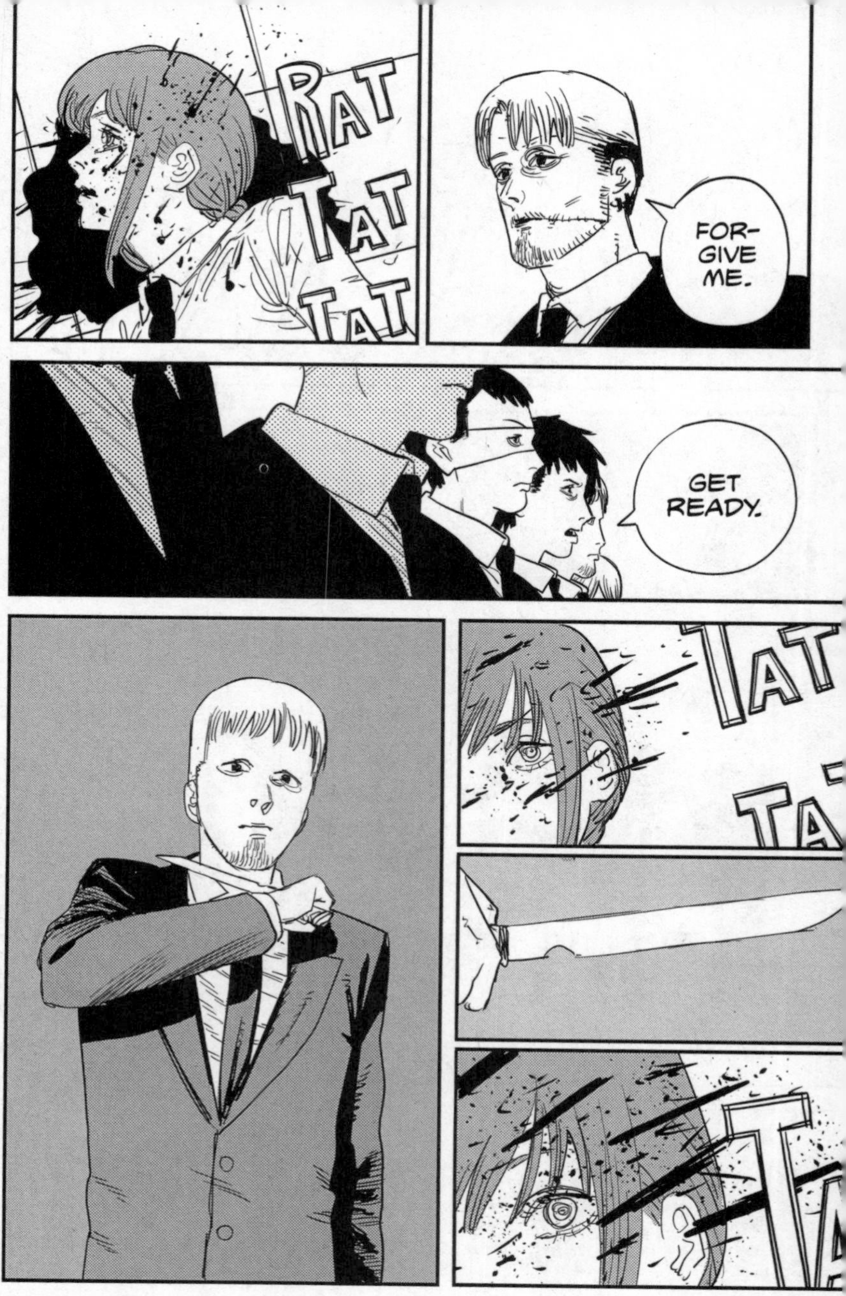
FOR-GIVE ME.
RAT TAT TAT
GET READY.
TAT TA
TA

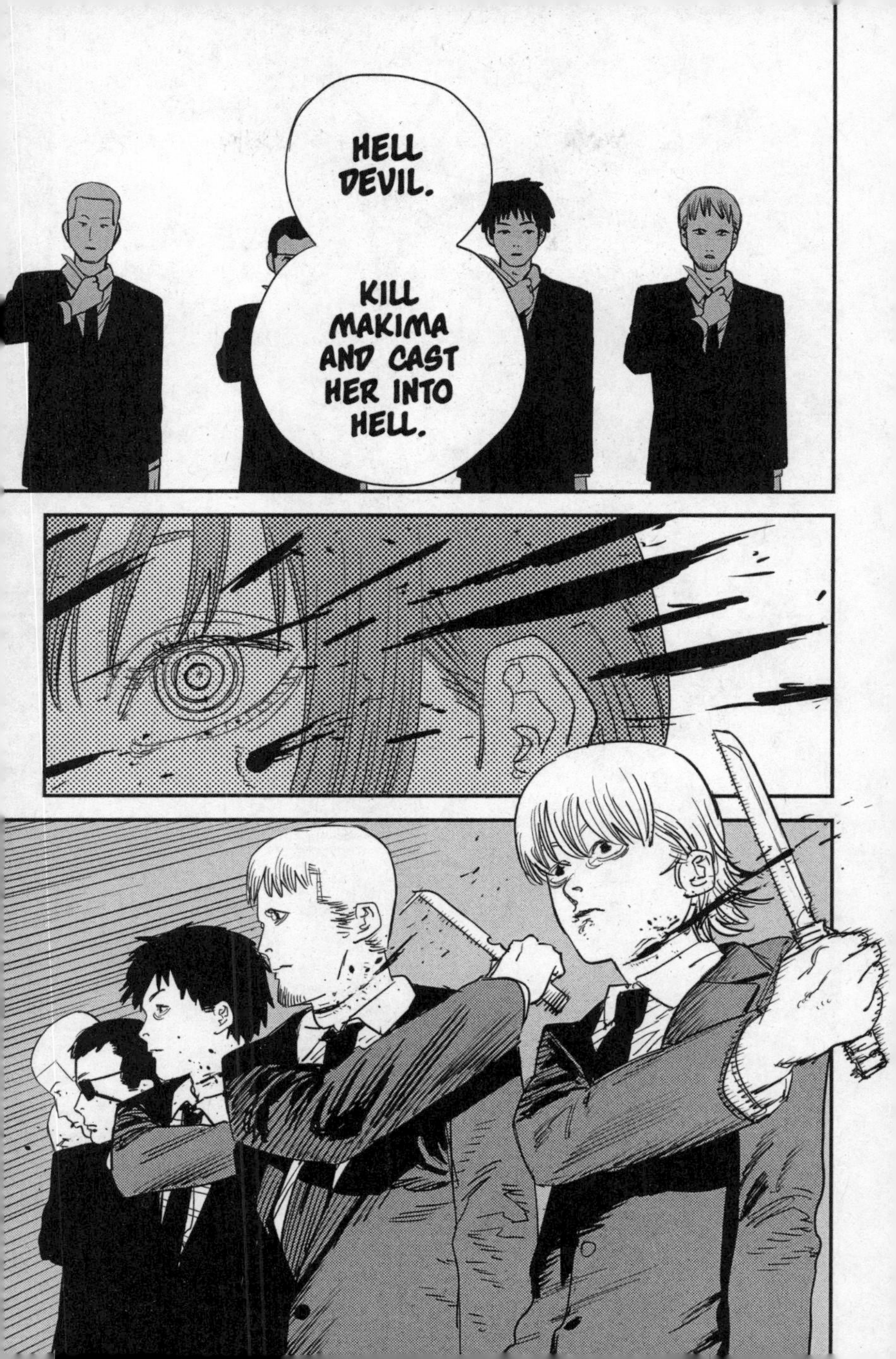
HELL DEVIL.
KILL MAKIMA AND CAST HER INTO HELL.

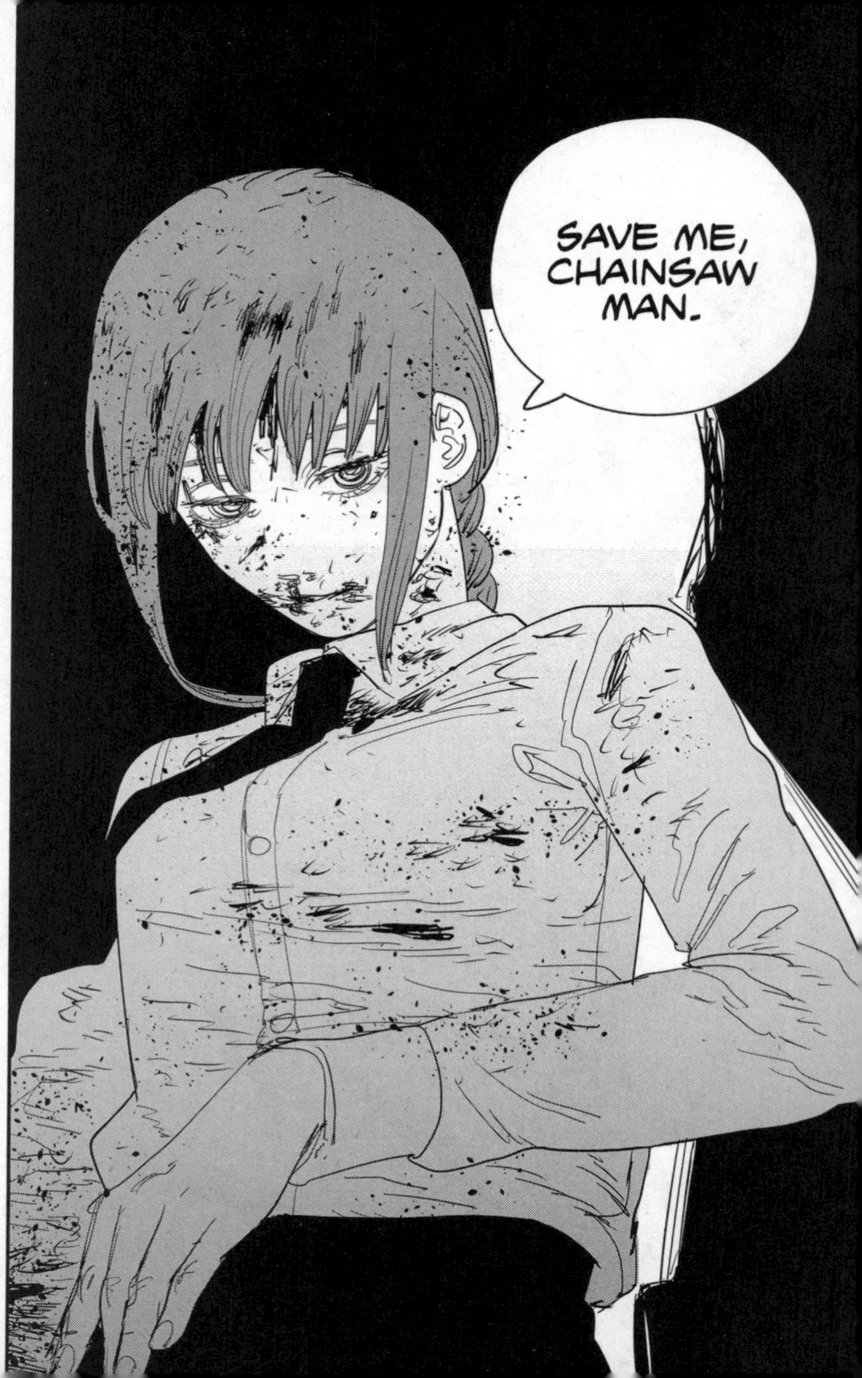
SAVE ME, CHAINSAW MAN.

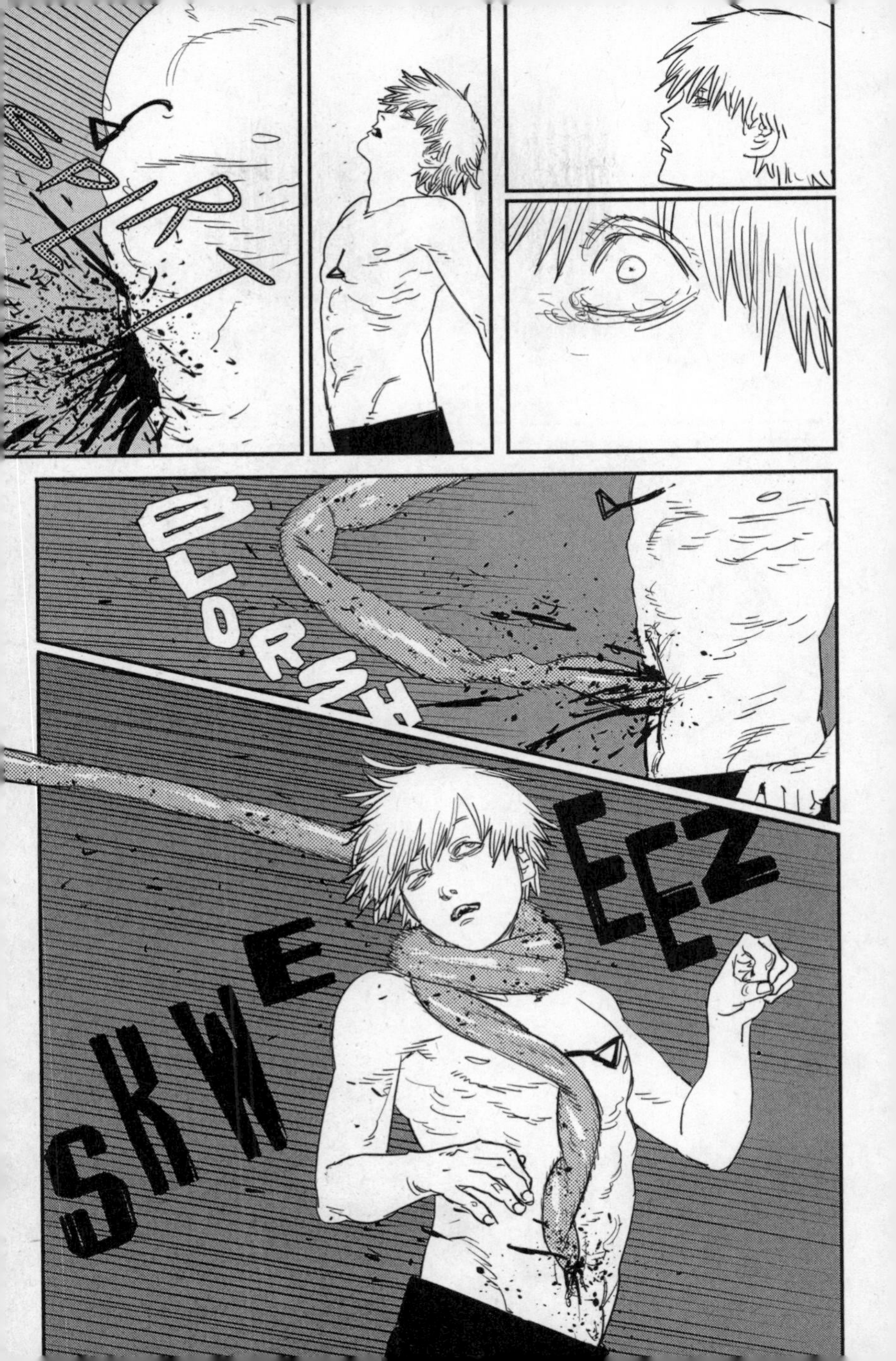
SPLRT
BLORSH
SKWEEZ

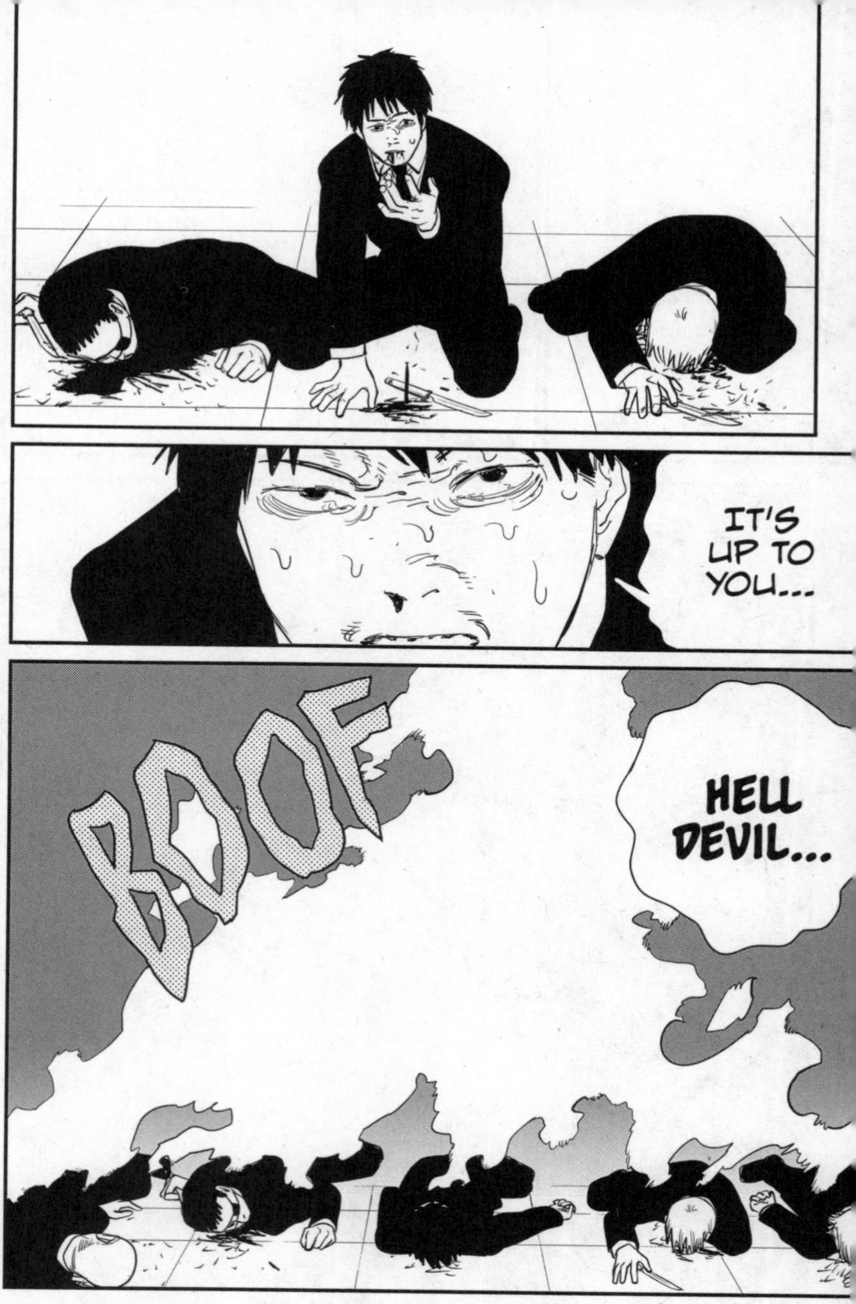
IT'S UP TO YOU...
BOOF
HELL DEVIL...

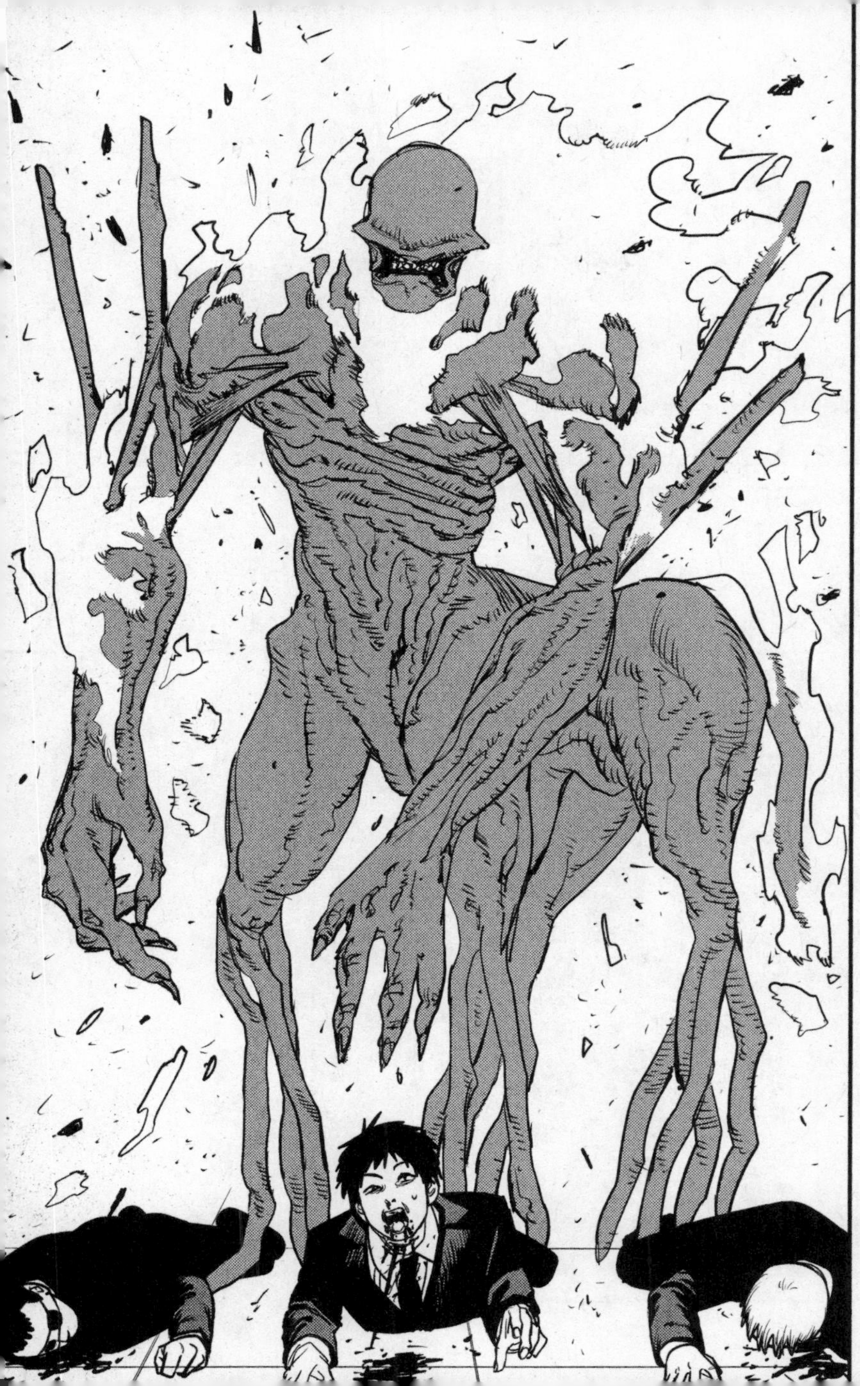

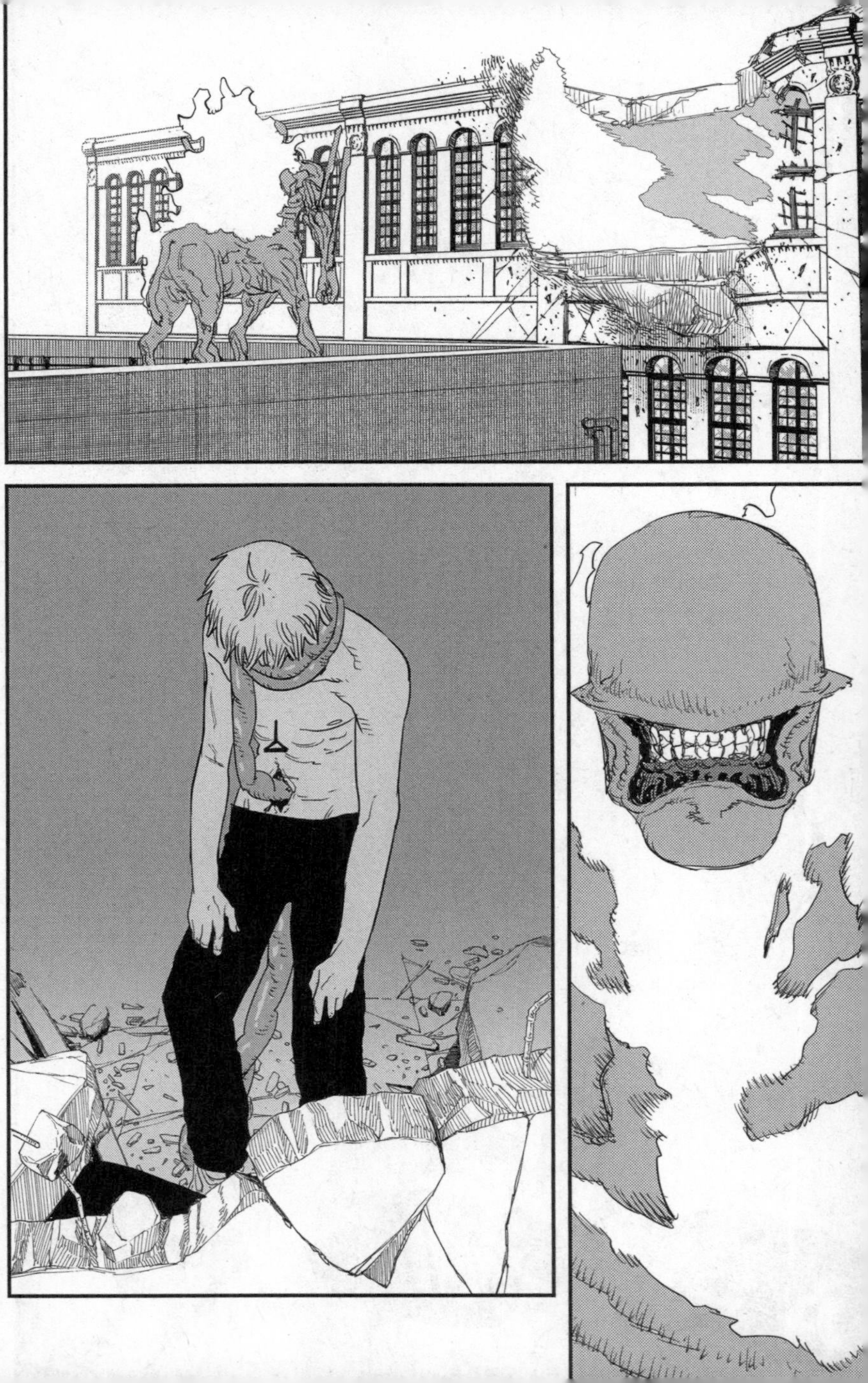

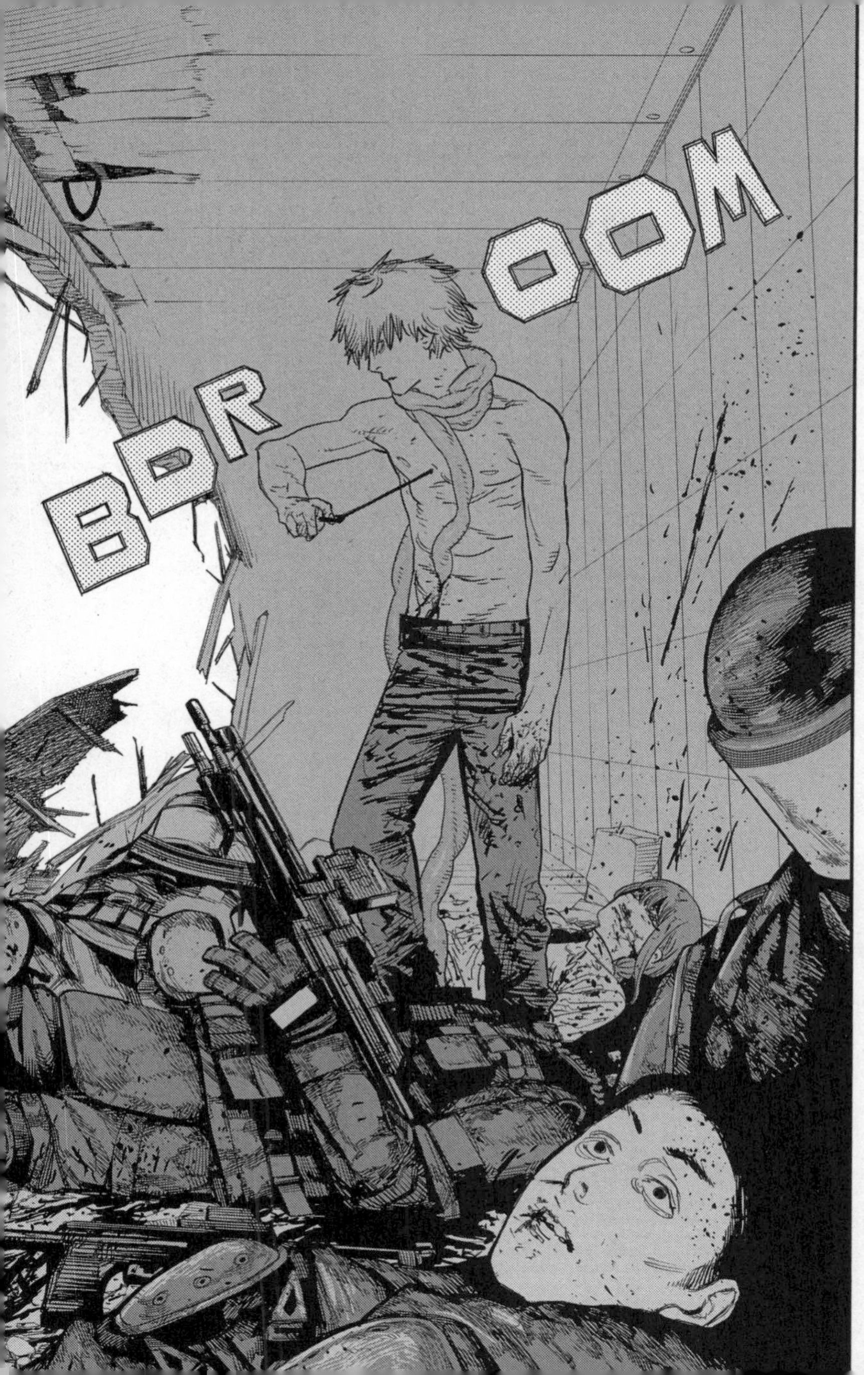
BDR
OOM

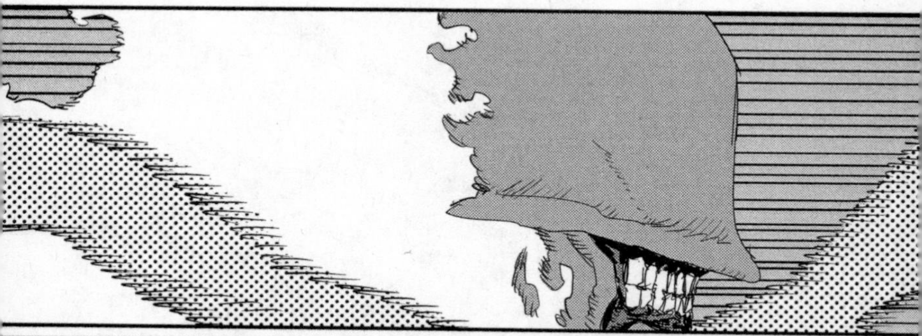
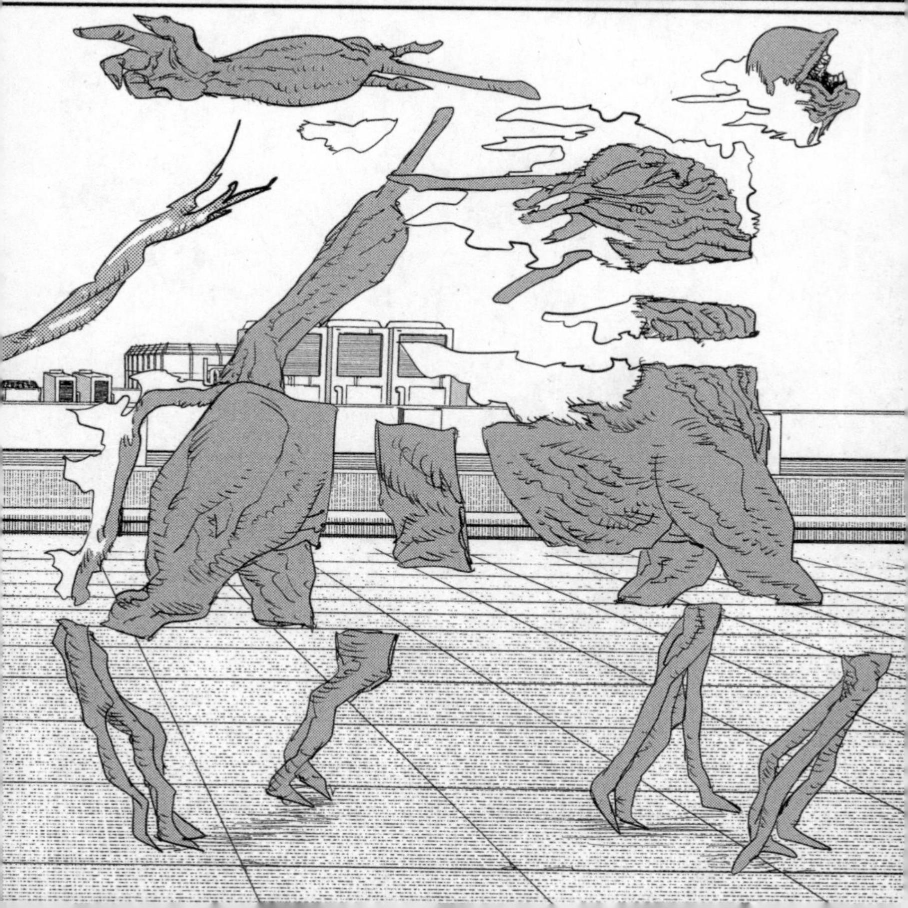

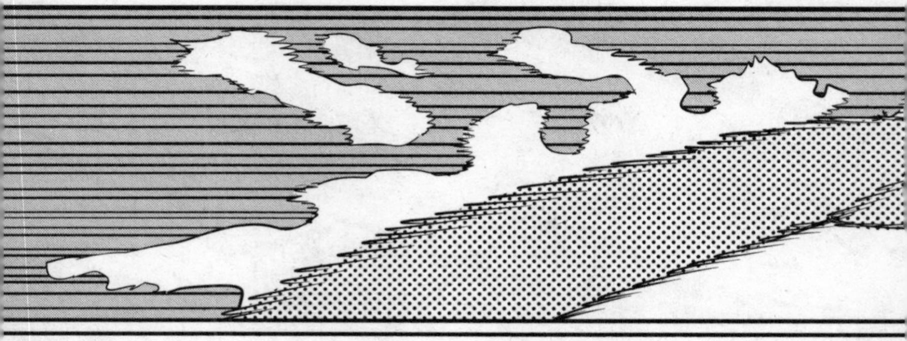

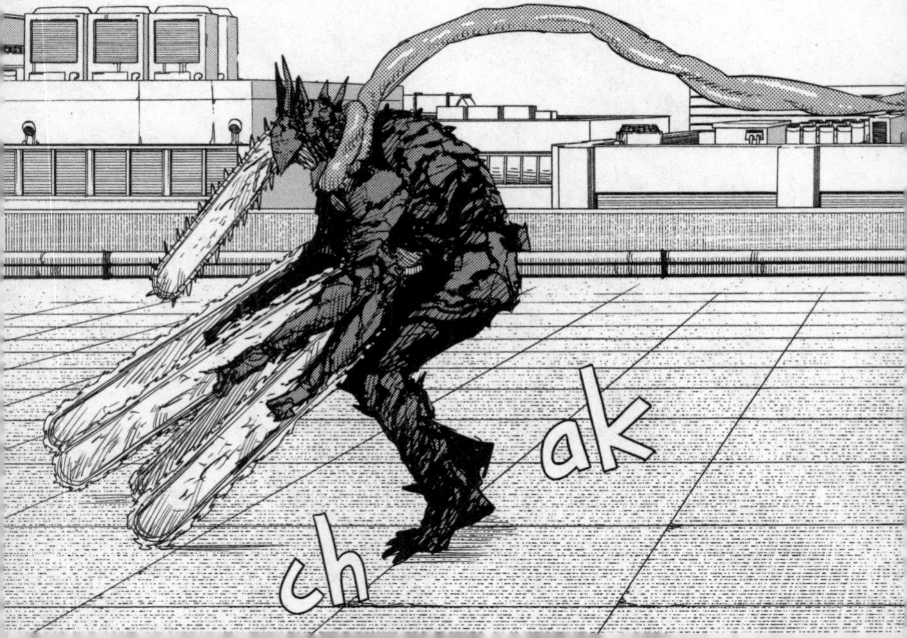
ch ak

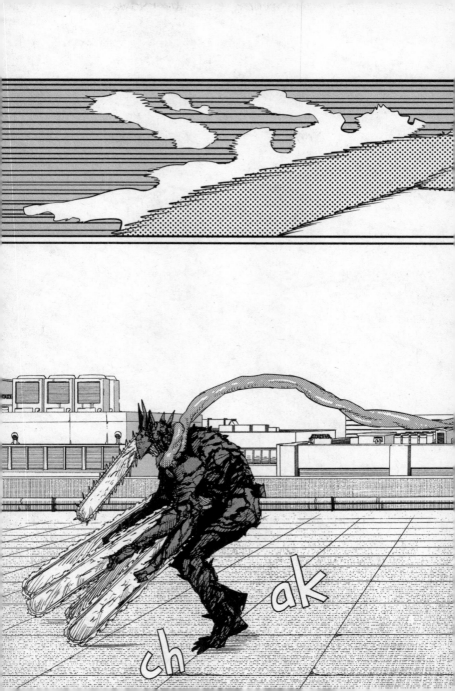

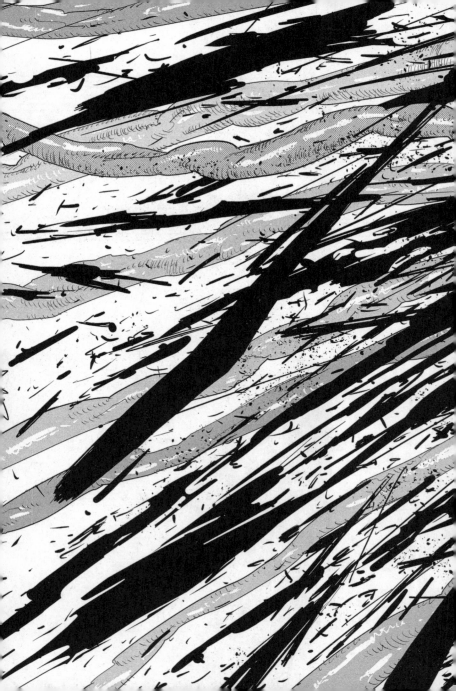

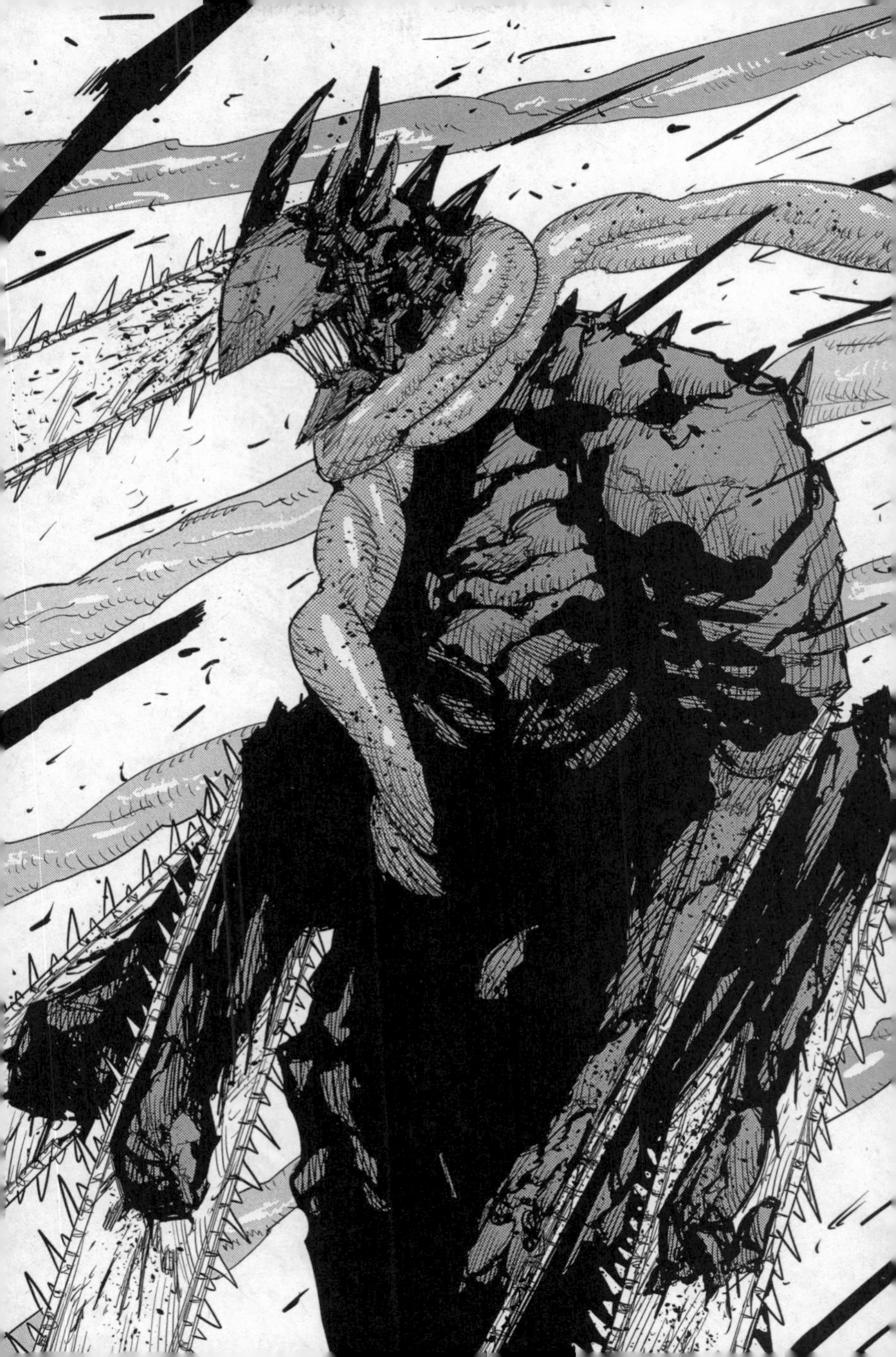

CHAINSAW MAN

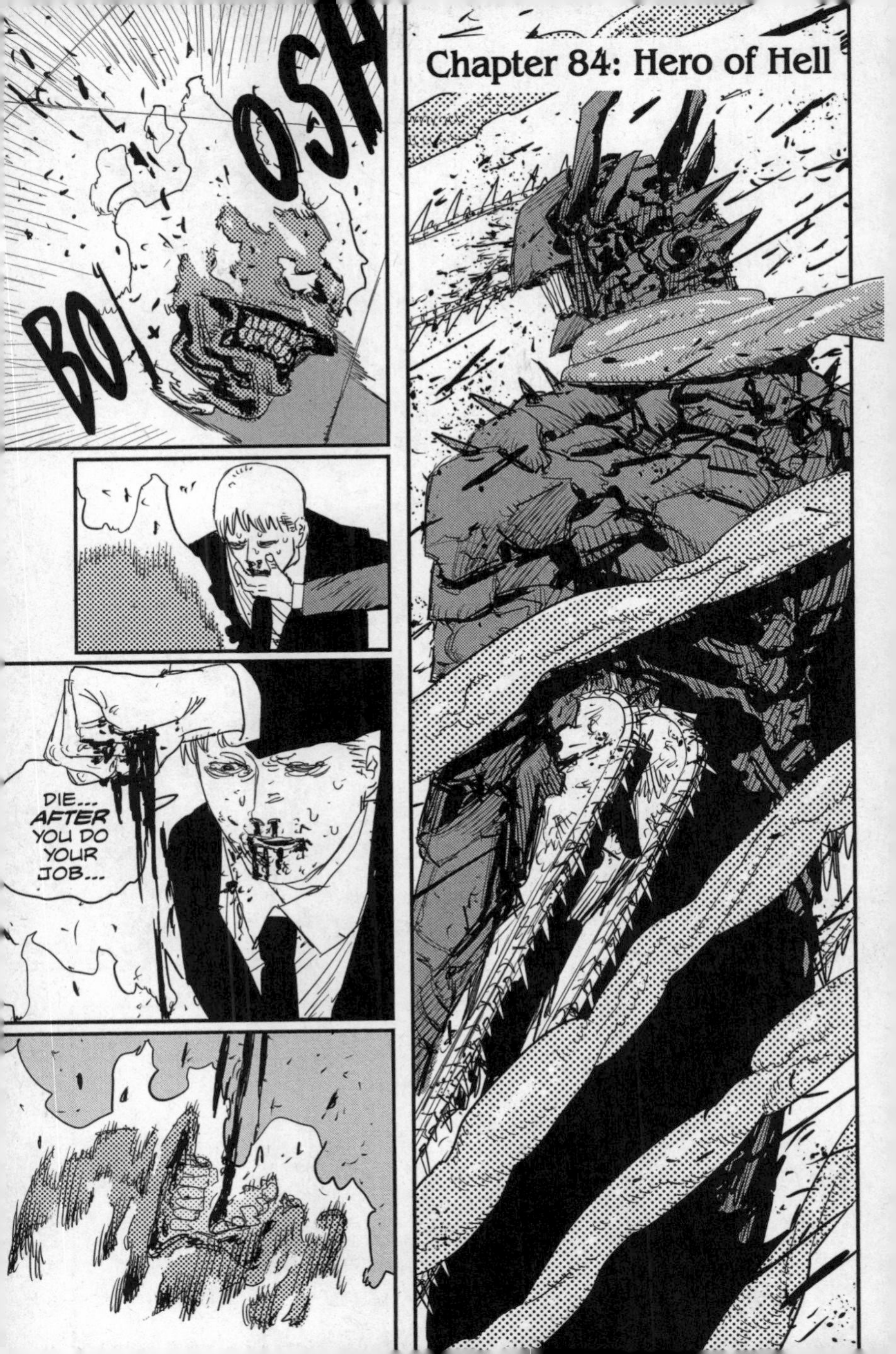
Chapter 84: Hero of Hell
BOOSH
DIE... AFTER YOU DO YOUR JOB...

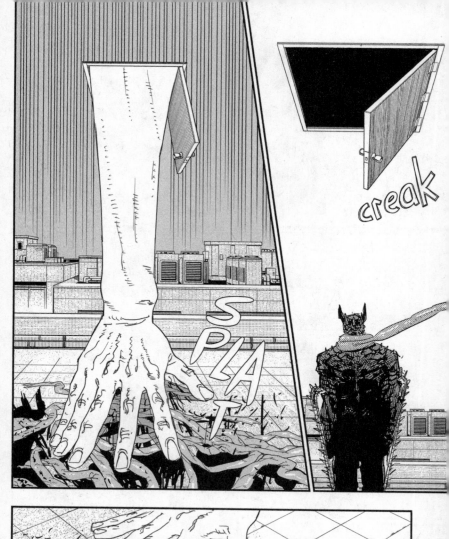

creak

SPLAT

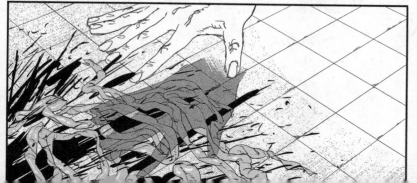

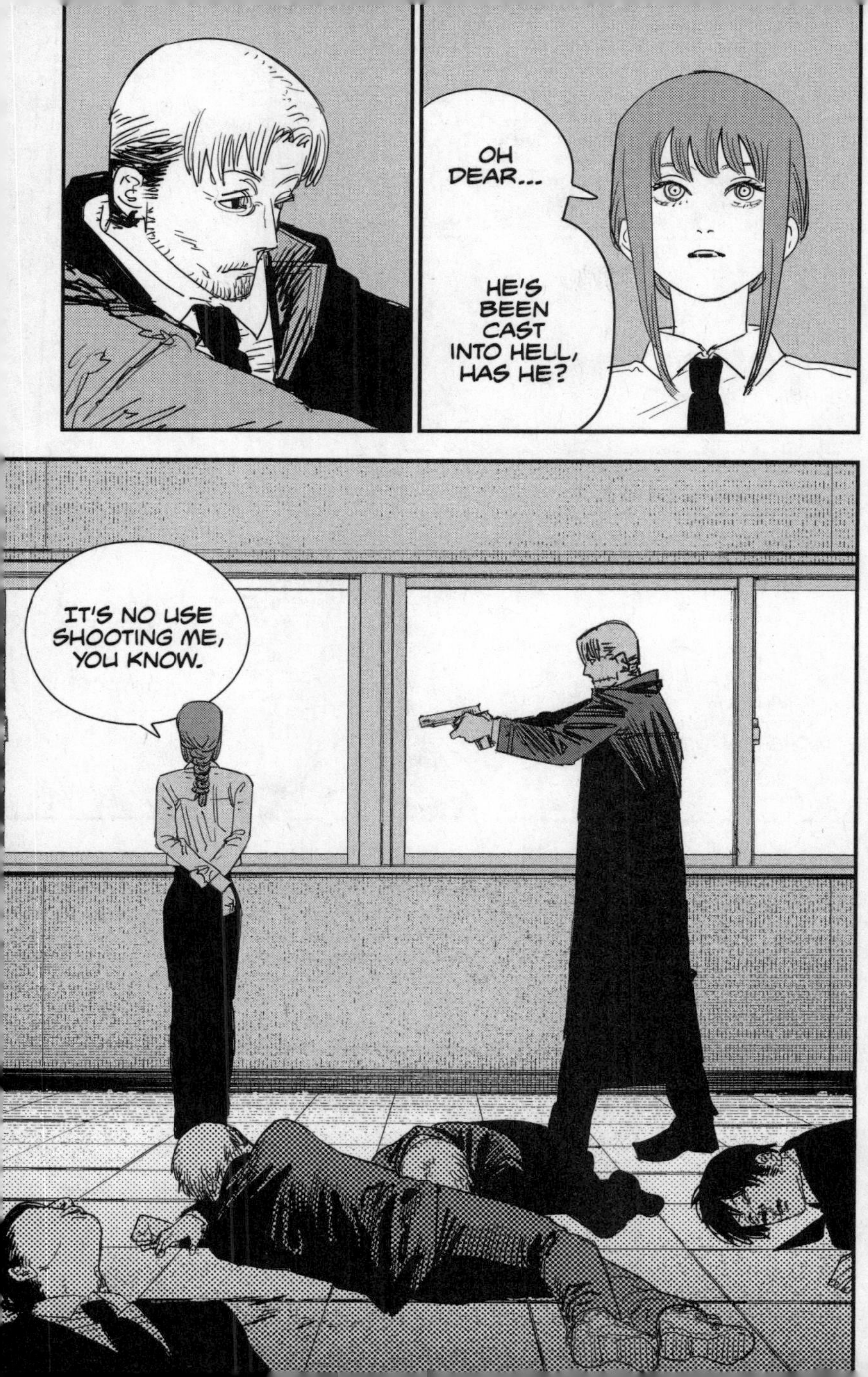
OH DEAR...
HE'S BEEN CAST INTO HELL, HAS HE?
IT'S NO USE SHOOTING ME, YOU KNOW.

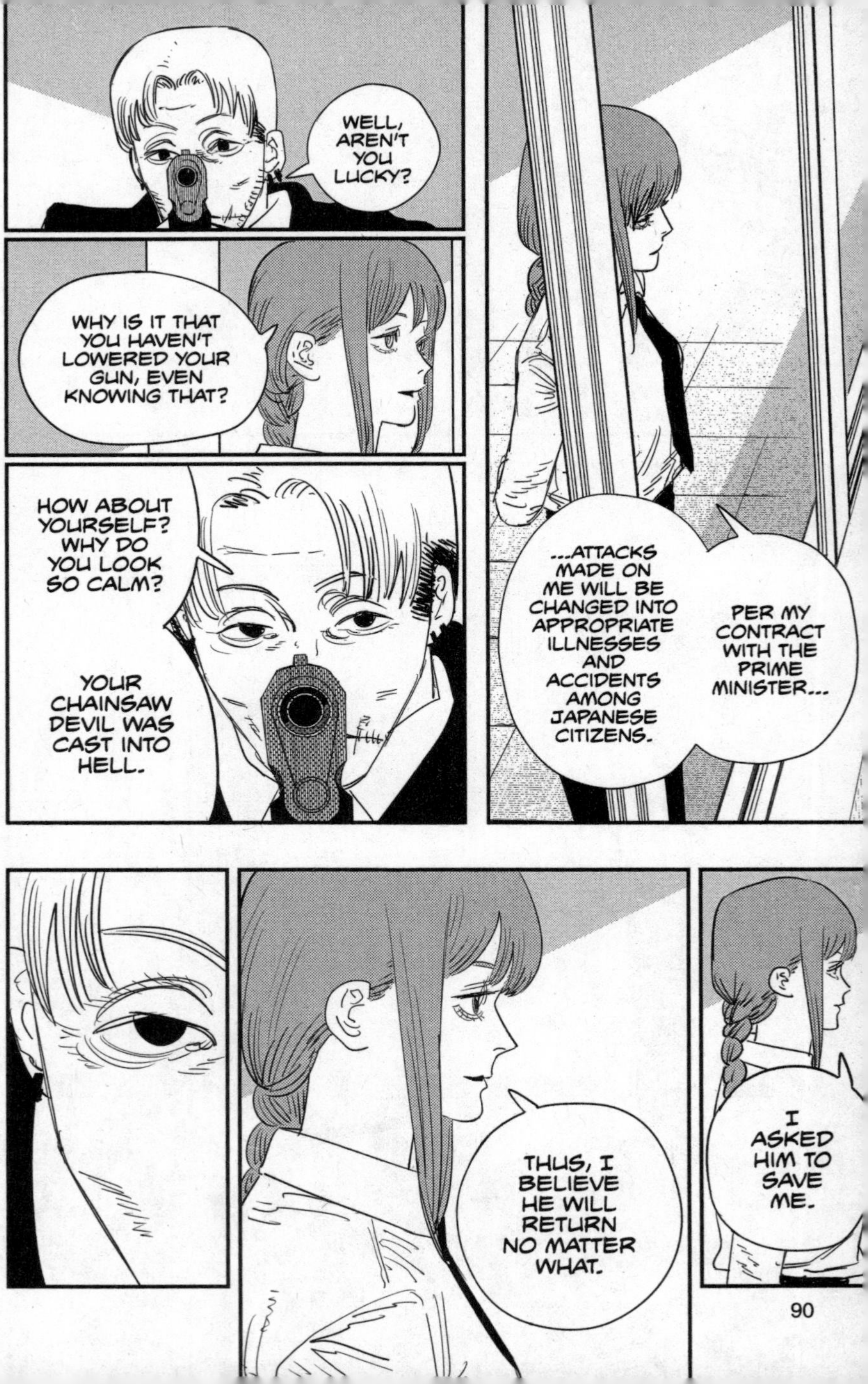
PER MY CONTRACT WITH THE PRIME MINISTER...
...ATTACKS MADE ON ME WILL BE CHANGED INTO APPROPRIATE ILLNESSES AND ACCIDENTS AMONG JAPANESE CITIZENS.
WELL, AREN'T YOU LUCKY?
WHY IS IT THAT YOU HAVEN'T LOWERED YOUR GUN, EVEN KNOWING THAT?
HOW ABOUT YOURSELF? WHY DO YOU LOOK SO CALM?
YOUR CHAINSAW DEVIL WAS CAST INTO HELL.
I ASKED HIM TO SAVE ME.
THUS, I BELIEVE HE WILL RETURN NO MATTER WHAT.

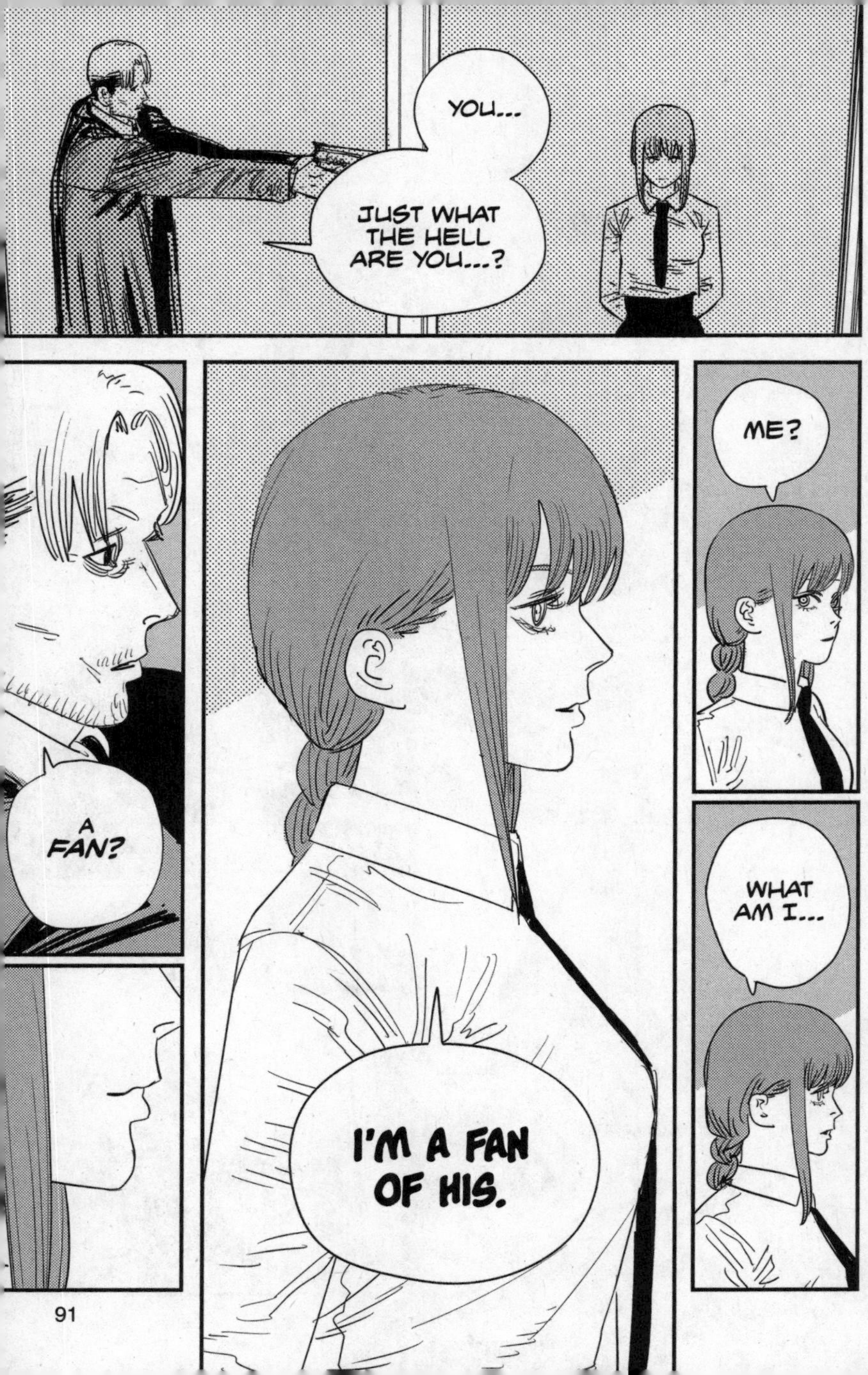
YOU...
JUST WHAT THE HELL ARE YOU...?
ME?
WHAT AM I...
I'M A FAN OF HIS.
A FAN?

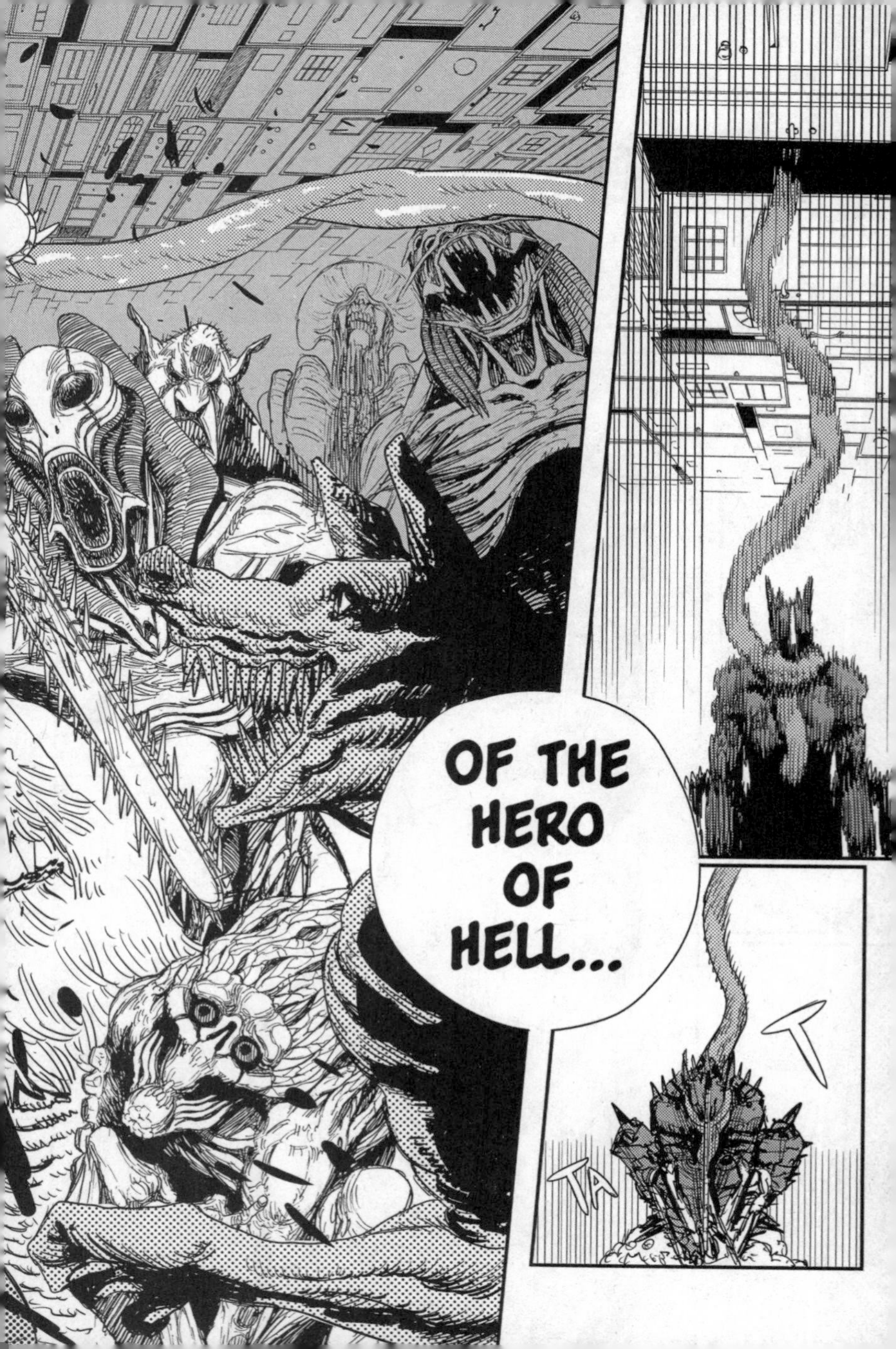
OF THE HERO OF HELL...
TA
T

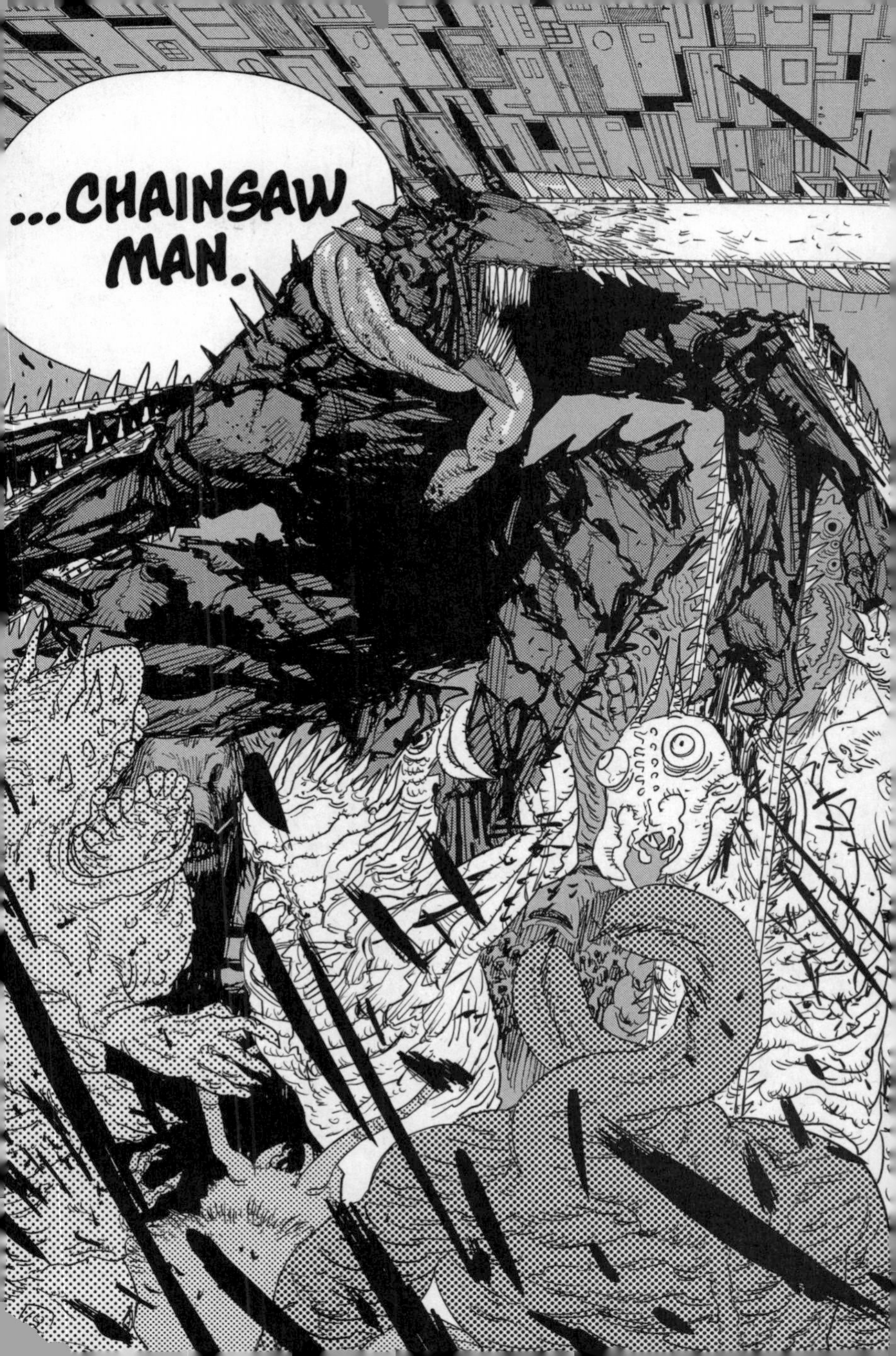
...CHAINSAW MAN.

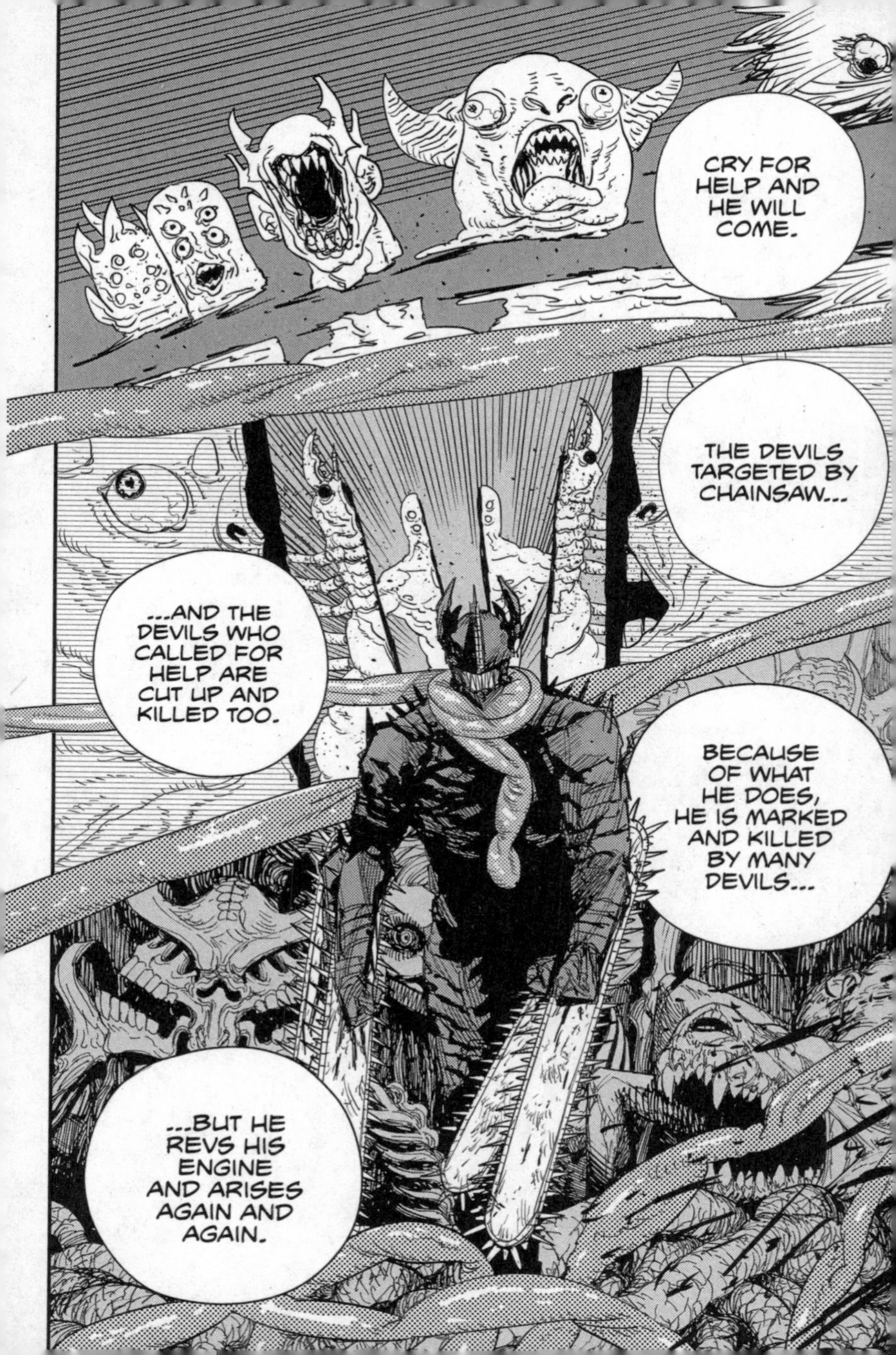
CRY FOR HELP AND HE WILL COME.
THE DEVILS TARGETED BY CHAINSAW...
...AND THE DEVILS WHO CALLED FOR HELP ARE CUT UP AND KILLED TOO.
BECAUSE OF WHAT HE DOES, HE IS MARKED AND KILLED BY MANY DEVILS...
...BUT HE REVS HIS ENGINE AND ARISES AGAIN AND AGAIN.

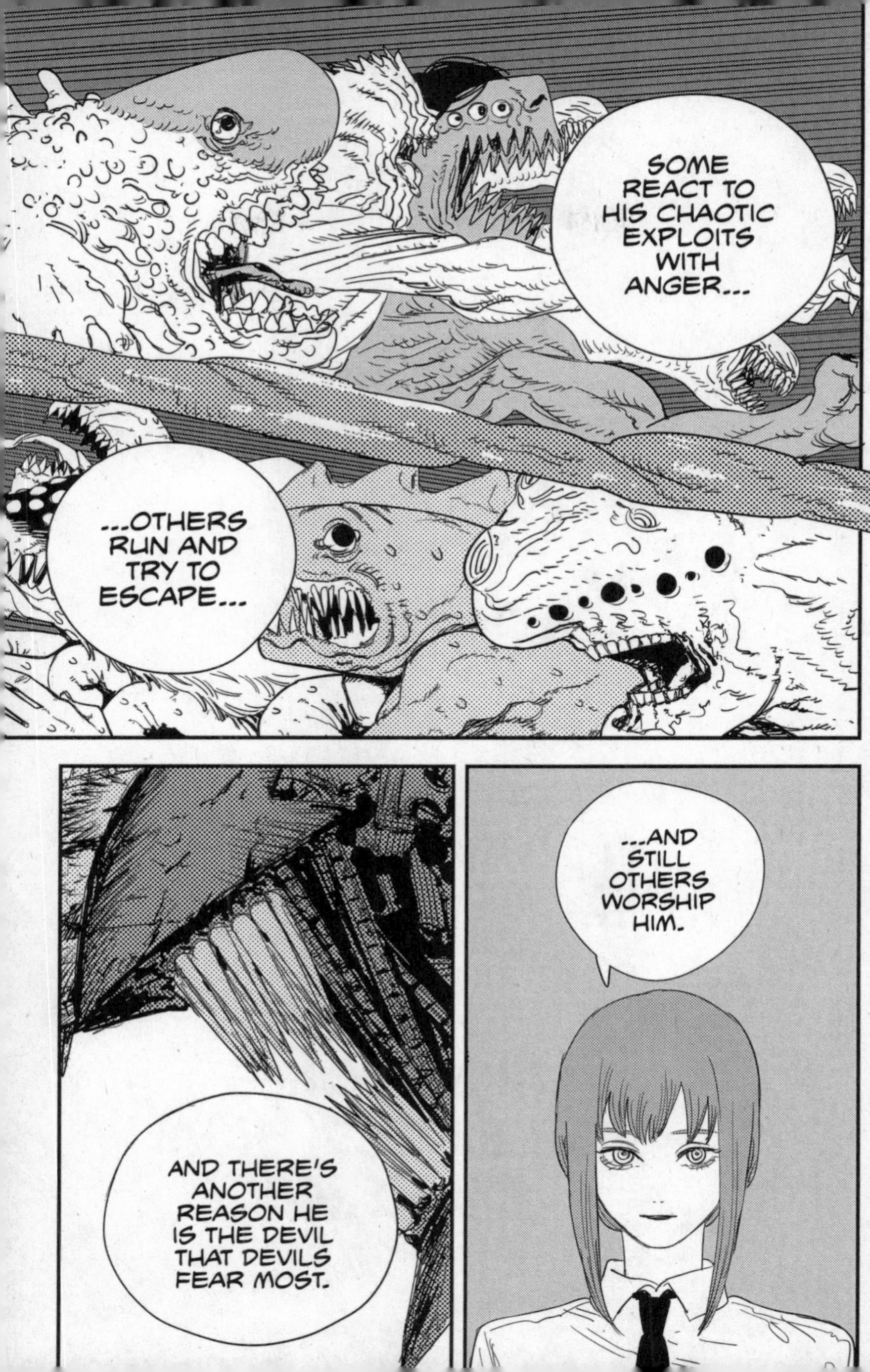
SOME REACT TO HIS CHAOTIC EXPLOITS WITH ANGER...
...OTHERS RUN AND TRY TO ESCAPE...
...AND STILL OTHERS WORSHIP HIM.
AND THERE'S ANOTHER REASON HE IS THE DEVIL THAT DEVILS FEAR MOST.

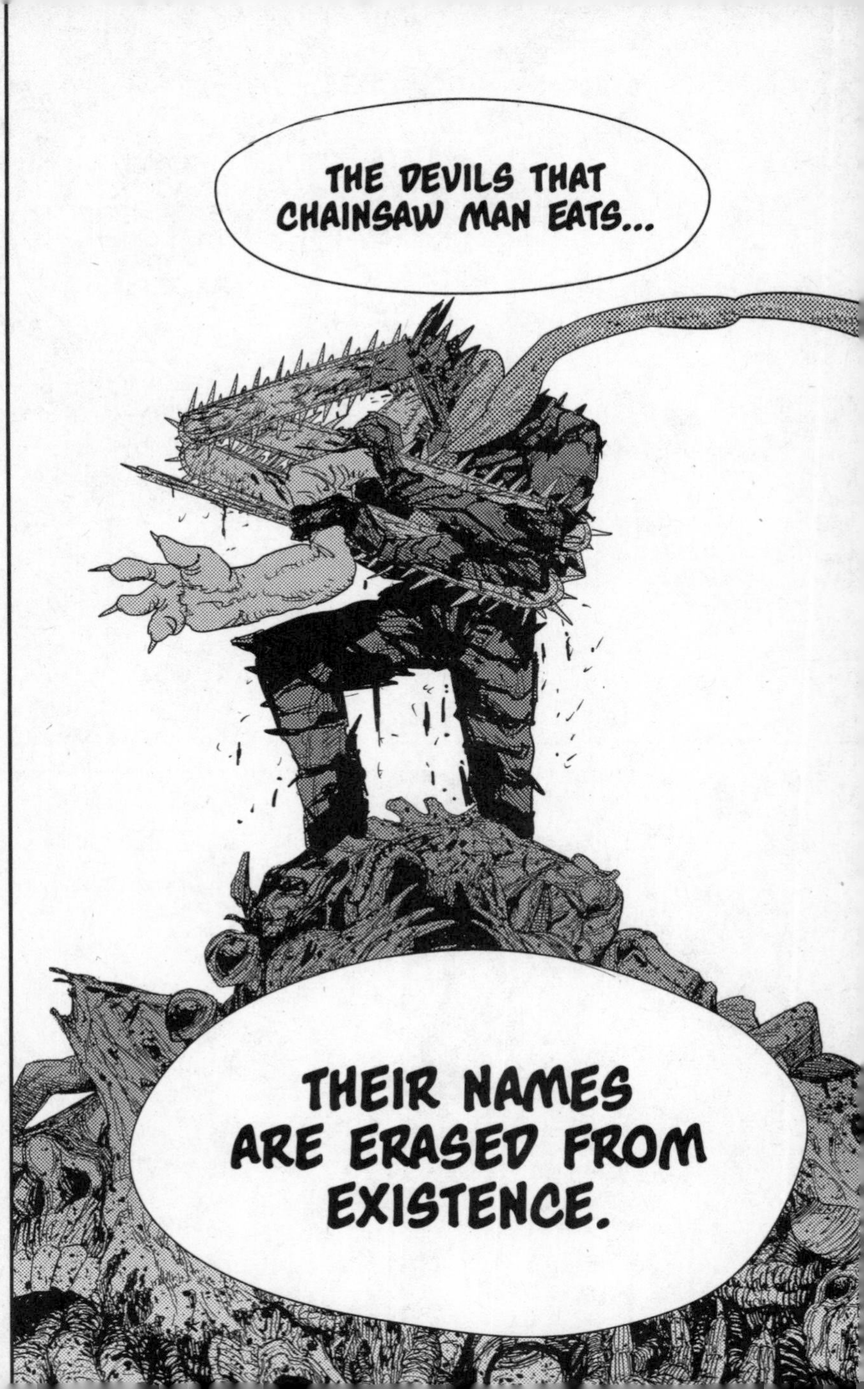
THE DEVILS THAT CHAINSAW MAN EATS...
THEIR NAMES ARE ERASED FROM EXISTENCE.

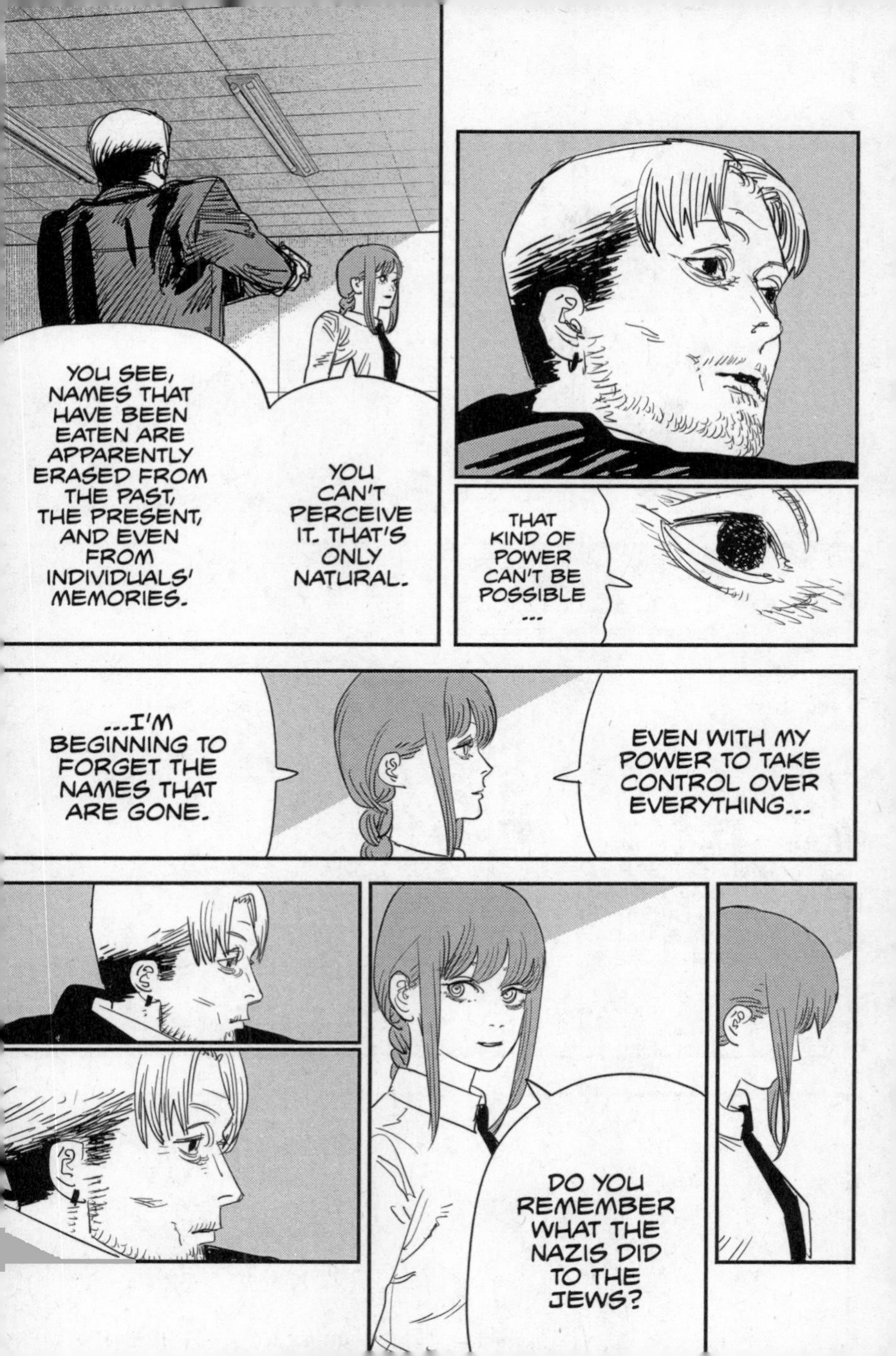
THAT KIND OF POWER CAN'T BE POSSIBLE...
YOU SEE, NAMES THAT HAVE BEEN EATEN ARE APPARENTLY ERASED FROM THE PAST, THE PRESENT, AND EVEN FROM INDIVIDUALS' MEMORIES.
YOU CAN'T PERCEIVE IT. THAT'S ONLY NATURAL.
EVEN WITH MY POWER TO TAKE CONTROL OVER EVERYTHING...
...I'M BEGINNING TO FORGET THE NAMES THAT ARE GONE.
DO YOU REMEMBER WHAT THE NAZIS DID TO THE JEWS?

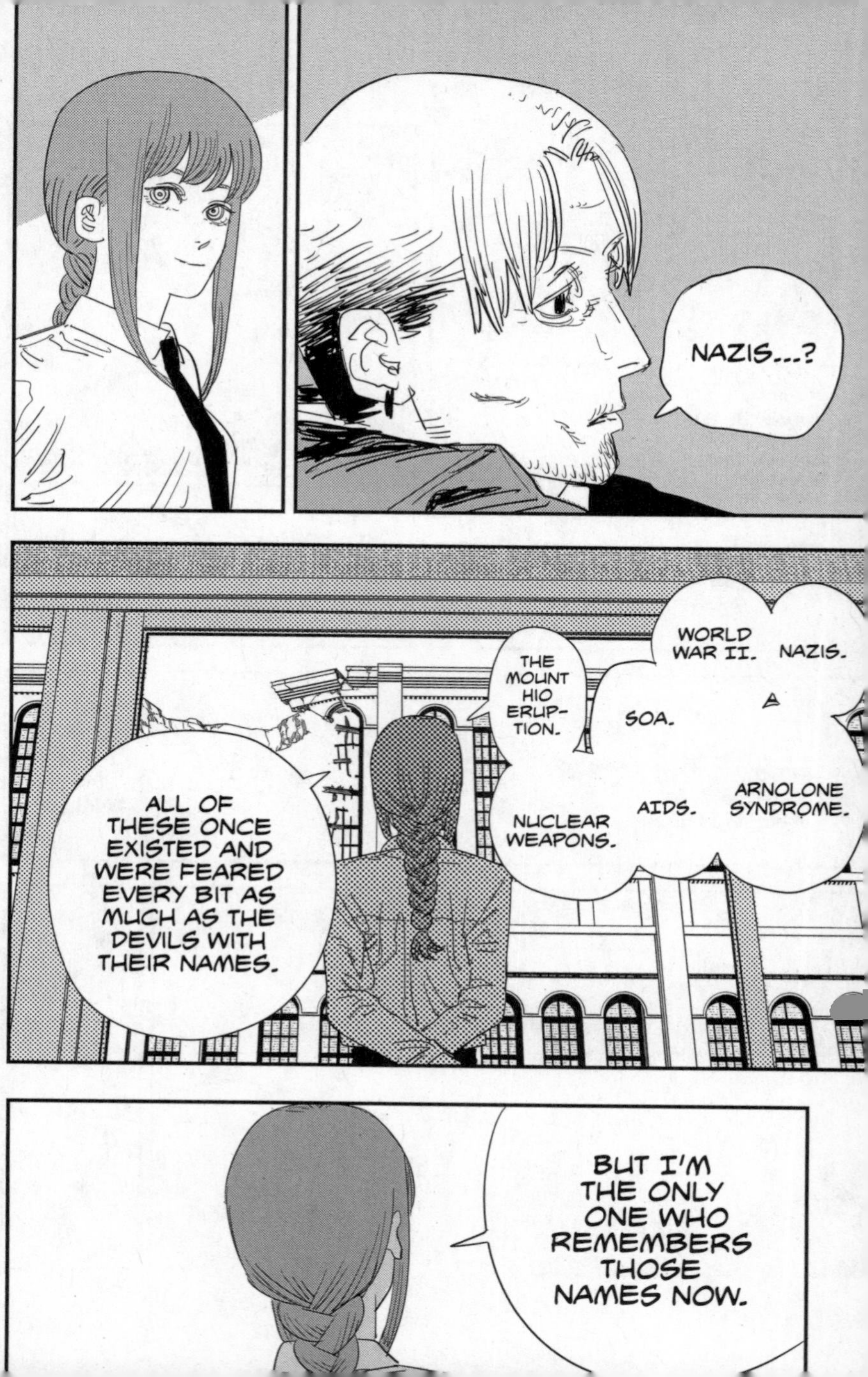
NAZIS...?
WORLD WAR II.
NAZIS.
A
SOA.
ARNOLONE SYNDROME.
AIDS.
NUCLEAR WEAPONS.
THE MOUNT HIO ERUPTION.
ALL OF THESE ONCE EXISTED AND WERE FEARED EVERY BIT AS MUCH AS THE DEVILS WITH THEIR NAMES.
BUT I'M THE ONLY ONE WHO REMEMBERS THOSE NAMES NOW.

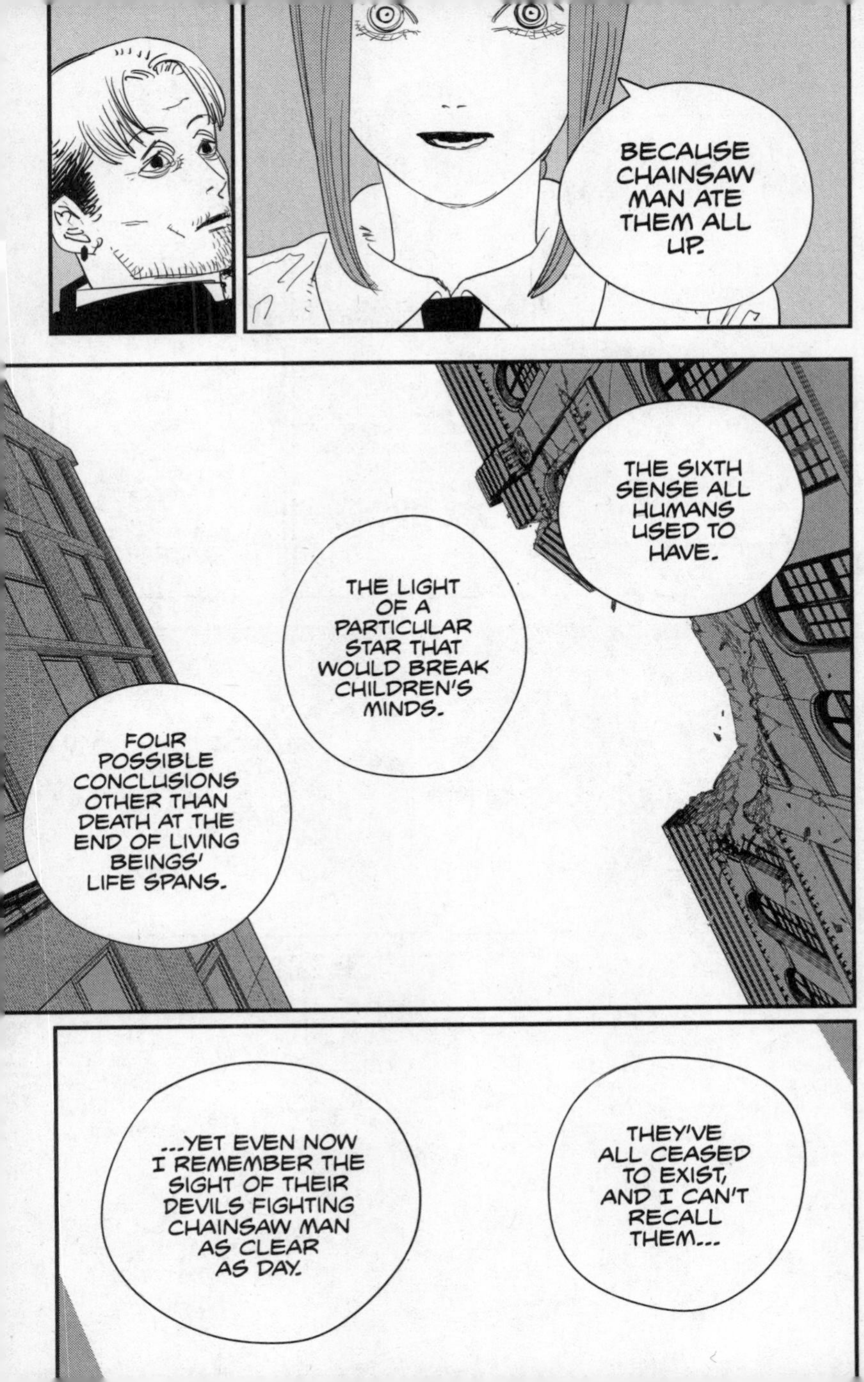
BECAUSE CHAINSAW MAN ATE THEM ALL UP.
THE SIXTH SENSE ALL HUMANS USED TO HAVE.
THE LIGHT OF A PARTICULAR STAR THAT WOULD BREAK CHILDREN'S MINDS.
FOUR POSSIBLE CONCLUSIONS OTHER THAN DEATH AT THE END OF LIVING BEINGS' LIFE SPANS.
THEY'VE ALL CEASED TO EXIST, AND I CAN'T RECALL THEM...
...YET EVEN NOW I REMEMBER THE SIGHT OF THEIR DEVILS FIGHTING CHAINSAW MAN AS CLEAR AS DAY.

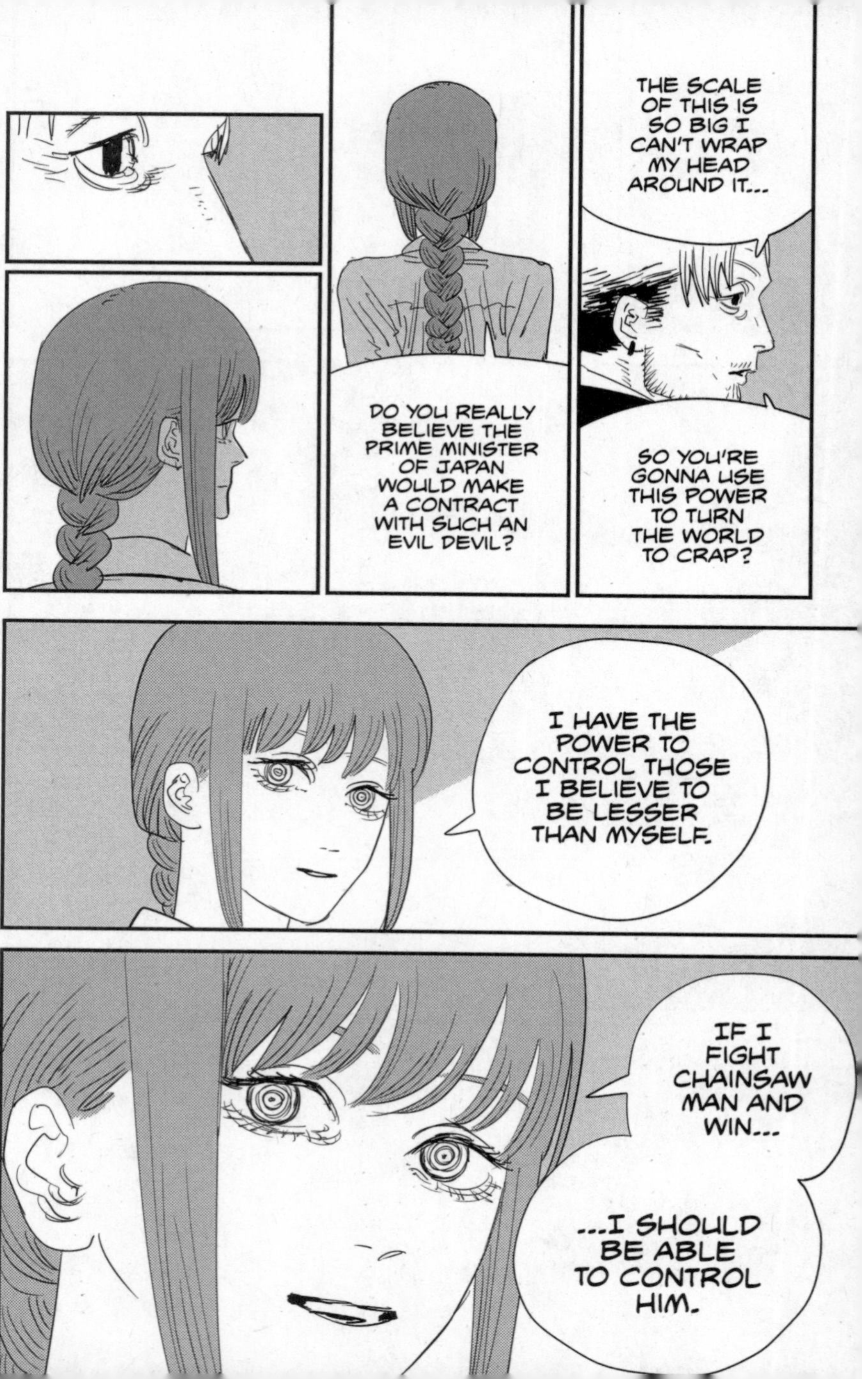
THE SCALE OF THIS IS SO BIG I CAN'T WRAP MY HEAD AROUND IT...
SO YOU'RE GONNA USE THIS POWER TO TURN THE WORLD TO CRAP?
DO YOU REALLY BELIEVE THE PRIME MINISTER OF JAPAN WOULD MAKE A CONTRACT WITH SUCH AN EVIL DEVIL?
I HAVE THE POWER TO CONTROL THOSE I BELIEVE TO BE LESSER THAN MYSELF.
IF I FIGHT CHAINSAW MAN AND WIN...
...I SHOULD BE ABLE TO CONTROL HIM.

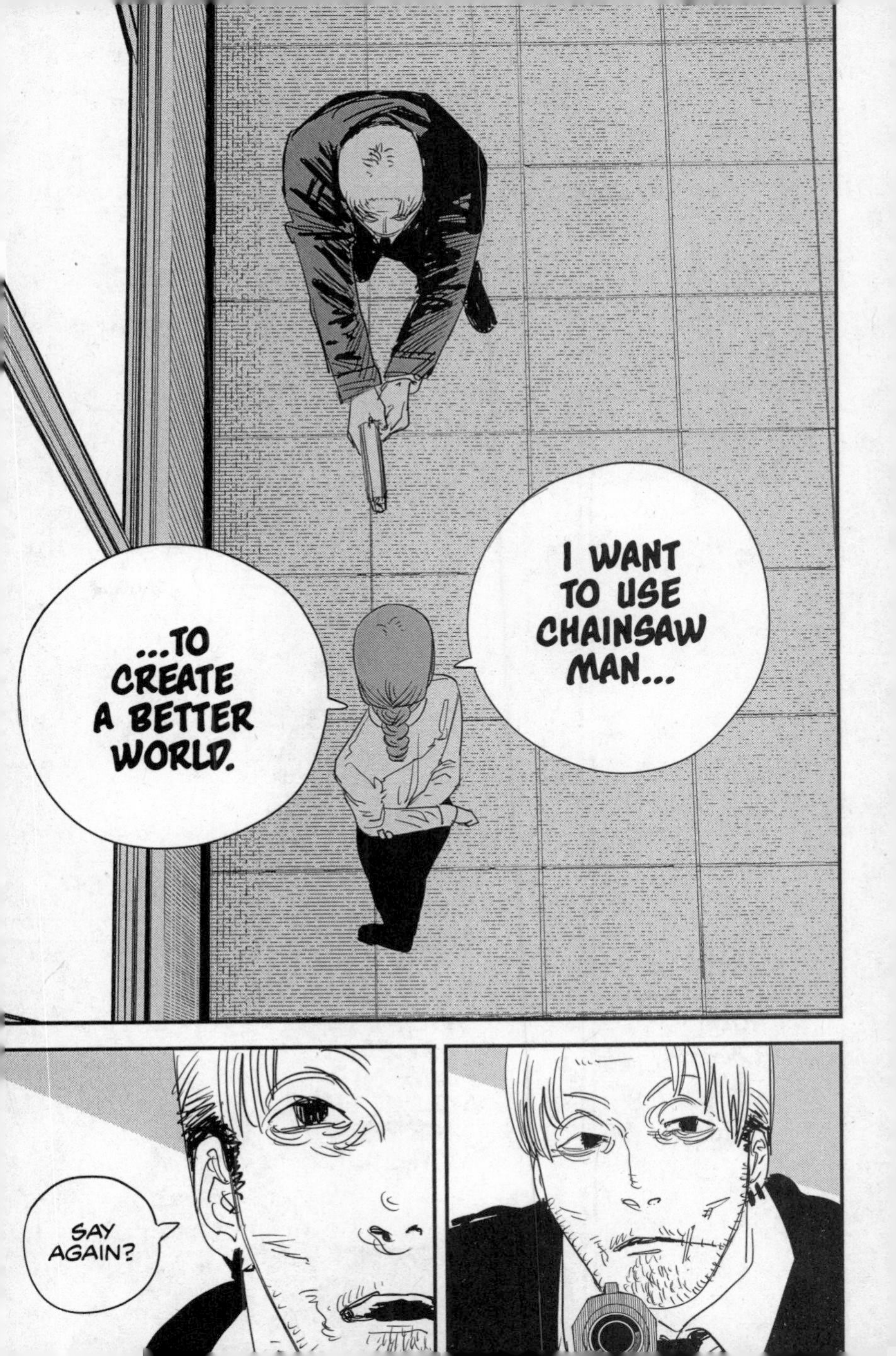
I WANT TO USE CHAINSAW MAN...
...TO CREATE A BETTER WORLD.
SAY AGAIN?

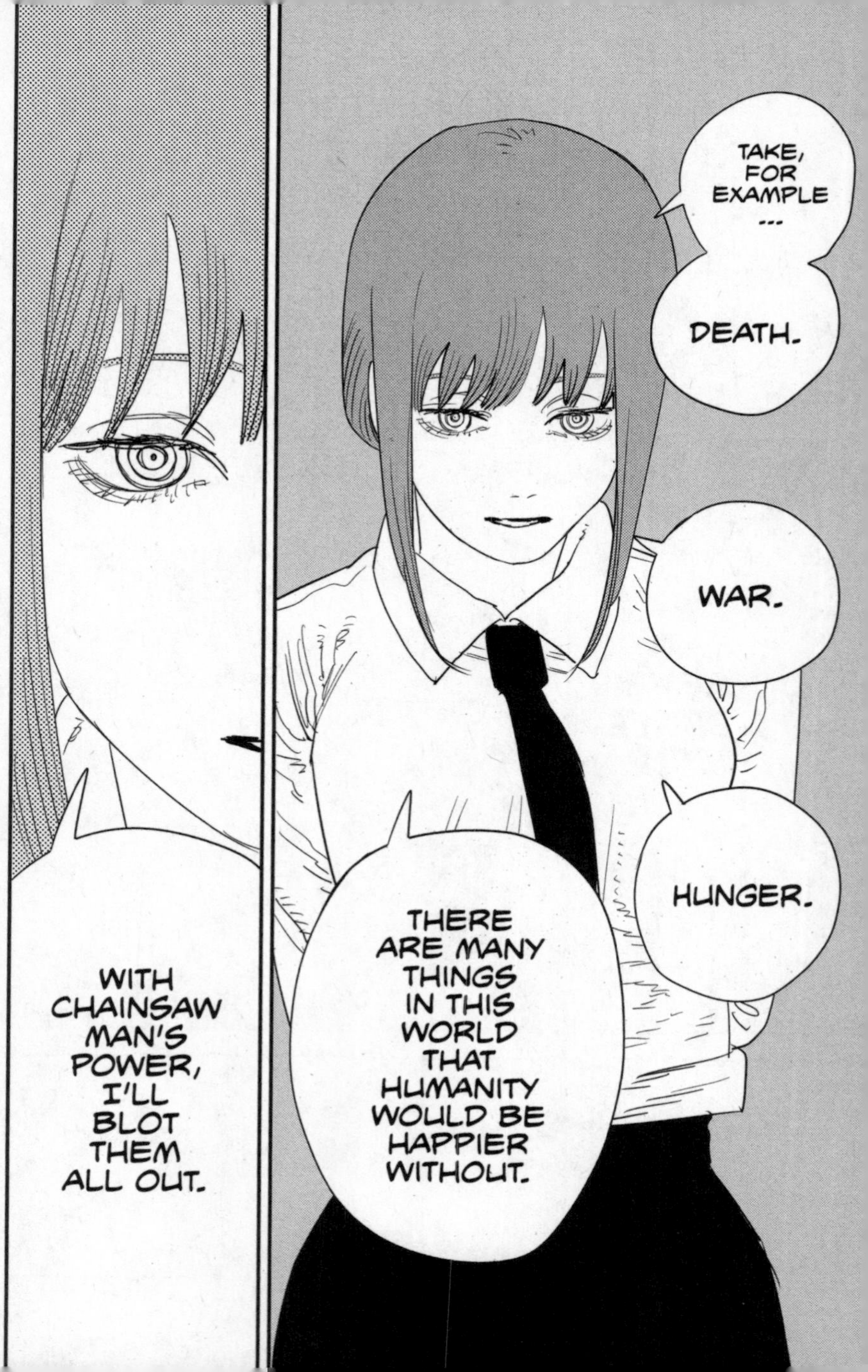
TAKE, FOR EXAMPLE...
DEATH.
WAR.
HUNGER.
THERE ARE MANY THINGS IN THIS WORLD THAT HUMANITY WOULD BE HAPPIER WITHOUT.
WITH CHAINSAW MAN'S POWER, I'LL BLOT THEM ALL OUT.

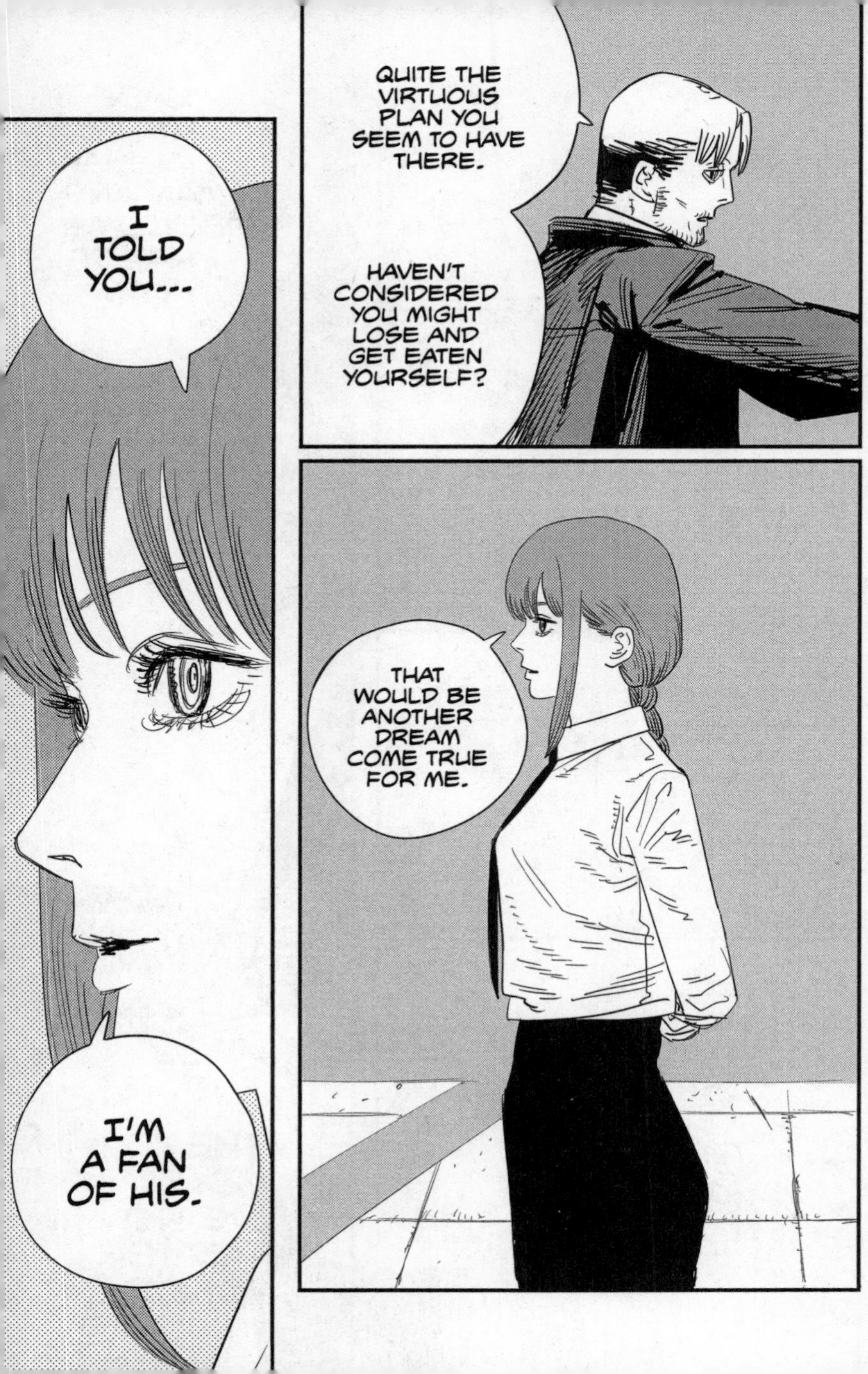
QUITE THE VIRTUOUS PLAN YOU SEEM TO HAVE THERE.
HAVEN'T CONSIDERED YOU MIGHT LOSE AND GET EATEN YOURSELF?
THAT WOULD BE ANOTHER DREAM COME TRUE FOR ME.
I TOLD YOU...
I'M A FAN OF HIS.

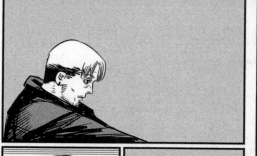

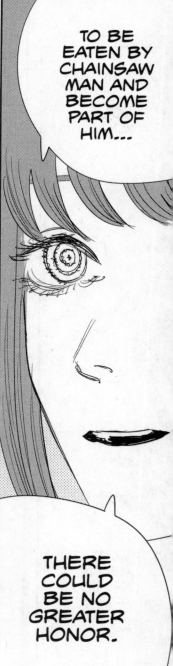

TO BE EATEN BY CHAINSAW MAN AND BECOME PART OF HIM...
THERE COULD BE NO GREATER HONOR.
NOW, IT SEEMS THE TIME FOR OUR LITTLE CHAT HAS COME TO AN END.
HE HAS RETURNED.
KR
AK
KRAK
KRAK
KRAK
KRAK

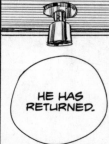

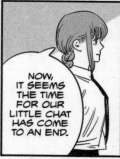

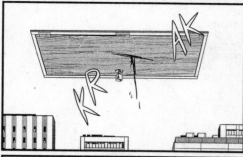

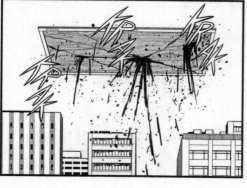

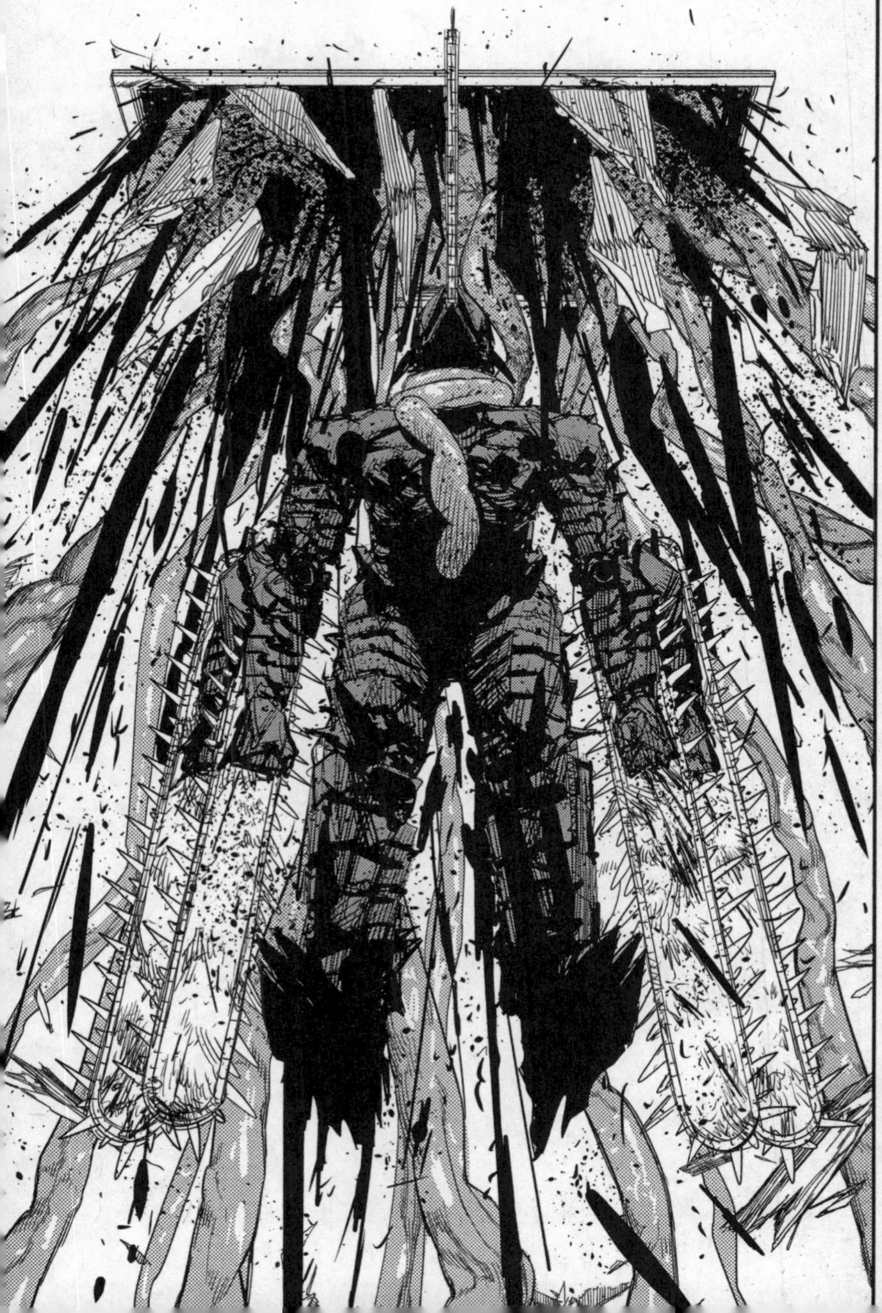

CHAINSAW MAN

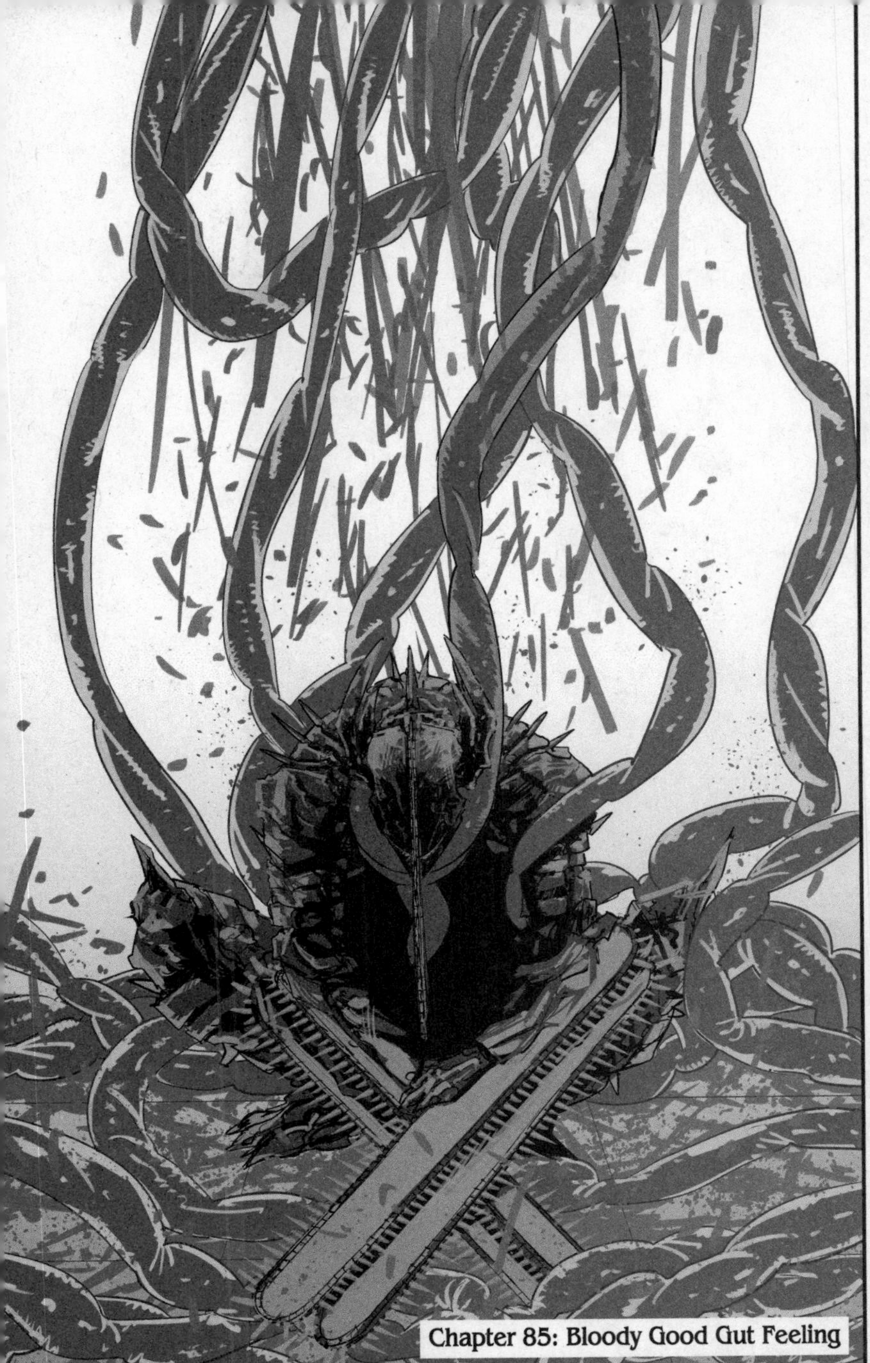

Chapter 85: Bloody Good Gut Feeling

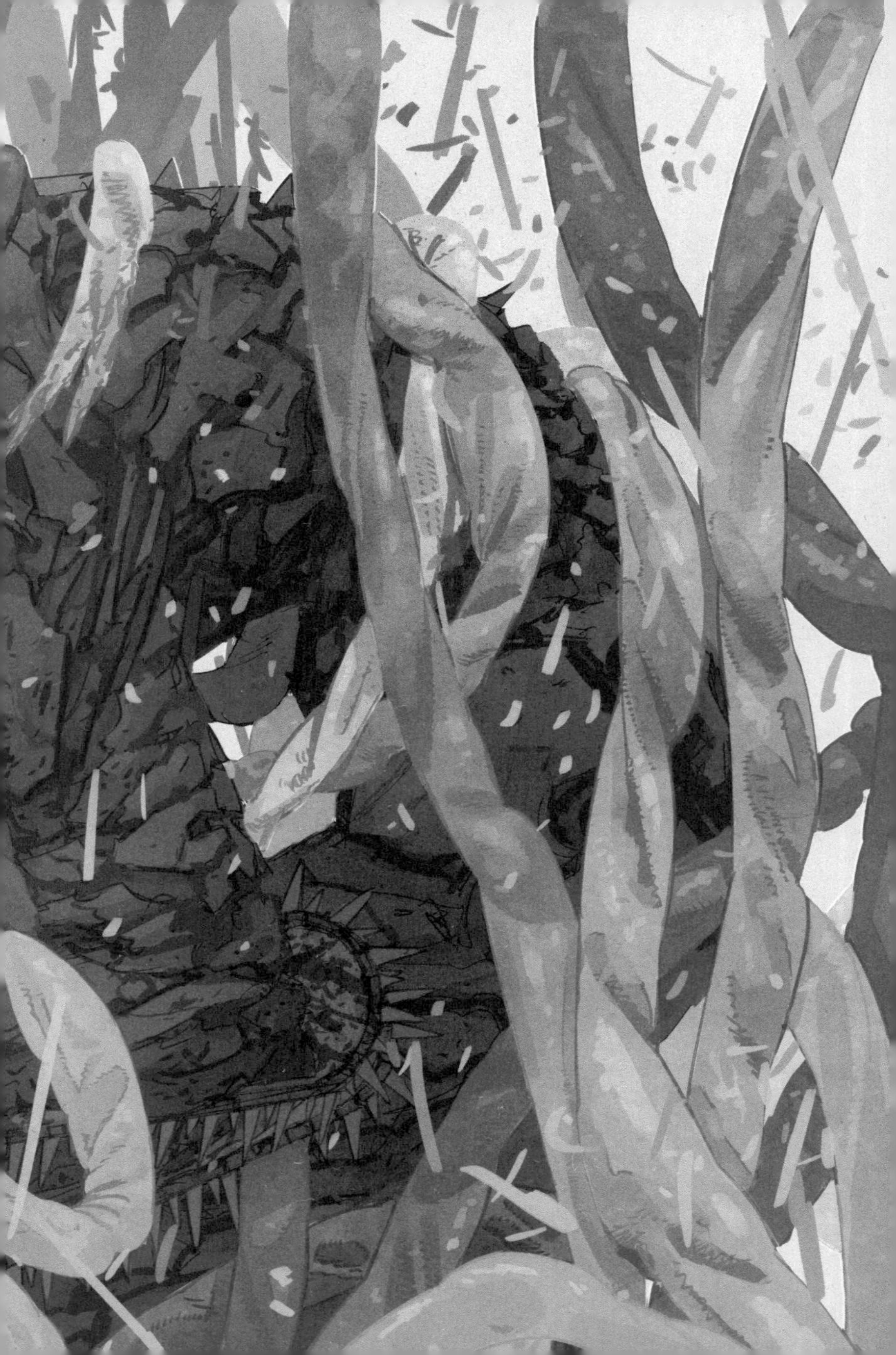

Chapter 85: Bloody Good Gut Feeling

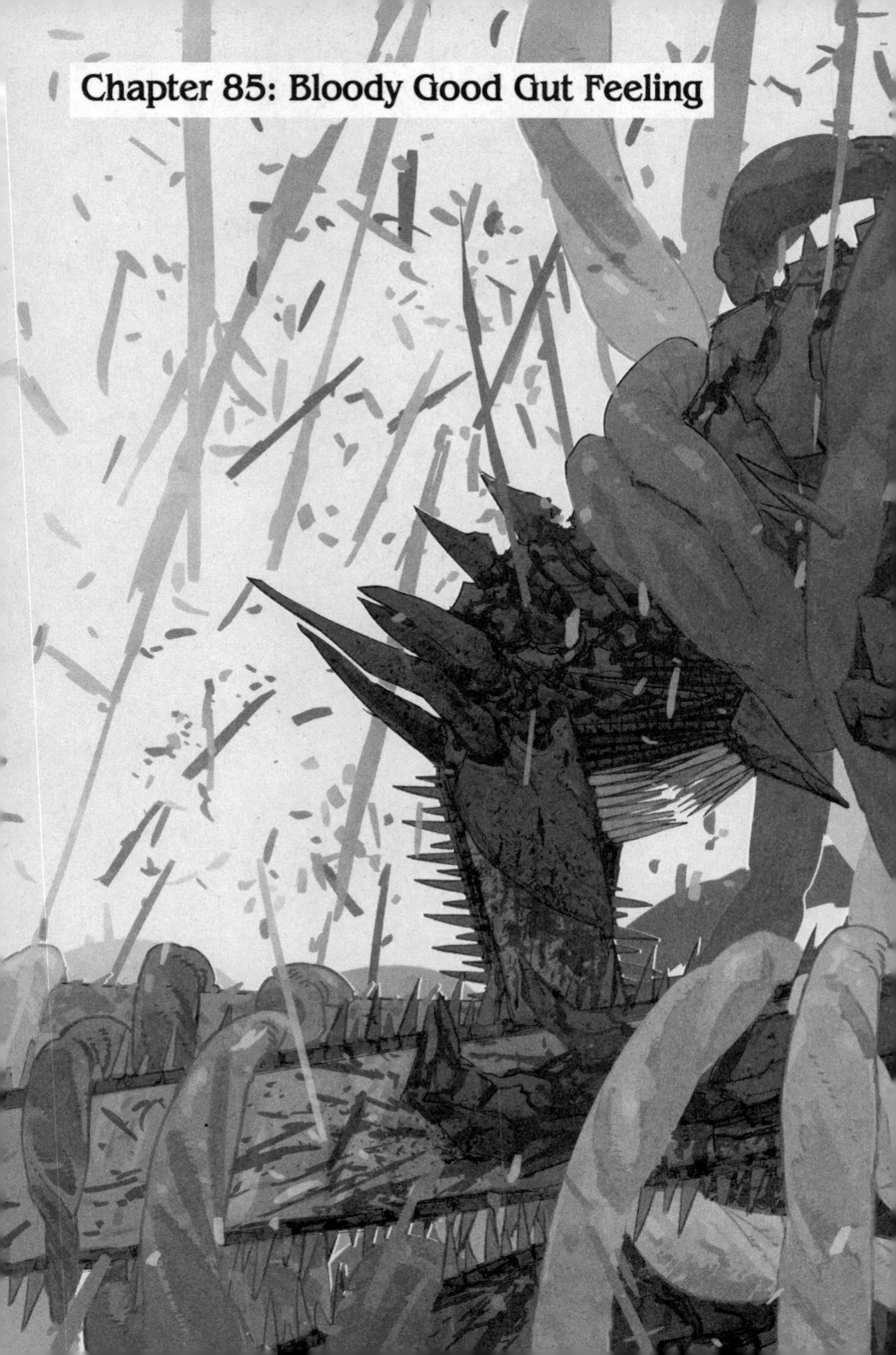

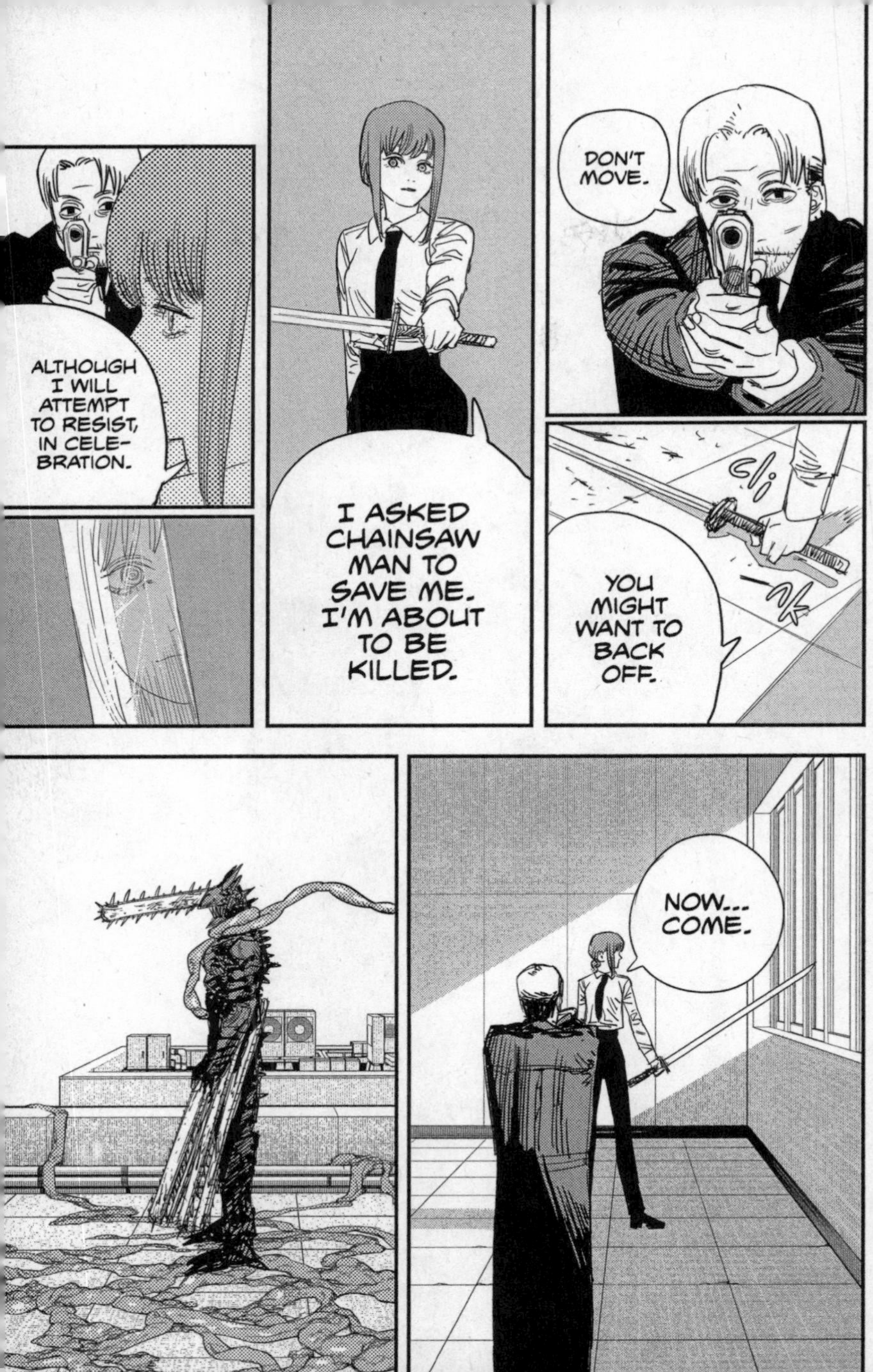
DON'T MOVE.
cli
—ck
YOU MIGHT WANT TO BACK OFF.
I ASKED CHAINSAW MAN TO SAVE ME. I'M ABOUT TO BE KILLED.
ALTHOUGH I WILL ATTEMPT TO RESIST, IN CELEBRATION.
NOW... COME.

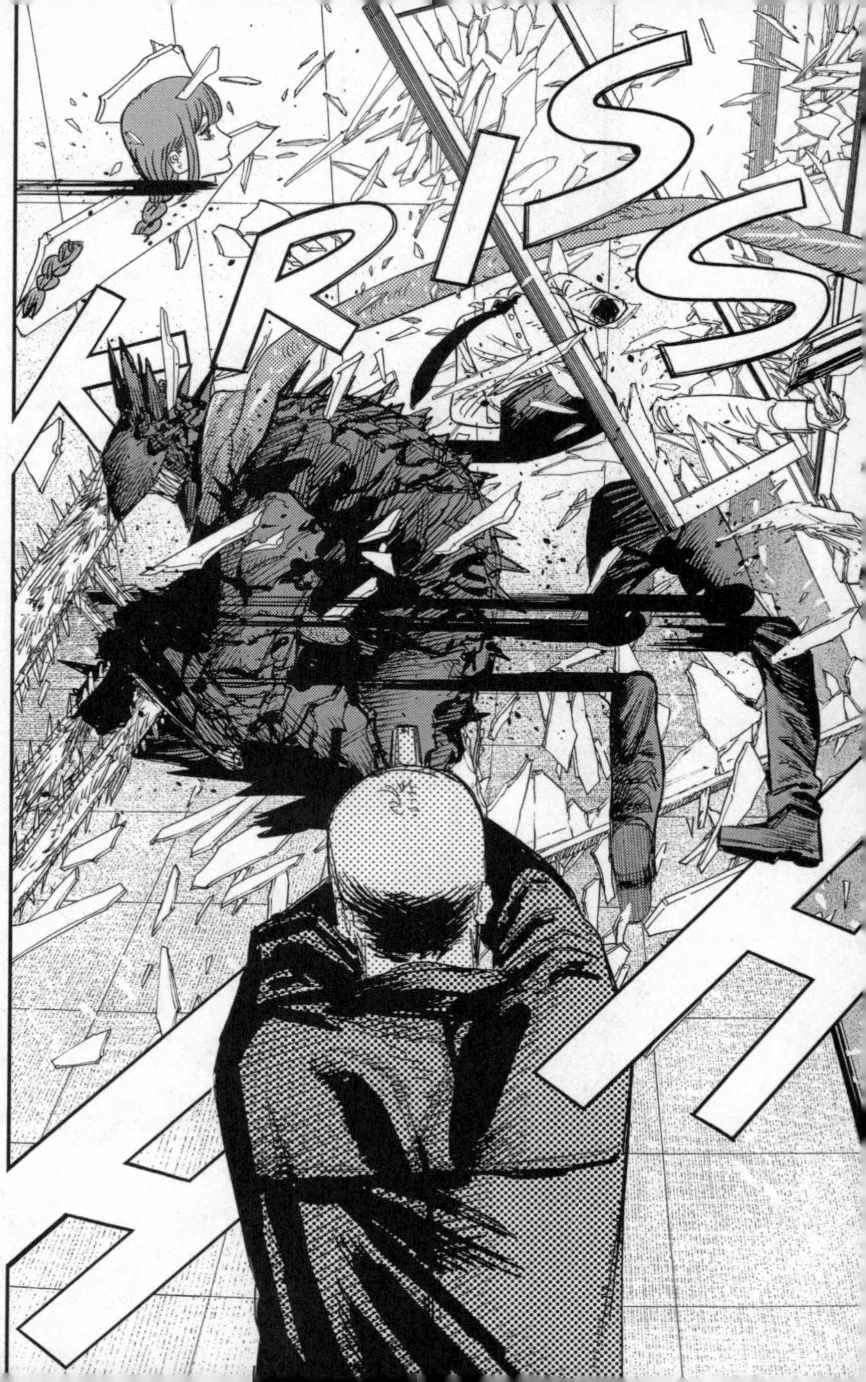
KRISSH

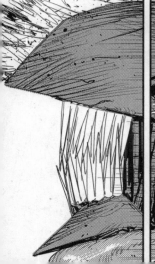

SAVE
ME...

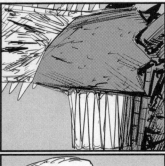

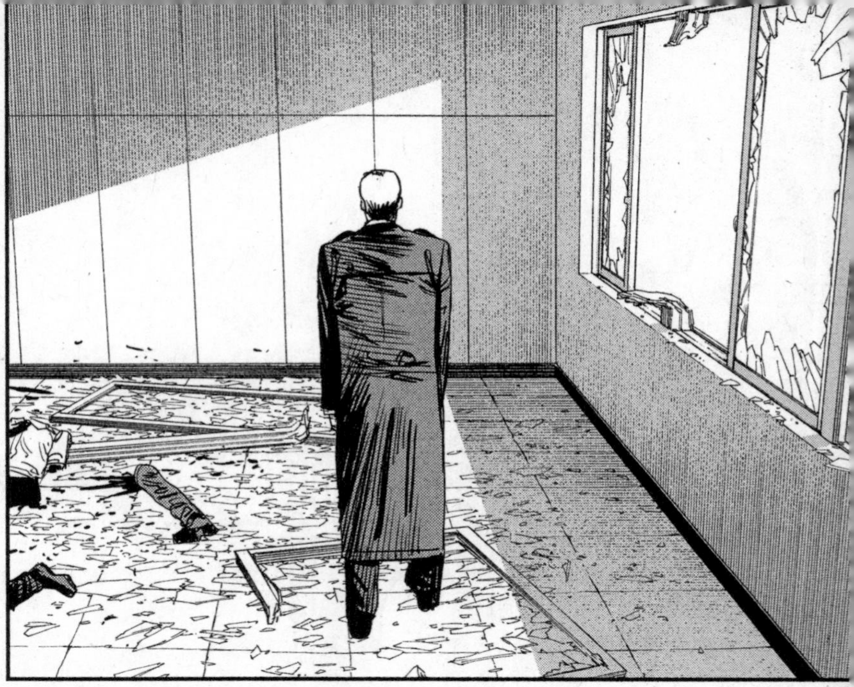
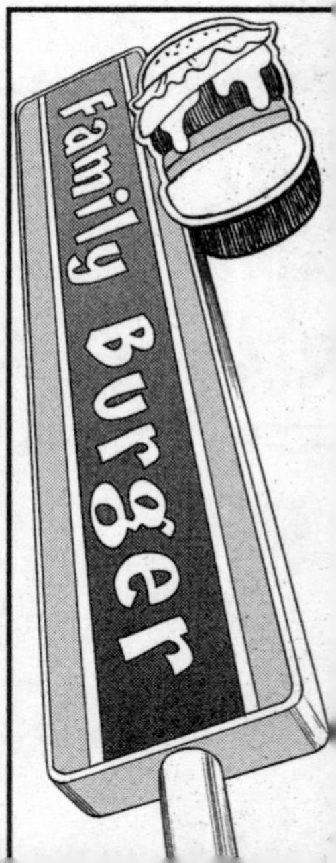
Family Burger
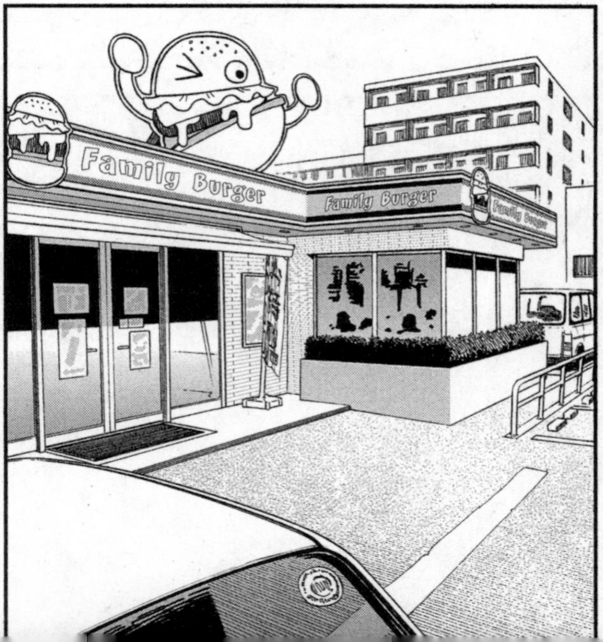
Family Burger
Family Burger
Family Burger

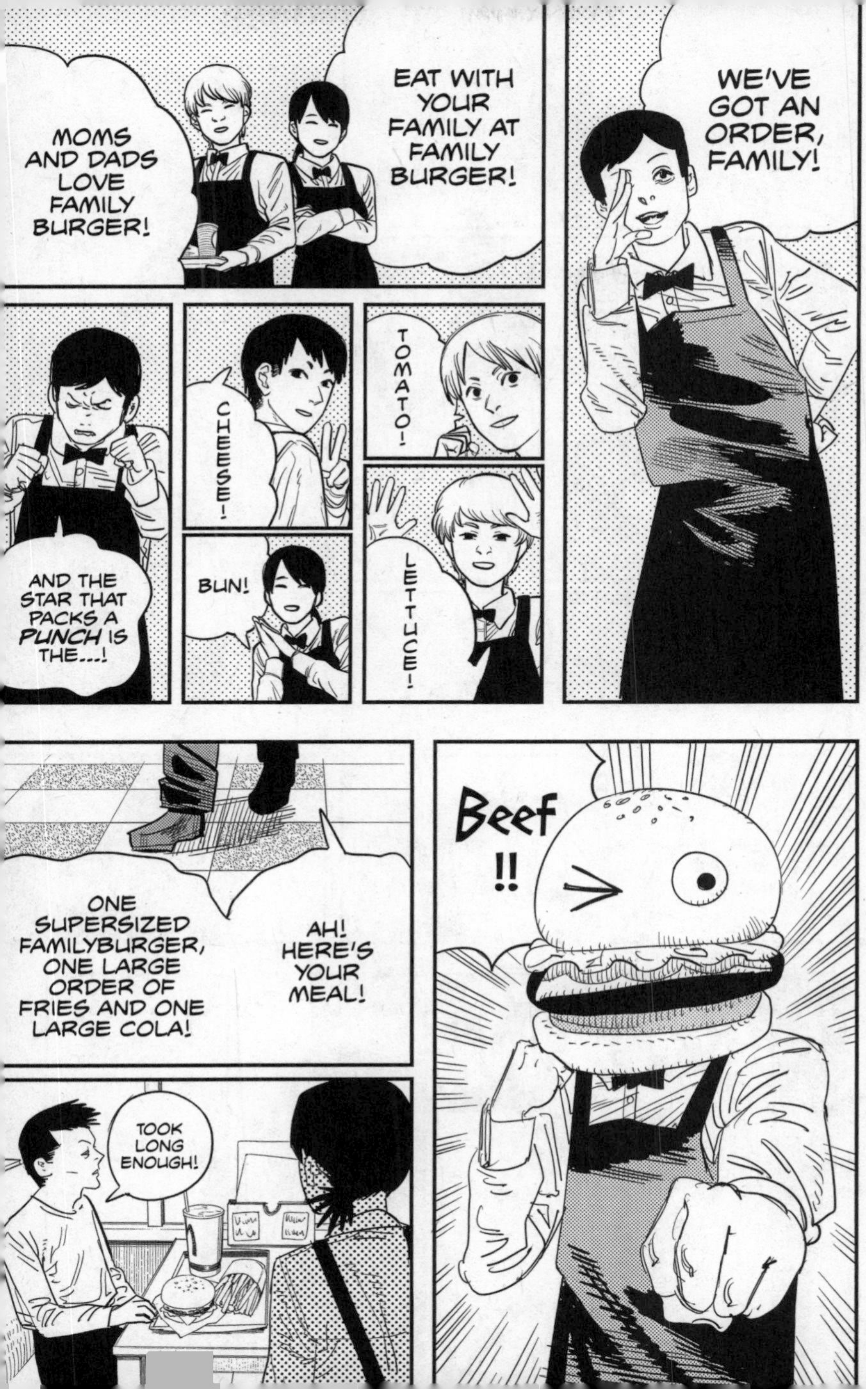
WE'VE GOT AN ORDER, FAMILY!
EAT WITH YOUR FAMILY AT FAMILY BURGER!
MOMS AND DADS LOVE FAMILY BURGER!
TOMATO!
LETTUCE!
CHEESE!
BUN!
AND THE STAR THAT PACKS A *PUNCH* IS THE...!
Beef !!
AH! HERE'S YOUR MEAL!
ONE SUPERSIZED FAMILYBURGER, ONE LARGE ORDER OF FRIES AND ONE LARGE COLA!
TOOK LONG ENOUGH!

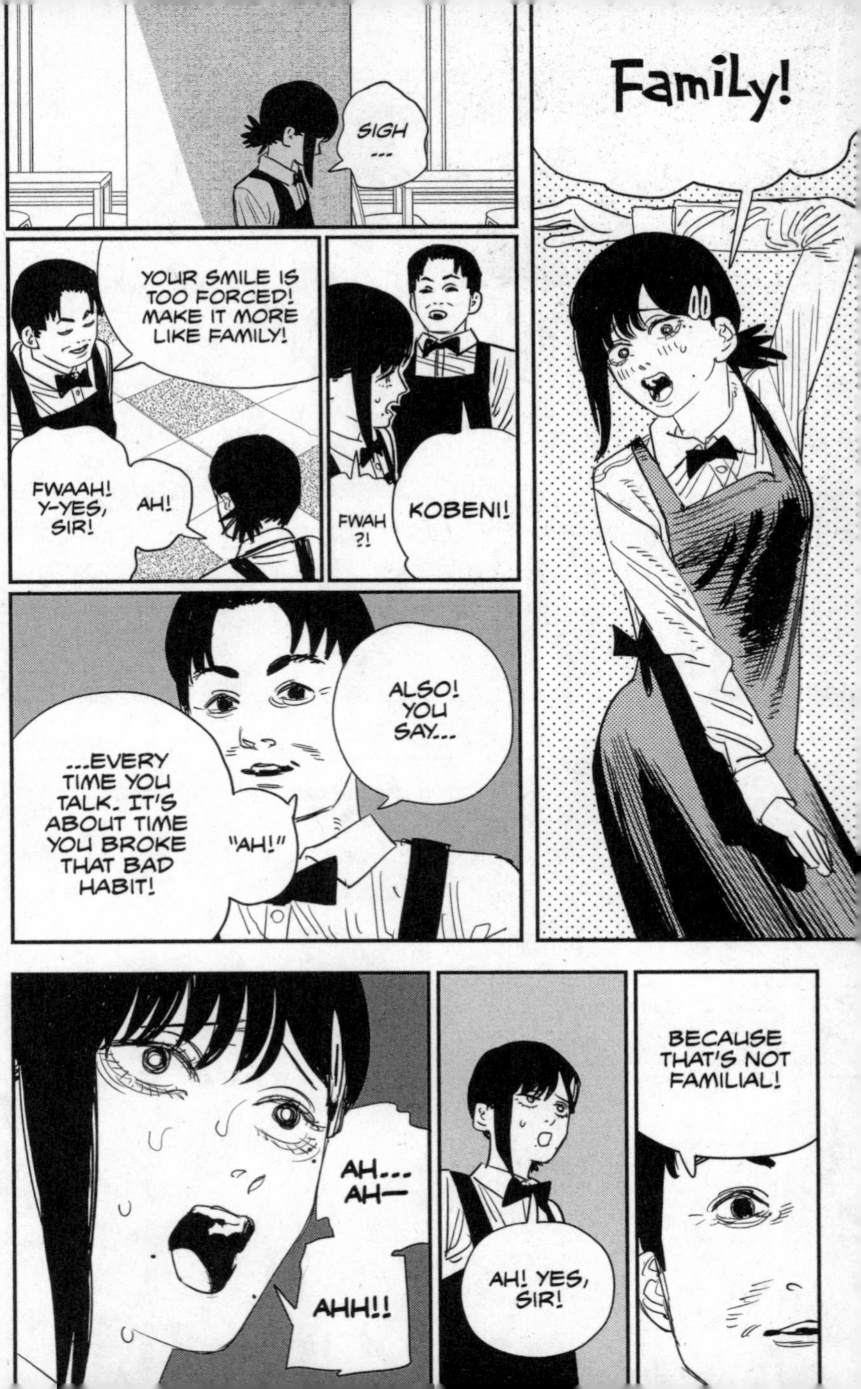
Family!
SIGH ...
KOBENI!
FWAH ?!
YOUR SMILE IS TOO FORCED! MAKE IT MORE LIKE FAMILY!
AH!
FWAAH! Y-YES, SIR!
ALSO! YOU SAY...
"AH!"
...EVERY TIME YOU TALK. IT'S ABOUT TIME YOU BROKE THAT BAD HABIT!
BECAUSE THAT'S NOT FAMILIAL!
AH! YES, SIR!
AH... AH—
AHH!!

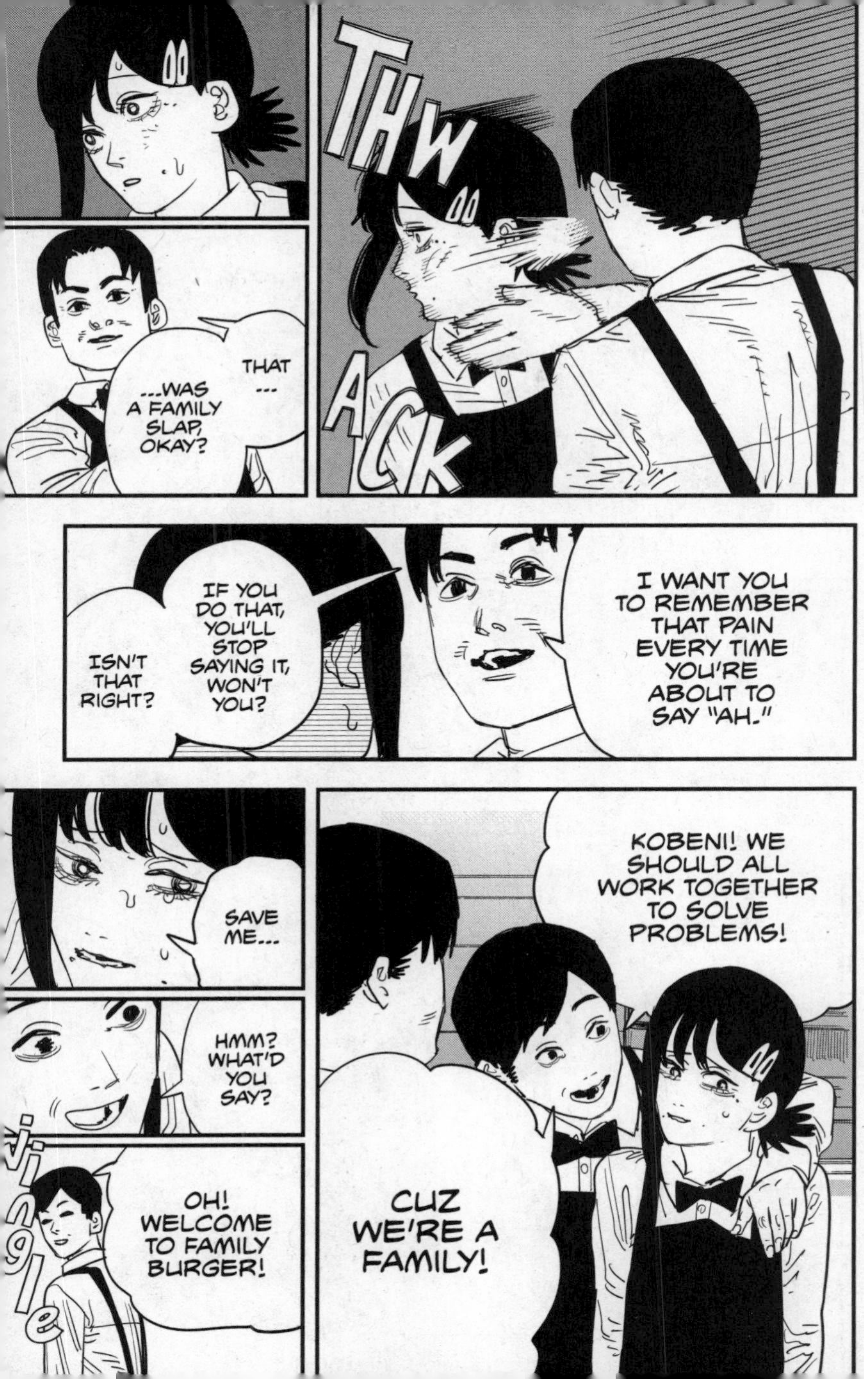
THWACK
THAT ...
...WAS A FAMILY SLAP, OKAY?
I WANT YOU TO REMEMBER THAT PAIN EVERY TIME YOU'RE ABOUT TO SAY "AH."
IF YOU DO THAT, YOU'LL STOP SAYING IT, WON'T YOU?
ISN'T THAT RIGHT?
KOBENI! WE SHOULD ALL WORK TOGETHER TO SOLVE PROBLEMS!
CUZ WE'RE A FAMILY!
SAVE ME...
HMM? WHAT'D YOU SAY?
Jingle
OH! WELCOME TO FAMILY BURGER!

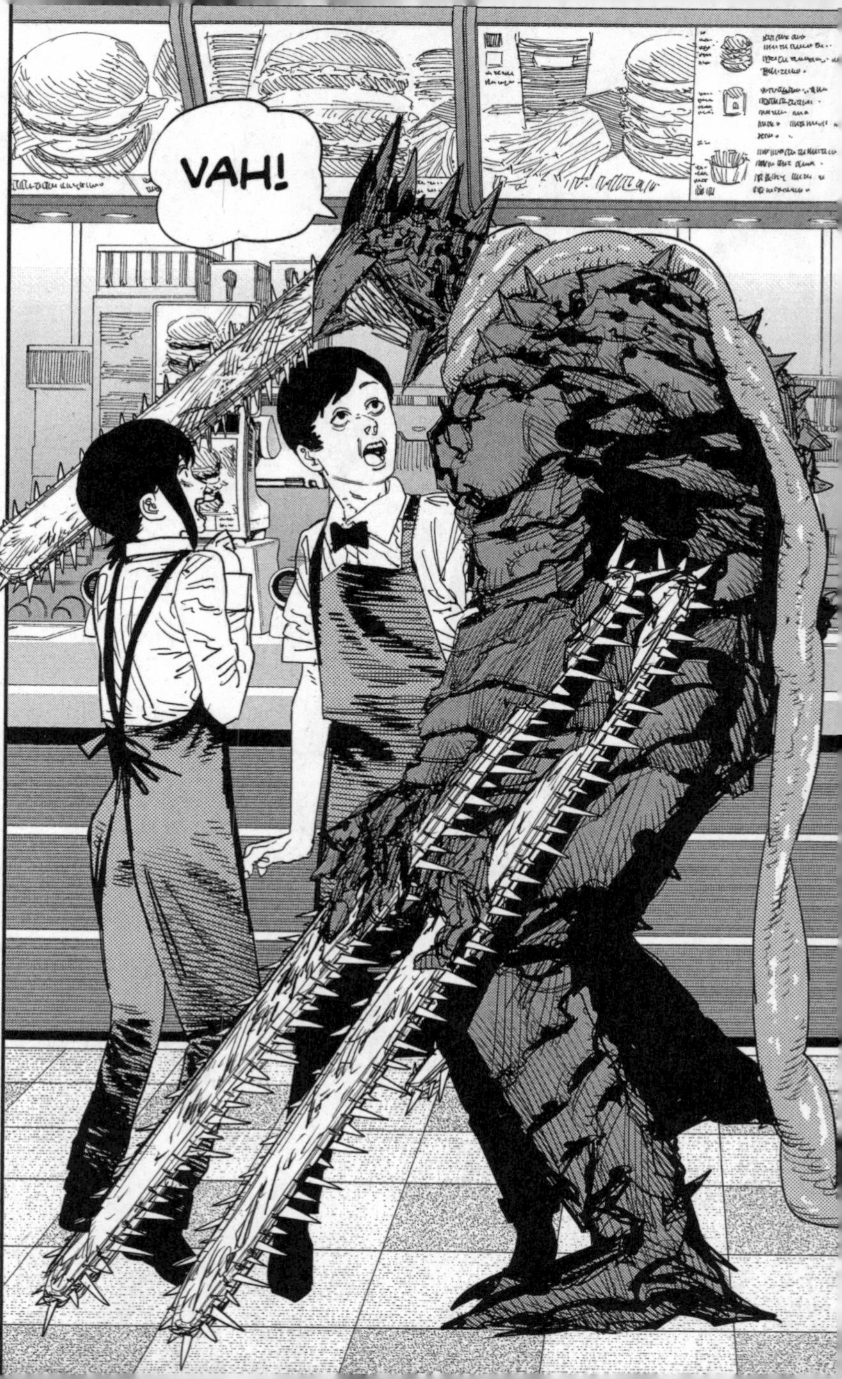
VAH!

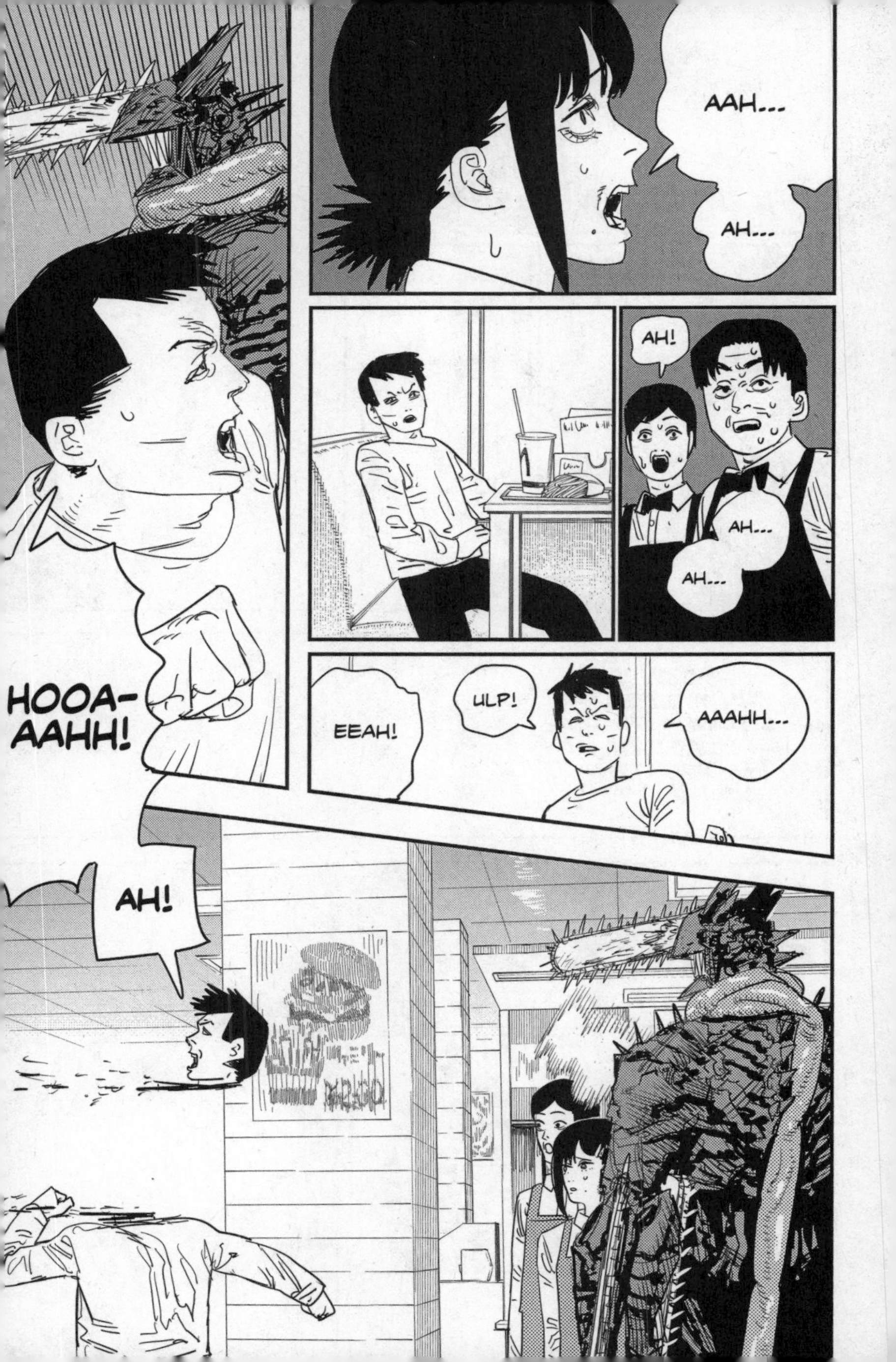
AAH...
AH...
HOOA-AAHH!
AH!
AH...
AH...
AAAHH...
ULP!
EEAH!
AH!

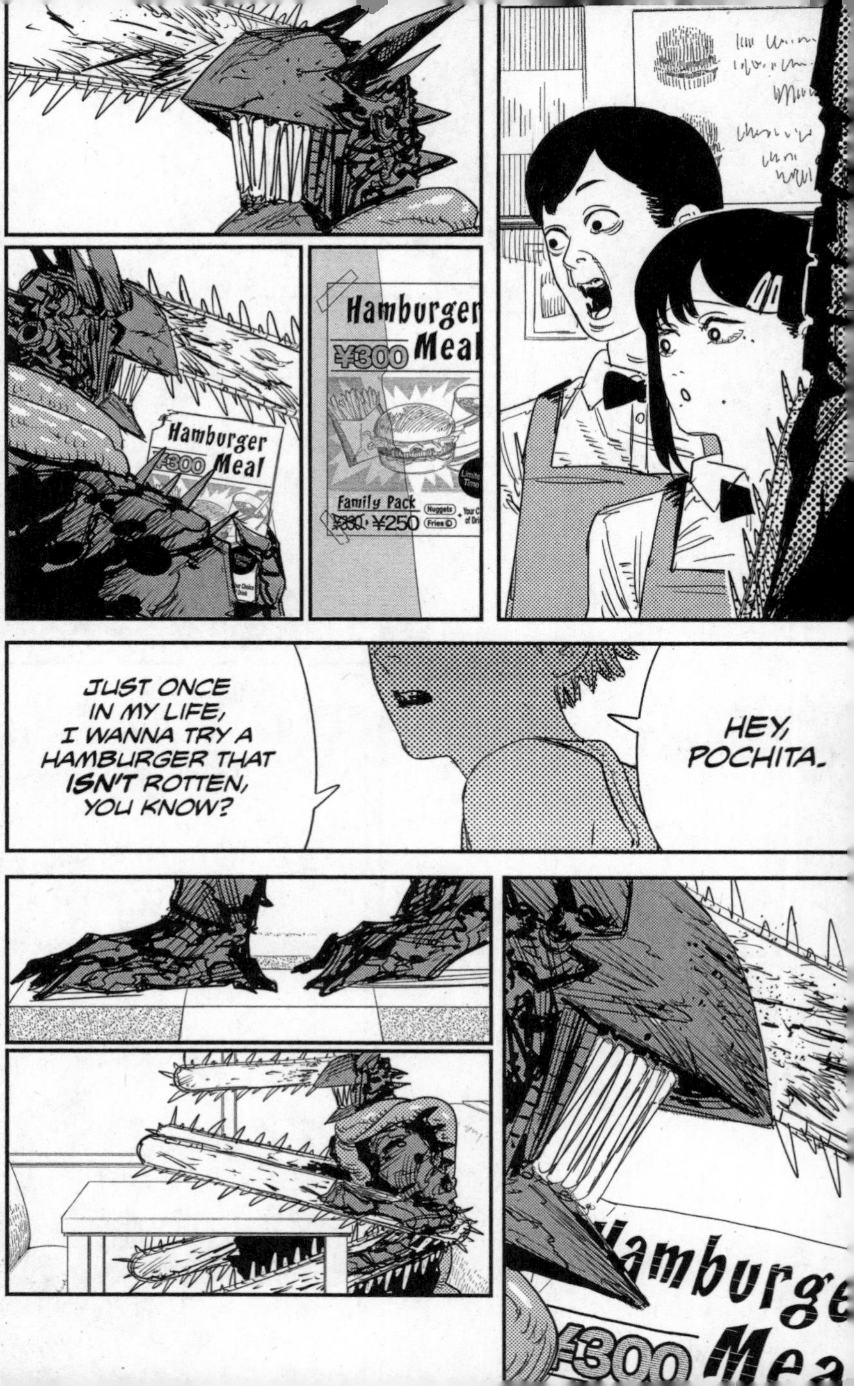
Hamburger Meal
¥300
Family Pack
¥300 ¥250
Nuggets
Fries
Hamburger Meal
¥300
HEY, POCHITA...
JUST ONCE IN MY LIFE, I WANNA TRY A HAMBURGER THAT ISN'T ROTTEN, YOU KNOW?

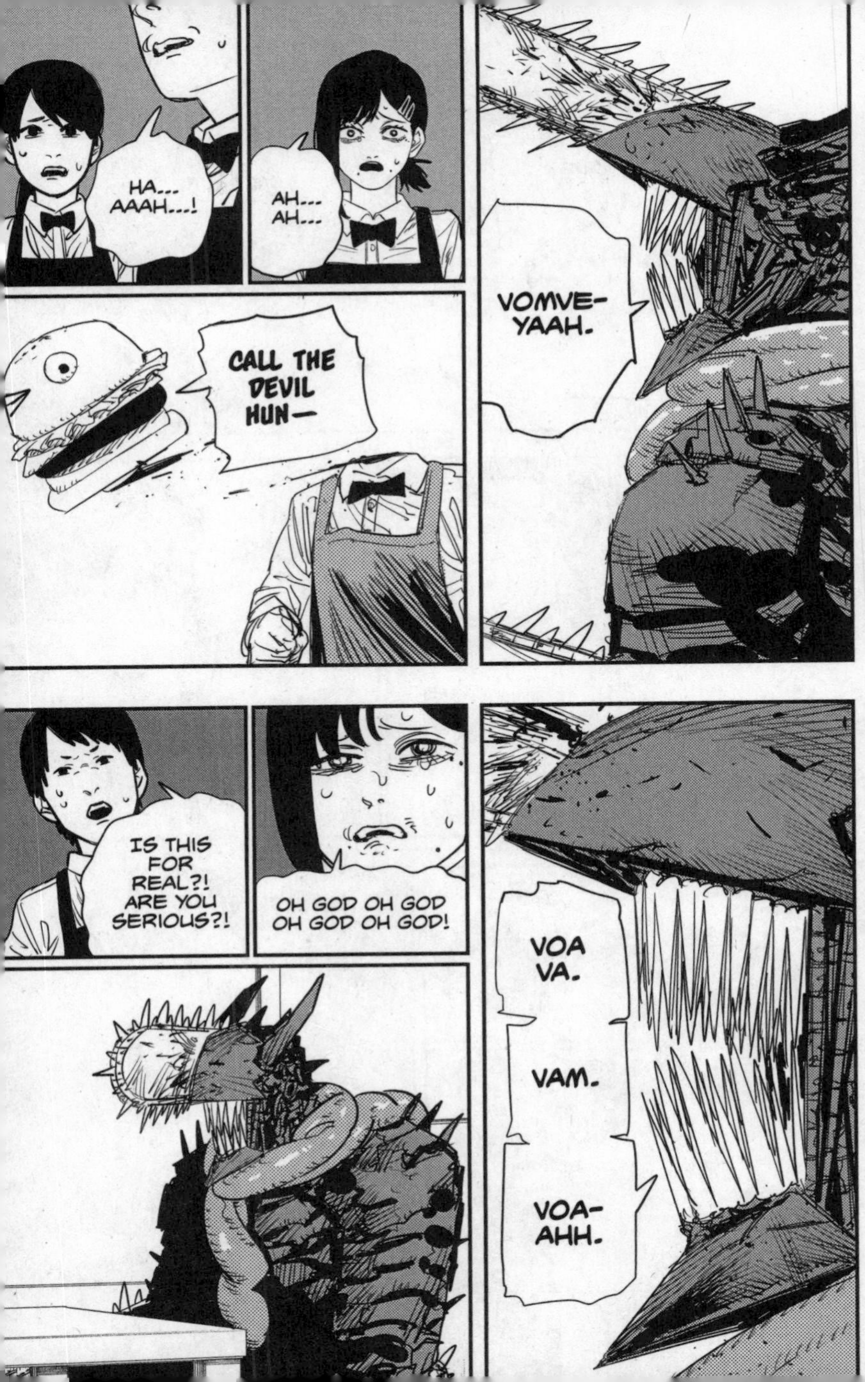
VOMVE-YAAH.
AH... AH...
HA... AAAH...!
CALL THE DEVIL HUN—
VOA VA.
VAM.
VOA-AHH.
OH GOD OH GOD OH GOD OH GOD!
IS THIS FOR REAL?! ARE YOU SERIOUS?!

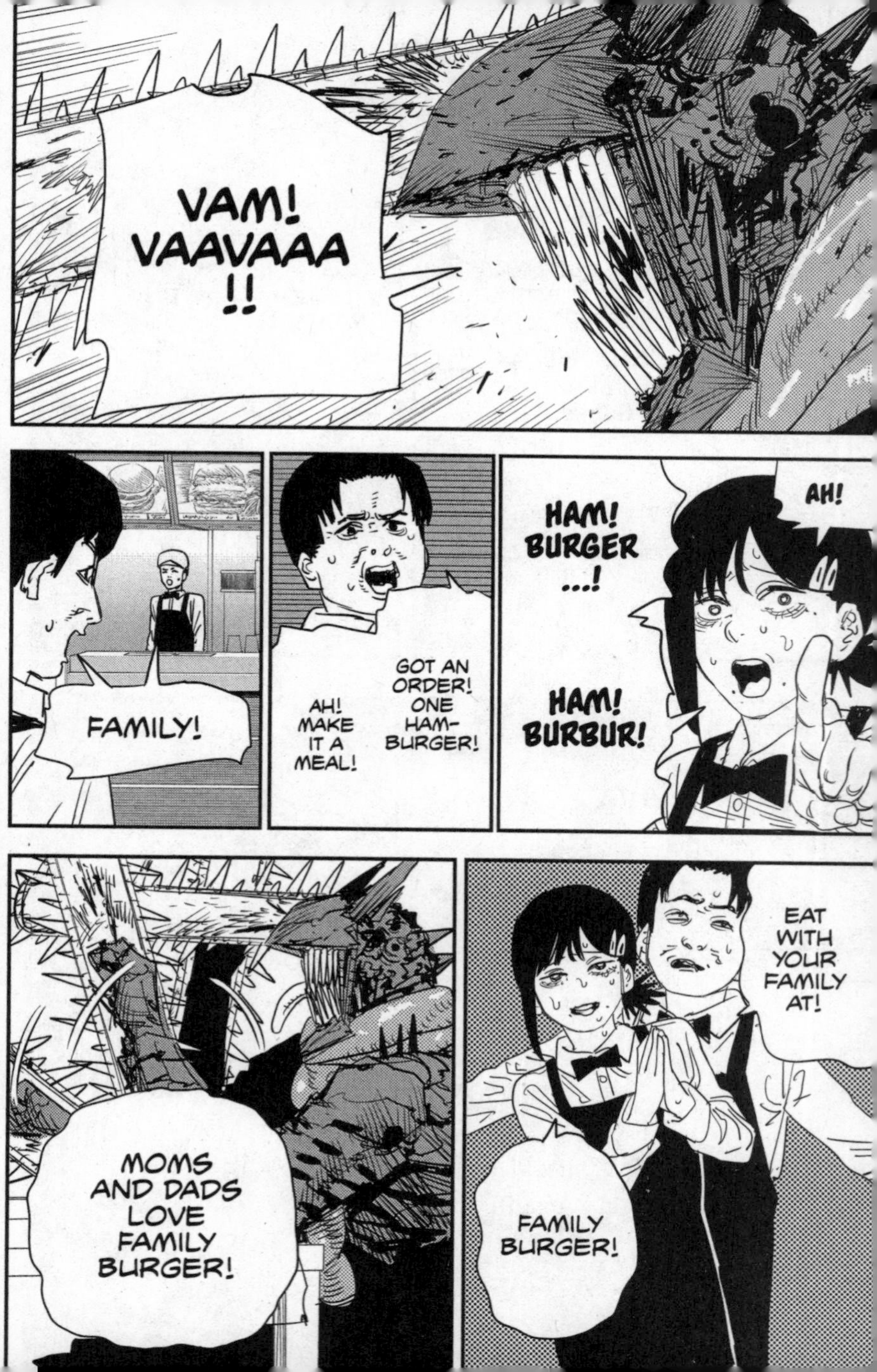
VAM! VAAVAAA !!
AH!
HAM! BURGER ...!
HAM! BURBUR!
GOT AN ORDER! ONE HAM-BURGER!
AH! MAKE IT A MEAL!
FAMILY!
EAT WITH YOUR FAMILY AT!
FAMILY BURGER!
MOMS AND DADS LOVE FAMILY BURGER!

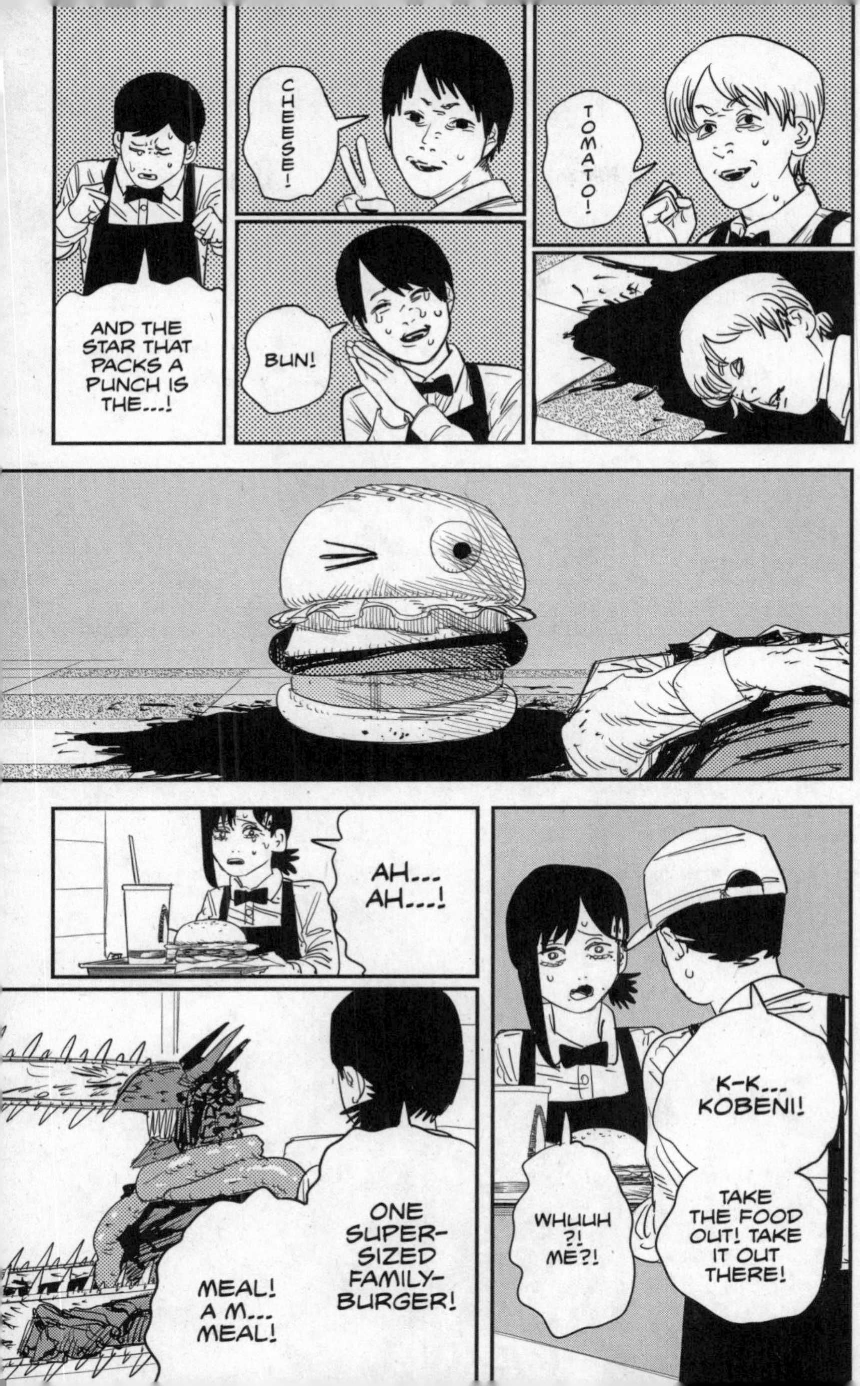
TOMATO!
CHEESE!
BUN!
AND THE STAR THAT PACKS A PUNCH IS THE...!
K-K... KOBENI!
TAKE THE FOOD OUT! TAKE IT OUT THERE!
WHUUH?! ME?!
AH... AH...!
ONE SUPER-SIZED FAMILY-BURGER!
MEAL! A M... MEAL!

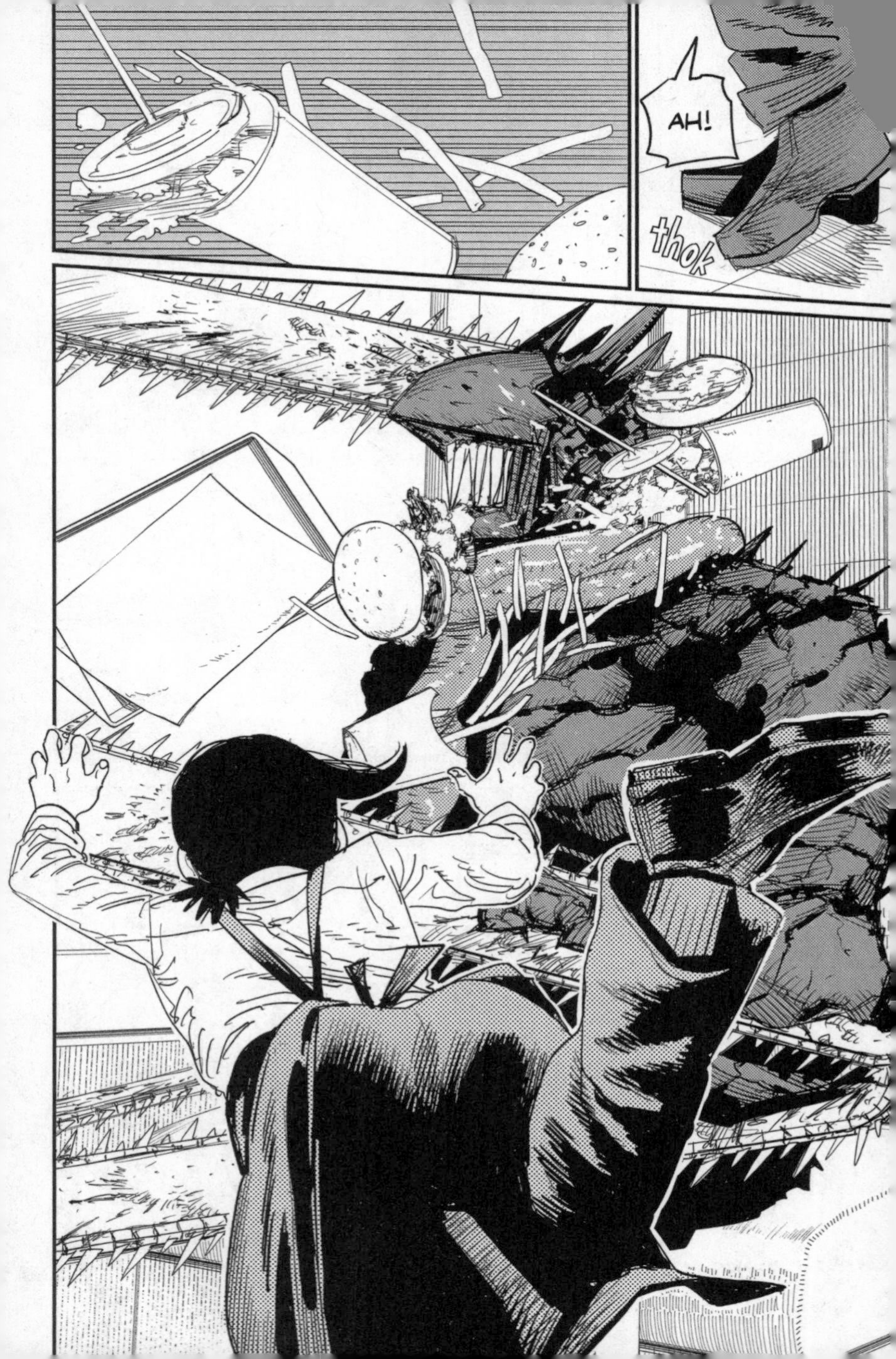
AH!
thok

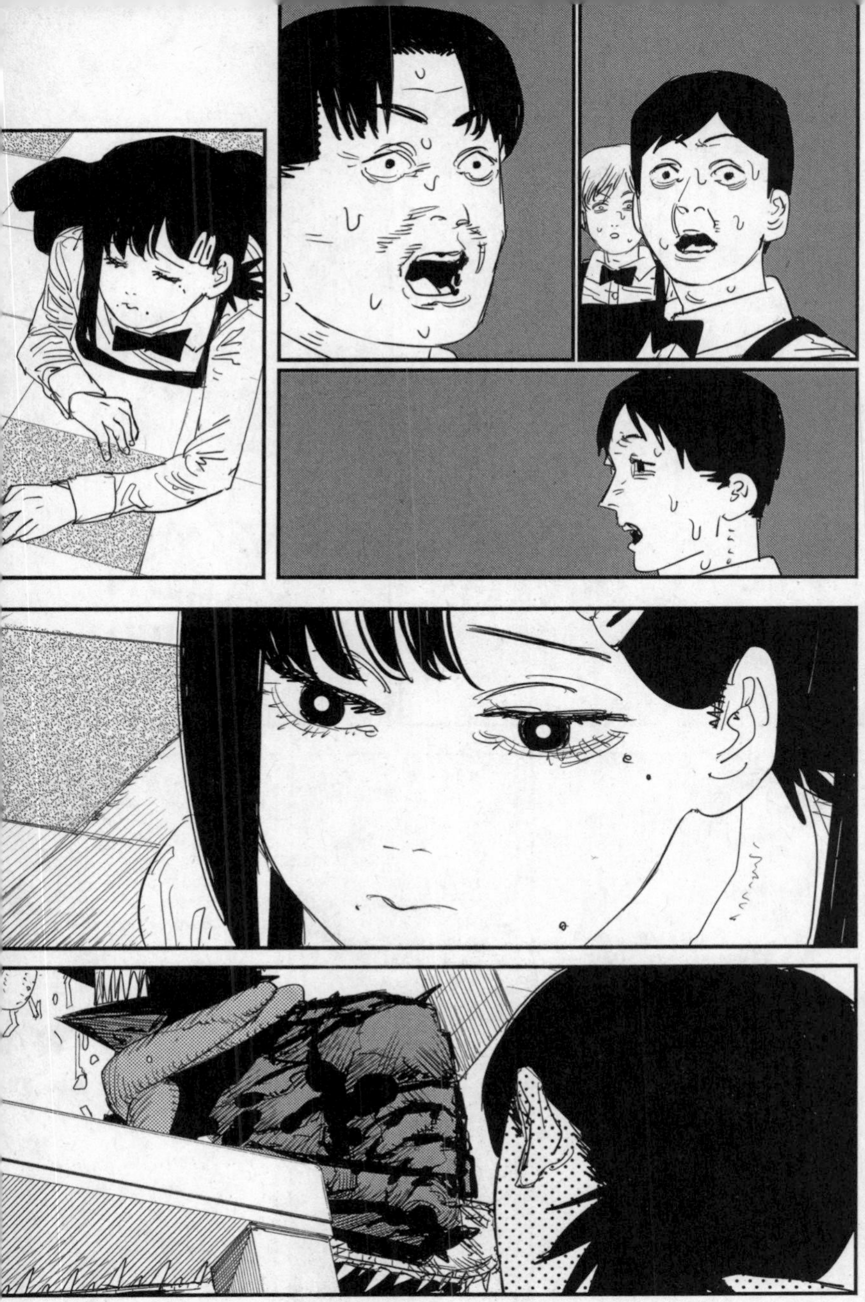

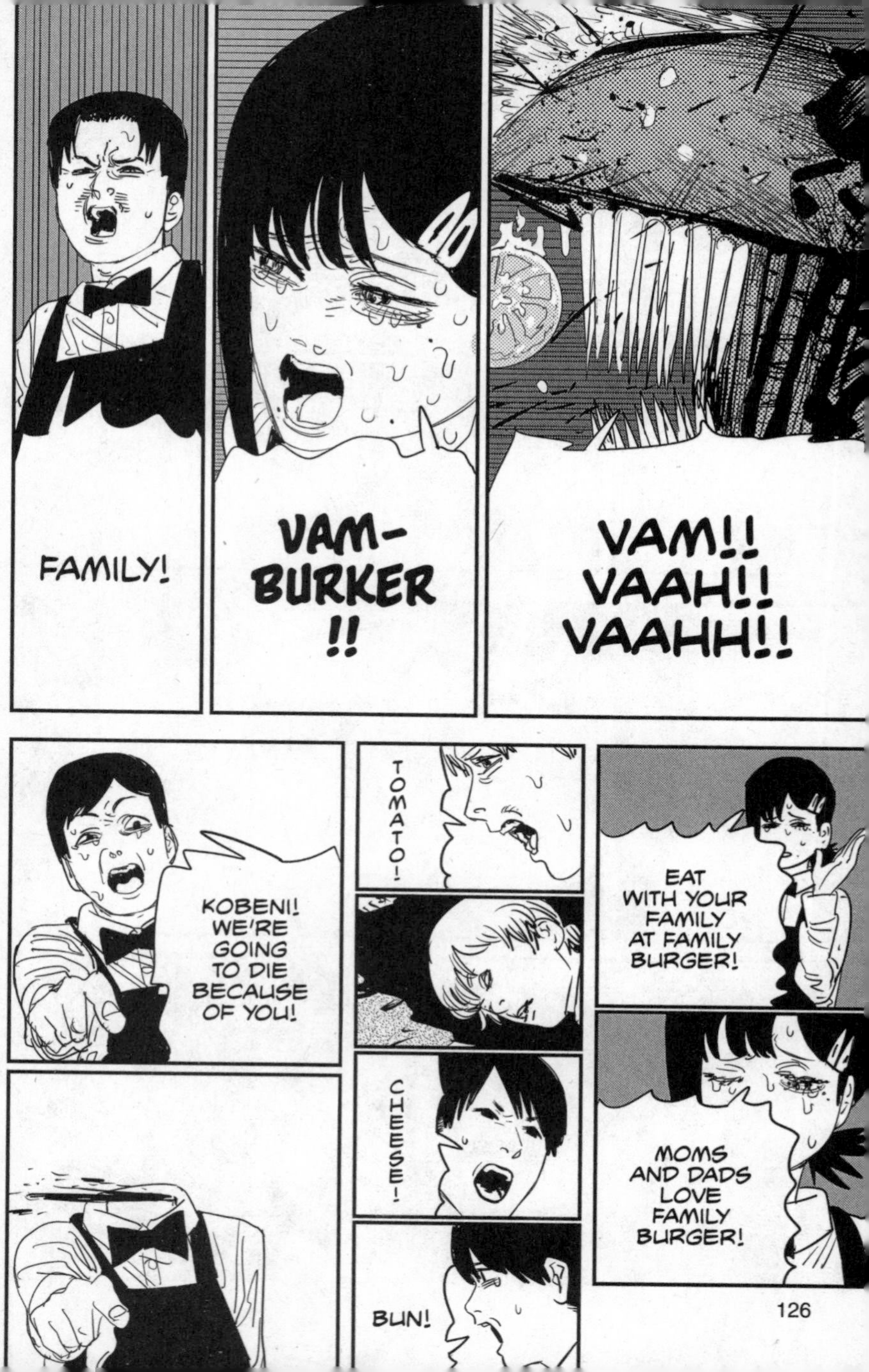
VAM!! VAAH!! VAAHH!!
VAM-BURKER!!
FAMILY!
EAT WITH YOUR FAMILY AT FAMILY BURGER!
MOMS AND DADS LOVE FAMILY BURGER!
TOMATO!
CHEESE!
BUN!
KOBENI! WE'RE GOING TO DIE BECAUSE OF YOU!

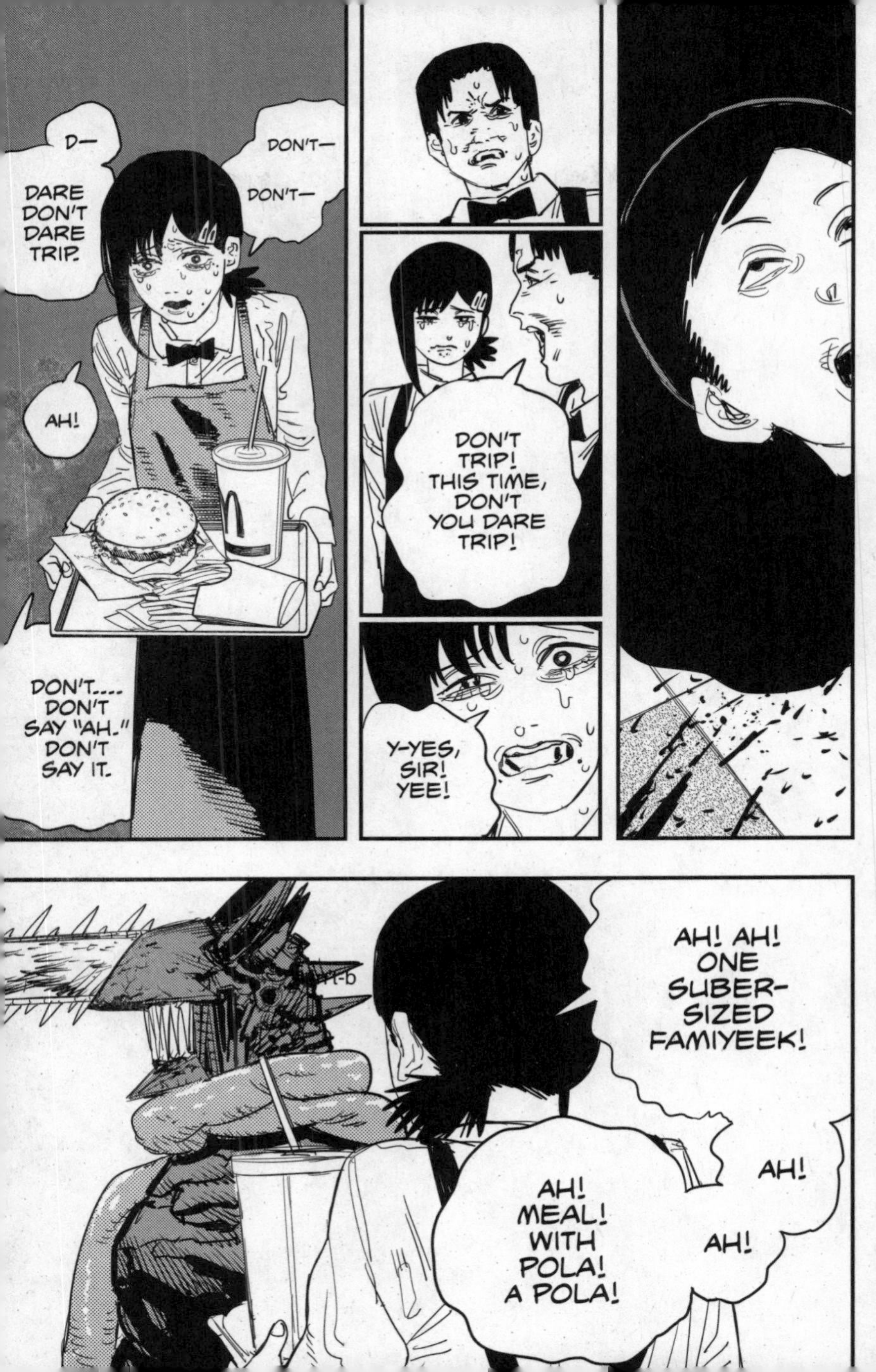
DON'T TRIP! THIS TIME, DON'T YOU DARE TRIP!
Y-YES, SIR! YEE!
DON'T—
DON'T—
D—
DARE DON'T DARE TRIP.
AH!
DON'T.... DON'T SAY "AH." DON'T SAY IT.
AH! AH! ONE SUBER-SIZED FAMIYEEK!
AH!
AH!
AH! MEAL! WITH POLA! A POLA!

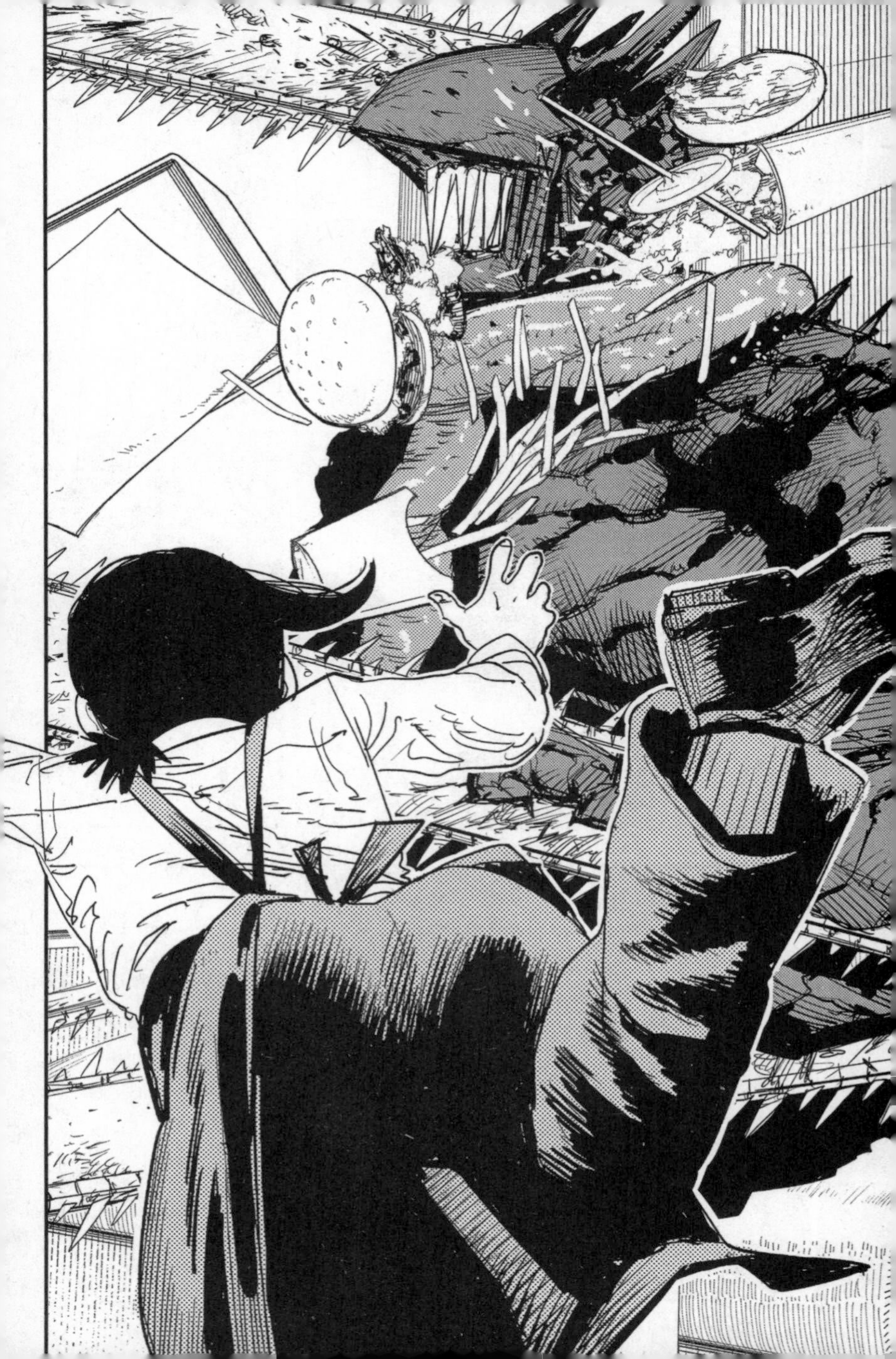

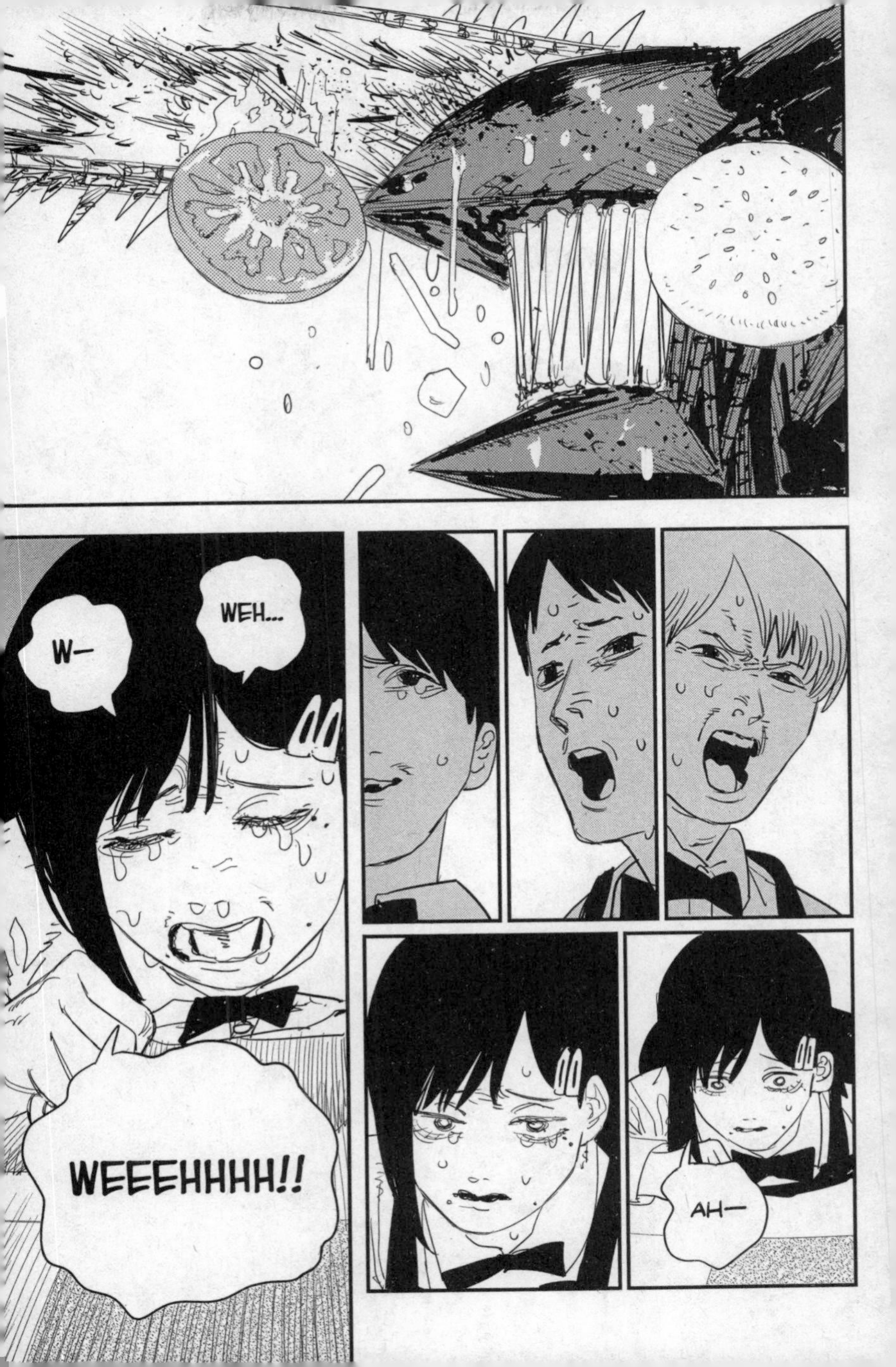
AH—
W—
WEH...
WEEEHHHH!!

CHAINSAW MAN

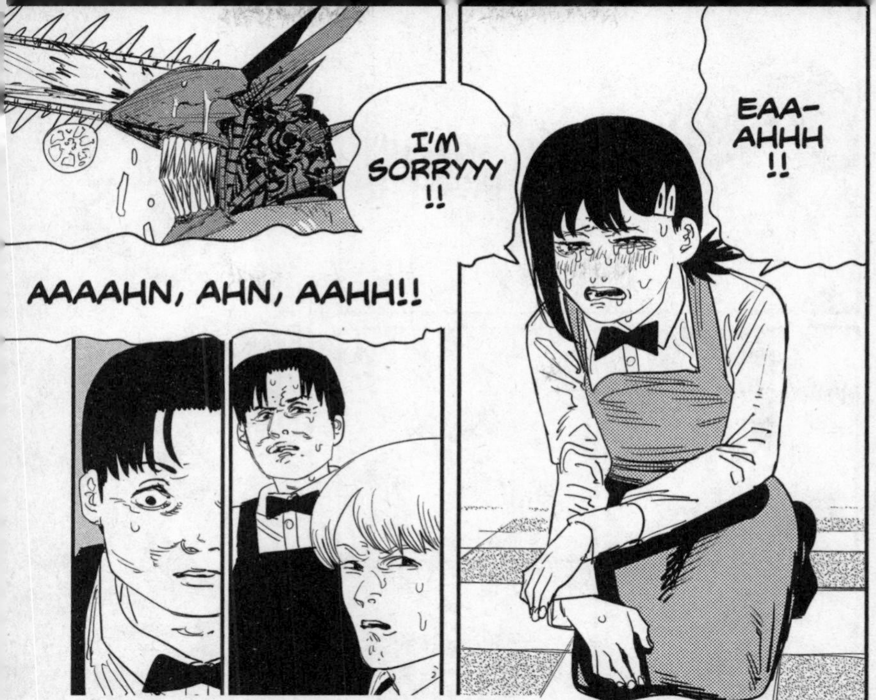
EAA-AHHH!!
I'M SORRYYY!!
AAAAHN, AHN, AAHH!!

Chapter 86: Date Chainsaw

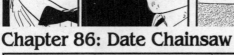

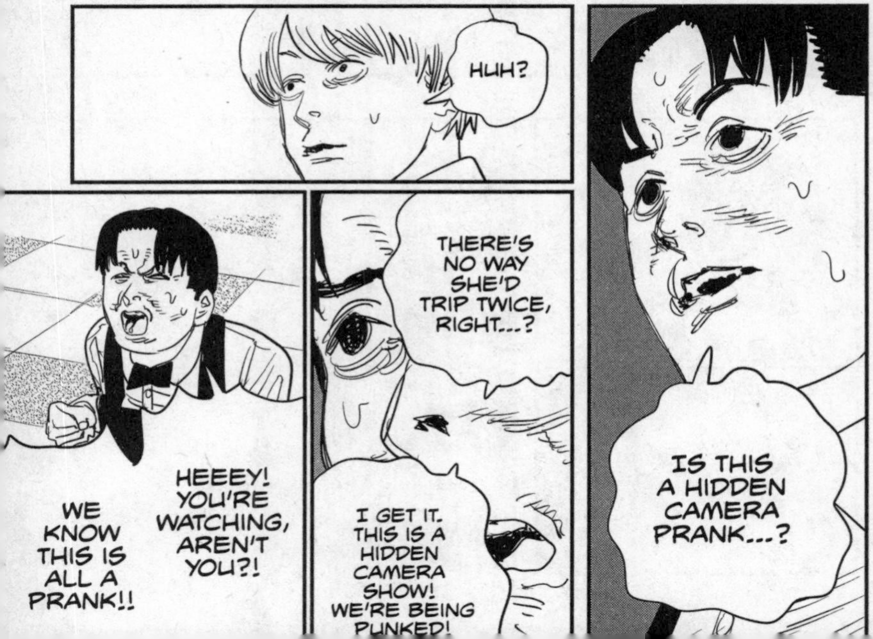
IS THIS A HIDDEN CAMERA PRANK...?
HUH?
THERE'S NO WAY SHE'D TRIP TWICE, RIGHT...?
I GET IT. THIS IS A HIDDEN CAMERA SHOW! WE'RE BEING PUNKED!
HEEEY! YOU'RE WATCHING, AREN'T YOU?!
WE KNOW THIS IS ALL A PRANK!!

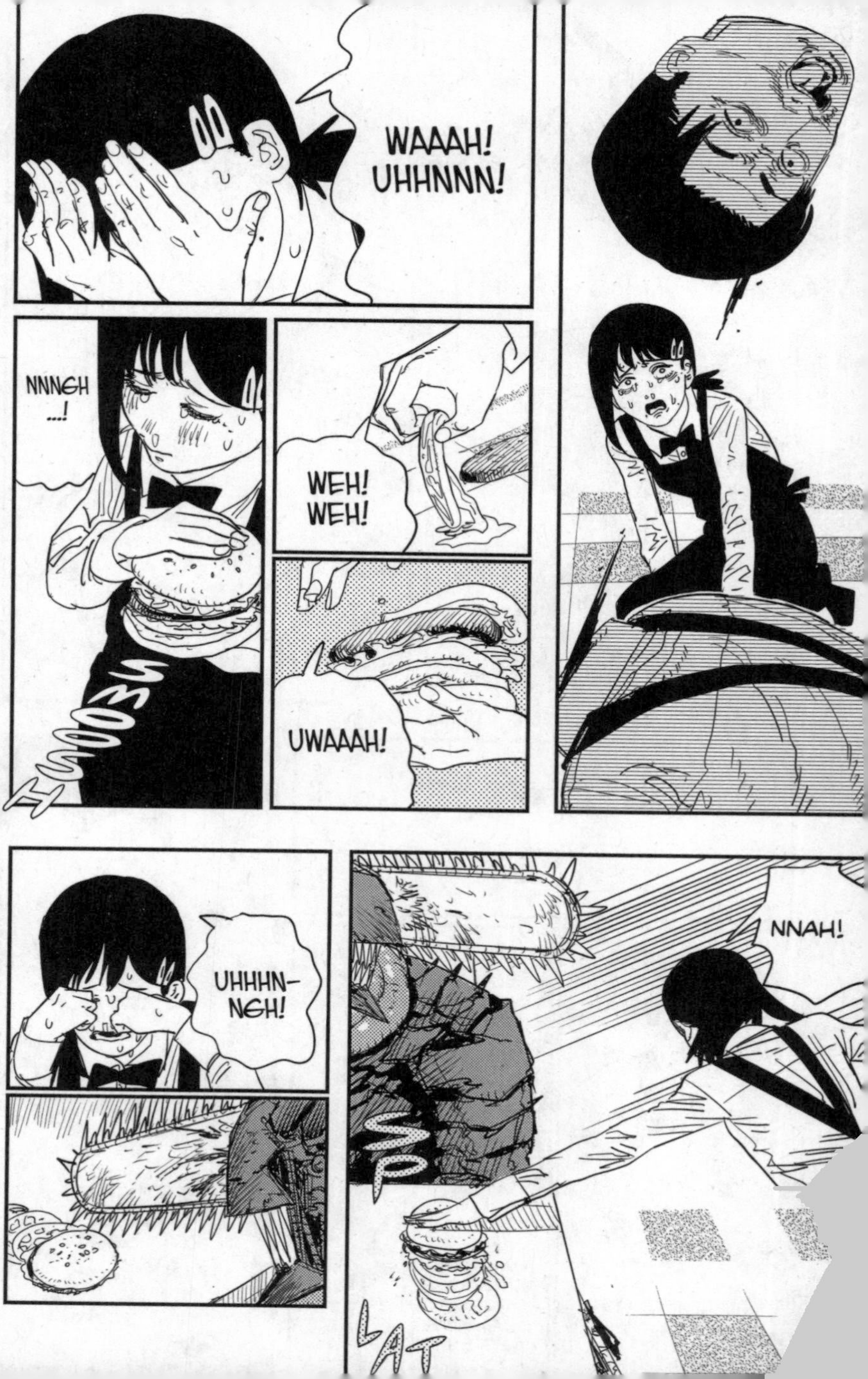
WAAAH! UHHNNN!
WEH! WEH!
UWAAAH!
NNNGH ...!
SWOOSH
NNAH!
SPLAT
UHHHN-NGH!

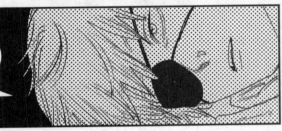

I WANNA GO ON A DATE WITH A GIRL SO BAD...

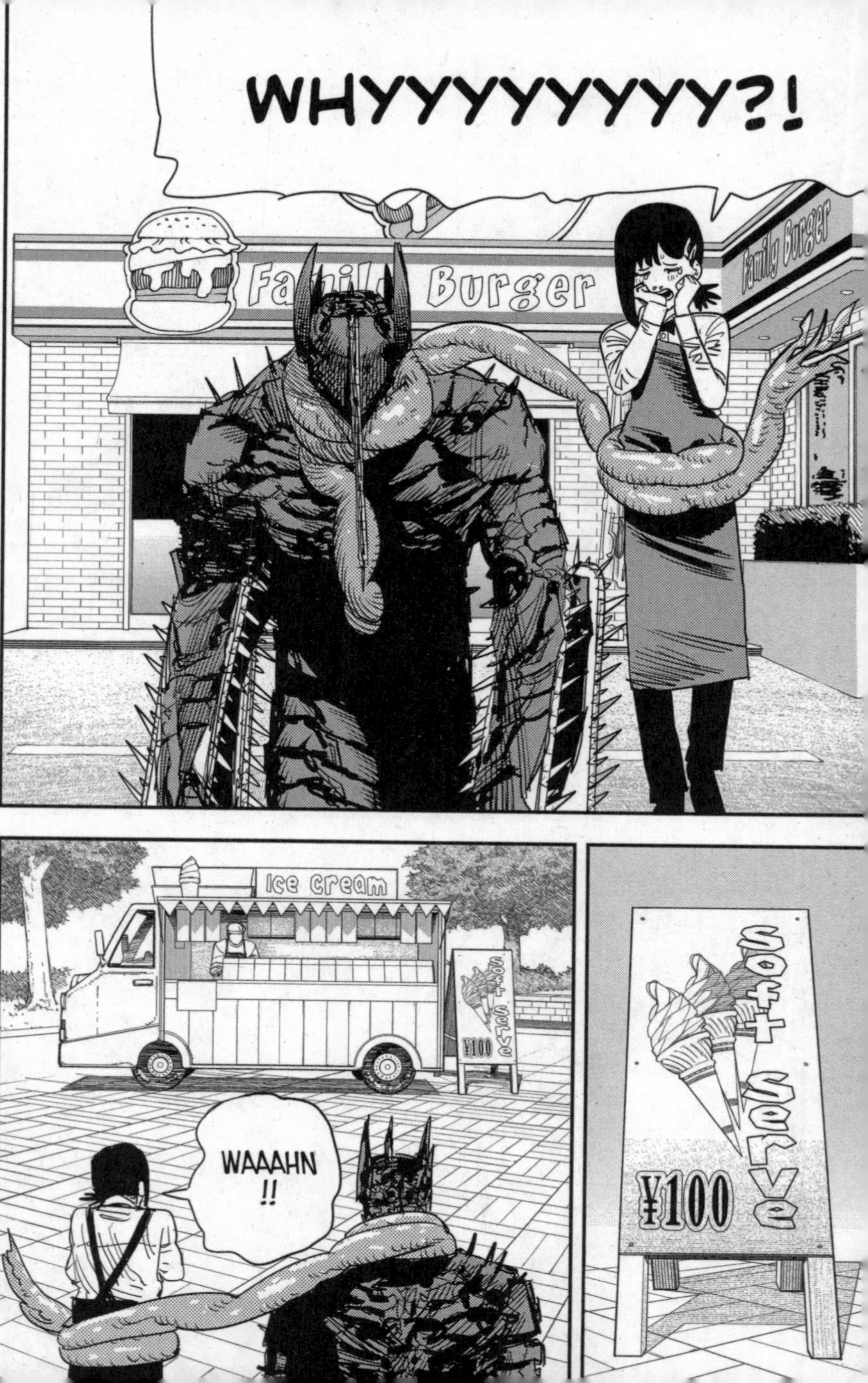
WHYYYYYYYY?!
Family Burger
Family Burger
Soft Serve
¥100
Ice cream
Soft Serve
¥100
WAAAHN !!

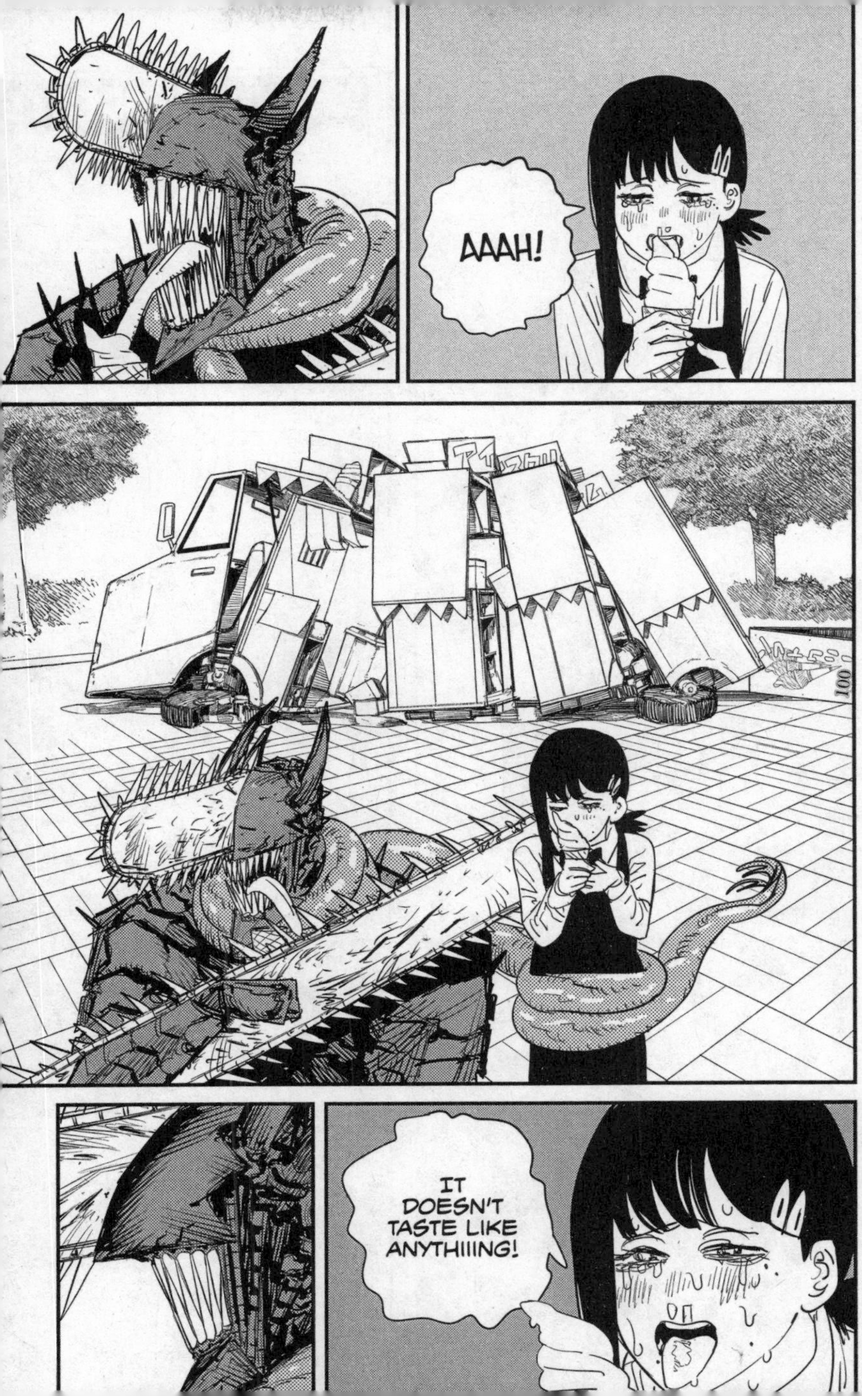
AAAH!
IT DOESN'T TASTE LIKE ANYTHIIING!

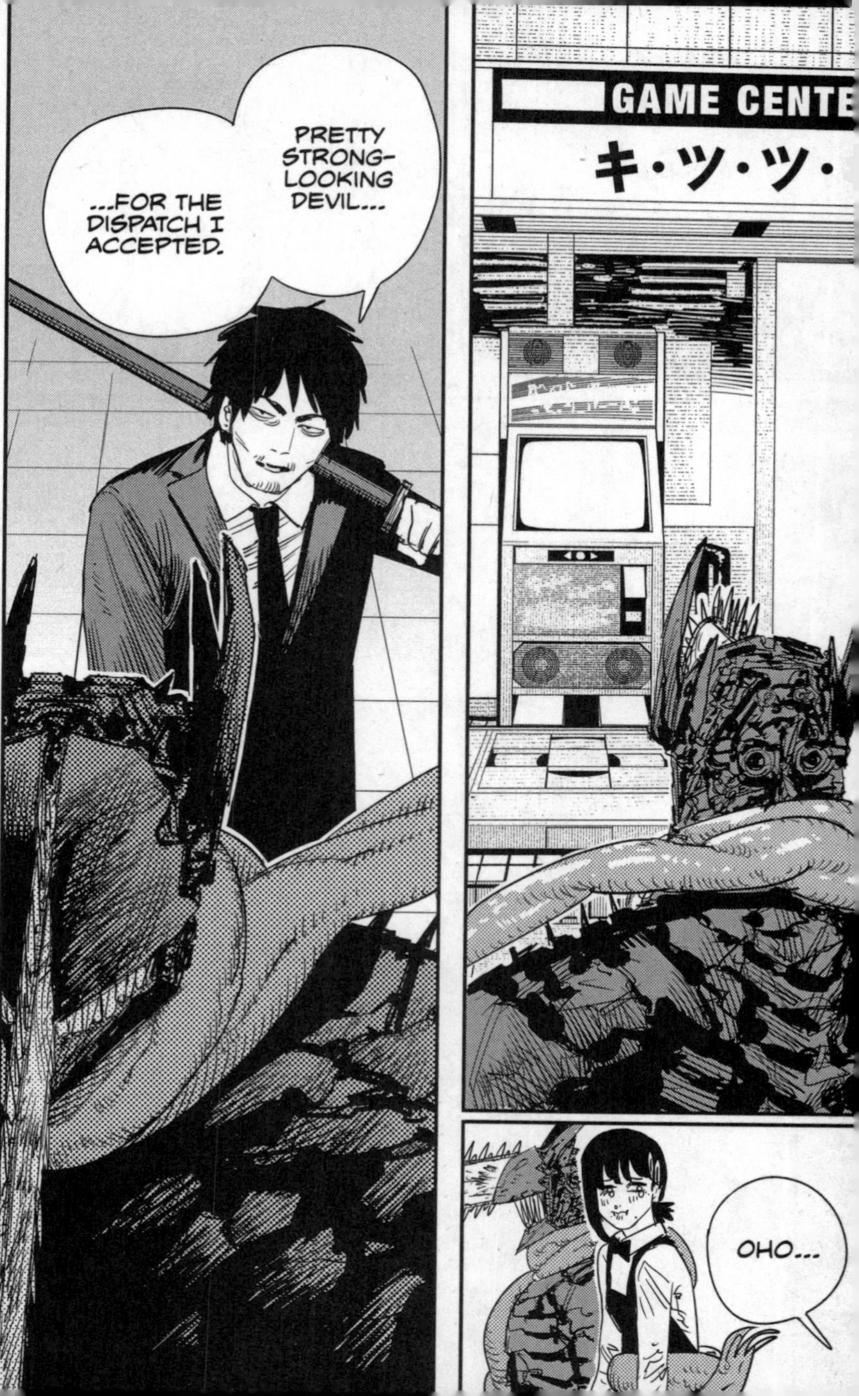
GAME CENTE
キ・ツ・ツ・
OHO...
PRETTY STRONG-LOOKING DEVIL...
...FOR THE DISPATCH I ACCEPTED.

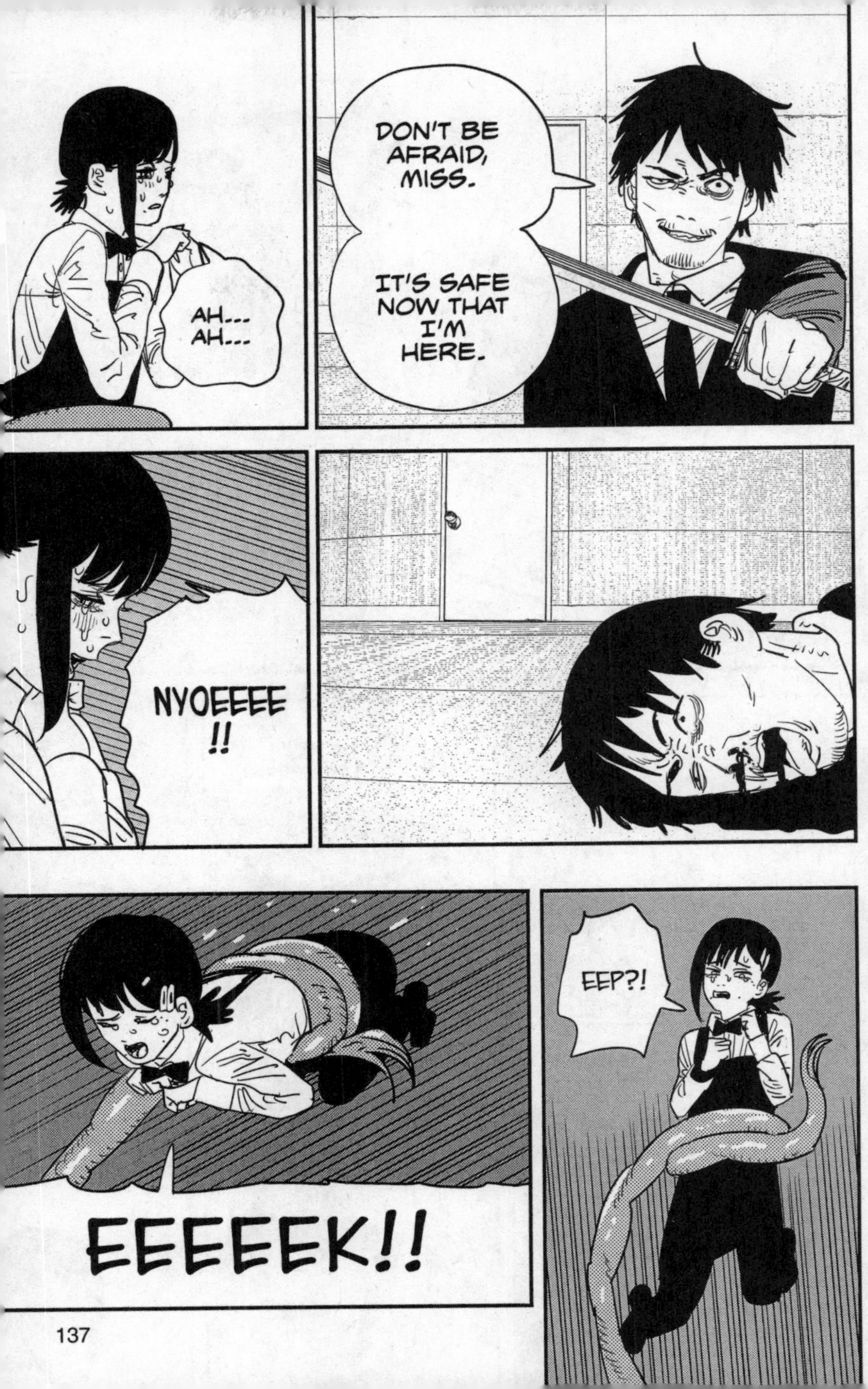
DON'T BE AFRAID, MISS.
IT'S SAFE NOW THAT I'M HERE.
AH... AH...
NYOEEEE !!
EEP?!
EEEEEK!!

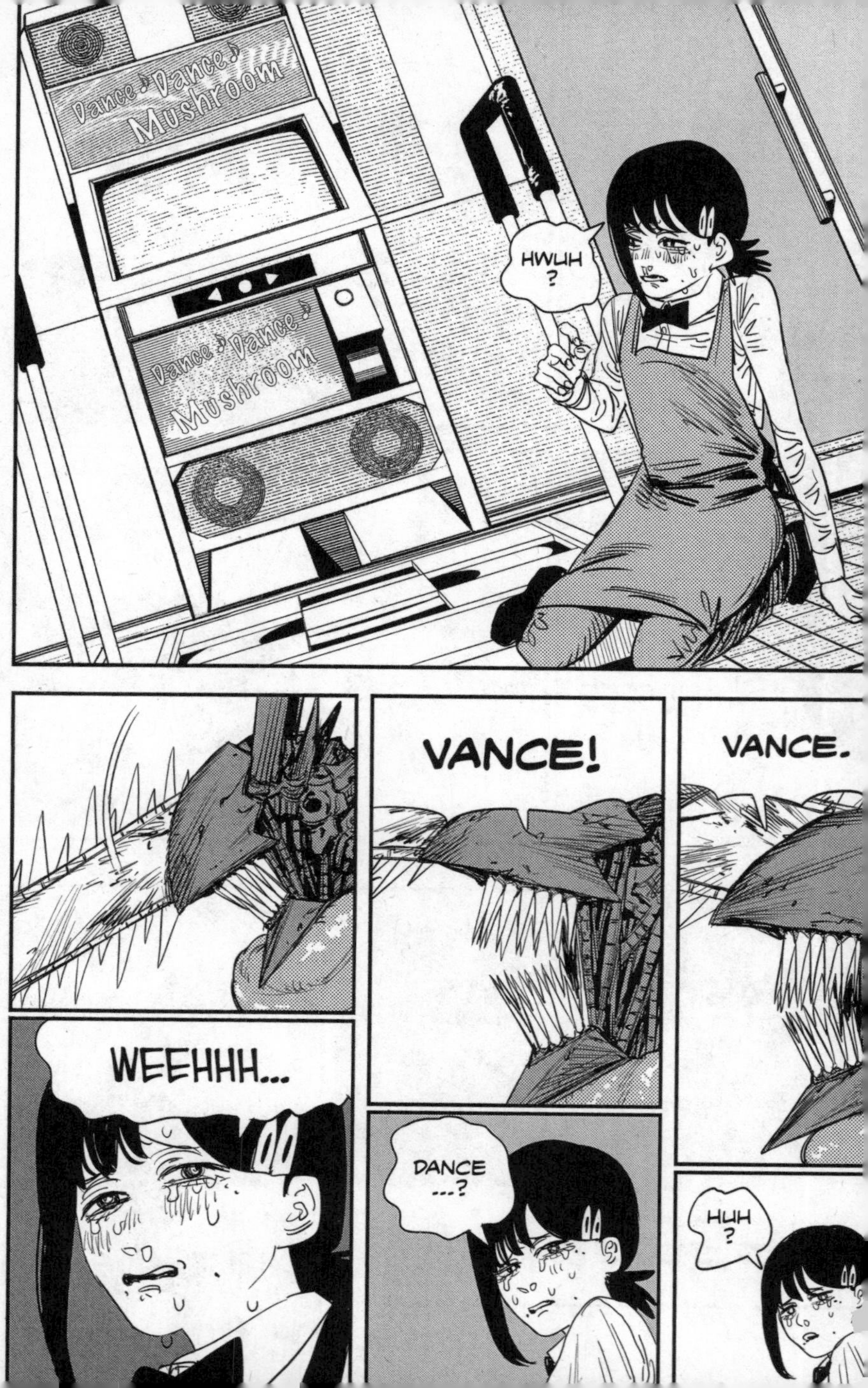
Dance♪Dance♪ Mushroom
Dance♪Dance♪ Mushroom
HWUH?
VANCE.
HUH?
VANCE!
DANCE...?
WEEHHH...

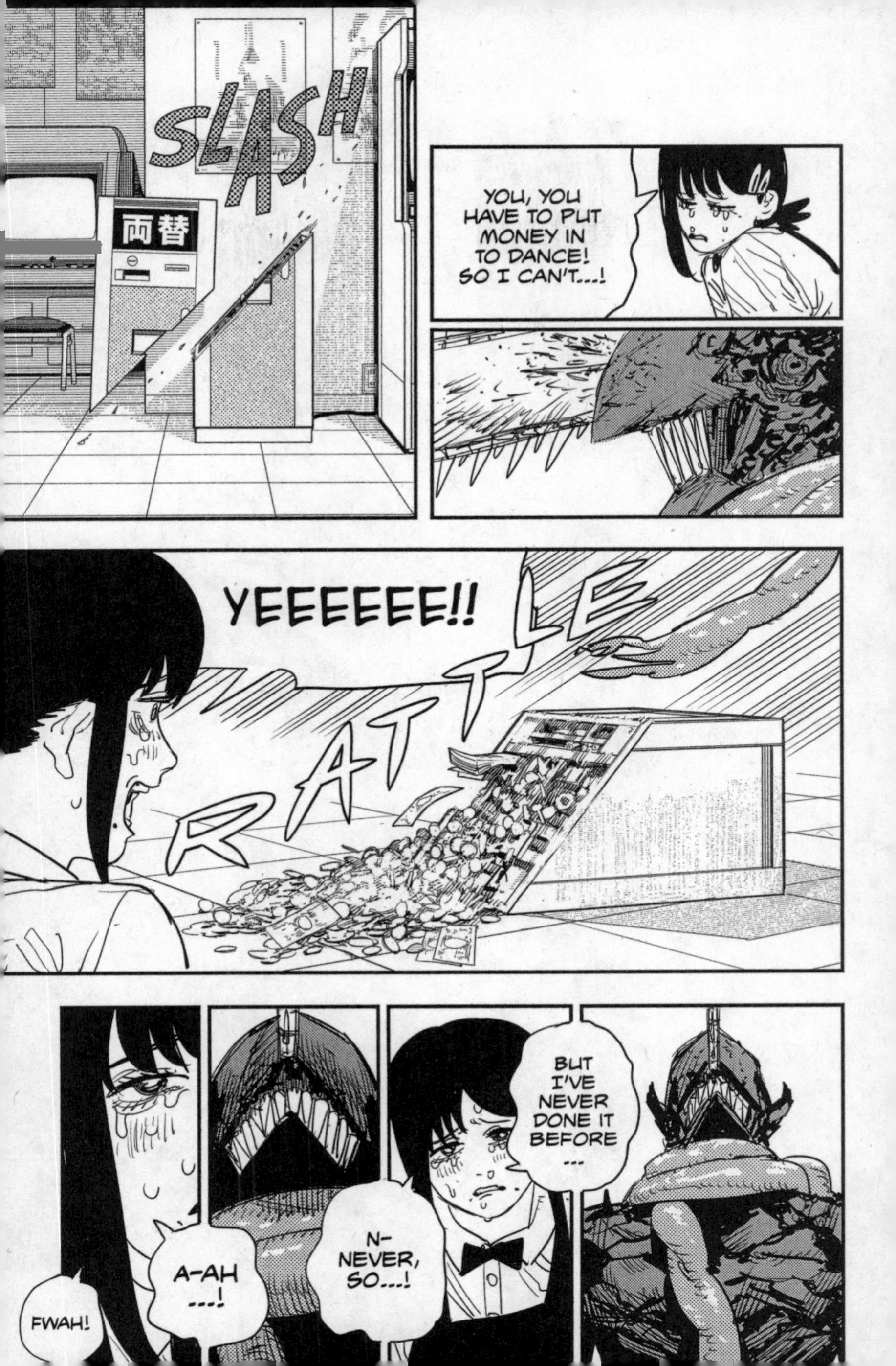
YOU, YOU HAVE TO PUT MONEY IN TO DANCE! SO I CAN'T...!
SLASH
両替
YEEEEEEE!!
RATTLE
BUT I'VE NEVER DONE IT BEFORE ...
N-NEVER, SO...!
A-AH ...!
FWAH!

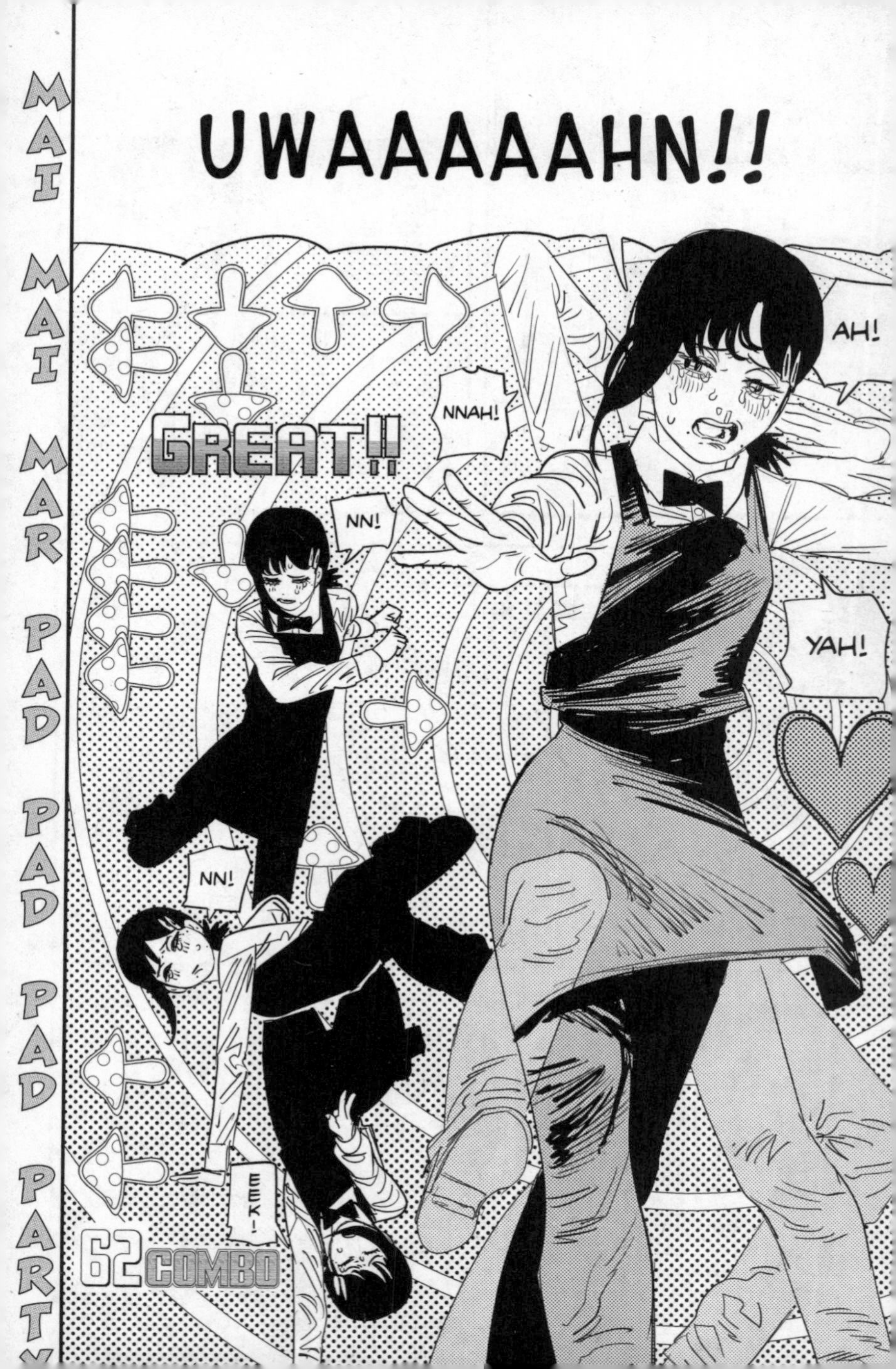
MAI MAI MAR PAD PAD PAD PAD PARTY
UWAAAAAAHN!!
AH!
NNAH!
GREAT!!
NN!
YAH!
NN!
EEK!
62 COMBO

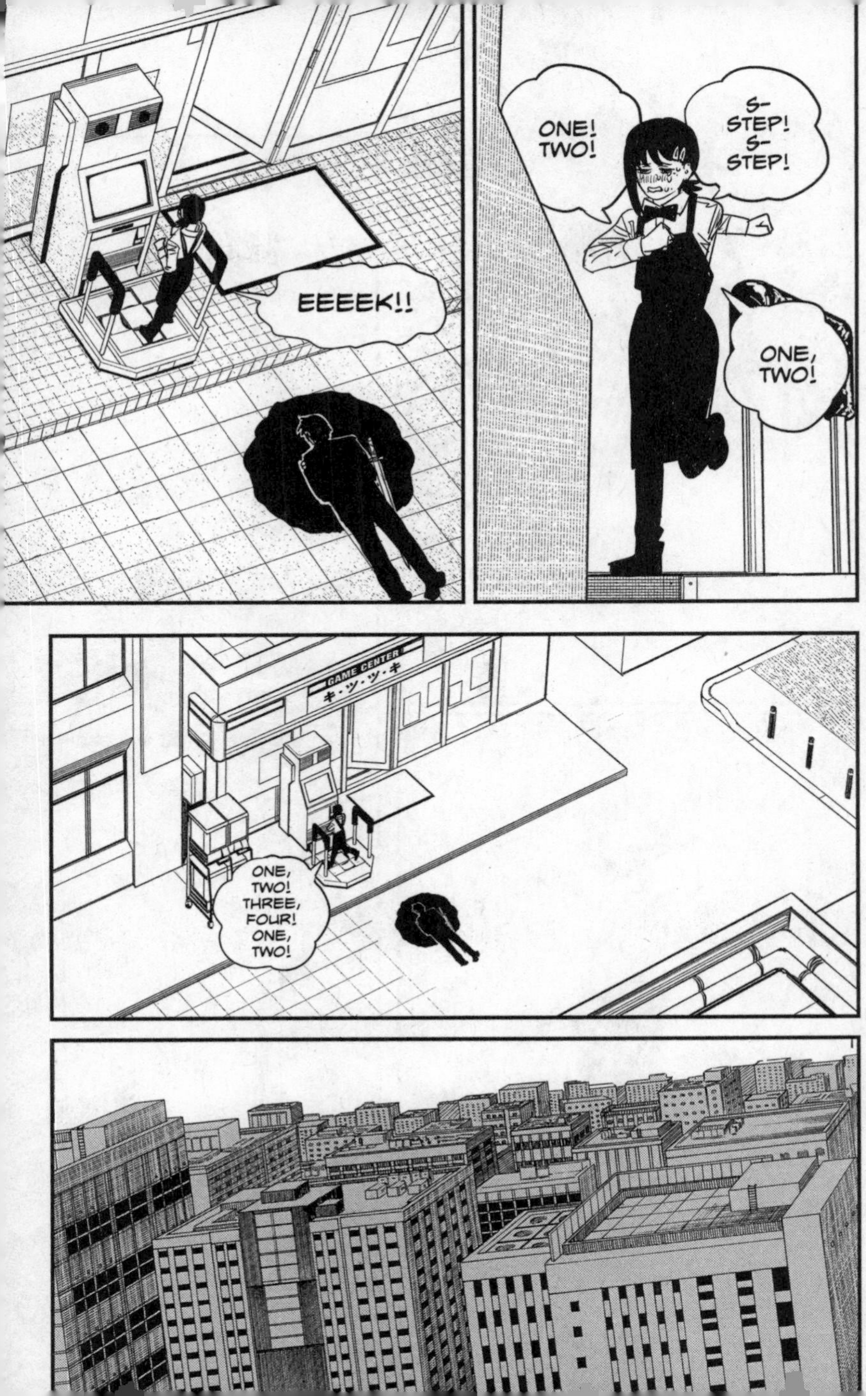
S-STEP! S-STEP!
ONE! TWO!
ONE, TWO!
EEEEK!!
GAME CENTER
キ・ツ・ツ・キ
ONE, TWO! THREE, FOUR! ONE, TWO!

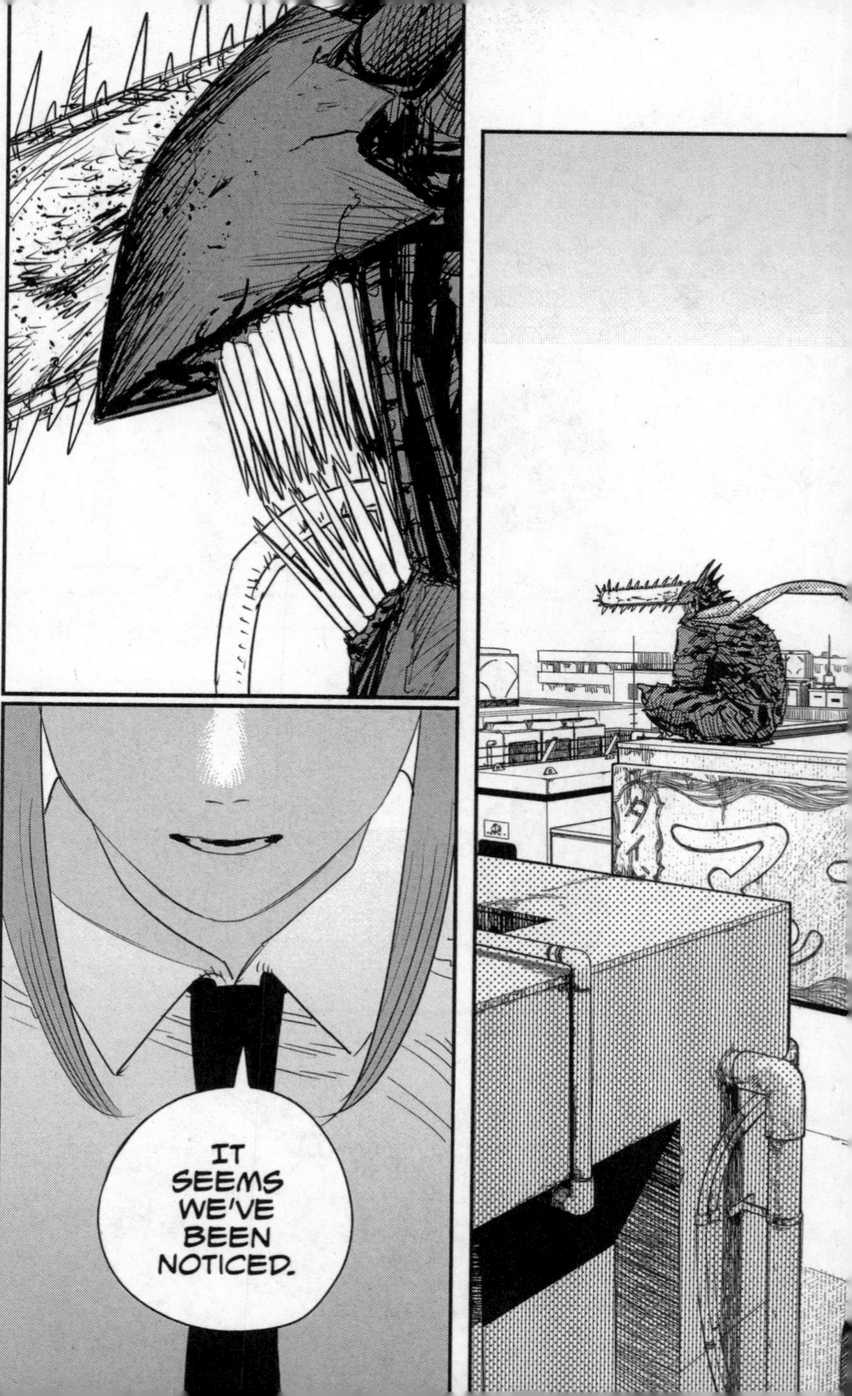
IT SEEMS WE'VE BEEN NOTICED.

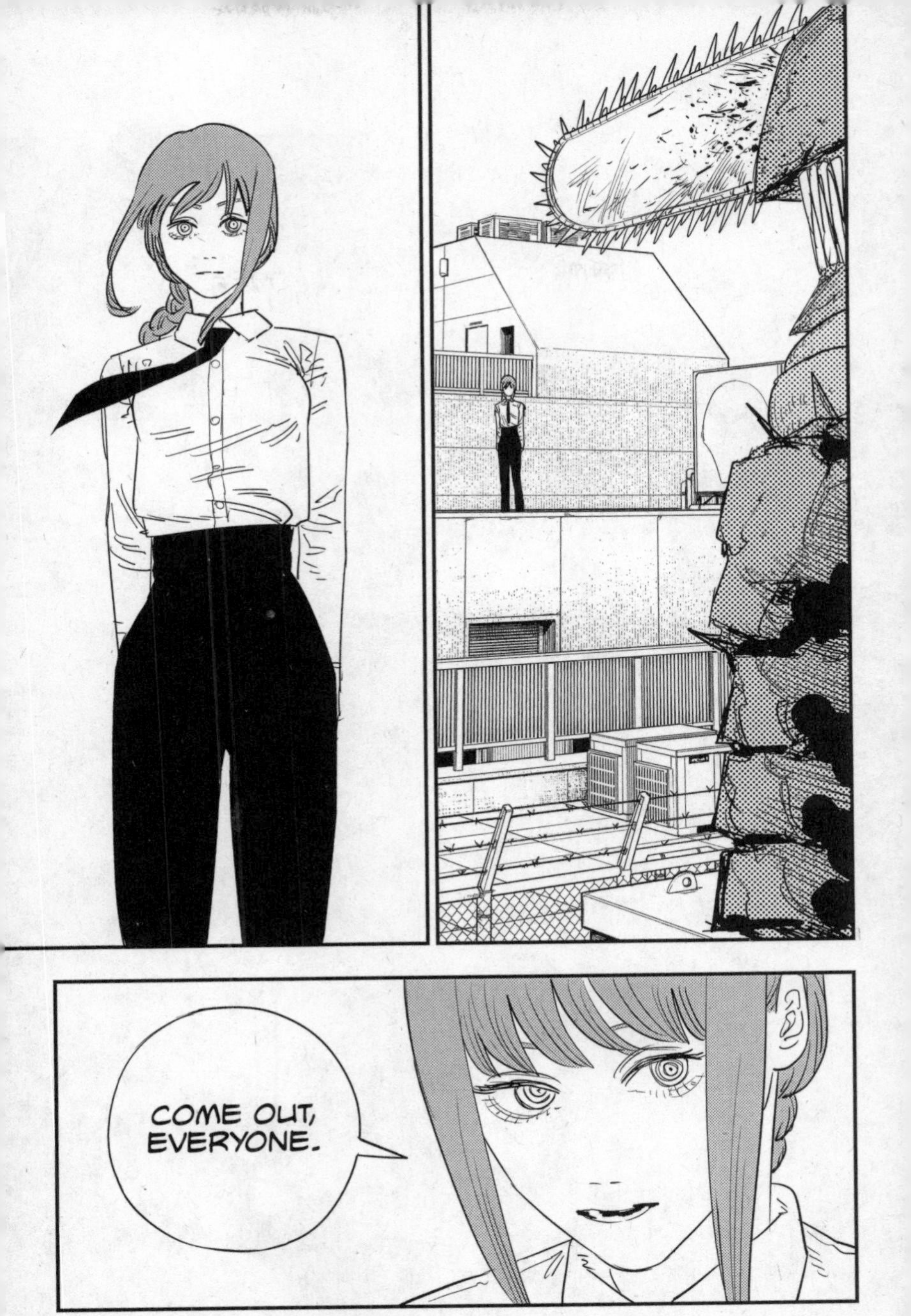
COME OUT, EVERYONE.

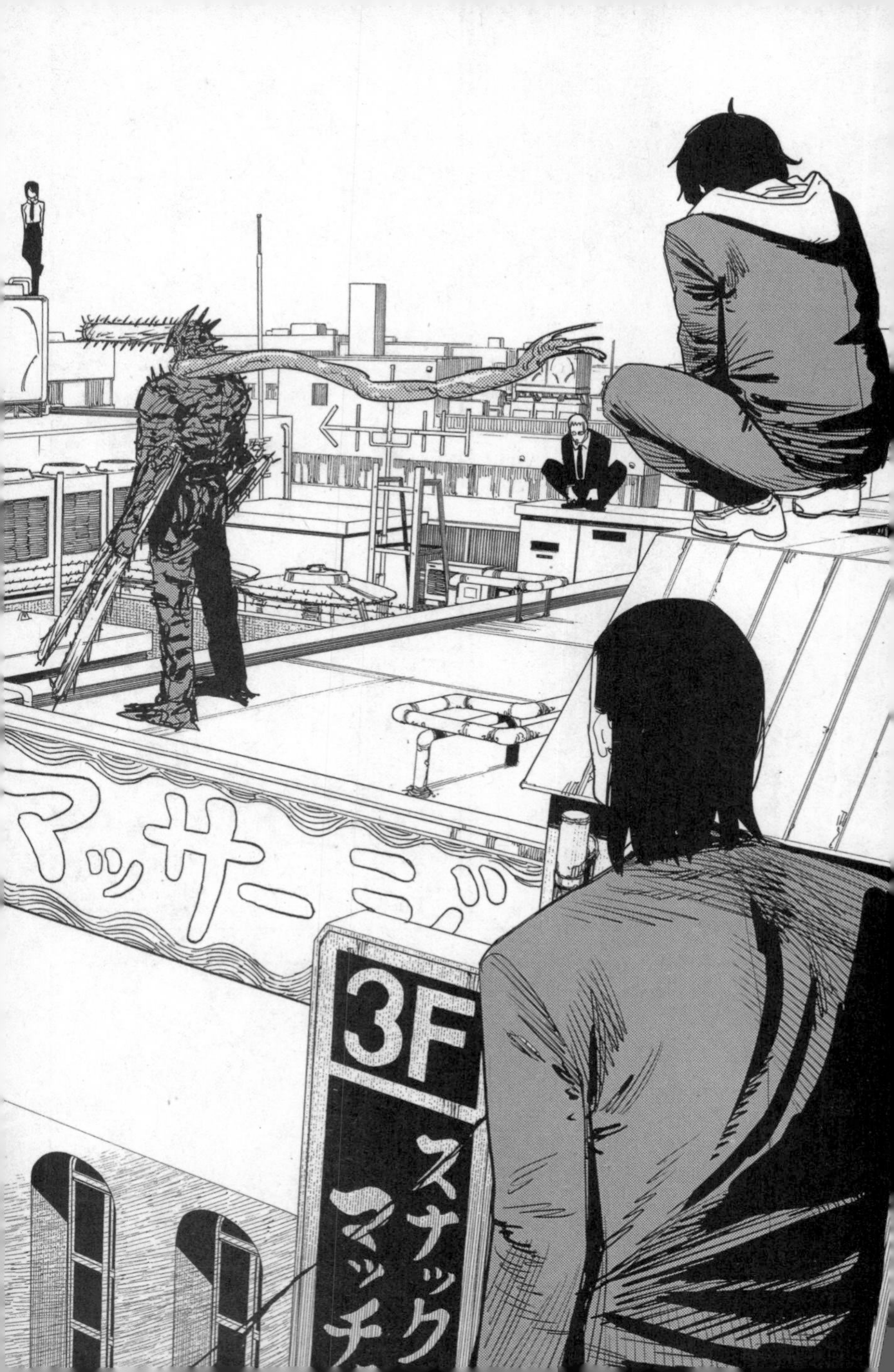
3F
スナック

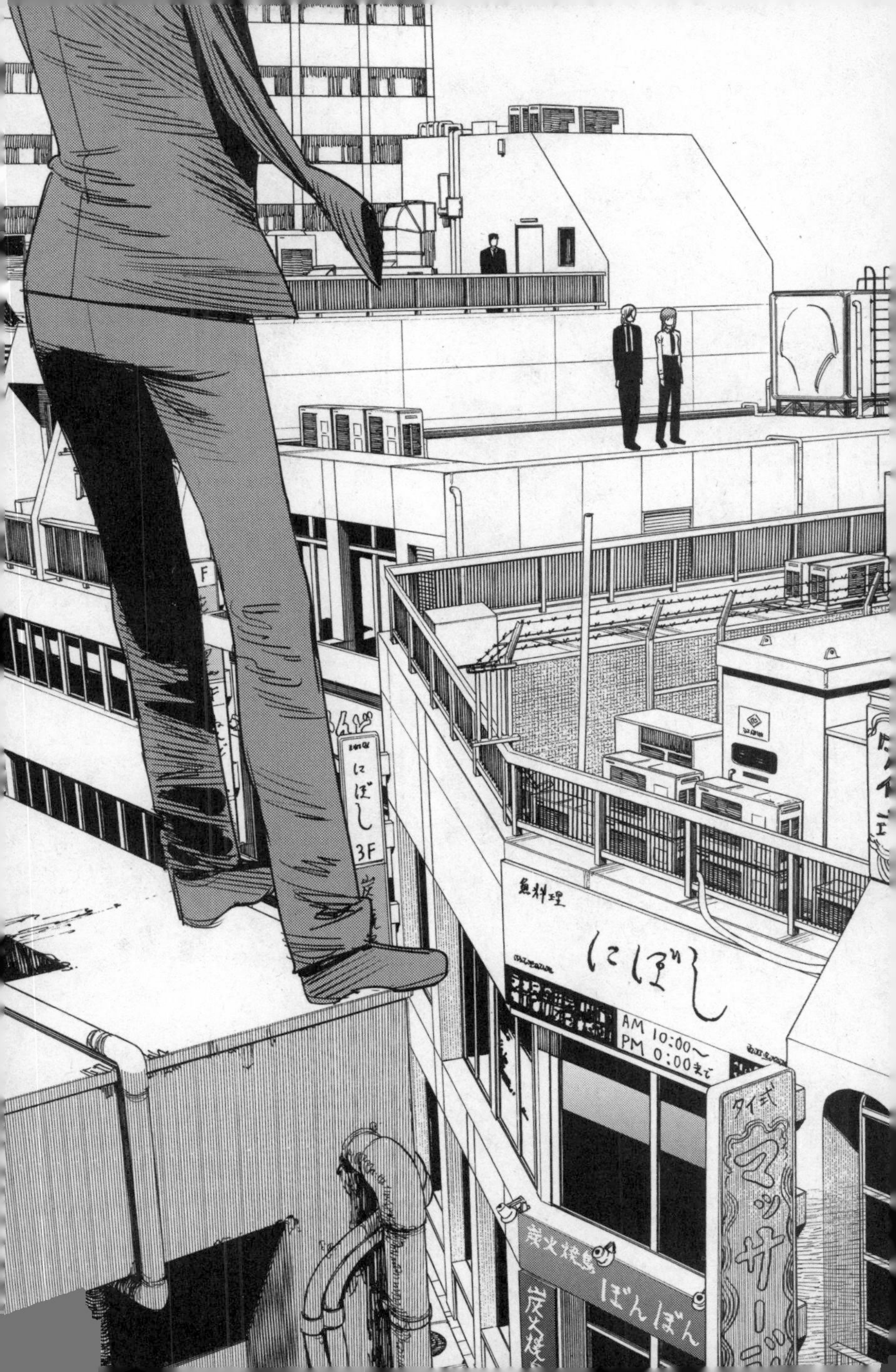

にぼし
3F
魚料理
にぼし
AM 10:00〜
PM 0:00まで
タイ式
マッサー
炭火焼鳥
ぼんぼん

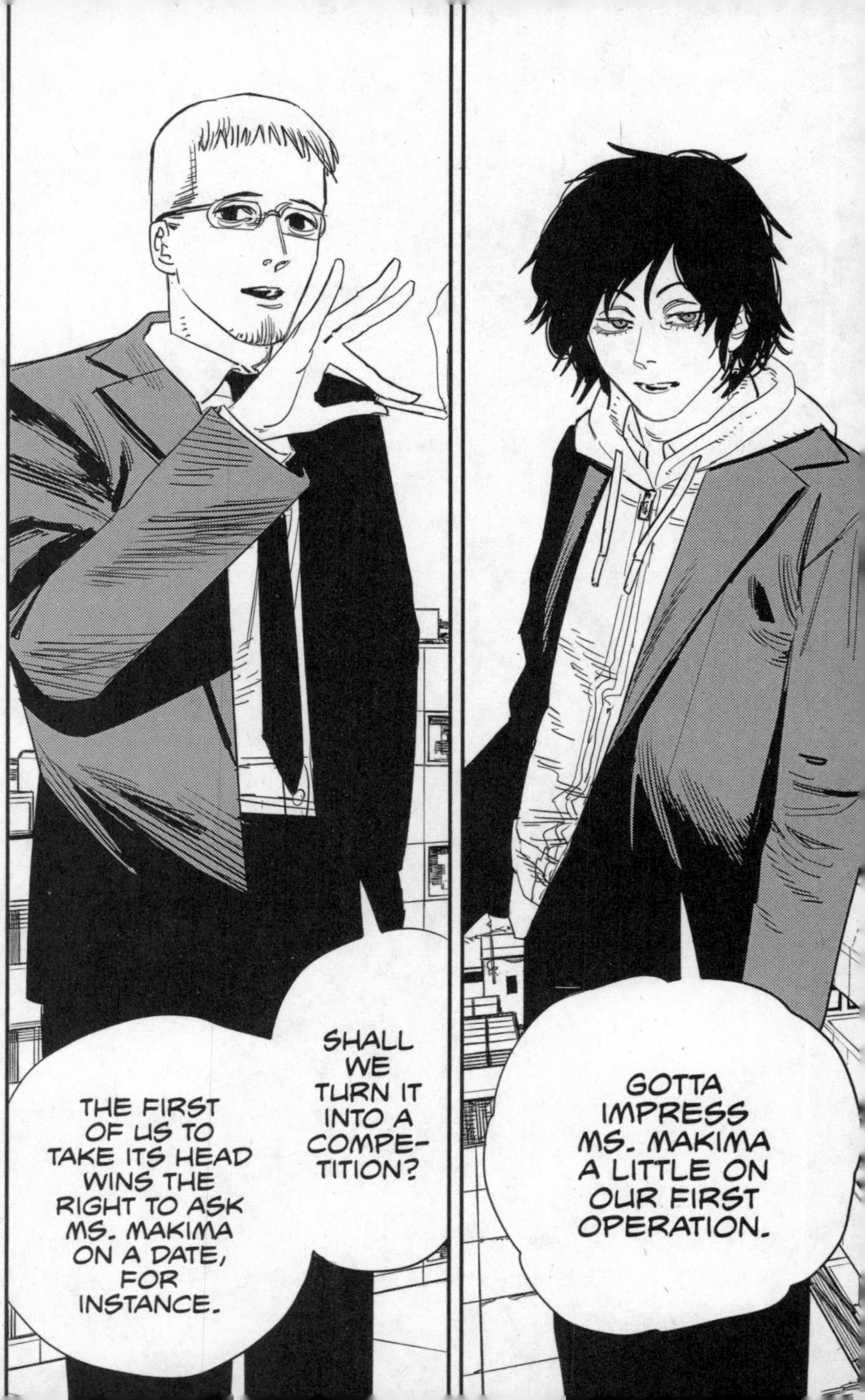
GOTTA IMPRESS MS. MAKIMA A LITTLE ON OUR FIRST OPERATION.
SHALL WE TURN IT INTO A COMPE-TITION?
THE FIRST OF US TO TAKE ITS HEAD WINS THE RIGHT TO ASK MS. MAKIMA ON A DATE, FOR INSTANCE.

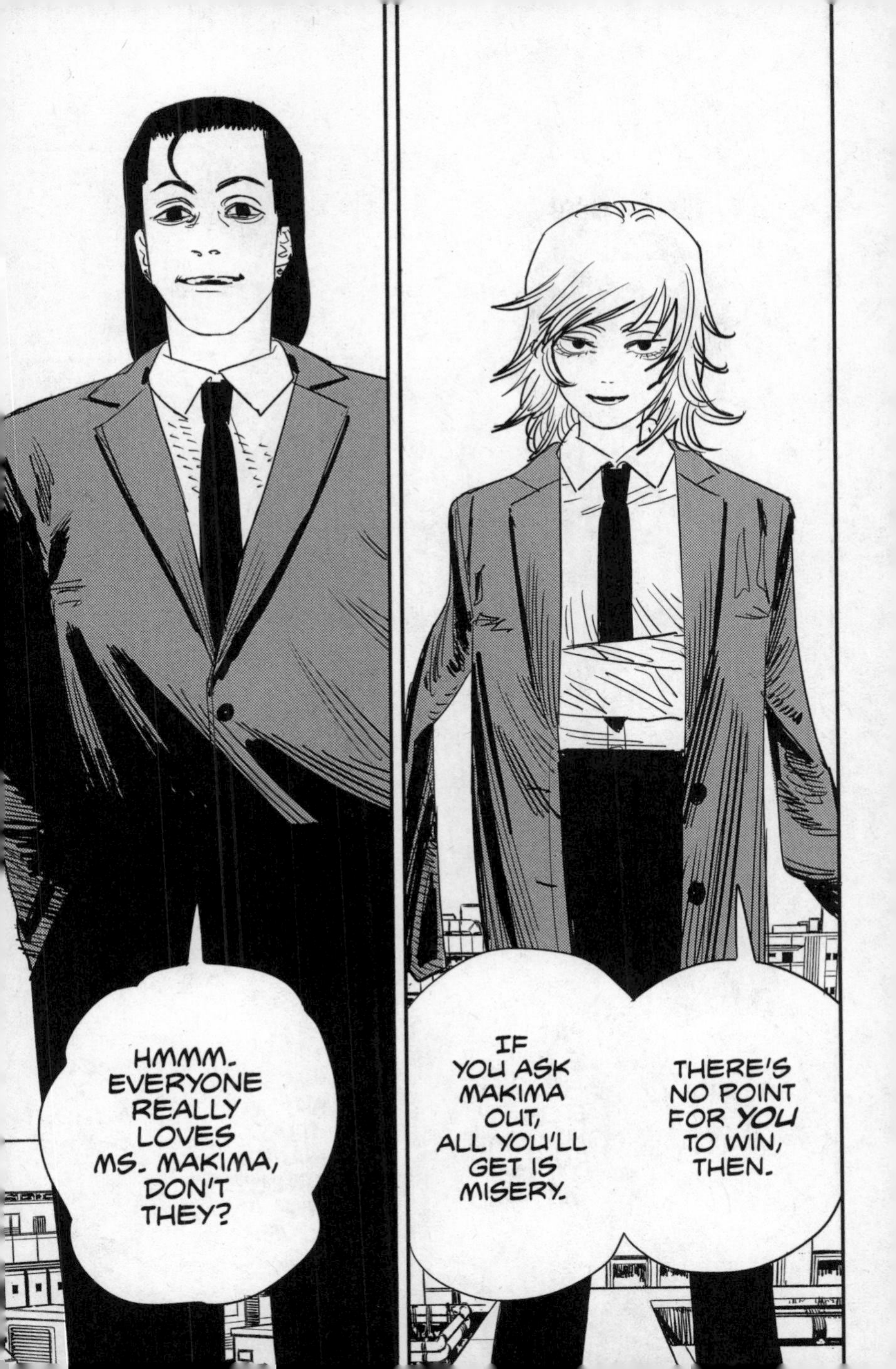
THERE'S NO POINT FOR YOU TO WIN, THEN.
IF YOU ASK MAKIMA OUT, ALL YOU'LL GET IS MISERY.
HMMM. EVERYONE REALLY LOVES MS. MAKIMA, DON'T THEY?

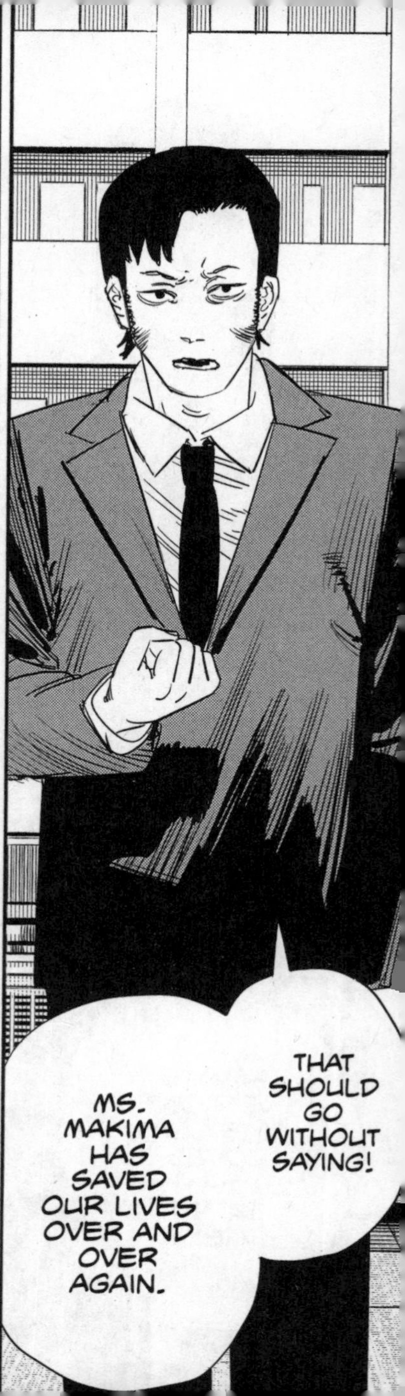
THAT SHOULD GO WITHOUT SAYING!
MS. MAKIMA HAS SAVED OUR LIVES OVER AND OVER AGAIN.

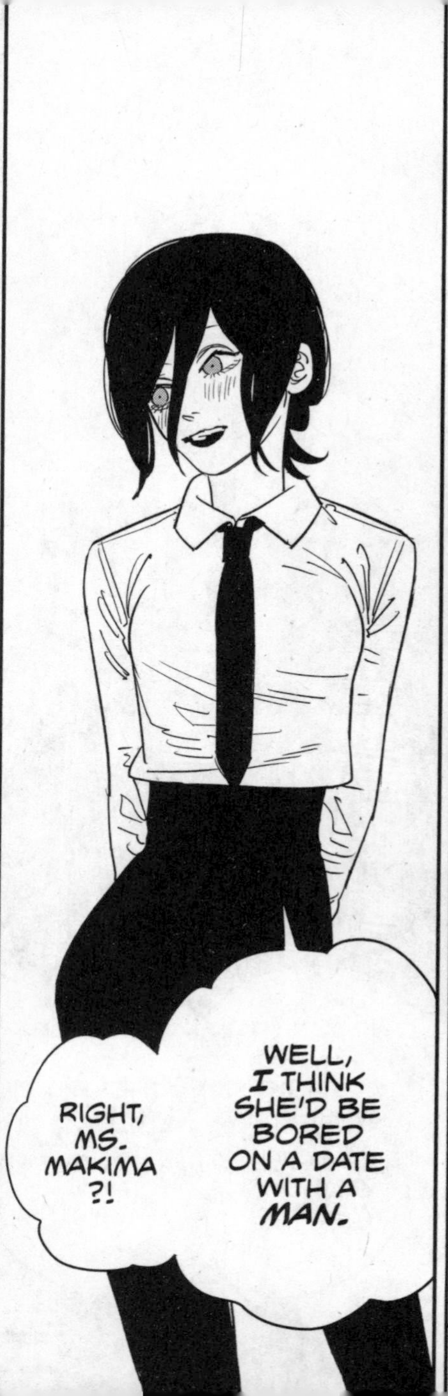
WELL, I THINK SHE'D BE BORED ON A DATE WITH A MAN.
RIGHT, MS. MAKIMA?!

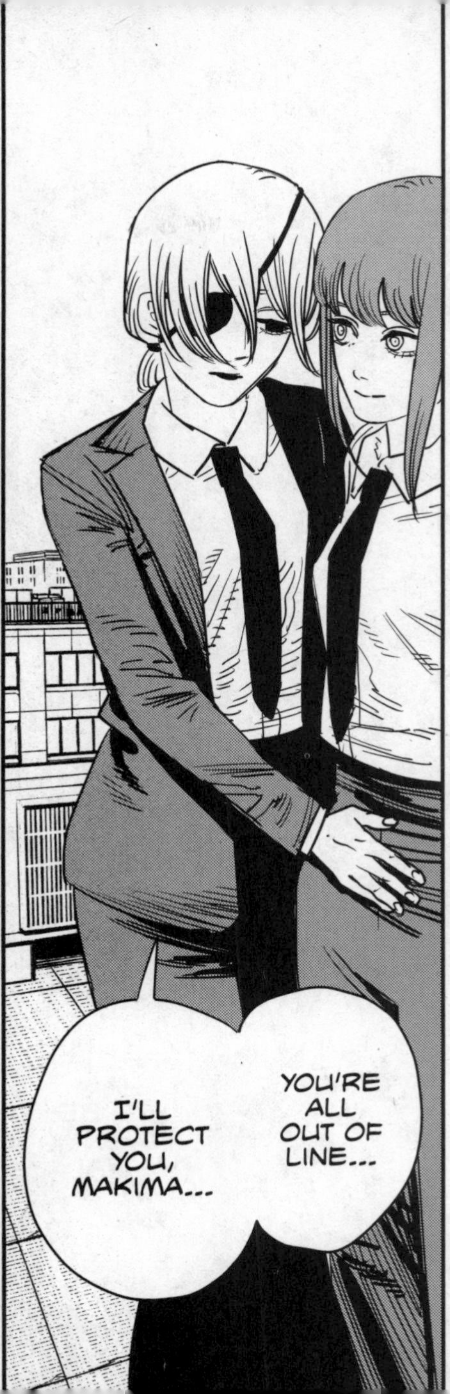
YOU'RE ALL OUT OF LINE...
I'LL PROTECT YOU, MAKIMA...
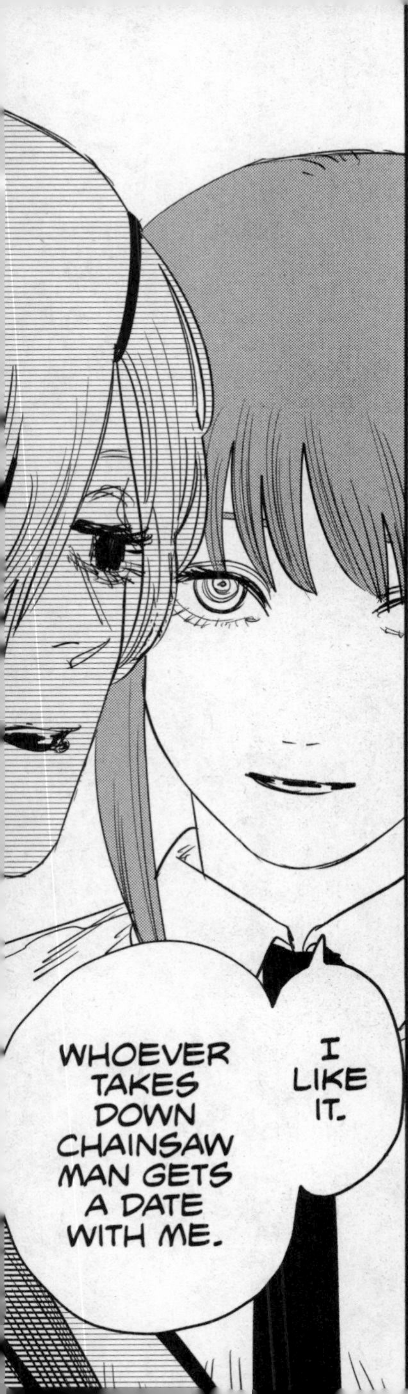
I LIKE IT.
WHOEVER TAKES DOWN CHAINSAW MAN GETS A DATE WITH ME.

CHAINSAW MAN

Chapter 87: Chainsaw Man vs. the Horrifying Weapon Humans

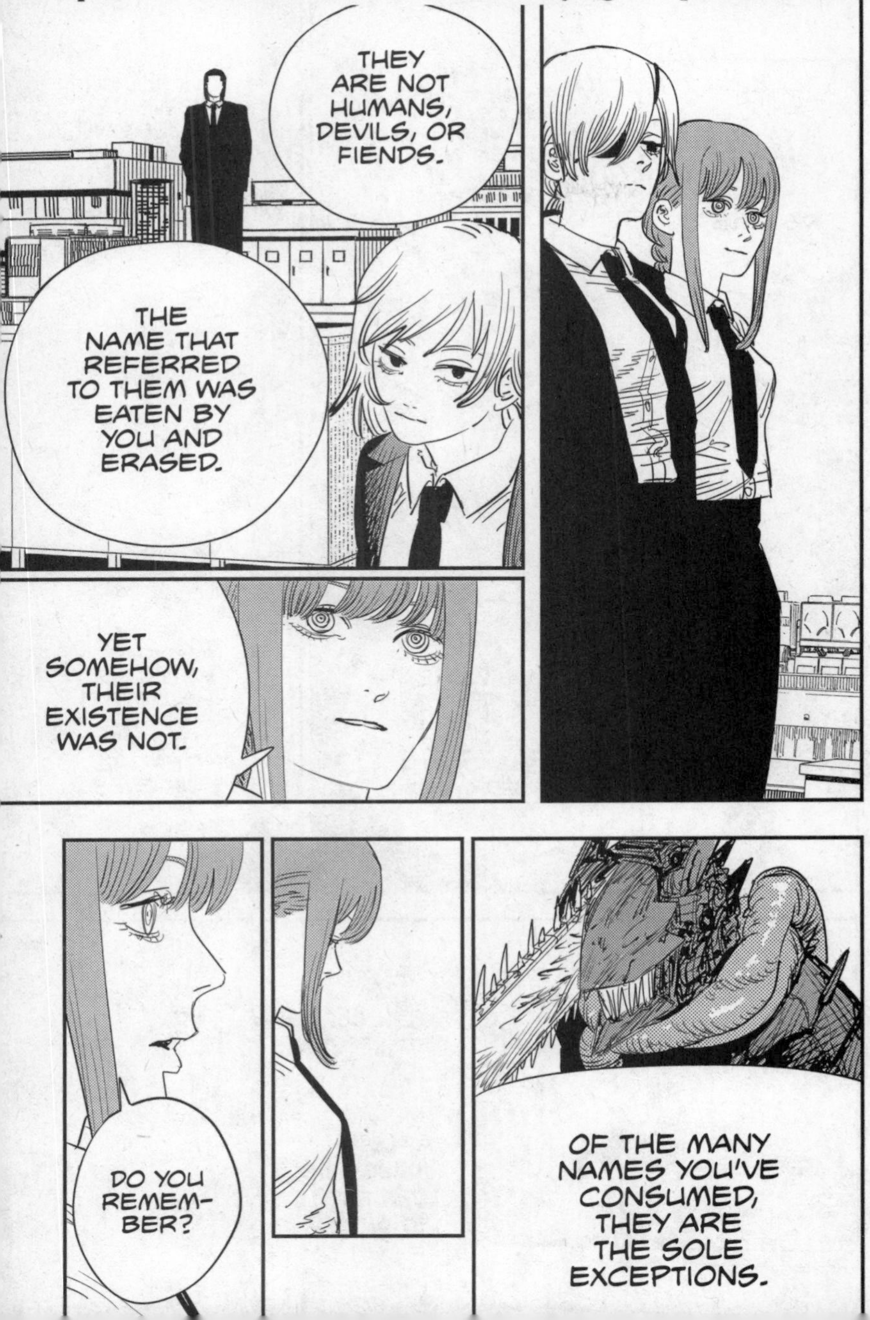
THEY ARE NOT HUMANS, DEVILS, OR FIENDS.
THE NAME THAT REFERRED TO THEM WAS EATEN BY YOU AND ERASED.
YET SOMEHOW, THEIR EXISTENCE WAS NOT.
OF THE MANY NAMES YOU'VE CONSUMED, THEY ARE THE SOLE EXCEPTIONS.
DO YOU REMEM-BER?

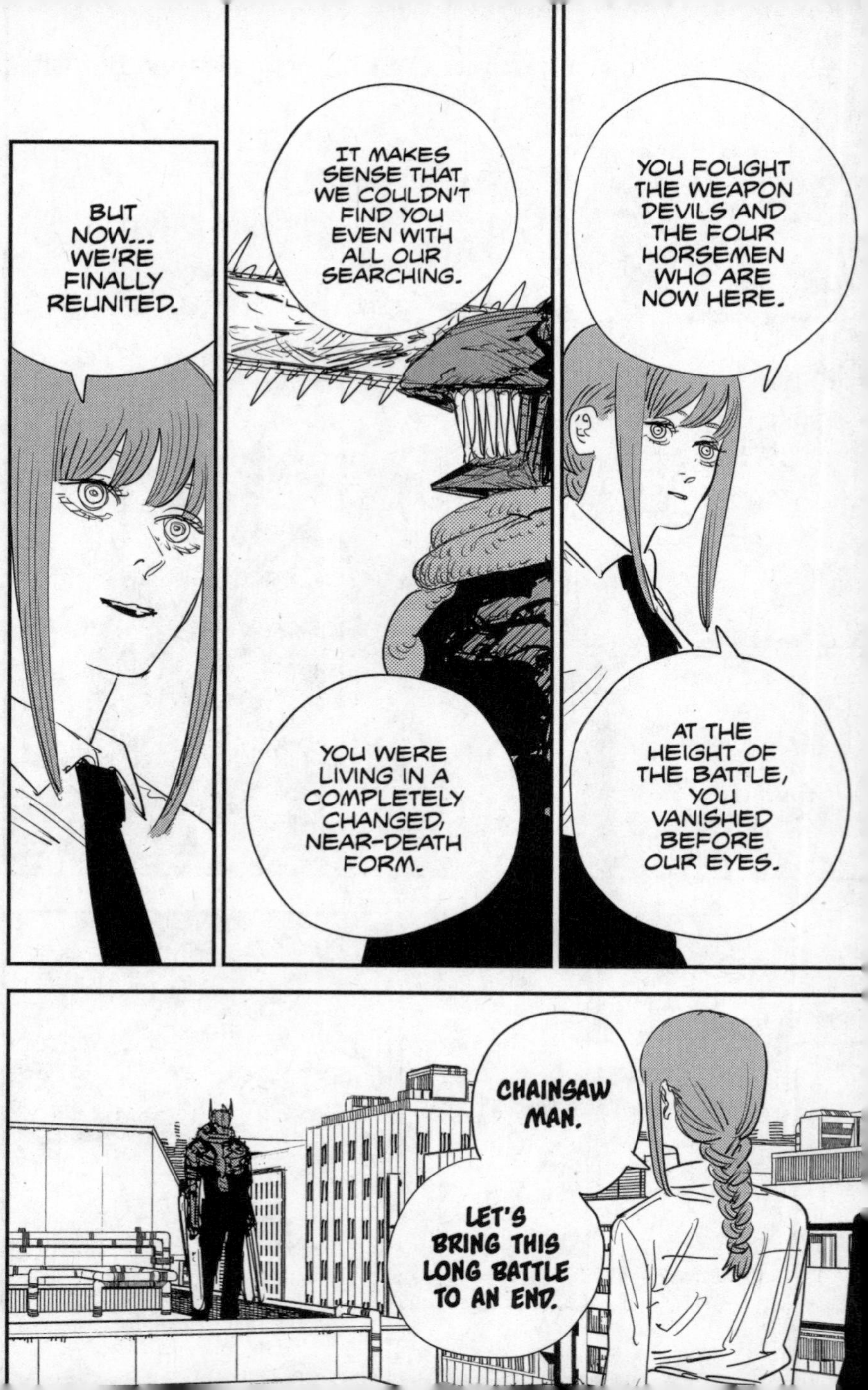
YOU FOUGHT THE WEAPON DEVILS AND THE FOUR HORSEMEN WHO ARE NOW HERE.
AT THE HEIGHT OF THE BATTLE, YOU VANISHED BEFORE OUR EYES.
IT MAKES SENSE THAT WE COULDN'T FIND YOU EVEN WITH ALL OUR SEARCHING.
YOU WERE LIVING IN A COMPLETELY CHANGED, NEAR-DEATH FORM.
BUT NOW... WE'RE FINALLY REUNITED.
CHAINSAW MAN.
LET'S BRING THIS LONG BATTLE TO AN END.

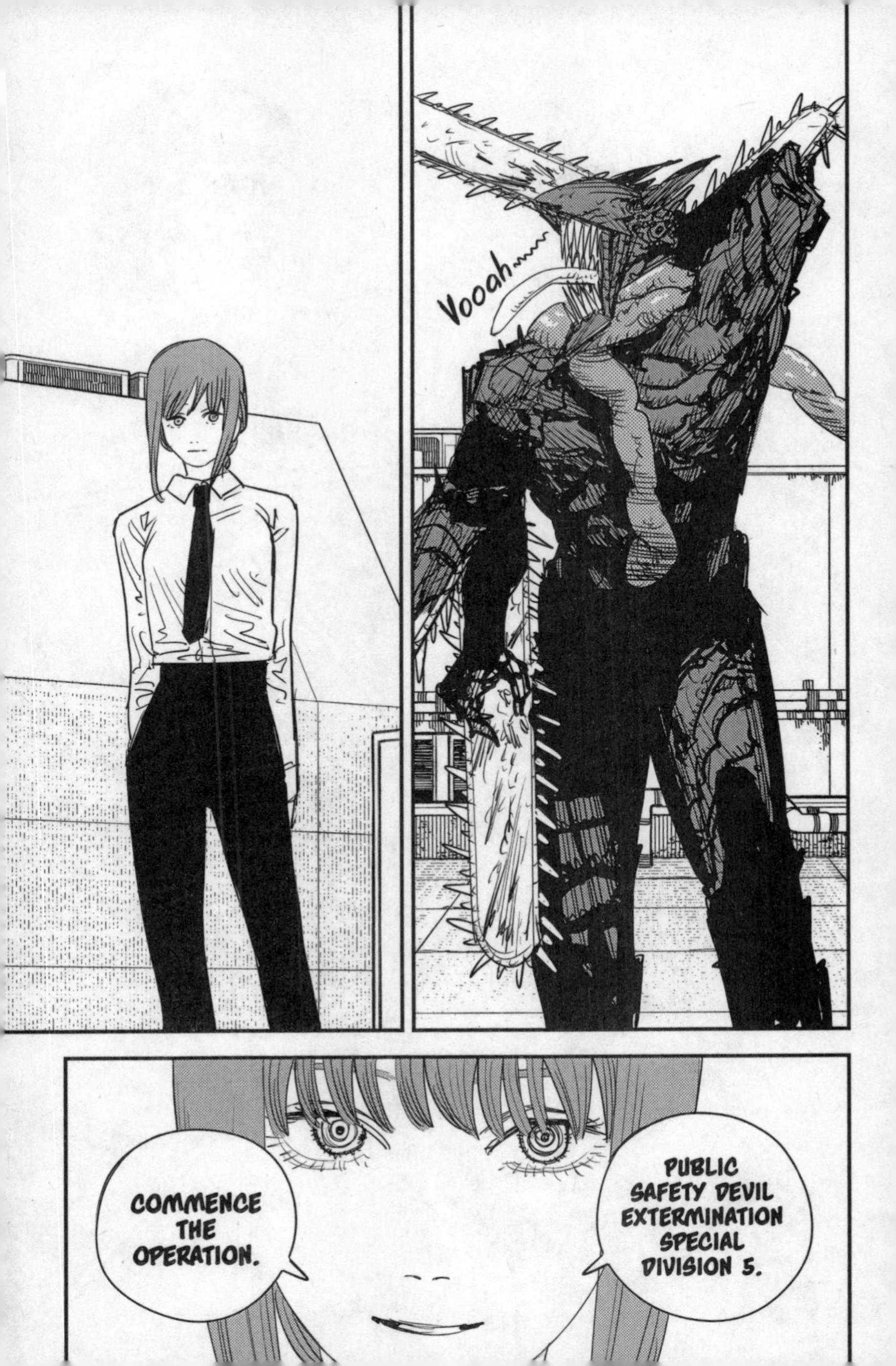
Vooah
Public safety devil extermination special division 5.
Commence the operation.

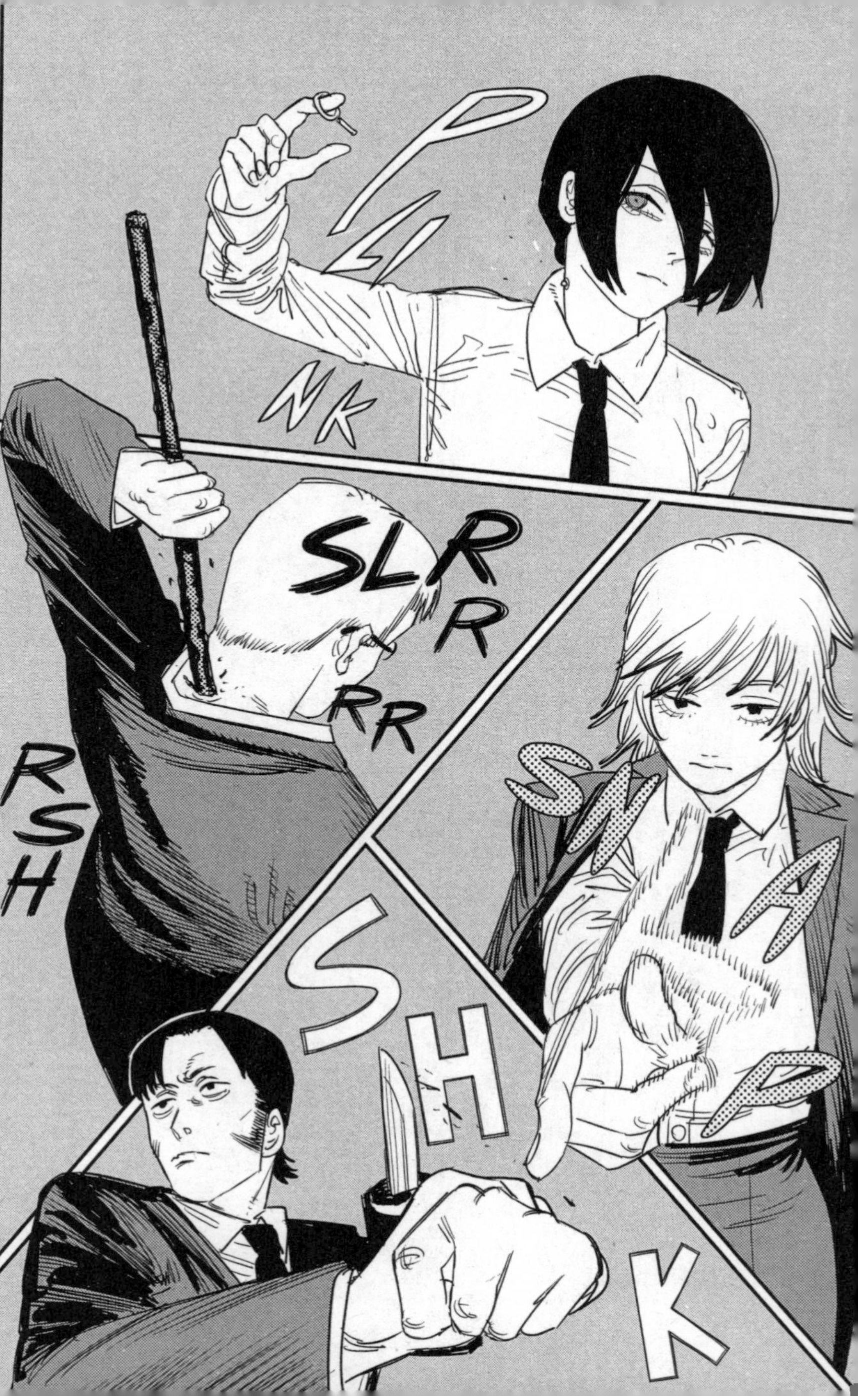
PLINK
SNAP
SLRRRR
RSH
SHK

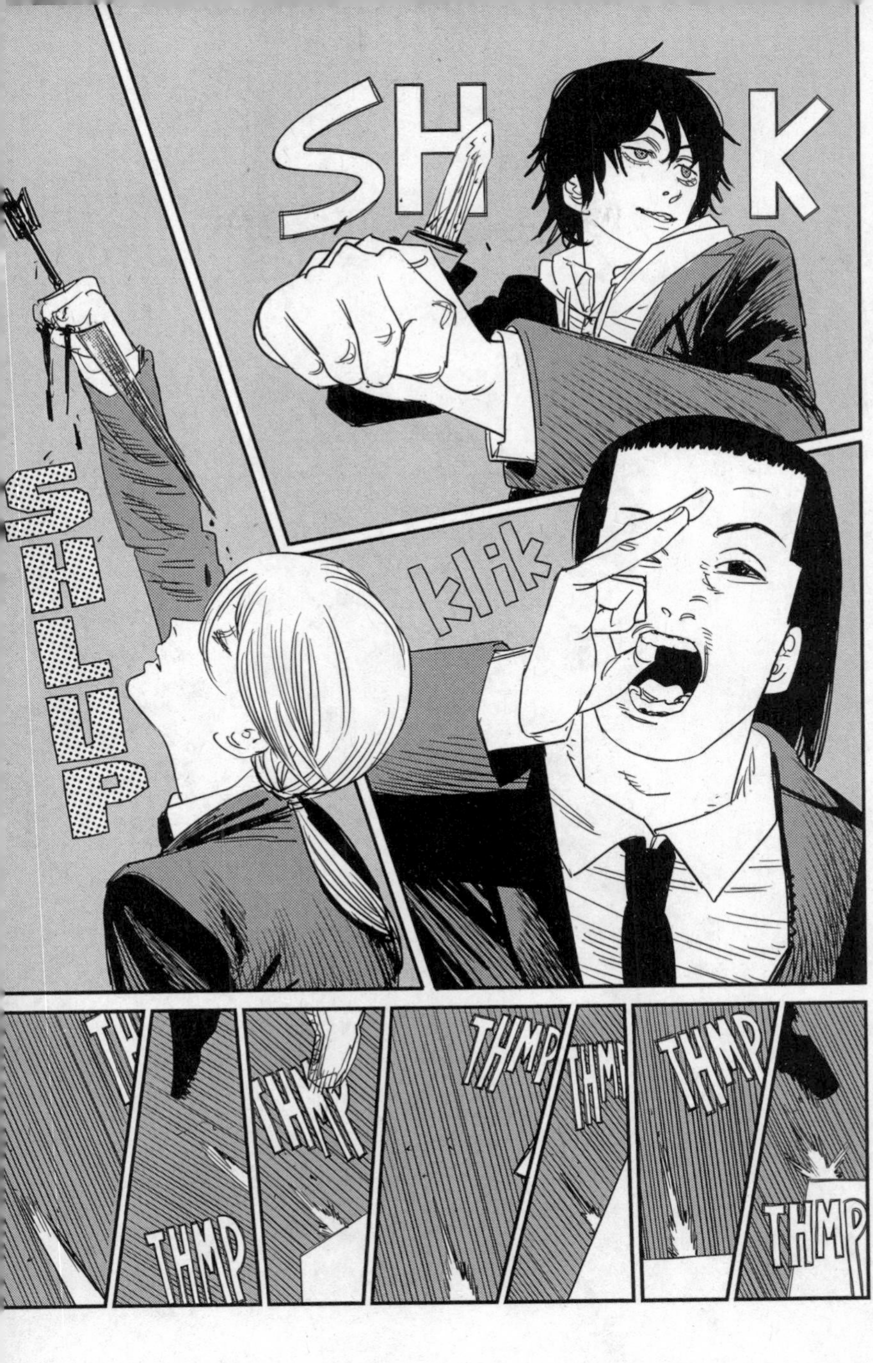
SHK
klik
SHLUP
THMP
THMP
THMP
THMP
THMP
THMP
THMP
TH

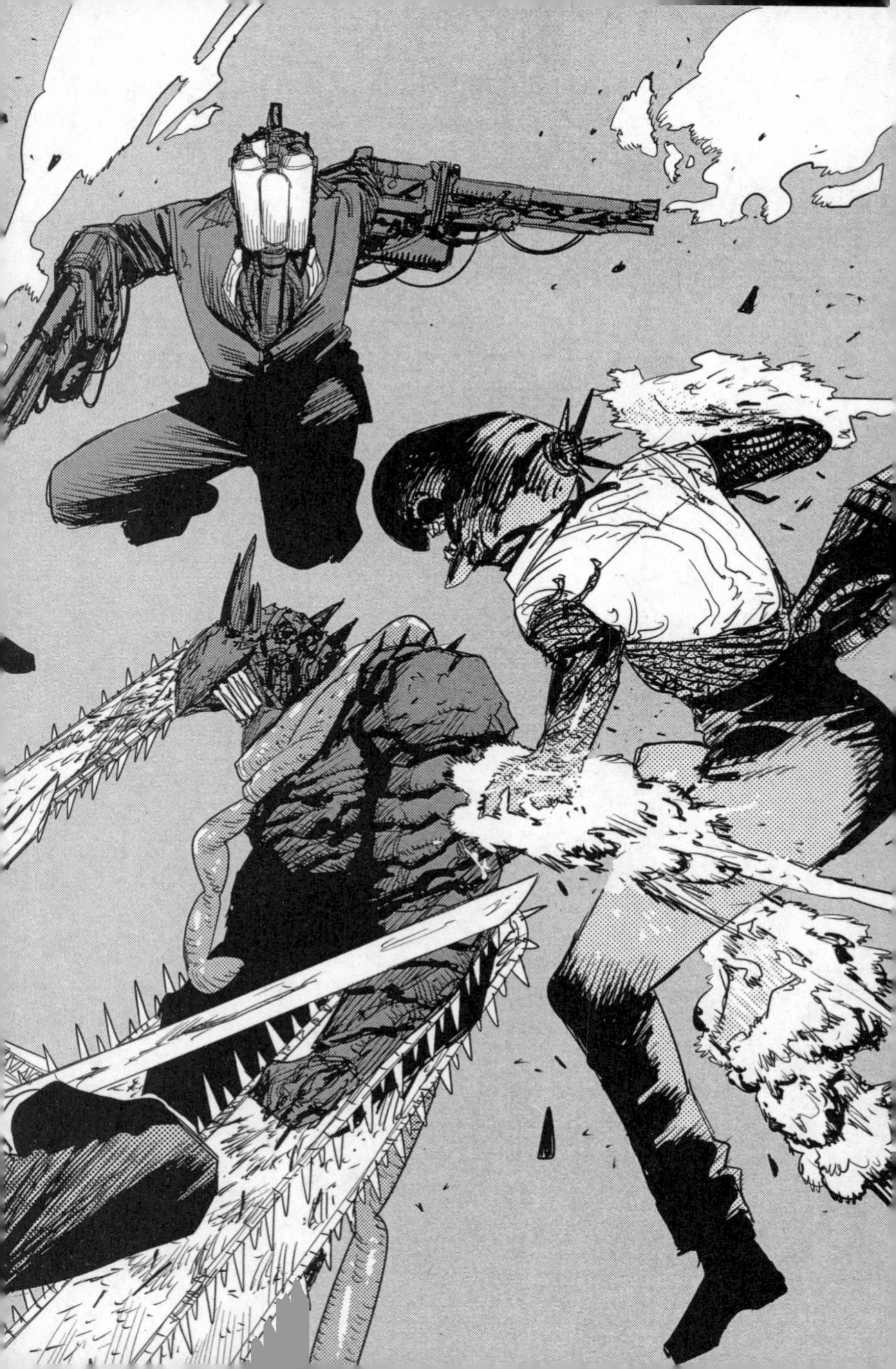

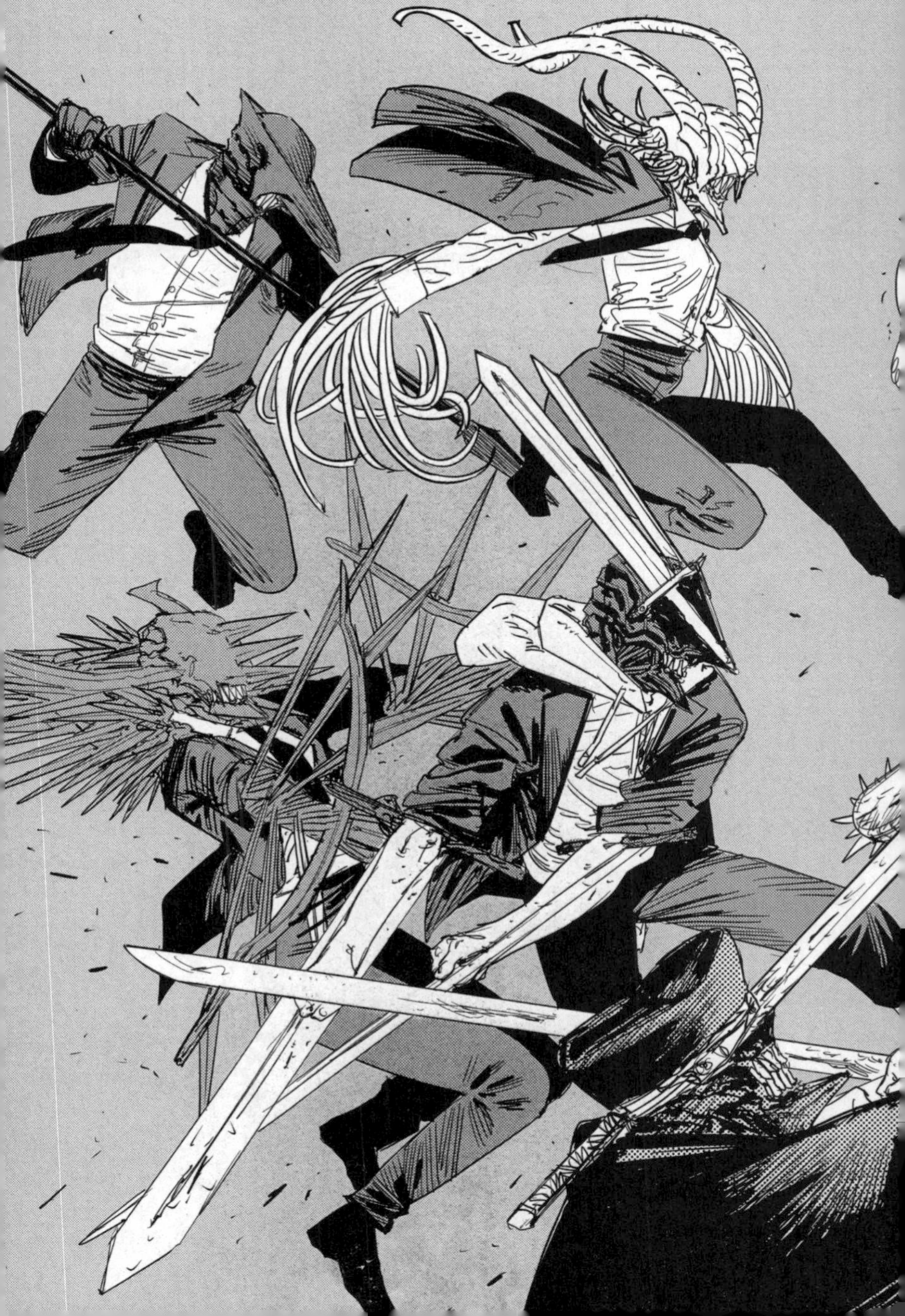

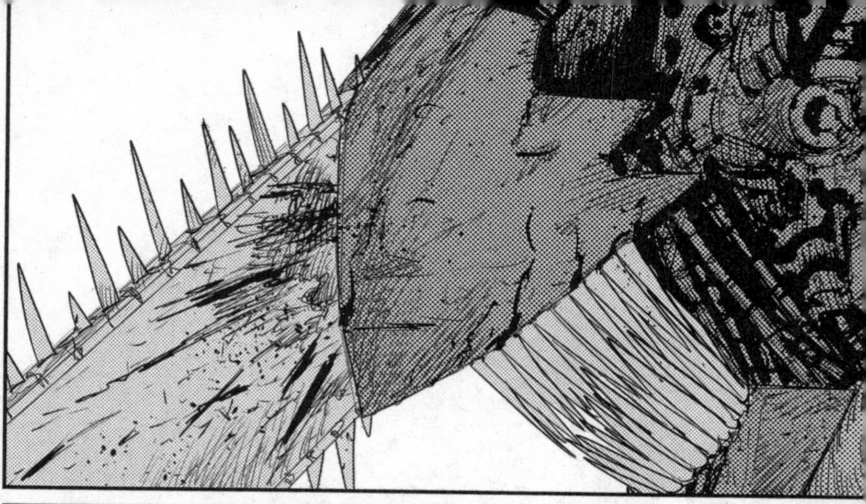

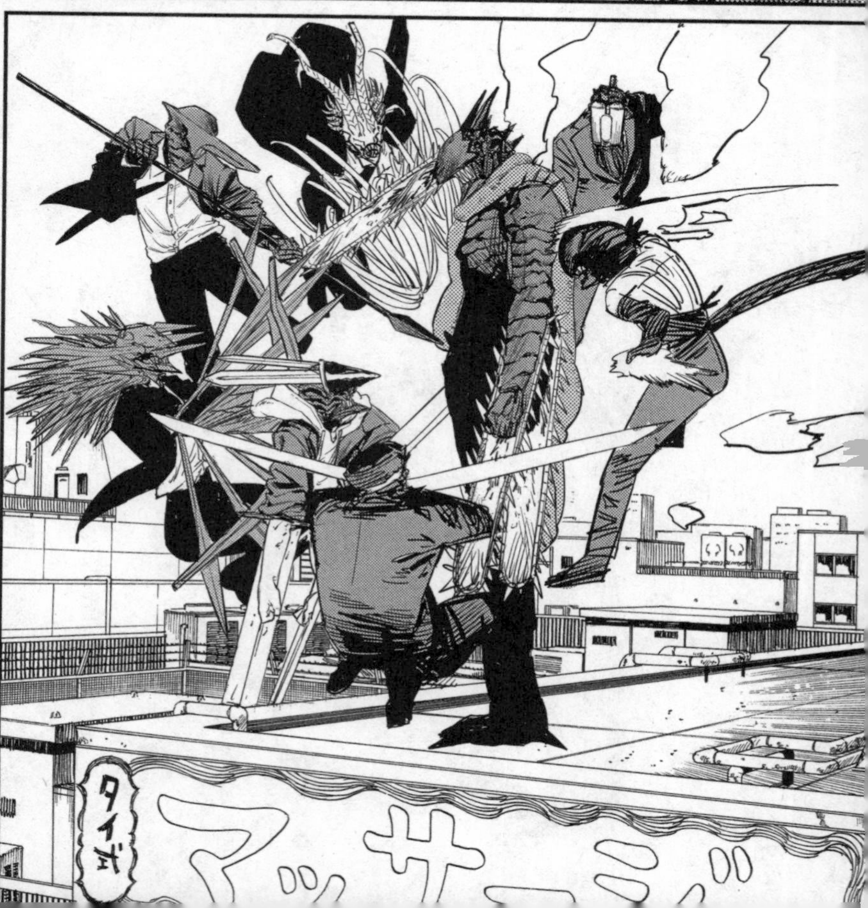
タイ式
マッサージ

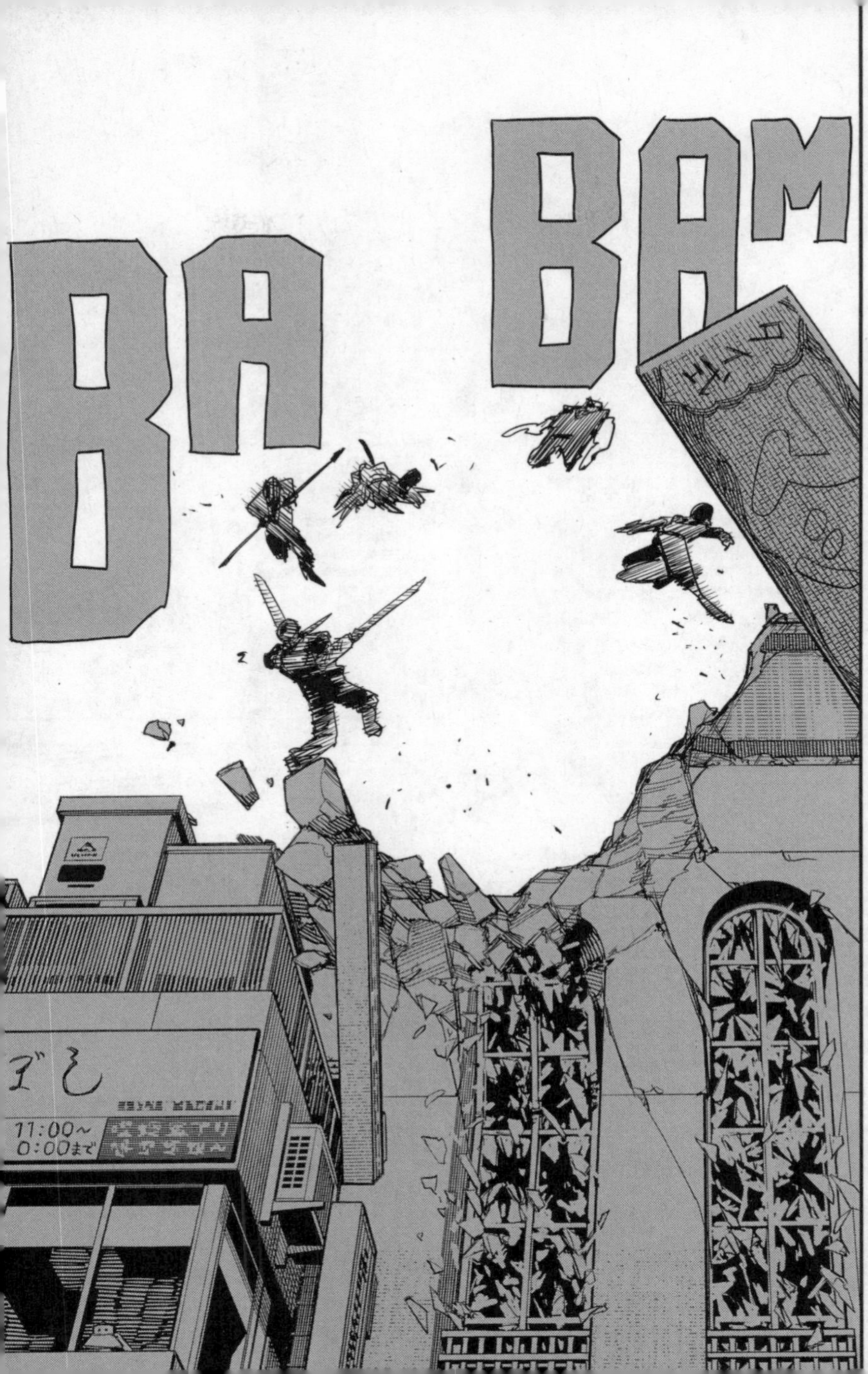
BA BABAM
11:00~
0:00まで

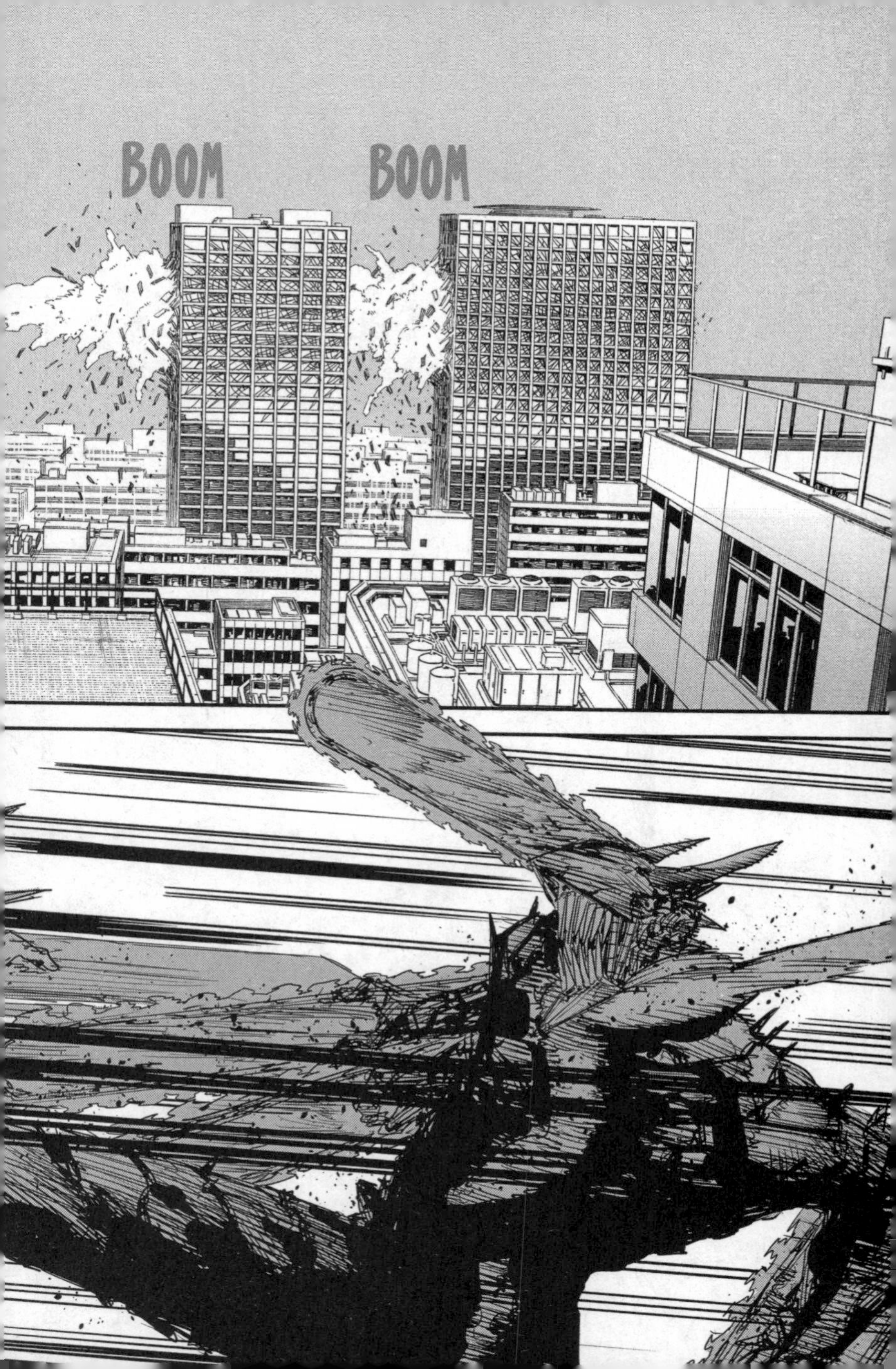
BOOM
BOOM

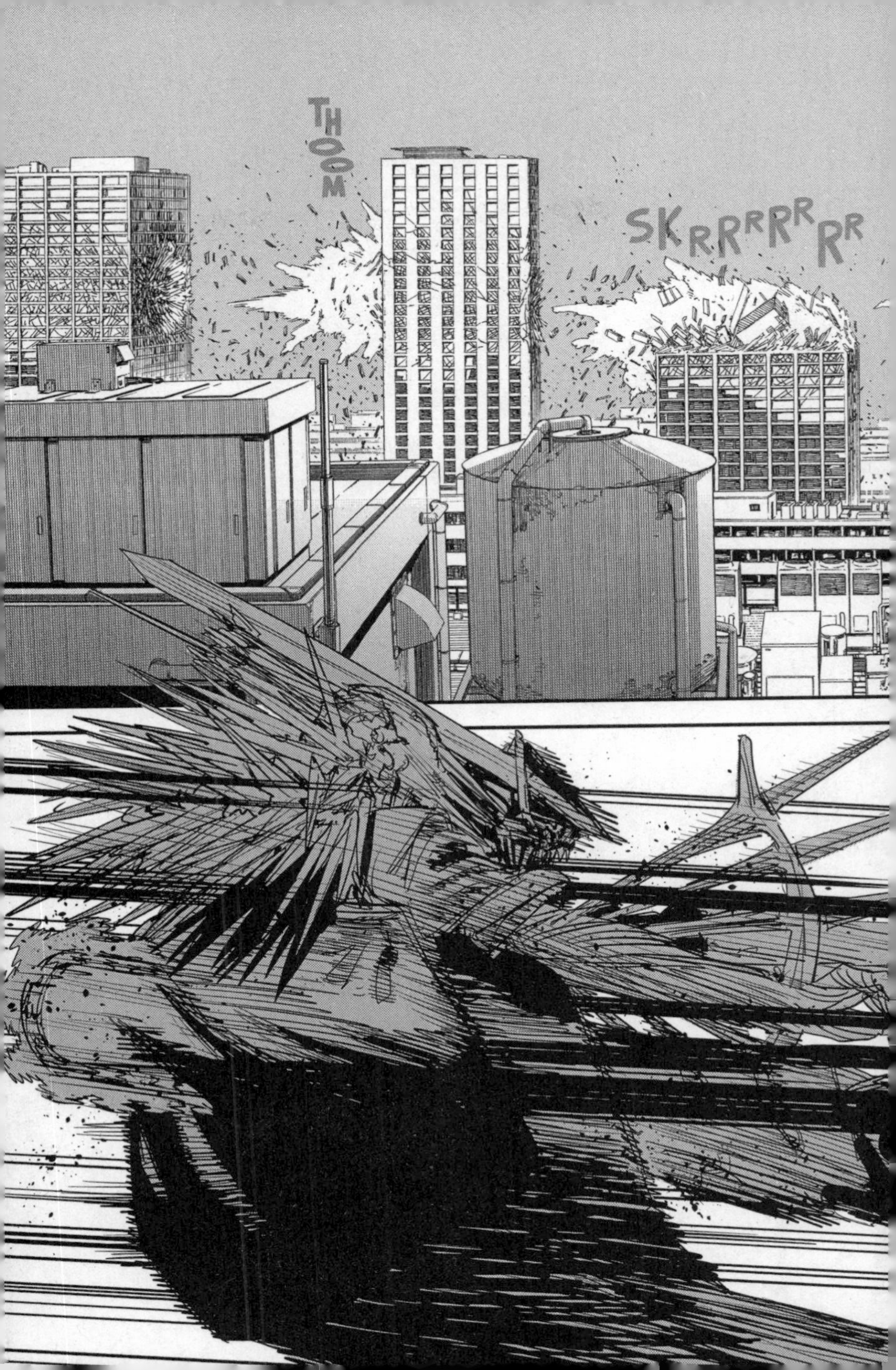
THOOM
SKRRRRRRR

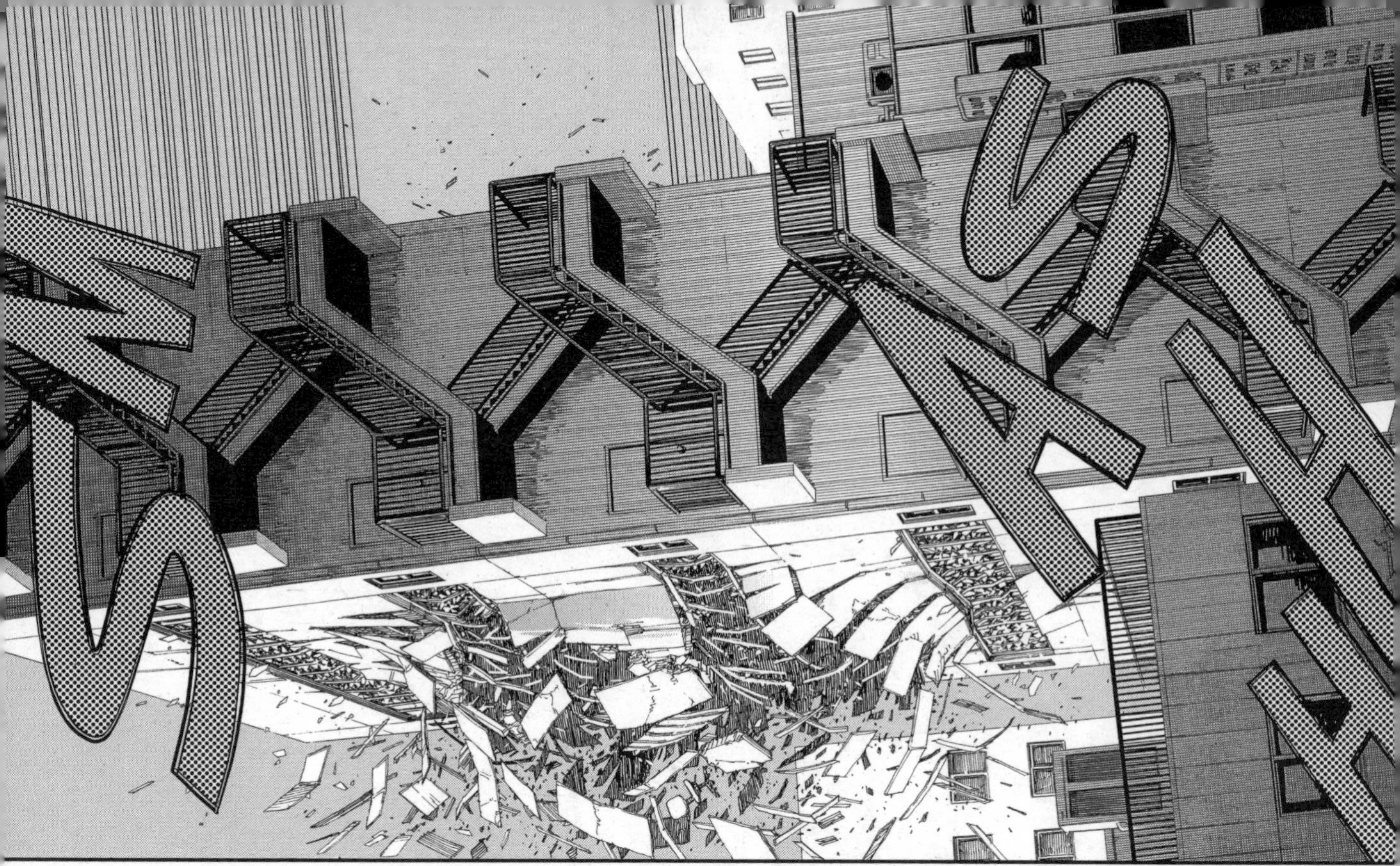
SMASH

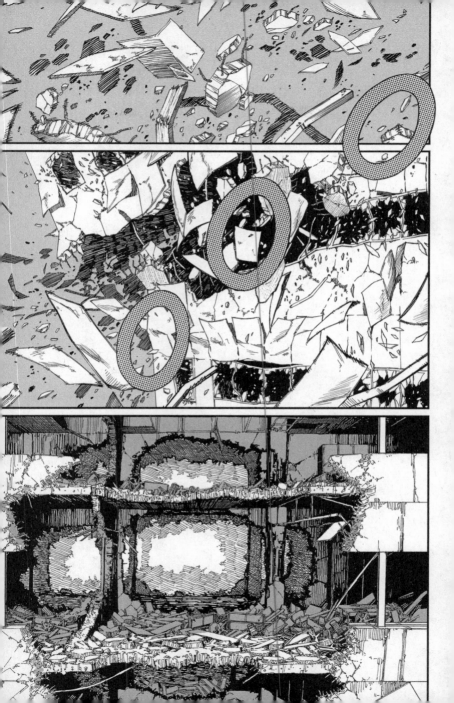

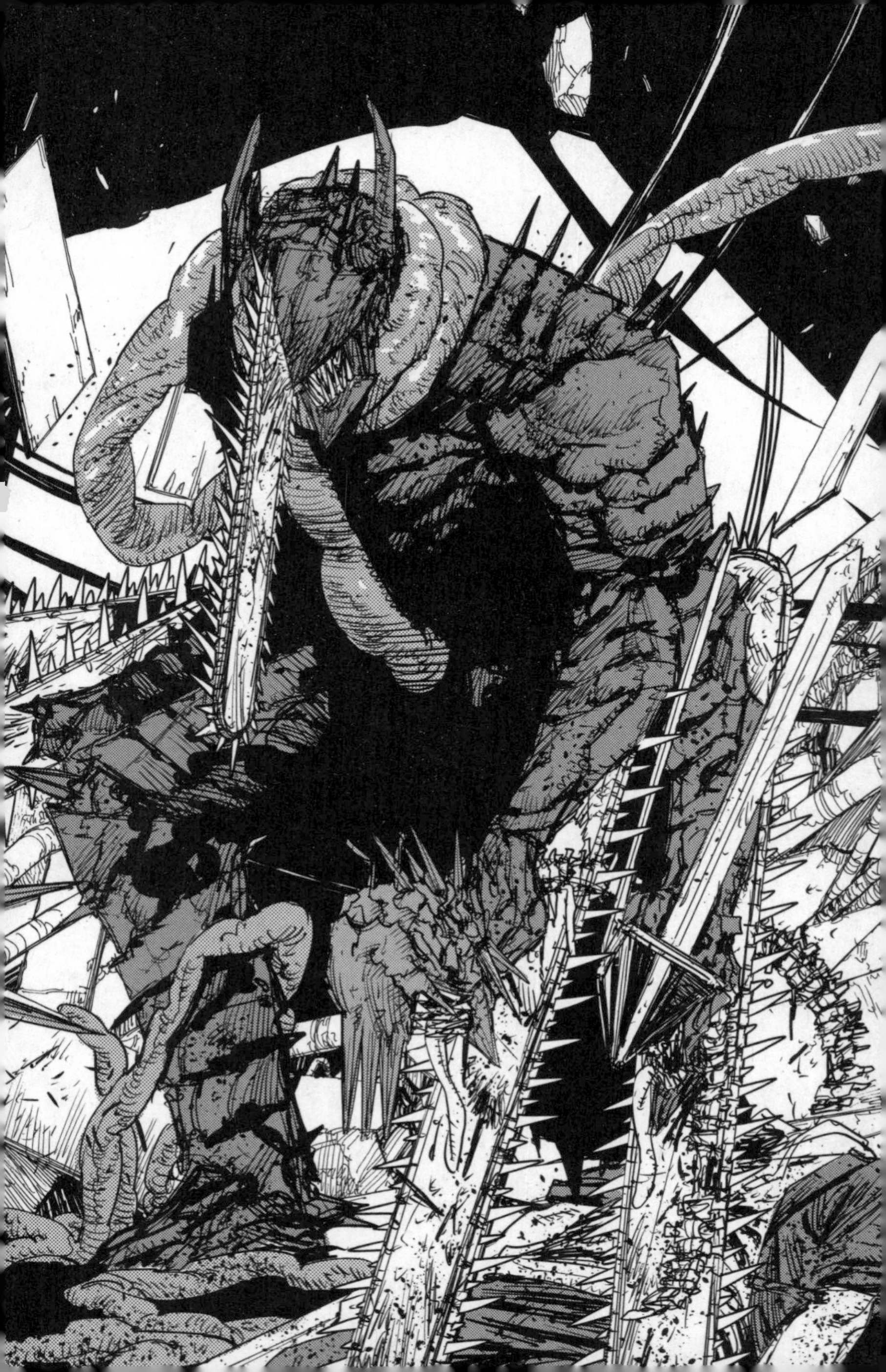

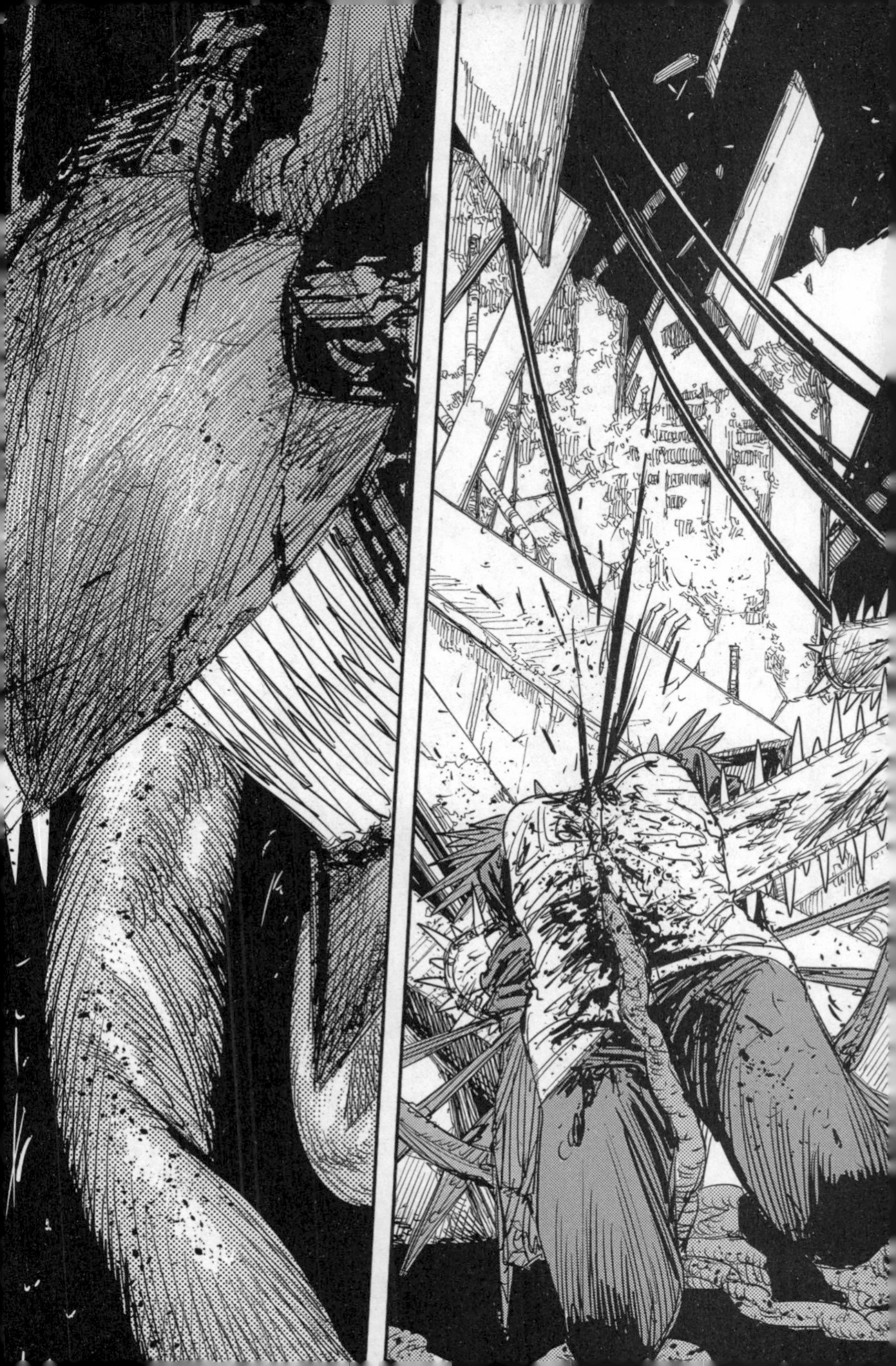

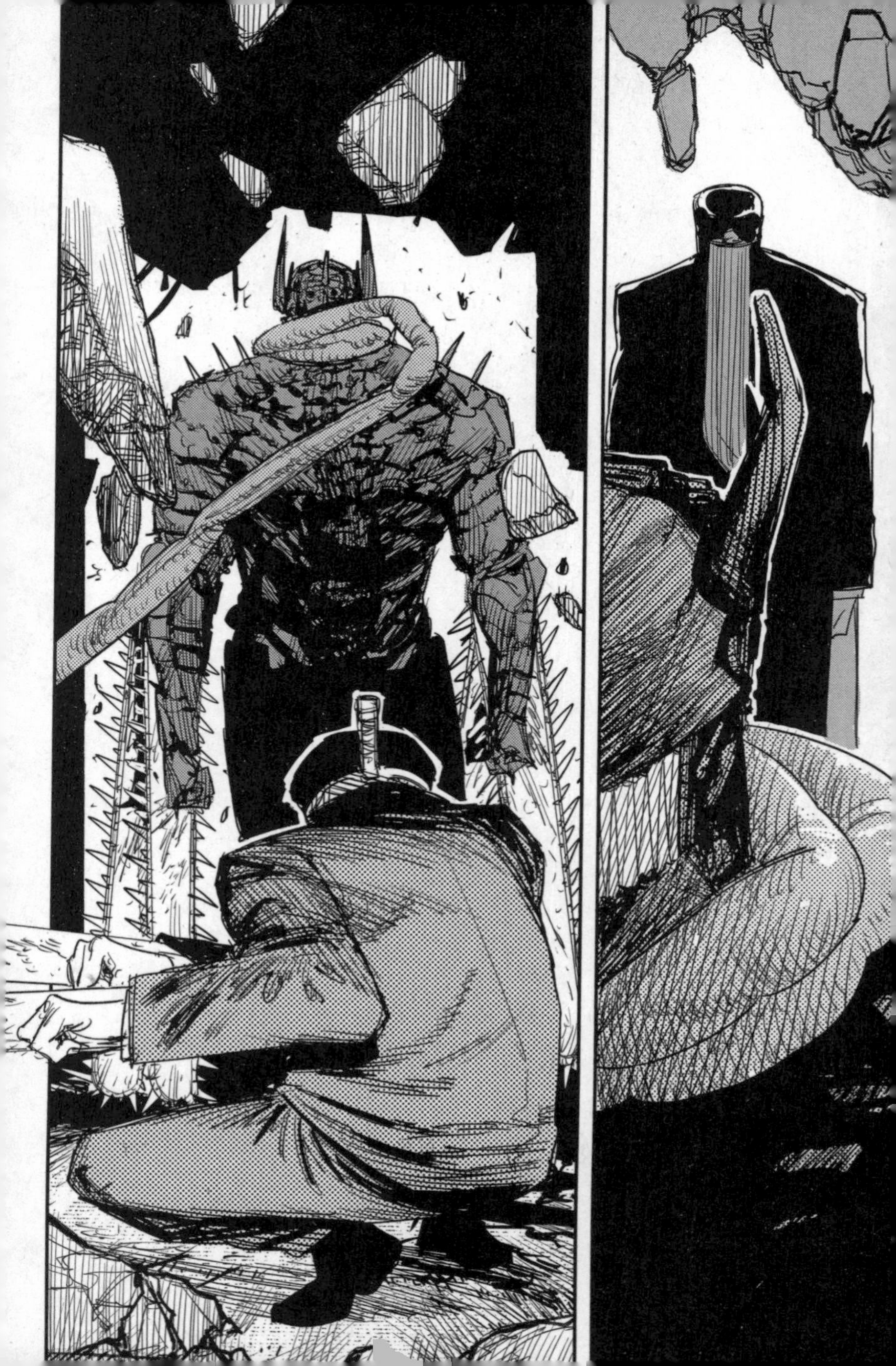

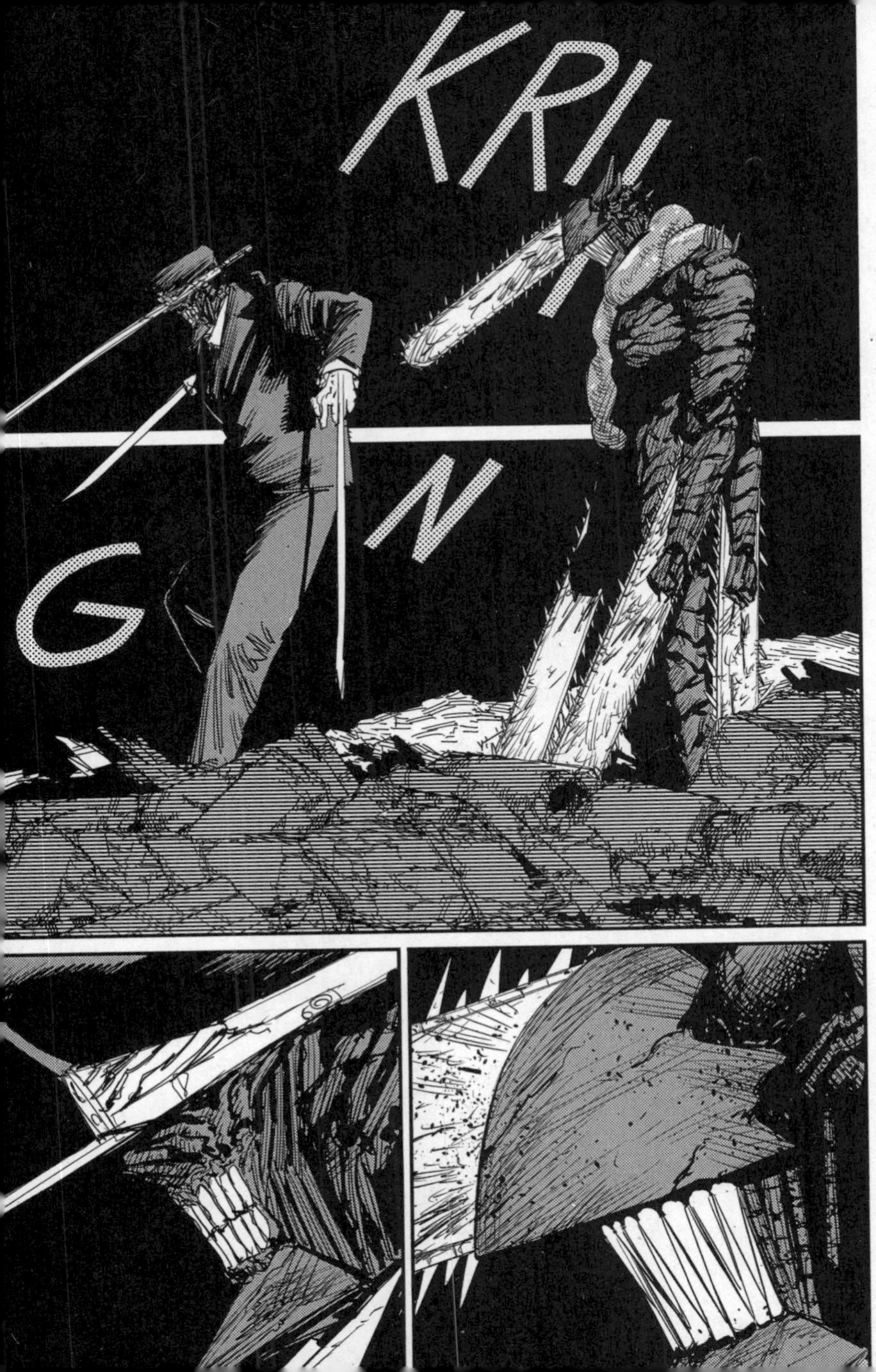
KRIIINNG

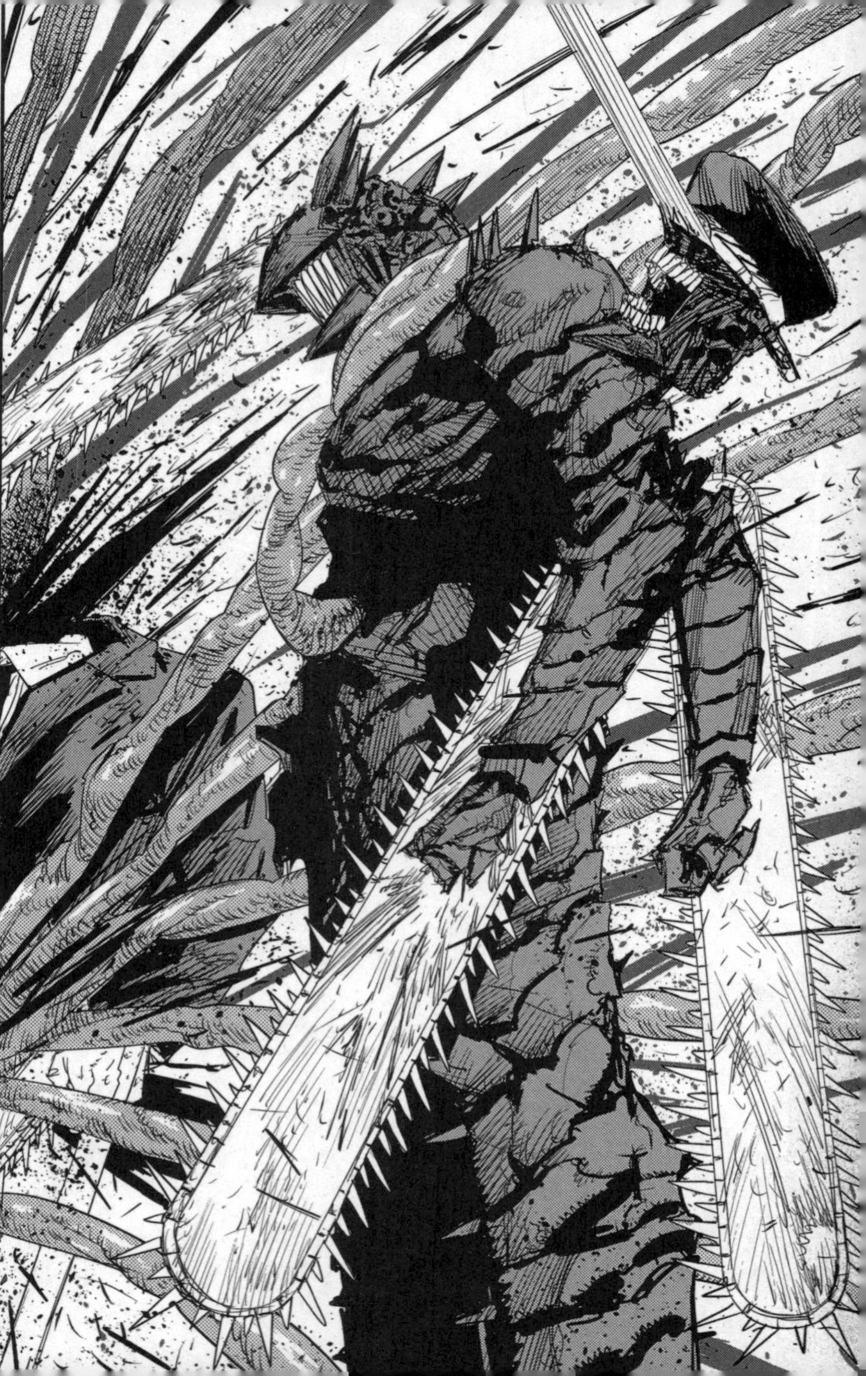

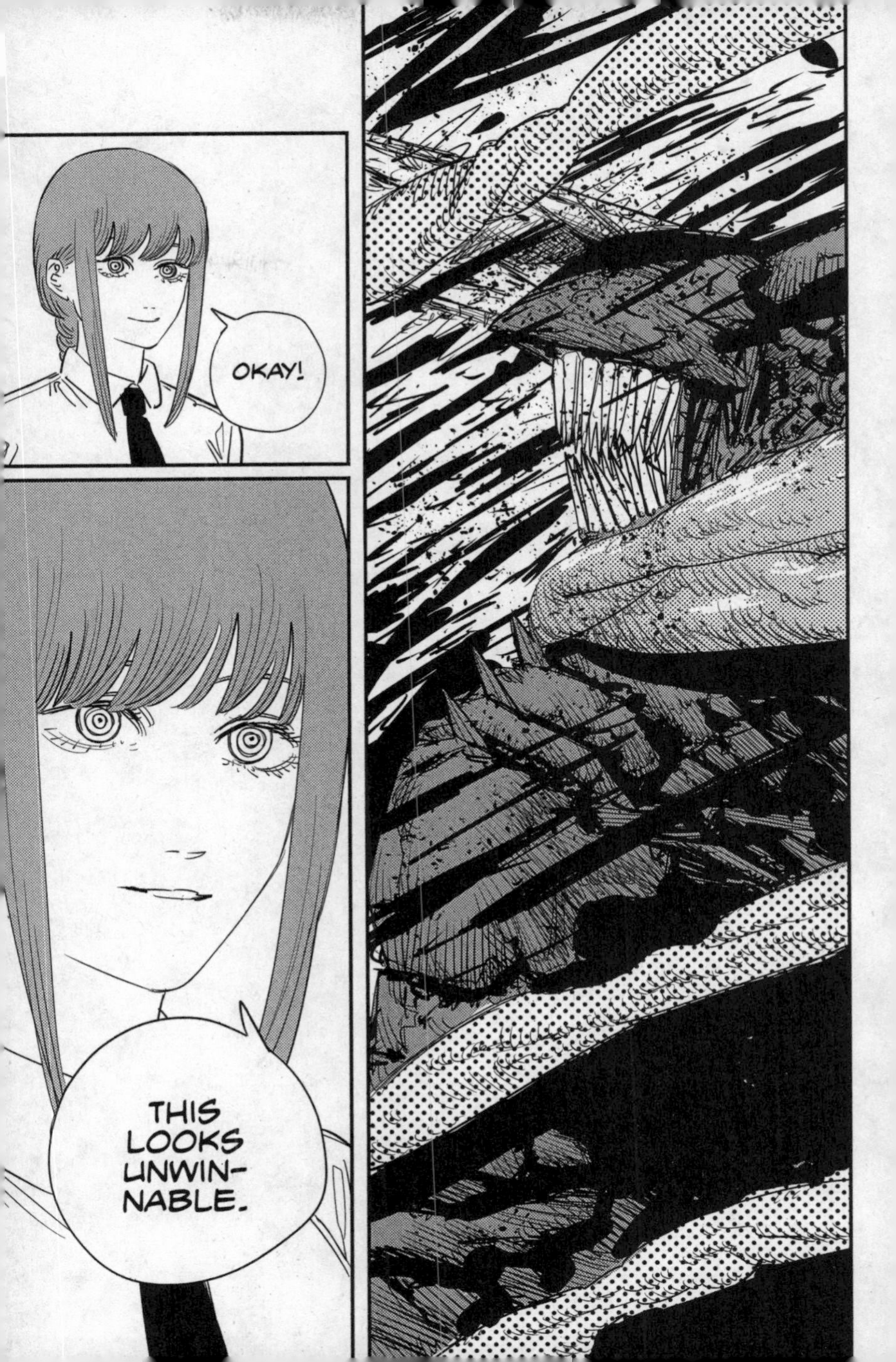
OKAY!
THIS LOOKS UNWIN-NABLE.

CHAINSAW MAN

Chapter 88: Star Chainsaw

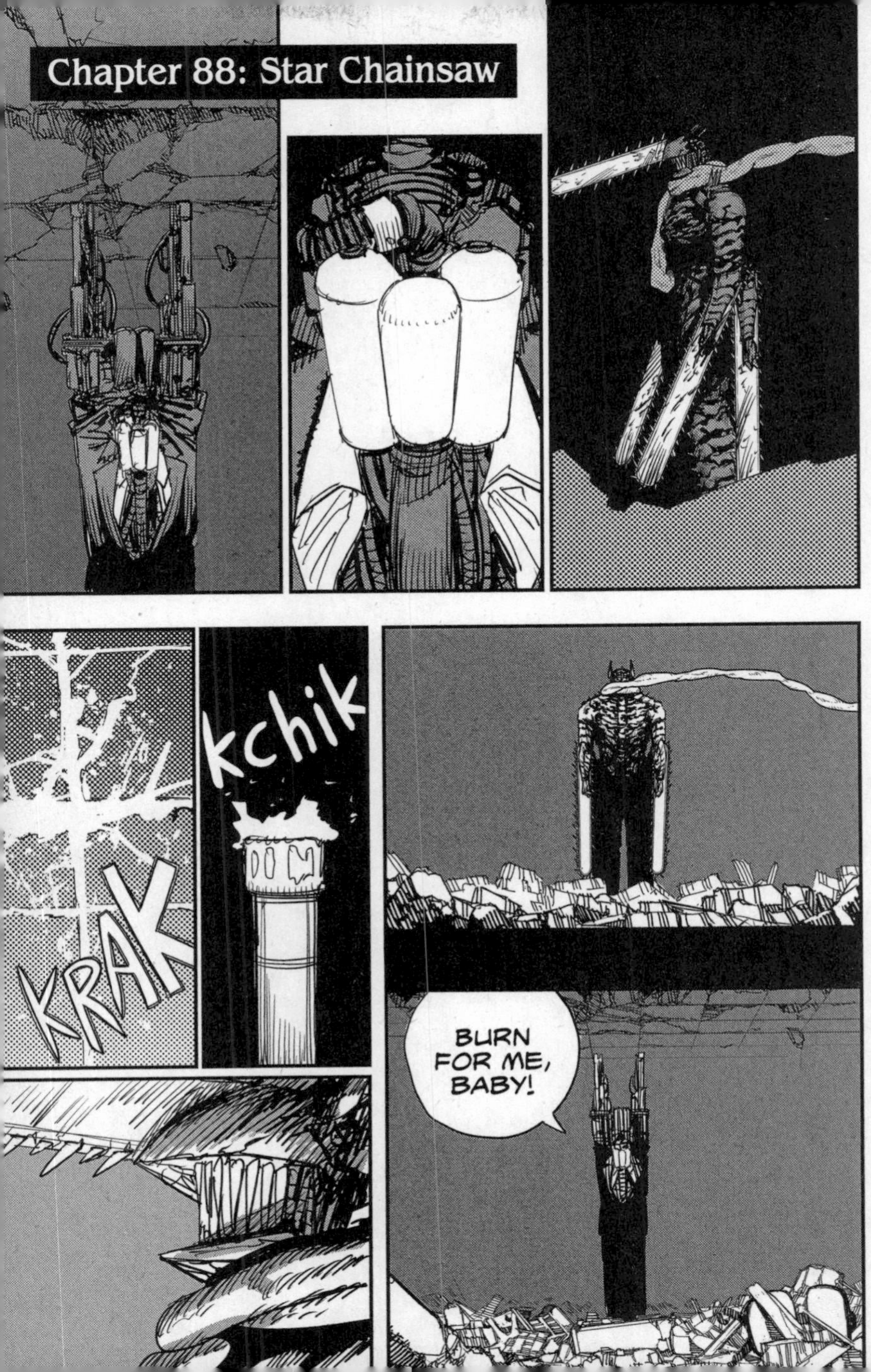
kchik
KRAK
BURN FOR ME, BABY!

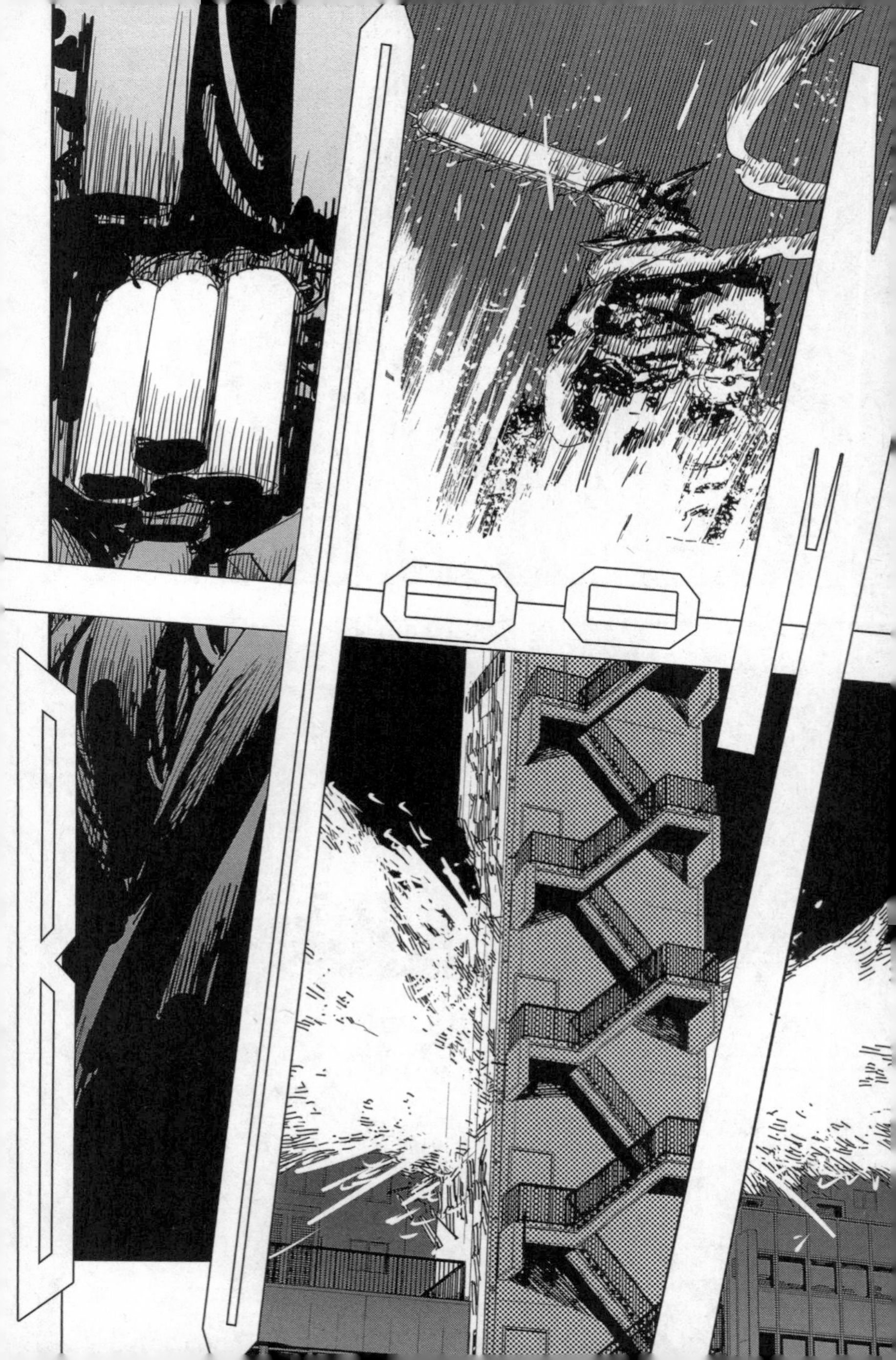

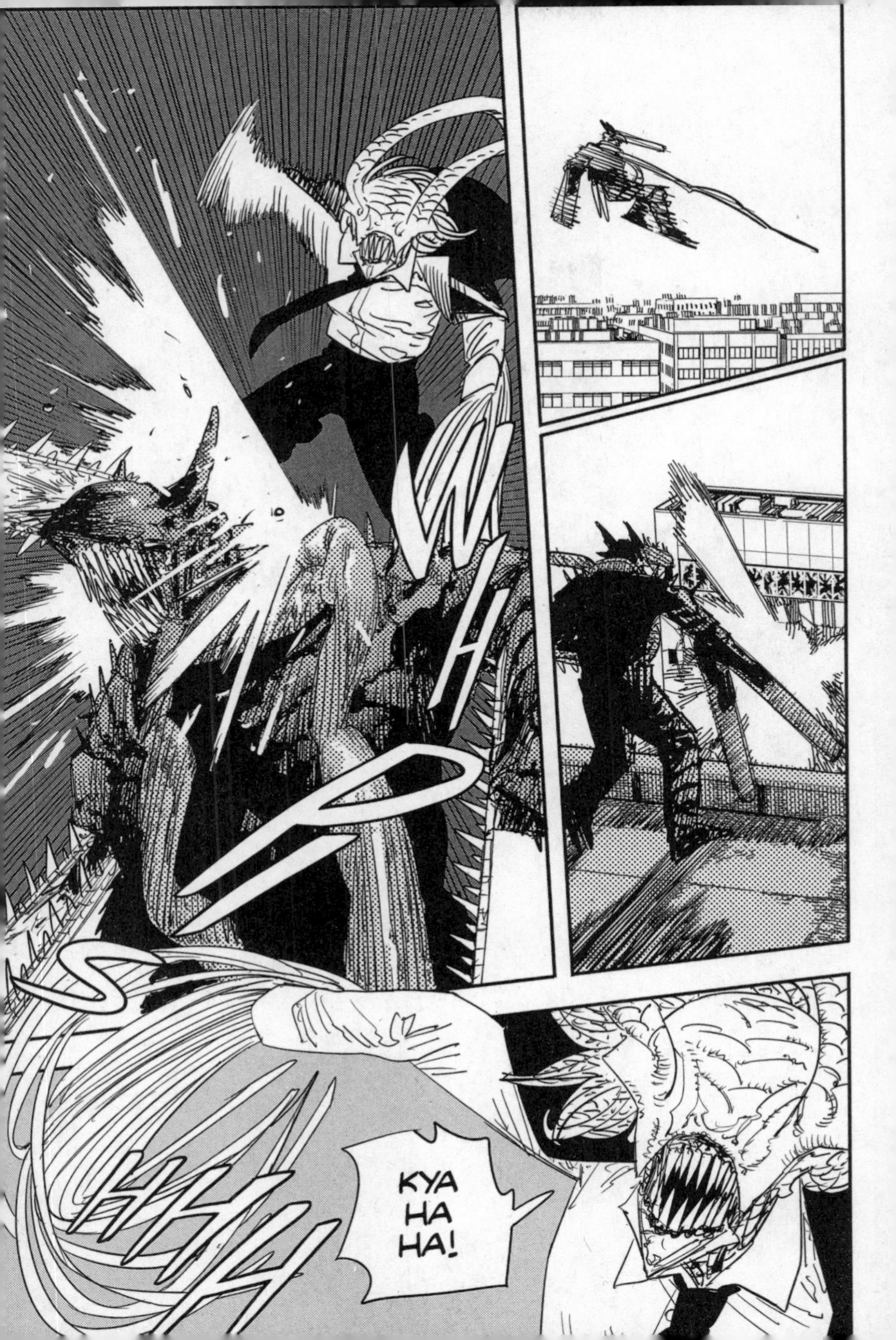
KYA
HA
HA!

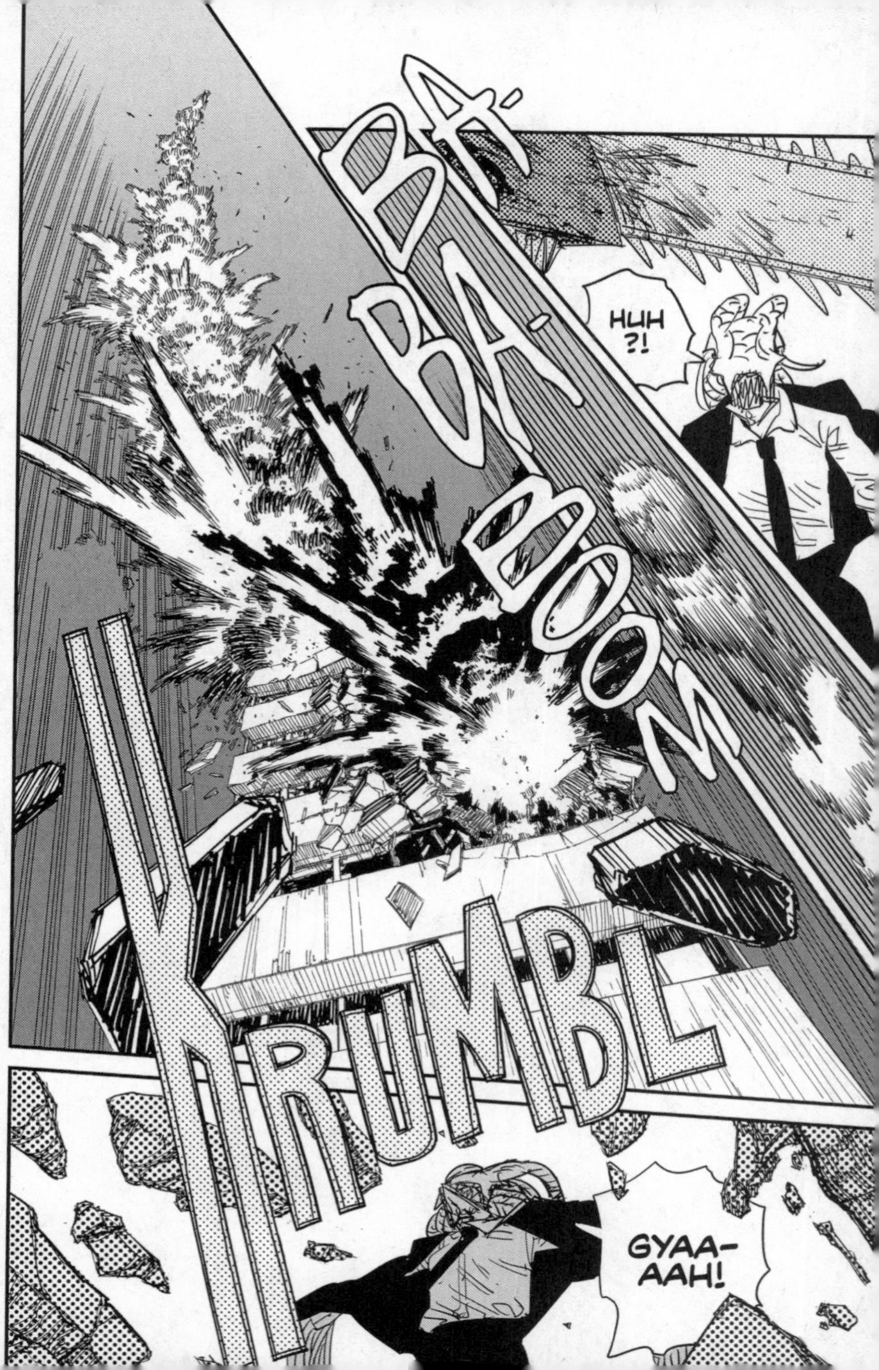
HUH ?!
BA-BA-BOOOM
KRUMBL
GYAA-AAH!

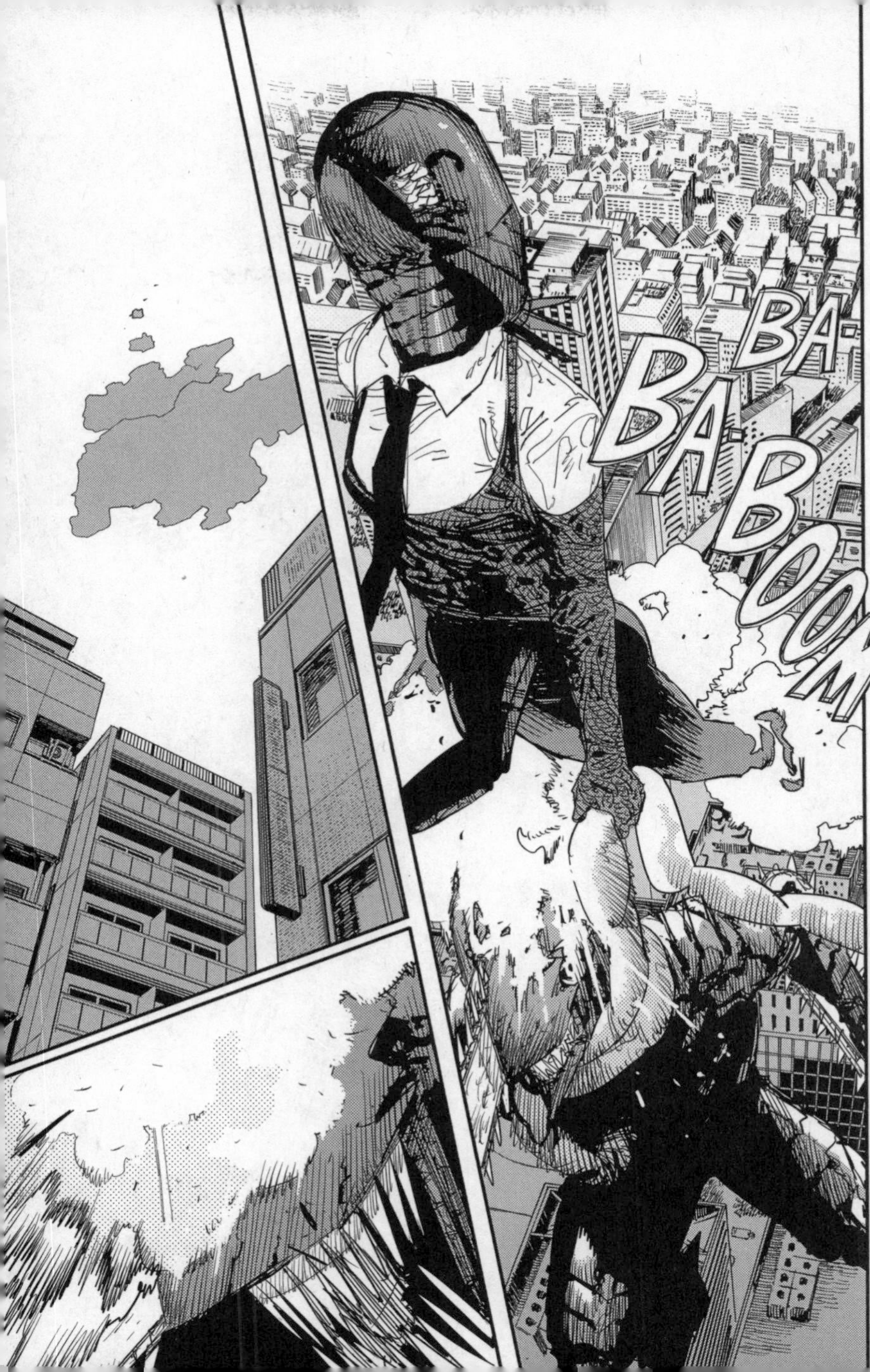
BA-BA-BA-BOOM

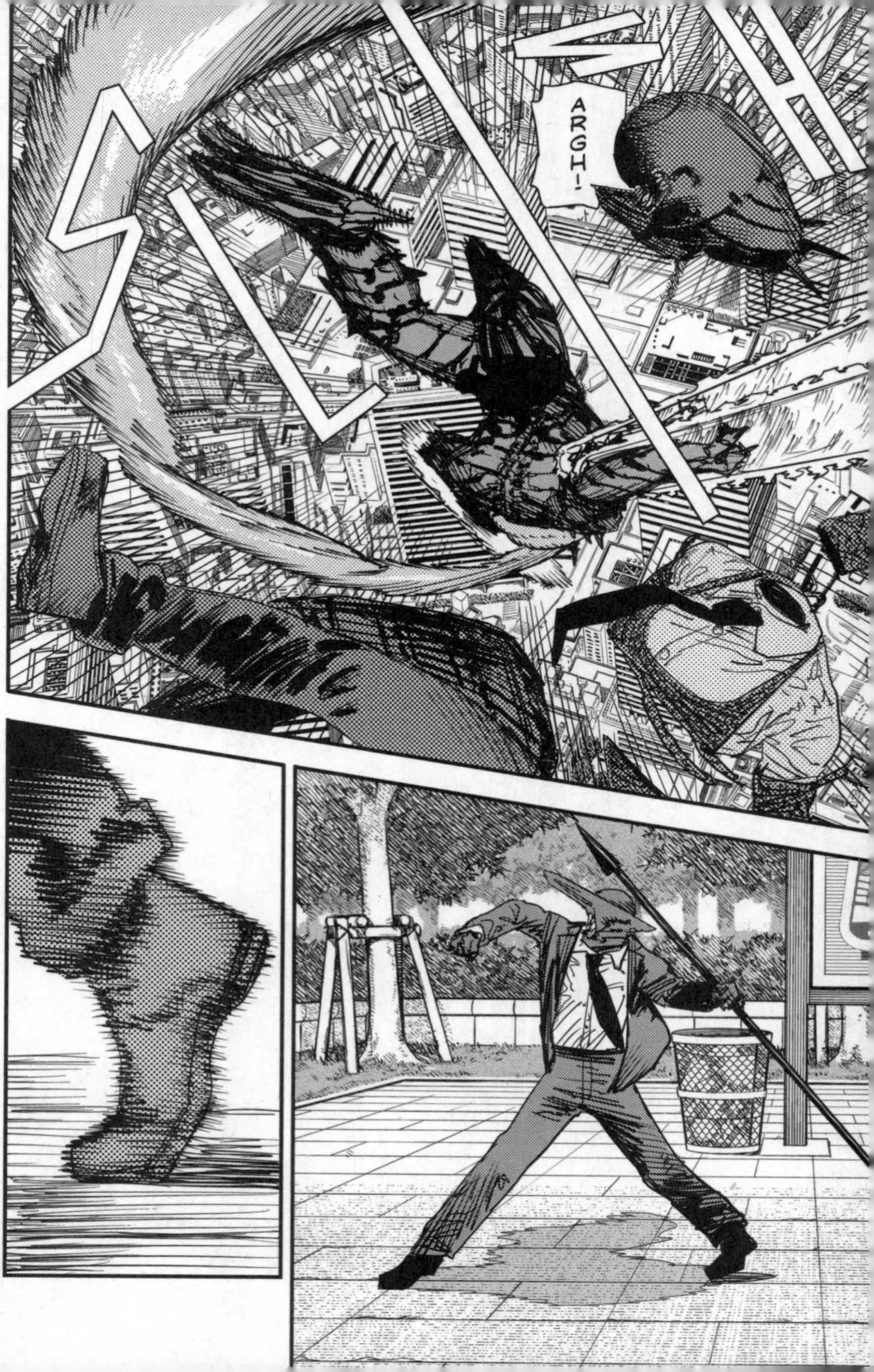
ARGH!

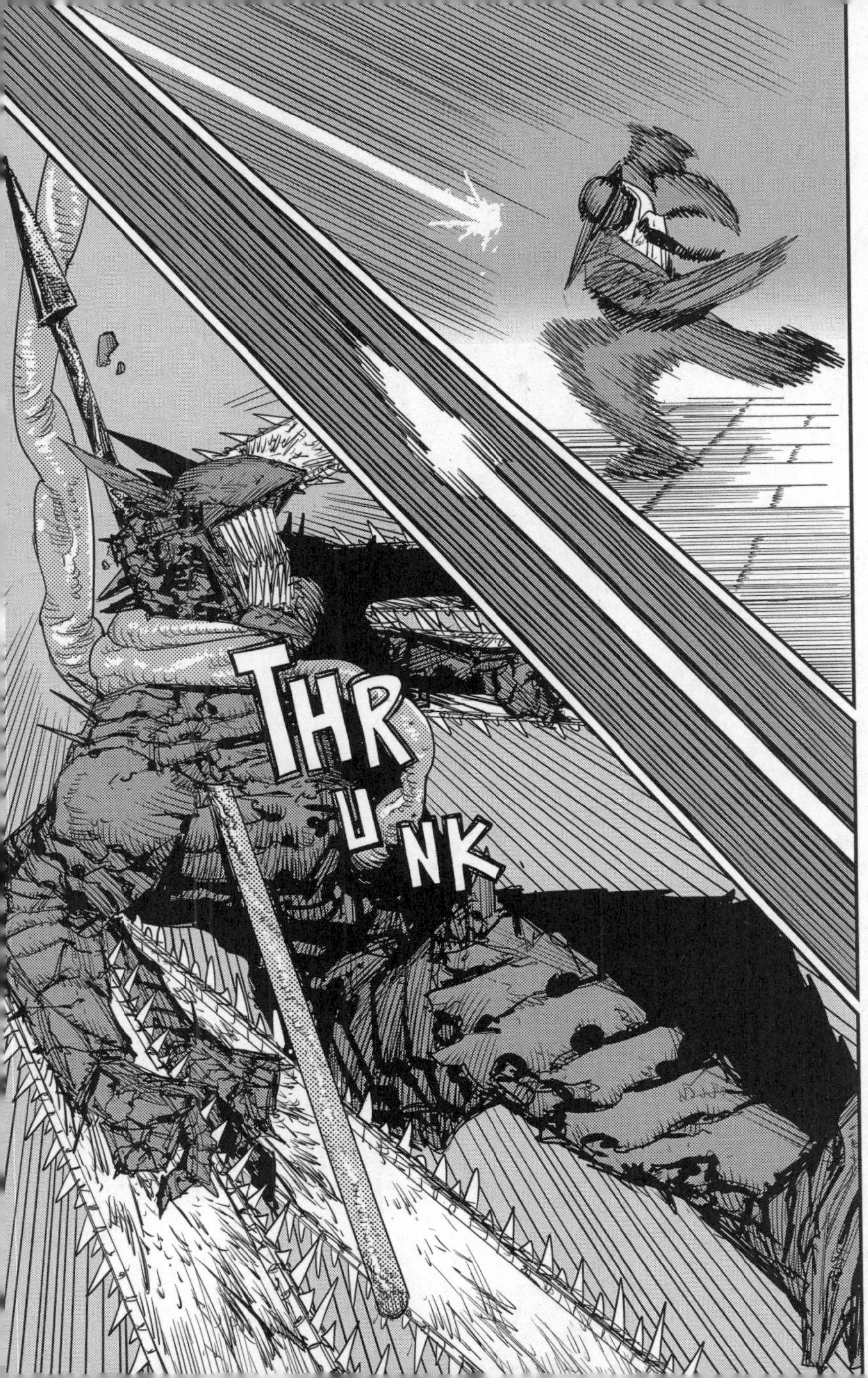
THRUNK

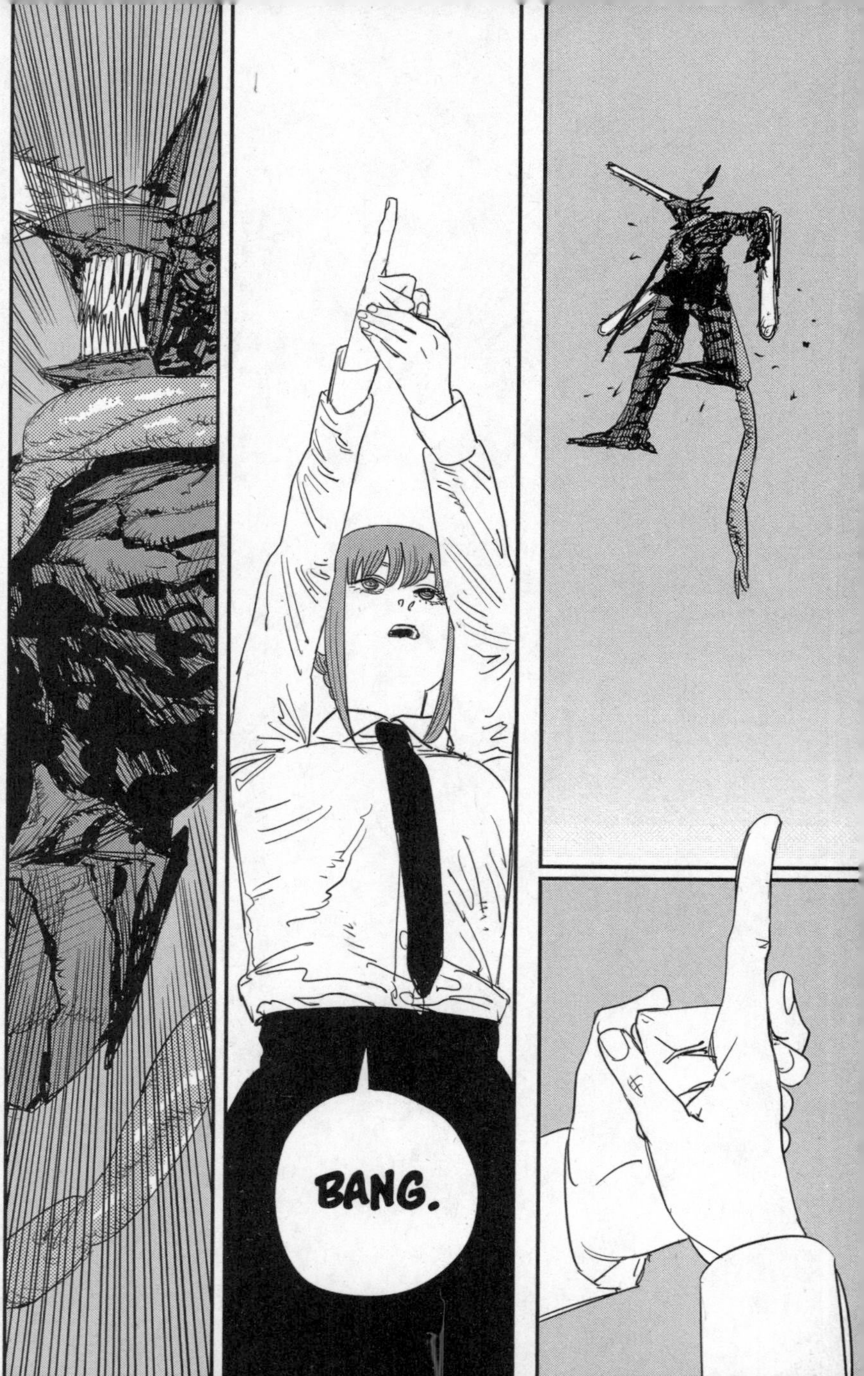
BANG.

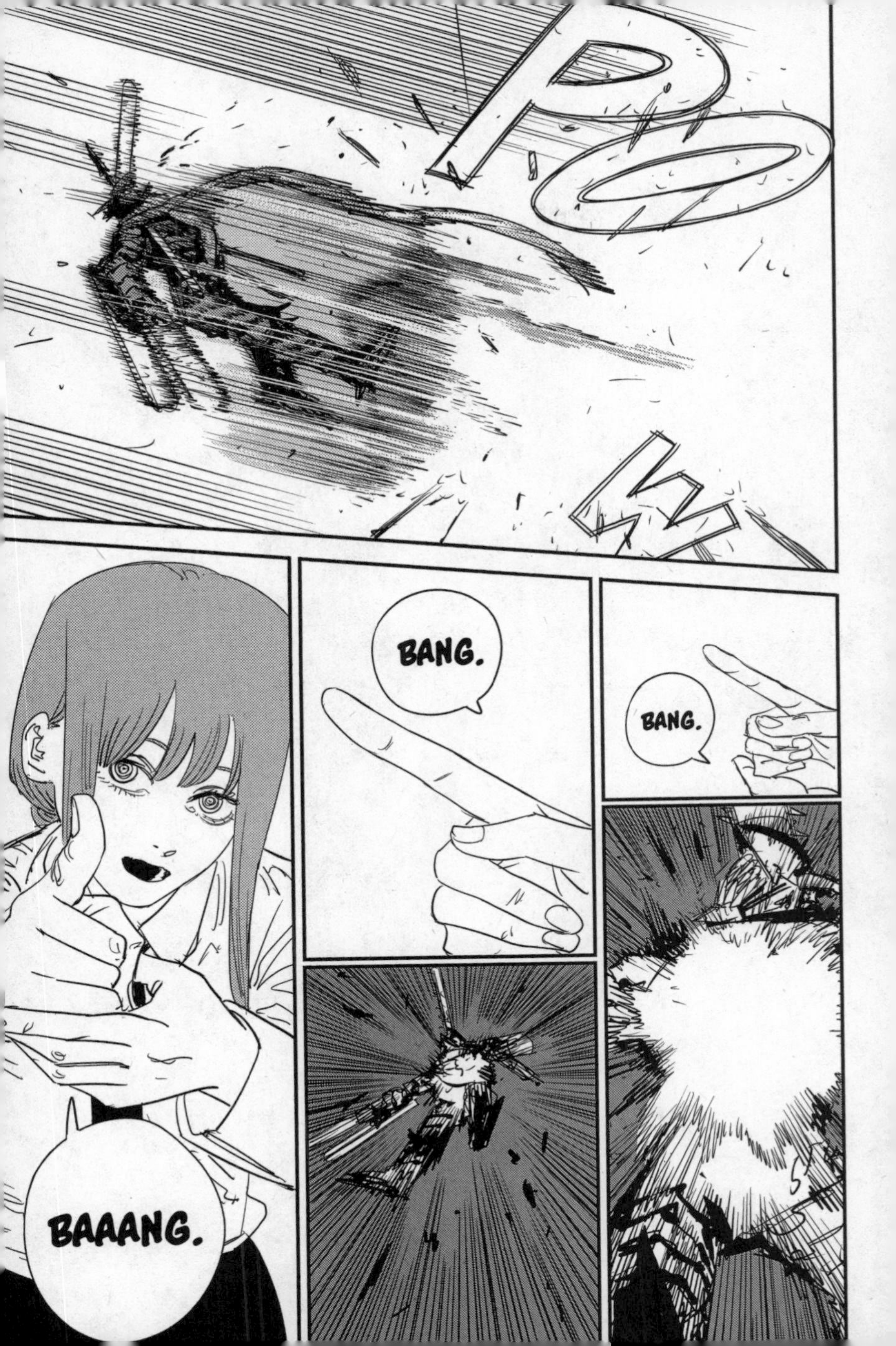
POW
BANG.
BANG.
BAAANG.

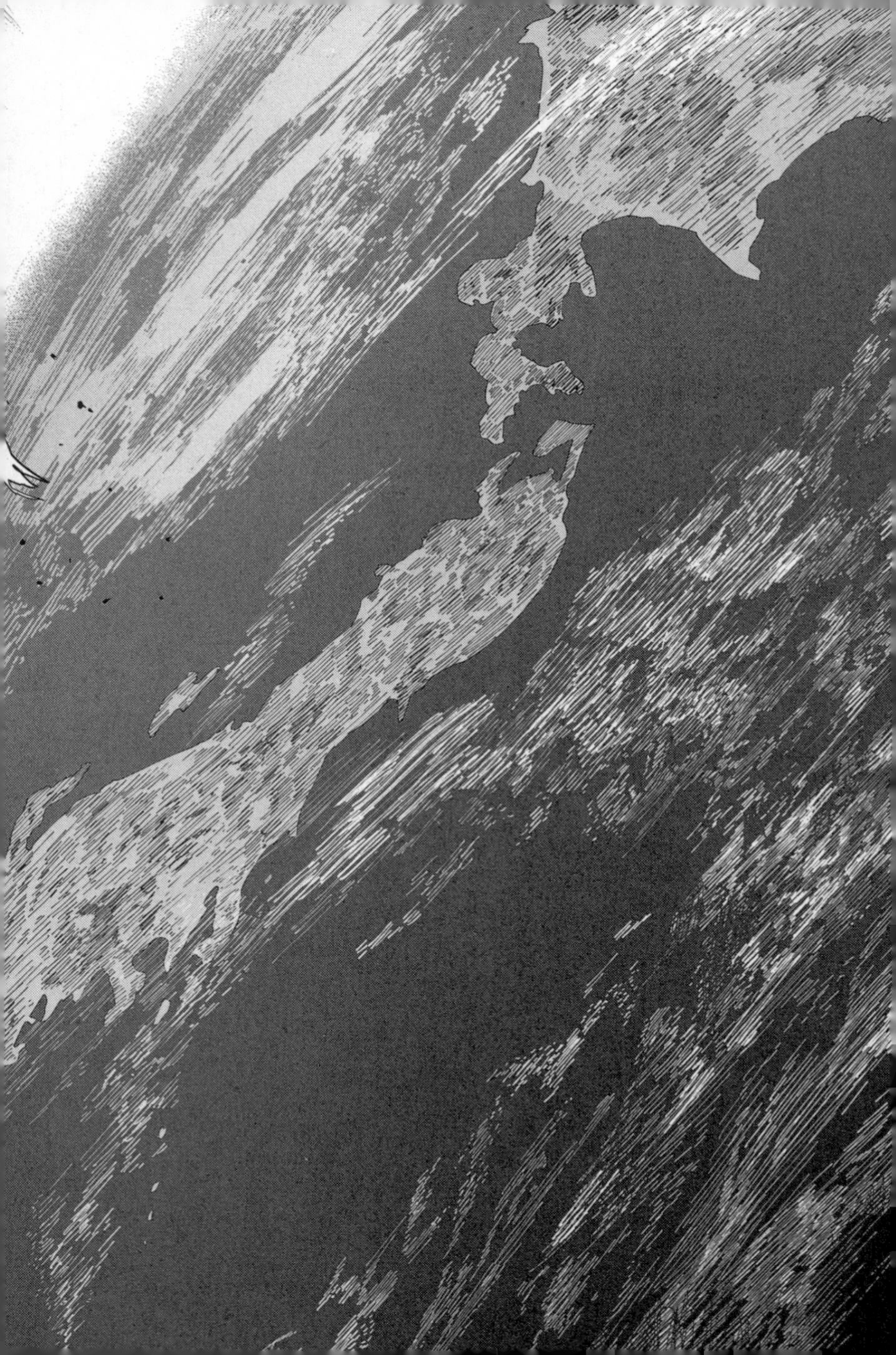

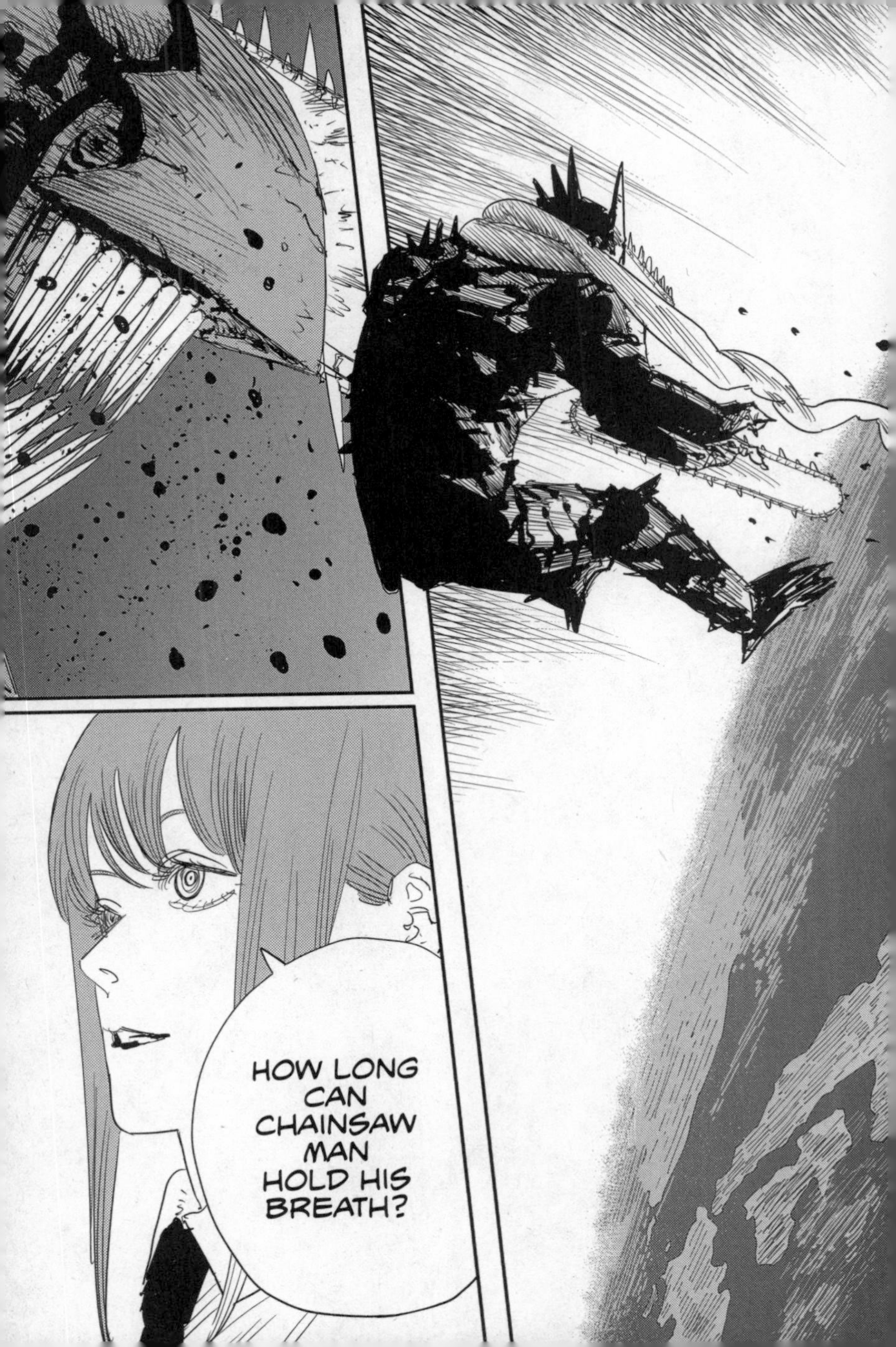
HOW LONG CAN CHAINSAW MAN HOLD HIS BREATH?

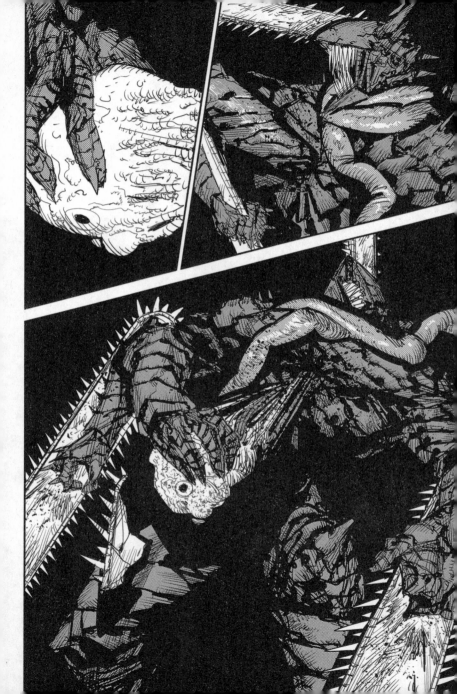

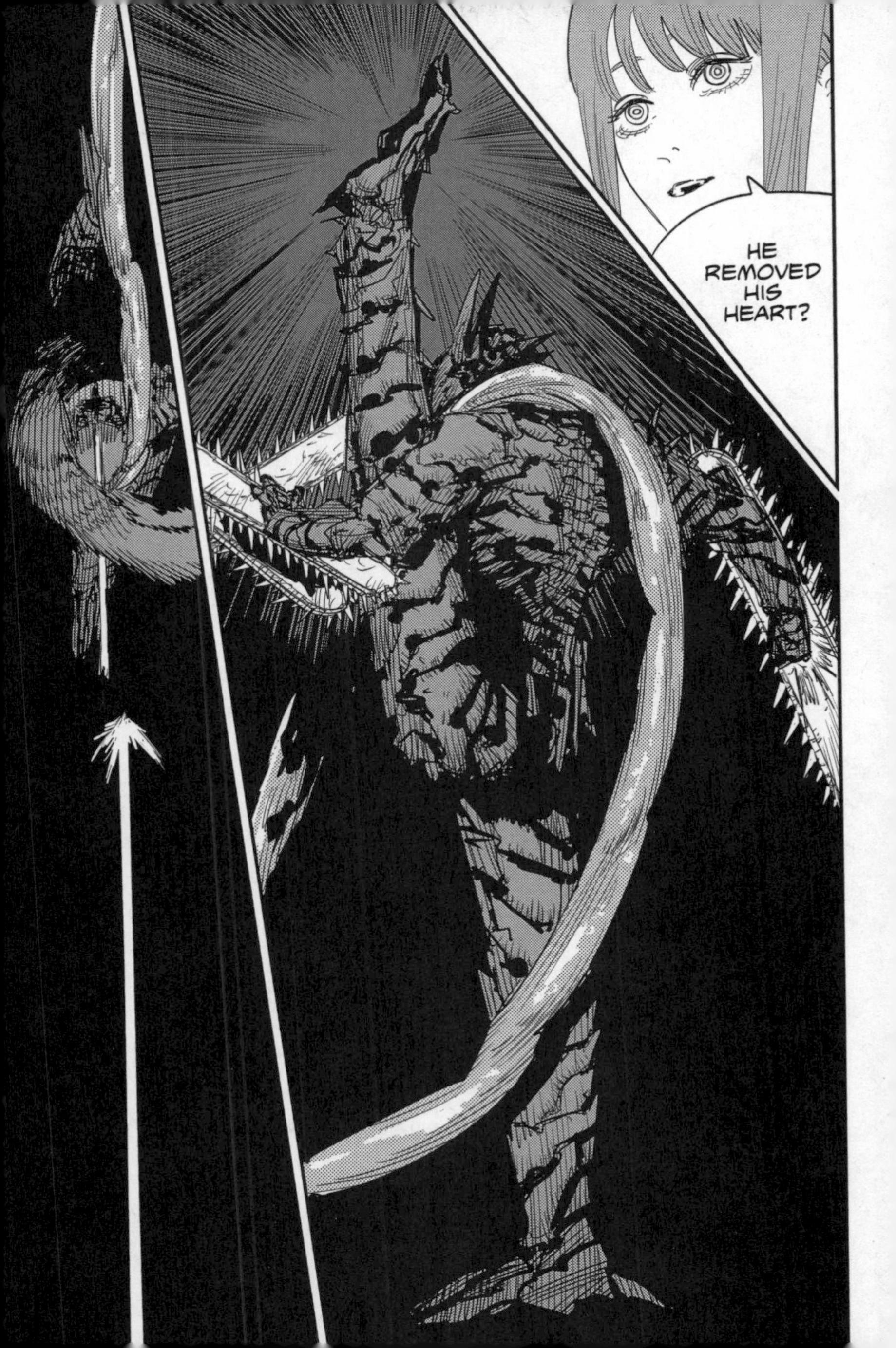
HE REMOVED HIS HEART?

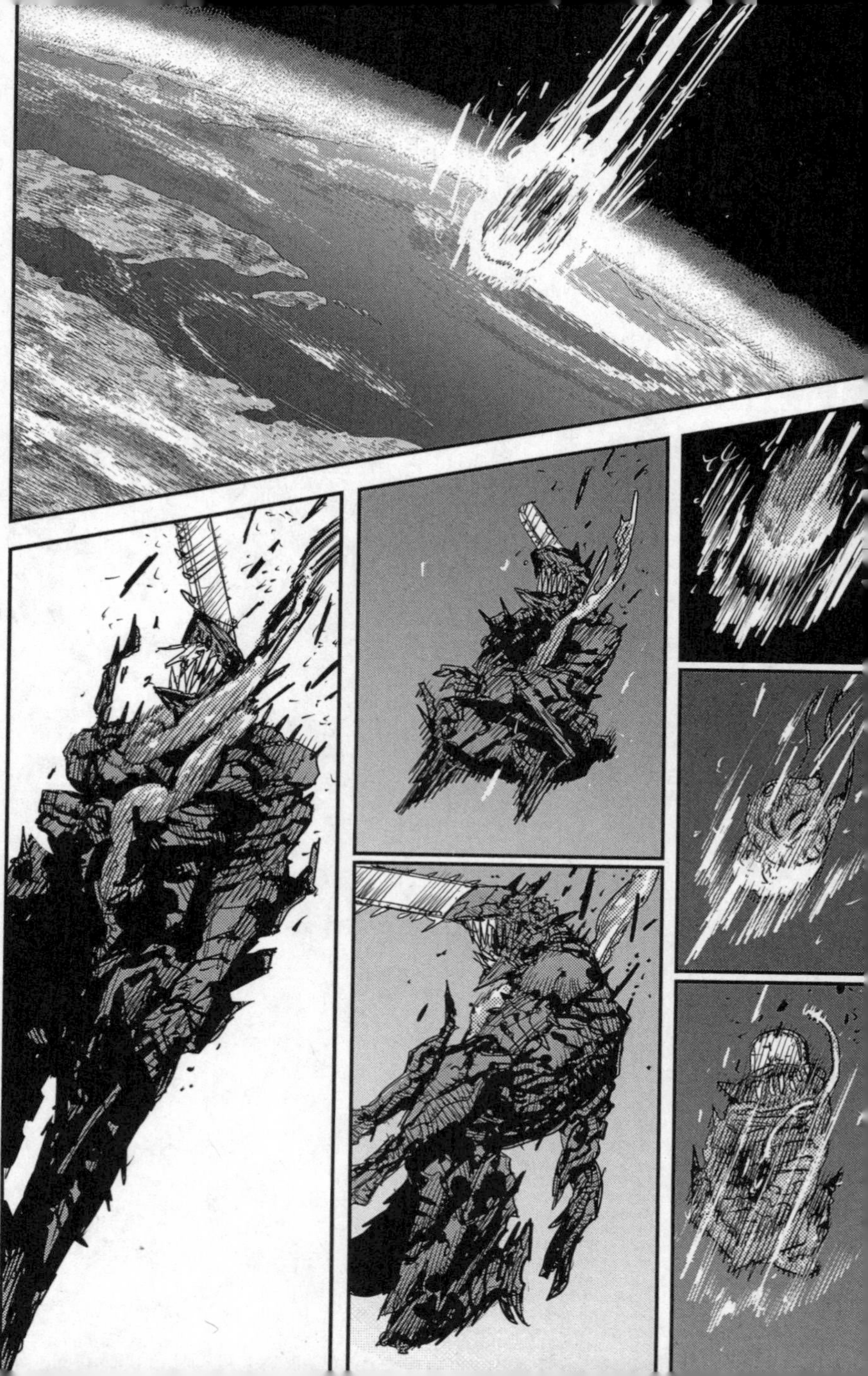

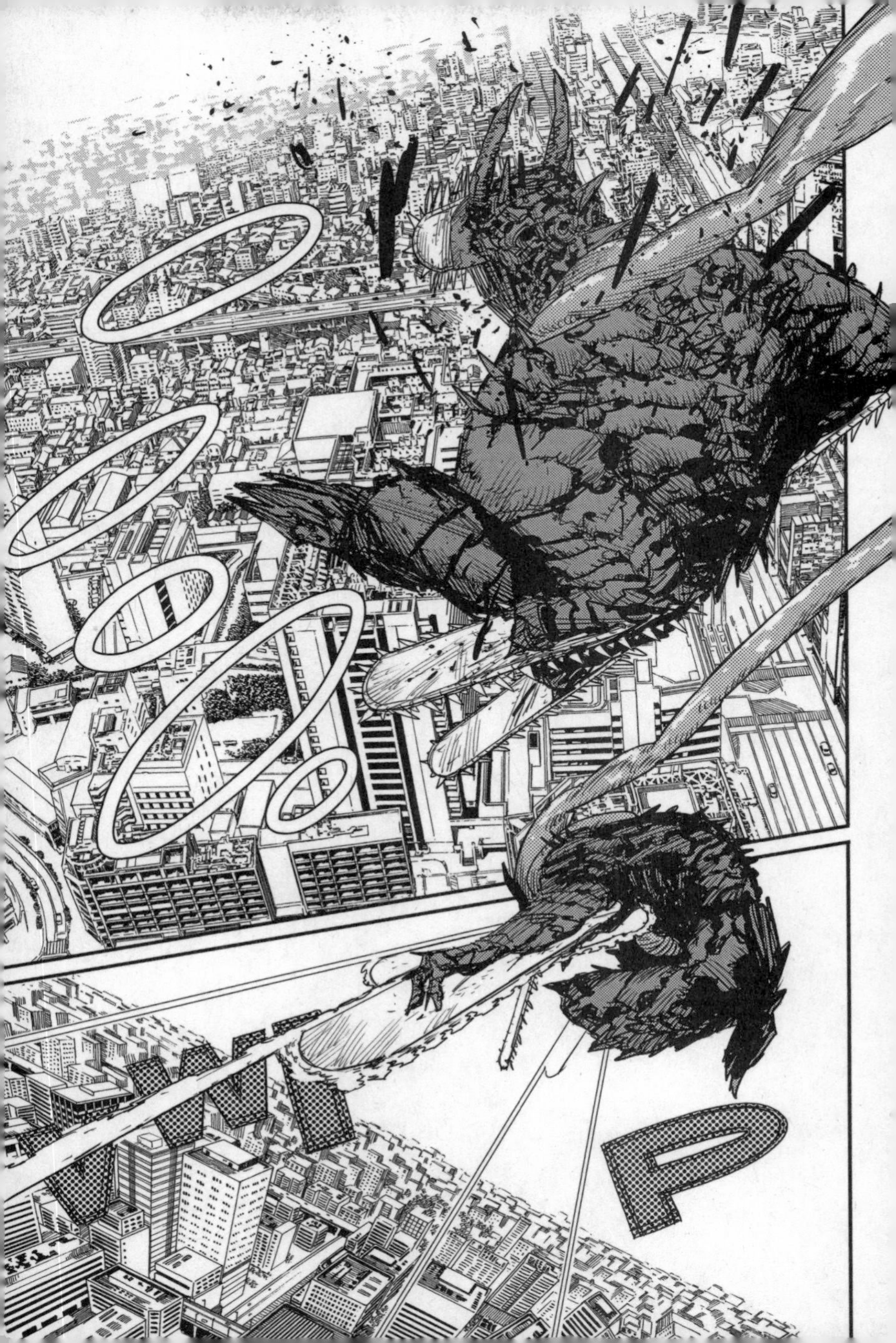

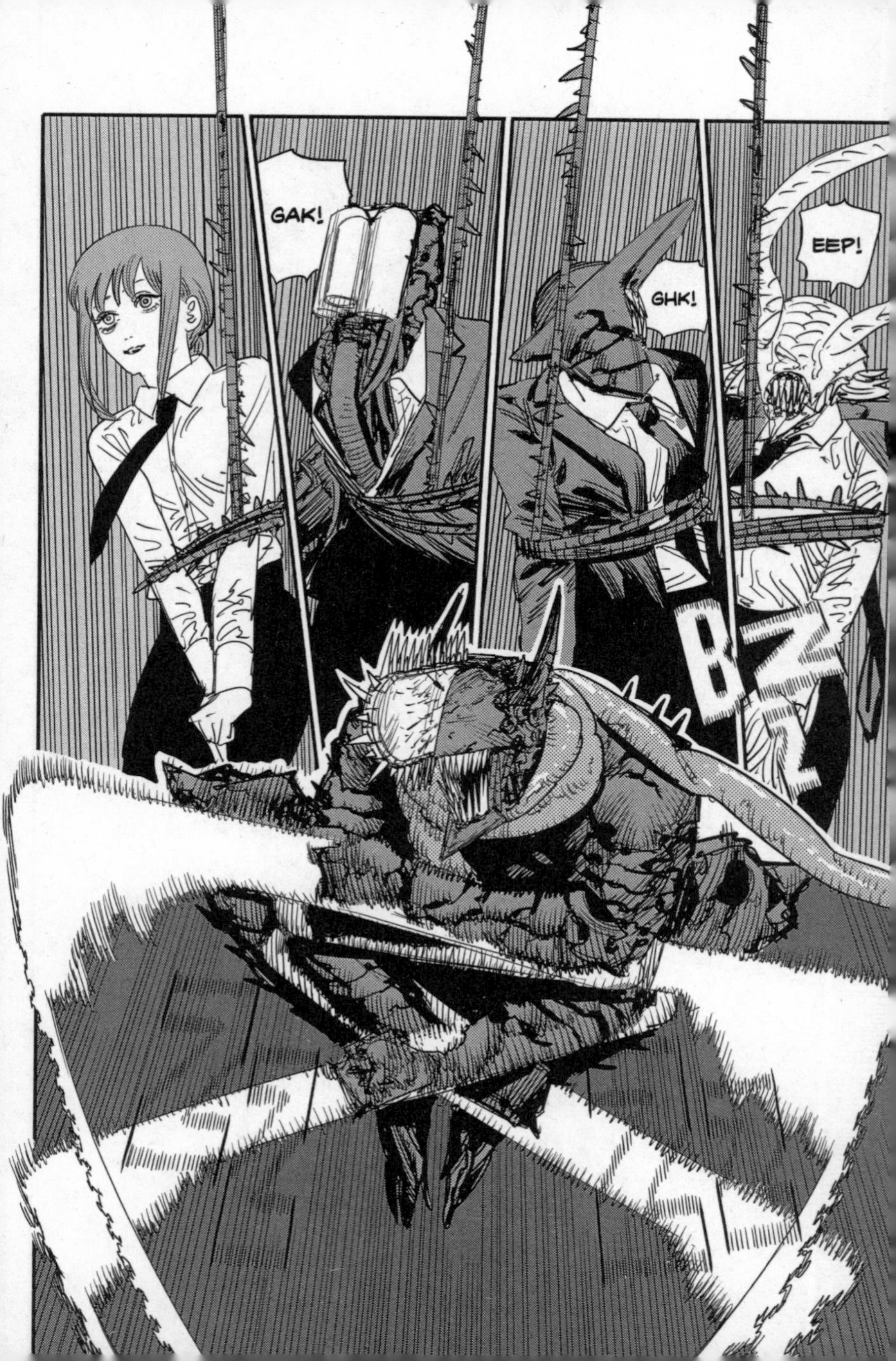
EEP!
GHK!
BZZ
GAK!

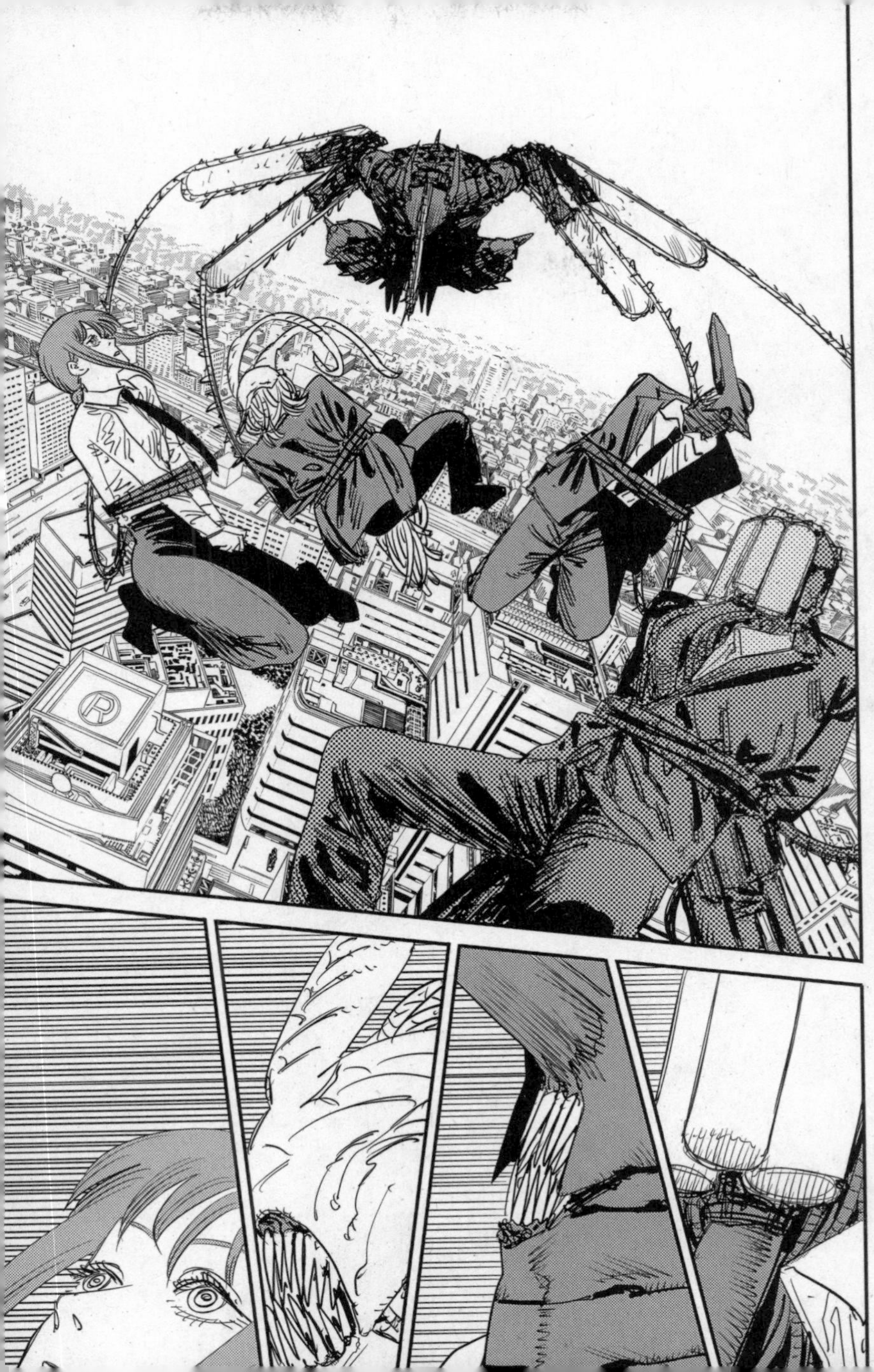

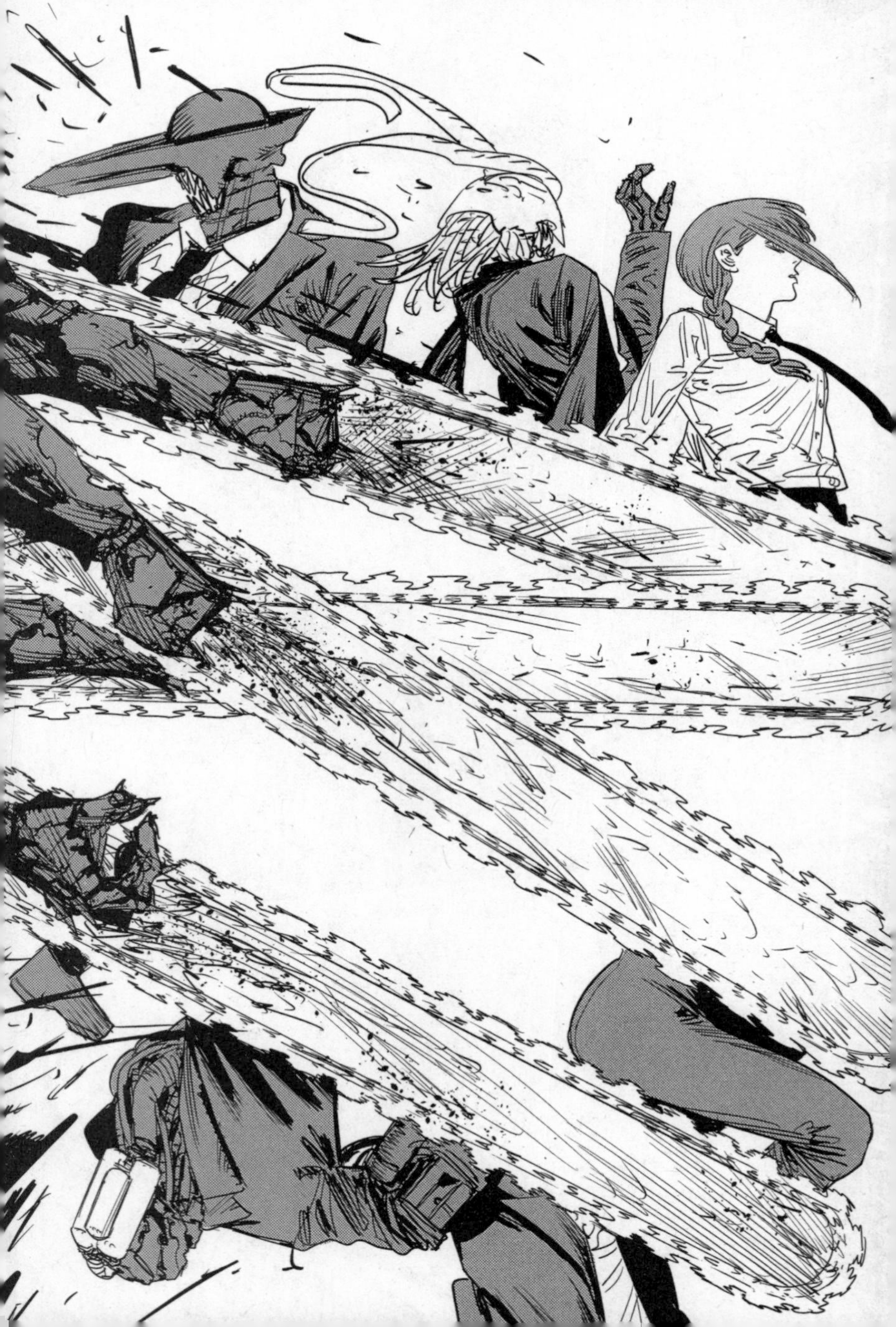

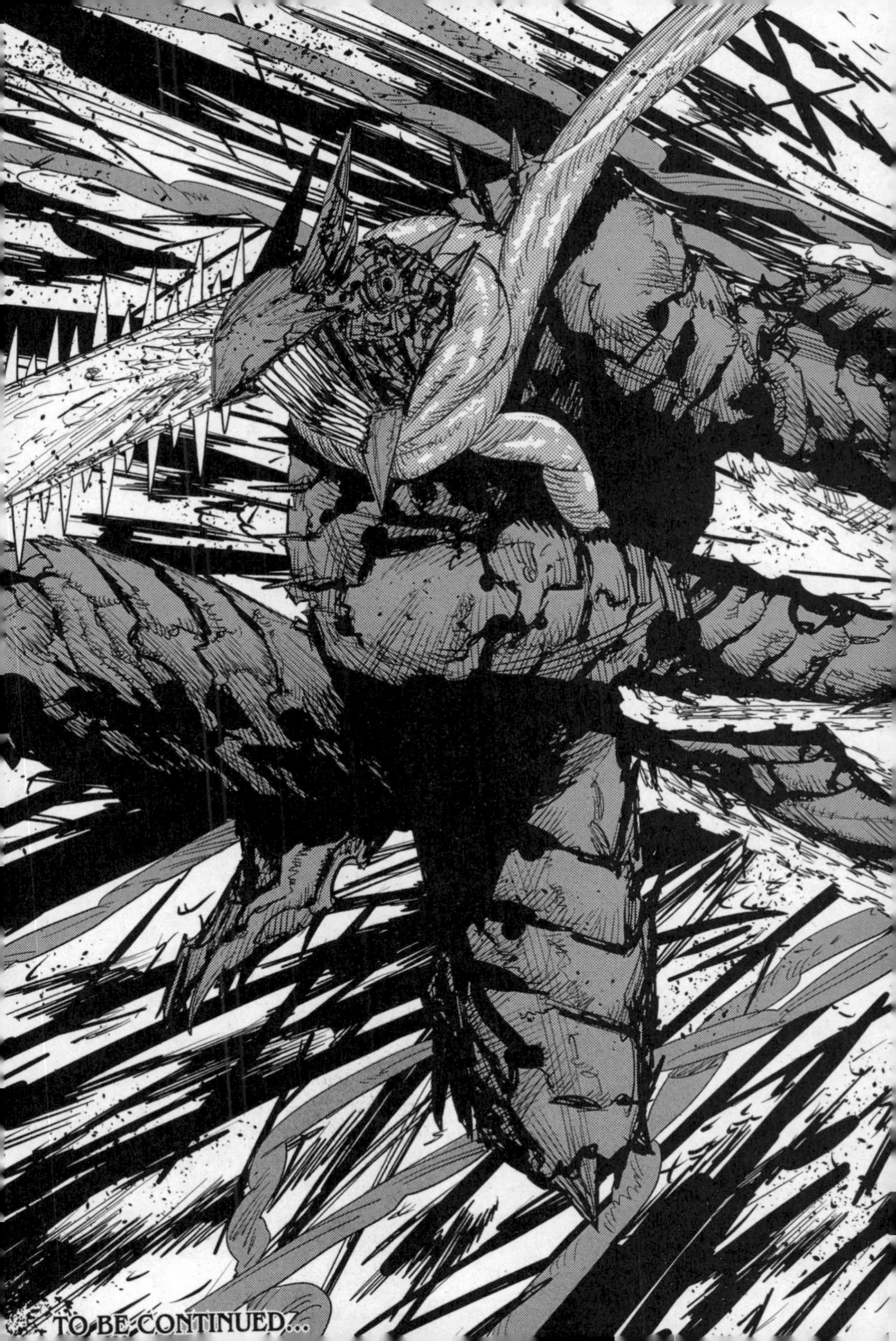
TO BE CONTINUED...

CHAINSAW MAN

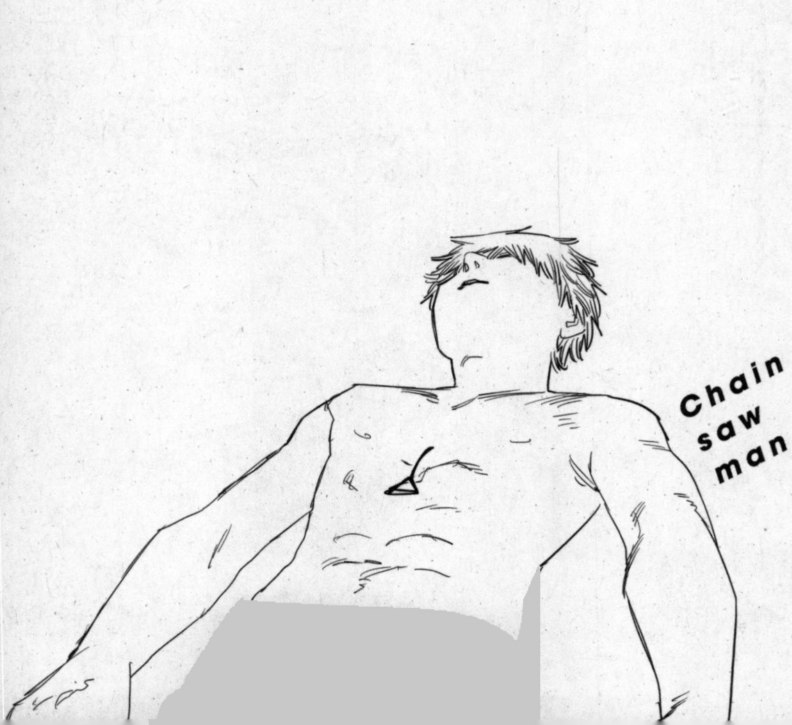Chain
saw
man

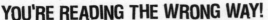

YOU'RE READING THE WRONG WAY!

CHAINSAW MAN

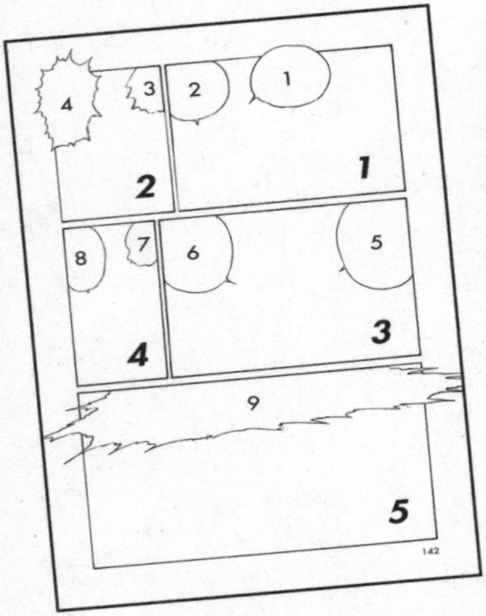
1
2
3
4
1
2
5
6
7
8
3
4
9
5
142

Chainsaw Man reads from right to left, starting in the upper-right corner. Japanese is read from right to left, meaning that action, sound effects, and word-balloon order are completely reversed from English order.

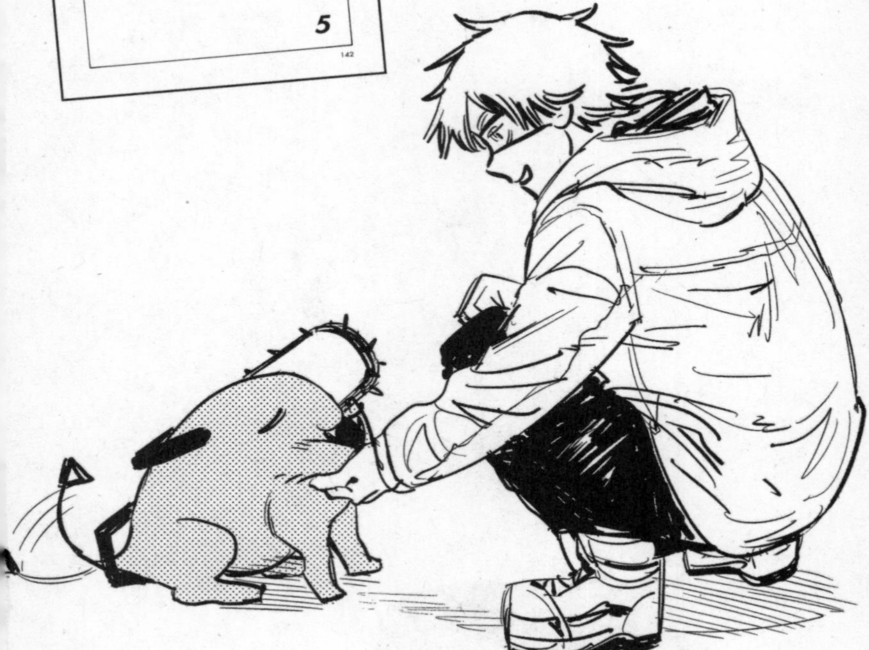